TEACH BRILLIANTLY

SMALL SHIFTS
THAT LEAD TO
BIG GAINS
IN STUDENT
LEARNING

JAMES A. NOTTINGHAM

Solution Tree | Press

Copyright © 2024 by Solution Tree Press

All rights reserved, including the right of reproduction of this book in whole or in part in any form.

555 North Morton Street
Bloomington, IN 47404
800.733.6786 (toll free) / 812.336.7700
FAX: 812.336.7790

email: info@SolutionTree.com
SolutionTree.com

Printed in the United States of America

Library of Congress Cataloging-in-Publication Data
Names: Nottingham, James, author.
Title: Teach brilliantly : small shifts that lead to big gains in student learning / James A. Nottingham.
Description: Bloomington, IN : Solution Tree Press, 2024. | Includes bibliographical references and index.
Identifiers: LCCN 2023045731 (print) | LCCN 2023045732 (ebook) | ISBN 9781960574749 (paperback) | ISBN 9781960574756 (ebook)
Subjects: LCSH: Effective teaching. | Motivation in education. | Teacher-student relationships.
Classification: LCC LB1025.3 .N678 2024 (print) | LCC LB1025.3 (ebook) | DDC 371.102--dc23/eng/20231012
LC record available at https://lccn.loc.gov/2023045731
LC ebook record available at https://lccn.loc.gov/2023045732

Solution Tree
Jeffrey C. Jones, CEO
Edmund M. Ackerman, President

Solution Tree Press
President and Publisher: Douglas M. Rife
Associate Publishers: Todd Brakke and Kendra Slayton
Editorial Director: Laurel Hecker
Art Director: Rian Anderson
Copy Chief: Jessi Finn
Senior Production Editor: Sarah Foster
Proofreader: Charlotte Jones
Text and Cover Designer: Rian Anderson
Acquisitions Editors: Carol Collins and Hilary Goff
Assistant Acquisitions Editor: Elijah Oates
Content Development Specialist: Amy Rubenstein
Associate Editor: Sarah Ludwig
Editorial Assistant: Anne Marie Watkins

Acknowledgments

I find acknowledgments a curious thing. How does one decide who to include and who not to?

I have a similar skepticism about "best teacher" awards. What exactly are the criteria? Are they to do with being the most popular (In whose eyes?); the most effective (According to what—grade outcomes, discipline, student growth?); or the most dedicated (Whatever that means)? If it is true that it takes a whole village to raise a child, then how on earth do we celebrate one teacher more than another?

I have felt this tension while choosing who to acknowledge in this book, not because I can't think of anyone to mention—I can think of hundreds—but because I don't know how to include *everyone* who should be thanked. My wonderful family and dearest friends deserve the first mention, of course. After all, I am who I am because of them.

Yet, when I look back at the eleven books I've written before this, I can't help but notice the people I *didn't* mention—the ones who should've been thanked and weren't.

So, perhaps I can go for thanking those who played a direct role in the production of *this* book. The close confidants who have so generously gifted encouraging critiques; the guardian angels who have protected my time so that I can write; and the fabulous team at Solution Tree who have brought this book to life all deserve my gratitude.

Then again, all who have ever influenced me deserve thanks, for they, too, have contributed to this book. Their encouragement, challenges, critiques, and quirks have been and continue to be influential. It may take ten months from me starting to write this book to it being printed, but *before that* came thirty years of thinking, exploring, experimenting, and researching. Those who have inspired me on this journey all deserve recognition.

Then, there is you, dear colleague. By being a teacher, you have chosen to do everything in your power to help those around you engage and thrive. It ain't easy, the pay is lousy, and the worries never end. But where on earth would the world be without you?

You deserve the biggest vote of thanks. This acknowledgment and this book is for you.

Thank you!

Table of Contents

About the Author ix

INTRODUCTION
Learning Is Driven by What Teachers and Students
Do Together xi

    How This Book Is Organized xii

CHAPTER 1
When You Adjust Your *Teaching*, It Transforms
Students' *Learning* 1

    1.0 Remember Your *Why* 2

    1.1 Pay Attention to Your *What* 3

    1.2 Choose *When* 5

    1.3 Justify Your Choices 6

    1.4 Understand Why Some Interventions Are More Equal Than Others 9

    1.5 Use a Benchmark 10

    1.6 Check the Reliability of Your Choices 13

    1.7 Learn About Effect Sizes: To Use or Not to Use 14

    1.8 Glossary of Terms 15

    1.9 Next Steps 16

    1.10 *Teach Brilliantly* Top Ten: *Learning* 17

CHAPTER 2
When You *Engage* Your Students, Their Learning
Gains *Purpose* 19

    2.0 Understand Student Engagement 21

    2.1 Use Questioning to Boost Engagement 30

    2.2 Use Dialogue to Build Engagement 49

    2.3 Choose the Right Time to Engage Students in Dialogue 56

    2.4 Use Strategies to Help Students Make Connections 58

    2.5 Use Strategies to Help Students Sort and Classify 67

    2.6 Use Strategies to Help Students Think About Concepts 76

    2.7 Use Strategies to Help Students Examine Opinions 80

    2.8 Understand Not All Those Who Wonder Are Lost 85

    2.9 Dialogue Summary 88

    2.10 *Teach Brilliantly* Top Ten: *Engagement* 89

CHAPTER 3
When *Challenge* Is Just Right, Students' Abilities *Improve* . . 91

    3.0 Understand That Without Challenge, There Is No Learning 93

    3.1 Make Challenge More Desirable 95

    3.2 Learn What Research Says About Challenge 98

    3.3 Hold High Expectations for All Students 100

    3.4 Create Desirable Difficulties 102

    3.5 Set Appropriately Challenging Goals 106

    3.6 Give Students Control Over Their Learning 109

    3.7 Understand Challenge and the Learning Pit 113

    3.8 Create Challenge With the Learning Pit: A Step-by-Step Guide 124

    3.9 Challenge Summary 145

    3.10 *Teach Brilliantly* Top Ten: *Challenge* 145

CHAPTER 4
When *Feedback* Is Used Brilliantly, It Adds Significant *Value* 147

    4.0 What Is Feedback? 148

    4.1 Why Is Feedback So Complex? 149

    4.2 Feedback's Guiding Questions 150

    4.3 Feedback's Essential Qualities 151

4.4 Learning Intentions and Success Criteria 166

4.5 Self- and Peer Feedback 179

4.6 *Formative* and *Summative* 186

4.7 A Wide Variety of Feedback Types 188

4.8 Feedback and the Learning Pit 195

4.9 The Seven Steps to Feedback 198

4.10 *Teach Brilliantly* Top Ten: *Feedback* 213

CHAPTER 5
When *Expectations* Are High, Everybody *Prospers* 215

5.0 Do You Hold Great Expectations for All Students? 216

5.1 Ability Is Not Genetic (Well, It Is Sort Of!) 220

5.2 We're All on a Continuum 222

5.3 The World of Intelligence Testing Is Murky 227

5.4 Is Growth Mindset Worth the Hype? 230

5.5 Improve Everyone's Learning by Amplifying Progress . . . 240

5.6 Group Students for Maximum Growth 247

5.7 Know How to Praise and What to Reward 251

5.8 Turn Mistakes and Failure Into Learning Opportunities . . 257

5.9 Boost Self-Efficacy and Collective Efficacy 263

5.10 *Teach Brilliantly* Top Ten: *Expectations* 267

CHAPTER 6
When There Is *Equity*, There Is *Fairness* 269

6.0 Equity, Equality, and Fairness 269

6.1 Preview Strategies 272

6.2 Growth Mindset for Low-Socioeconomic-Status Students . . 280

6.3 Further Strategies to Boost Equity 282

6.4 Cognitive Load Theory 287

6.5 Equity Summary 292

EPILOGUE
Post-Credit Encores 299

References and Resources 303

Index 325

About the Author

 **James A. Nottingham** is the creator of the Learning Pit®, one of the most widely used models for teaching to emerge in the 21st century. He is also the author of twelve books, is a Fellow of the Royal Society of Arts, and is listed in *The Future 500*, which lists the United Kingdom's most forward-thinking and creative innovators.

James is driven by the desire to make education a better experience than the one he encountered. Having attended four primary schools and been expelled from two high schools, James was a student who fell through the gap. He also failed at his first two jobs: pig farming and factory work. However, when volunteering at makeshift schools in South African squatter camps, he saw a different possibility for education, one that could inspire and transform lives.

Since then, he has been on a mission to discover and share the very best that education has to offer. Along the way, he has worked closely with professors Carol Dweck (growth mindset) and John Hattie (Visible Learning), been a teaching assistant in a school for deaf students, taught across ages three to nineteen, and held a range of leadership positions in schools. At the end of the 1990s, a BBC documentary featured his work, leading to an invitation to design a new approach to teaching and learning that would raise the aspirations and achievements of students in low-socioeconomic-status schools. The success of this project was noticed beyond the United Kingdom, and so, in 2006, James started an independent company to share his approaches farther afield. Over the course of the next fifteen years, James built his company into an organization employing thirty staff in seven countries working with preK–12 schools and community groups.

James has returned to being an independent author-consultant once more. (He feels a little like a principal returning to the classroom!) He is a sought-after keynote speaker, workshop leader, and in-school consultant. He also runs demonstration lessons. Give him any class, any age, and he will be delighted to show you any of the techniques he has written about, working in situ with your students.

James is married and has three children, five mini-dachshunds (at last count), and four frizzle hens.

You can find James's work at https://learningpit.org, https://uk.linkedin.com/in/james nottingham, and @LearningPit on Instagram.

To book James A. Nottingham for professional development, contact pd@SolutionTree.com.

INTRODUCTION

Learning Is Driven by What Teachers and Students Do Together

Learning is driven by what teachers and students do together. Other people have an influence: families, leaders, administrators, and the wider community. They all play a role. But without a doubt, the interactions between teaching staff and their students make the biggest difference to the success of educational experiences. (*Teaching staff* means everyone directly involved with instruction, including teaching assistants, learning support mentors, and coaches, as well as teachers.) So, if you are interested in raising standards and improving learning outcomes, then the effectiveness of the teaching and learning process has to take center stage.

How does one improve the teaching and learning process? Thousands of theories and packaged programs promise to help. Which of these have helped and which have hindered? John Hattie's (2023) synthesis of 2,100-plus meta-analyses indicates that almost everything has worked, even the placebos. Therefore, in a sense, it matters not what we choose. Except that it does matter. It matters a lot.

We have only a short span of time with our students (despite the sense that some lessons will never end!). So, we must be discerning. We must pick the approaches that work best—not just the ones that work, but the ones that work *best*. Take the inputs we are given (students, resources, curriculum, and time), pick some approaches, work our magic, and presto—create some fabulous learning outcomes.

Oh, how easy that sounds. At least that's what commentators from afar (a long way afar!) would have us believe. It's not easy, though, is it? It's so complex that it is almost impossible to capture accurately. It's what professors Paul Black and Dylan Wiliam (1998b) called the *black box*:

> [Educational] policies . . . seem to treat the classroom as a black box. Certain inputs from the outside—pupils, teachers, other resources, management rules and requirements, parental anxieties, standards, tests with high stakes, and so on—are fed into the box. Some outputs are supposed to follow: pupils who

are more knowledgeable and competent, better test results, teachers who are reasonably satisfied, and so on.

But what is happening inside the box? How can anyone be sure that a particular set of new inputs will produce better outputs if we don't at least study what happens inside?

The answer usually given is that it is up to teachers: they have to make the inside work better. This answer is not good enough, for two reasons. First, it is at least possible that some changes in the inputs may be counterproductive and make it harder for teachers to raise standards. Second, it seems strange, even unfair, to leave the most difficult piece of the standards-raising puzzle entirely to teachers. If there are ways in which policy makers and others can give direct help and support to the everyday classroom task of achieving better learning, then surely these ways ought to be pursued vigorously. (p. 2)

Inside the Black Box (Black & Wiliam, 1998b) was published just a few years into my teaching career. The effect it had on my thinking still reverberates today. Back then, I wanted to know how to make the actions inside the black box as effective as possible. Today, I still want to know. With thirty-five years of teaching and consulting under my belt, I think I have a better idea.

A decade of speaking tours alongside professors Carol S. Dweck (expert on growth mindset) and John Hattie (creator of Visible Learning), as well as countless keynotes and workshops with other educational luminaries, have also afforded me a rare depth of insight as to what is likely to work best.

My first book, *Challenging Learning* (Nottingham, 2010), gave the Top Ten FACTS about Feedback, Application, Challenge, Thinking Skills, and Self-Esteem. This was also the first time I shared my concept of the Learning Pit®. Since then, I have written ten more books, each one giving an in-depth analysis of a single area of pedagogy.

Now, it's time to return to the beginning by sharing the most significant insights on a range of important topics. Each one stands separately. Together, they are more than the sum of their parts. They form a significant part of what ought to be taking place inside the black box.

Questions still abound, of course, but this book shares much of what I have learned.

How This Book Is Organized

To help you understand how this book is organized, this section provides some chapter highlights.

Chapter 1 (page 1): The way you think and the decisions you make as a teacher greatly influence your students' learning. This chapter shares some criteria you could use to help make those decisions wisely.

Chapter 2 (page 19): Student engagement has always been a concern, perhaps most so now. How can you recognize it when you see it, and perhaps more importantly, how do you improve it so that all students are ready to learn? This chapter includes ways to use questioning and dialogue to boost participation.

Chapter 3 (page 91): Learning begins when students go beyond their current abilities. Unfortunately, many students actively avoid taking on challenges for fear of failure or ridicule. This chapter shows how to make levels of challenge just right so that students more willingly step out of their comfort zone. It also includes Learning Pit approaches.

Chapter 4 (page 147): Feedback is already one of the most powerful effects on student learning, so why write more about it? Well, first, its quality is so variable that one-third of studies show negative effects from it! Second, many school and faculty policies focus on how to give feedback, whereas the way in which students use it matters much more. And third, timing is critical; give it too soon and you'll stop students from learning, but give it too late and it will rarely be used. This chapter shows how to put all of this right.

Chapter 5 (page 215): Every student is capable of growing and improving. They won't all achieve top grades, but they *can* all make excellent progress, so long as our expectations are high and we teach them with this prediction in mind. What does that mean for classroom practice and interactions? This chapter explains all!

Chapter 6 (page 269): Digging ever deeper into the meta-analyses I used to create this book, I noticed how time and again, the outcomes for the strategies I recommend are particularly impressive for students at risk of not graduating from K–12 education. These strategies work for everyone (I wouldn't share them if they didn't), but they are even more effective in creating equity in the classroom. This chapter tells you how and why.

To help set the scene, I have included three features in chapters 2–5: (1) purpose, (2) notice, and (3) timing. Sections 1.0–1.3 explain why I think these features are important.

CHAPTER 1

When You Adjust Your *Teaching*, It Transforms Students' *Learning*

 *More important than the curriculum is the question of the methods of teaching and the spirit in which the teaching is given.*

—Bertrand Russell

During October 1992, I experienced the first day of my teacher training course. After welcoming my peers and me, the tutor pointed to one of the hills in the distance—Wansfell Pike—and asked us to climb it! That was it: no poring over the national curriculum or learning about educational psychology as per our expectations. Instead, our mission was to climb to the top of a 1,600-foot hill, work out where we were, and then return ready to talk about it.

When we gathered back in the classroom, our tutor, Chris Rowley, asked us a series of questions, starting with, "Where were you?" The dialogue that flowed has stayed with me ever since.

Early answers were straightforward enough. We were on Wansfell Pike, one of the hills surrounding Ambleside, a town in the center of England's Lake District National Park, in the northern county of Cumbria (or the county of Westmorland, for the traditionalists among us). As we answered, Chris neither confirmed nor refuted the accuracy of assertions; he just listened. Now and again, he would ask clarification questions, but otherwise, he encouraged us to talk.

Less than five minutes into the discussion, we began arguing about our sense of place. Many of us were adamant that this part of the world was northern, but in the eyes of the Scottish students among us, it was a long way south. Some said it was traditionally Cumbrian, whereas others said locals couldn't afford to live in such a touristy place, and therefore, it could no longer be thought of as traditional.

As time went on, we covered a wide range of topics, including how long you must live somewhere for you to think of it as home and for you to be considered a local; where the North begins and where it ends; whether national parks are good for locals; and if a sense of place is anything other than someone's feelings about a place at a particular point in time.

Afterward, as we reflected on the discussion, Chris shared some curriculum documents identifying sense of place as a central topic in elementary school geography. We were blown away. We had assumed the activity was purely an icebreaker before the *real* studies began. Yet, his lesson design and well-timed questions had caused us to care deeply about and engage passionately in a topic that until then none of us had ever even thought about.

Throughout that year, Chris Rowley changed my view of education.

Initially, I had signed up for teacher training because I wanted to work with young people. There wasn't a subject I particularly wanted to teach, and I certainly wasn't keen on the idea of being back at school, having hated the experience so much as a kid. But I wanted to work with young people, and I thought teacher training was a good place to start.

I soon realized that being a teacher could also give me the opportunity to get kids to care about their learning, to be interested in the world around them, and to *want* to know more, just as Chris had done for me. His sense of purpose was as inspirational as it was clear—he wanted people to care. Not just go through the motions. Not just pass tests. Not just know the curriculum. But really, deeply, passionately care.

I should say that not every lesson was like the first. There were days that he drew attention to the minutiae of curriculum standards or helped us understand how to grade papers. On other occasions, he took a contrary approach to teaching in the hope that we would push back and show him what needed improving. In doing so, he showed us that there isn't just one way to teach in much the same way as there isn't one way to learn. Different contexts need different approaches.

Therefore, I would like to start off this first chapter by asking you to consider your purpose, your mission, and your approach (or approaches) to teaching, for what you do, why you do it, and how you think about it will make a big difference to your students' learning.

1.0 Remember Your *Why*

Our sense of purpose is all too often lost in the busyness of the black box. We put so much effort into making today run smoothly that tomorrow's aspirations are relegated to an afterthought. What outcomes do we want by the end of the term, by the end of the year, or by the end of our students' schooling? All become passing thoughts when the events of today distract us.

It is a similar story for our students. "What are you learning?" classroom visitors ask. "We're doing this," students reply. "Why?" ask the visitors. "Don't know," "Because it's on the test," and "Our teacher told us to" come the answers.

As Simon Sinek made famous in his TED Talk (Sinek, 2009a), as well as in his book (Sinek, 2009b), we should start with the *why*. Why are we teaching this? Why are we doing that? Why is this important to master? (One hopes our answers will be better than "Because it's on the curriculum!")

More fundamentally, why did we go into teaching in the first place? Why choose this career rather than another? For example, finance and business tend to pay more and demand less. Presumably, we chose it not for the paperwork or politics, nor for the one-hour meetings that last fifty-nine minutes longer than necessary!

Most of us went into teaching to make a difference; to help students learn; to put right what didn't work when we were students; or to follow in the footsteps of those who made a difference. Does this passion still propel us? Does the mission still guide us? Or have the bureaucrats ground us down?

As you read this book, you will notice that I am a fan of etymology. Reflecting on words' original meanings can add layers of significance. The word *disaster*, for example, comes from the Latin, *dis-astro*. The original meaning evolved at a time when navigation relied on position fixing using stars and other celestial bodies. Disaster, therefore, was likely when navigators lost sight of the stars.

Following this line of inquiry, which stars do you navigate your teaching by? Do they have something to do with the attitudes, skills, and knowledge you want your students to develop? Do they reflect the grades you hope your students will achieve? Do they perhaps involve the ways in which students engage in schooling with curiosity, eagerness, and confidence? Do they represent students' belief in themselves and the willingness to continue learning that they might develop by the time they leave your watchful eye? These are all big questions that I hope this book will provoke.

Questions about purpose don't necessarily have to be so elemental. They could also be about the purpose of the lesson, the topic, or the task. Connecting the *what* to the *why* will give meaning. It will situate. It will determine direction. Ultimately, it will lead to better understanding.

To give you a head start, each chapter begins with a statement of purpose. In chapter 4 (on feedback, page 147), for example, I start with the following.

- Feedback should help students decide on the next steps in their learning journey.
- Feedback ought to be offered constructively and compassionately.
- Feedback's value rests in being received thoughtfully and used wisely.

I also include an example vision statement that you could use to describe the purpose and direction of travel. These statements include a clear sense of the inherent values as well as the expected outcomes.

In the preceding example, I describe the purpose of feedback as helping people on their learning journey. I say this because feedback is at its most effective when used formatively to form the next steps. This becomes the guiding star. Feedback is about helping recipients improve. It's not about grading or making comments on past performances. It's about helping students (or staff) decide on their next steps so that they can improve their learning or performance. Having this purpose clear in our minds helps us determine which approaches to use *inside the black box* and which not to.

1.1 Pay Attention to Your *What*

Learning what to notice adds qualities to our life that didn't exist before. In the early 2000s, I began traveling to Australia and New Zealand for work. One thing I noticed was that teachers I met in that part of the world knew their wine. Not all did, of course, but certainly a significant number knew when a chardonnay is more fitting than a sauvignon blanc or when a shiraz is superior to a pinot noir. Back home, my mates and I went to the pub and had whatever local beer was on tap. This collective and seemingly ingrained knowledge intrigued me. So, I signed up for a series of wine-tasting courses.

For the first time in my life, I learned how to taste and smell with sensitivity. I moved beyond simple judgments of niceness to distinguishing between textures, flavors, and aromas. I learned to notice tannins and the ways in which they complement or overpower, to take a similar approach to acidity, and to notice a wine's body, its smells, and its complexity.

I found it all fascinating and frustrating in equal measure. How had I gotten to my thirties without ever learning this? Not about wine per se, but about tasting and smelling in general. Once upon a time, the process of eating and drinking had been principally utilitarian for me. I ate and drank because it was functional or social. But the more courses I did—and the more I learned what to notice—the more eating and drinking became an experience in itself.

I had a similar journey with photography. A friend of a friend just so happened to be an award-winning photographer. So, I made sure to hang out with him and to learn what I could. And guess what? He taught me what to notice. The sources of light and associated shadows; the relationships between objects; and different perspectives, additional reflections, and cropping change the essence of a photograph. I learned to capture a story in one shot—rarely posed, always contextual. I still take shoot-from-the-hip shots, but when I put my mind to it, I now also take photos that tell a story, celebrate a moment, and convey ideas, all because I know more about what to notice.

And just in the last week, as I have been writing this introduction, I have thought a lot about what to notice in art. I am not an arty person; in fact, I'm quite the opposite. I've spent much of my life believing I don't have an artistic bone in my body. When I was a teenager, my art teachers repeatedly implied I was talentless. Comparing my less-than-impressive efforts to those created by my talented peers further entrenched my belief. As an adult, I once queued for hours to see the *Mona Lisa* at the Louvre. I took one look and wondered what all the fuss is about. The same goes for the Sistine Chapel ceiling. Yes, the scale is impressive, but a vista of lakes and mountains wins my attention every time. I know how to appreciate nature, but art is beyond me. Or that's what I thought.

All it took to change my thinking was a post on X (formerly known as Twitter) by Joseph Fasano (2023), which read, "What's your favorite detail of any work of art? I think the right hand of Michelangelo's *David* is one of the greatest things ever made." Luckily for me, or else I would have scrolled on by, he included a photograph of the statue's hand, and, as I mentioned earlier, I like photography. So, I followed the thread of replies, and they were astonishing. Here were people from all around the world giving their recommendations about what is worth noticing.

Many of the replies struck me, but the two that really stood out were these:

> I used to live in Paris and one of the things I always marveled at was the carving on the *Victory of Samothrace*. It's amazing to make marble into something that looks like ripples of gauze over a beautiful body. (Sullivan, 2023)

> Michelangelo's *Moses* includes one very small muscle in the forearm—it contracts only when lifting the pinky, otherwise it's invisible. He's lifting his pinky finger, so the statue shows the tiny muscle is contracted. What a detail. (Connolly, 2023)

Both posts were accompanied by images of the sculptures they referred to. The pictures were breathtaking. They provoked a longing to see the sculptures up close and personal.

I subsequently shared the posts with my eldest daughter, who was equally fascinated. Like me, she has had art teachers who have implied she has little talent in the subject. However, these posts caused her to think that maybe adding a course on art history during her university degree might not be as preposterous as she first thought. That is the power of knowing what to notice. Knowing what to be passionate about.

In each chapter, I will help you decide what to notice. The topics I cover will be familiar to every teacher, but what to notice might not be. Every educator knows that learning should include feedback, dialogue, challenge, and self-esteem. Even growth mindset (Dweck, 2015) is de rigueur these days. But what are the vital features to notice? What is essential, and what is merely window dressing? These are some of the distinctions I will help you make.

1.2 Choose *When*

Once you've clarified your purpose and you know what to notice, your next step is identifying your priorities. Or, to put it another way, you know where you're going and what's important. Now, what should you do next and when? I will help you answer these questions throughout the book.

The majority of each chapter covers *what*. What is feedback (and how does it differ from assessment)? What is a growth mindset, and what can you do to build a growth mindset culture in your classroom? What is exploratory talk, and why is it the optimum form of dialogue in the context of learning? and so on.

However, I also draw attention to *when*. In fact, in some sections, I do this almost as much as I identify *what*. For example, deep learning is as necessary as surface knowledge, but the key is not to identify which is best but to know *when* to move students from one to the other. The same goes for challenge. All students need to be challenged, but no one should be challenged all day long. We need to know *when* to challenge and when to support, when to scaffold and when to encourage students to study independently. Timing is as crucial as the topic, sometimes even more so. Here are a few more examples to illustrate this point.

- **Making mistakes can be instructional (at the right time):** In chapter 5 (page 215), I share evidence that learning from mistakes can result in longer-lasting understanding. But *when* a student makes those mistakes is just as important as *how* they learn from them. When students make mistakes in high-stakes conditions, the impact is likely to be negative. For example, mistakes in a one-time-only exam could mean the difference between one grade and the next grade higher or lower, or a mistake crossing the road could lead to dangerous consequences. However, making the same mistakes in a practice exam, correcting them, and studying further is likely to lead to enhanced learning. Making mistakes identifying road hazards during a simulation can lead to similarly improved learning if the exam taker has the opportunity to revise and restudy.

- **Going into the Learning Pit can deepen learning (at the right time):** I created the Learning Pit to encourage my students to step more willingly out of their comfort zone. An exploration of my reasons for this, and why I call the process *going through the Learning Pit*, is shared in section 3.7 (page 113). For now, I think it's worth making the point that students shouldn't *always* go through the pit, which is the same as saying they shouldn't *always* be out of their comfort zone. They obviously need to go beyond their ability and comfort levels if they are to learn; but then sometimes, we don't want them to learn! Sometimes, we want them to consolidate and build confidence in their current abilities. Therefore, as with everything, there is a time and a place to go into the Learning Pit, and there are times to avoid it.

- **Dialogue can significantly improve learning (when used at the right time):** Dialogic teaching is one of the best ways to help students make meaning of their learning. The effect size of using dialogue strategies with students can be as high as d = 0.82, double the normal rate of progress (Murphy, Wilkinson, Soter, Hennessey, & Alexander, 2009). (If you're unfamiliar with effect sizes, you'll learn more about them in the next section.) However, this type of classroom talk works best when students are ready to move from surface knowledge to deep learning. Before then, it is nowhere near as effective. If students have little or no knowledge about a topic of study, then they will typically gain more from direct instruction or from reading about and researching the topic. Dialogue works best when your students are ready to make connections and apply their learning to new contexts. I cover all of this in chapter 2 (page 19).

These examples are but a few of the many included in this book. In fact, it would be fair to say that every strategy and approach to pedagogy I've recommended works well at some stages of the learning cycle but not at others. Just as there is truth to the saying, "There is no silver bullet in education," it is true to say that no strategy is suitable for every occasion.

1.3 Justify Your Choices

Subjective experiences rather than empirical data often guide teachers' beliefs. In our profession, we have to use both sources of evidence. Neither is solely accurate; a combined approach gives us a better chance of improving learning for all students:

> Teachers' beliefs have been shown to influence teaching and learning. If they differ substantially from results of school effectiveness research, we have reason to assume a negative effect on educational outcomes. For example, if a teacher undervalues a particular teaching method or overvalues surface structural aspects like class size, this could be a serious threat to effective teaching. (Fleckenstein, Zimmermann, Köller, & Möller, 2015, p. 28)

New Zealand professor John Hattie's work has been instrumental in helping teachers know not just what will work but what will work *best*. When he published *Visible Learning: A Synthesis of Over 800 Meta-Analyses Relating to Achievement*, he shared a synthesis of eight hundred meta-analyses in education (Hattie, 2009). (In 2023, Hattie released *Visible Learning: The*

Sequel, which includes more than 2,100 meta-analyses in its synthesis.) Placing the data from all this research onto an effect size scale, he calculated that the average gains students make in one school year are equivalent to an effect size of $d = 0.40$. Thus, if students make gains in the region of $d = 0.60$, this is equivalent to eighteen months of growth in twelve months. An effect size of $d = 0.80$ would be doubling the rate of learning, and so on.

This average effect of $d = 0.40$ became Hattie's benchmark or, as he calls it, the *hinge point* (Hattie, 2023). More than $d = 0.40$, and you could say your students are likely to achieve more-than-average gains across the school year. Less than $d = 0.40$ (but greater than zero), and you would still improve student learning but in a less-than-average way.

Effect sizes offer a useful measure of how effective one approach is likely to be compared to another. They don't tell the whole story, but they do give a sense of what is worth the investment of our focus and energies. They can also help justify one choice over another.

In chapter 2 (page 19), I share evidence that dialogue has an effect size of $d = 0.82$, which compared to the average effect size of $d = 0.40$ is equivalent to doubling the rate of learning. I use this statistic to support my claim that dialogue should be part of everyday classroom practice. In chapter 4 (page 147), I show that feedback has an overall effect size of $d = 0.62$ but that this varies according to the feedback's type, timing, and application. So, for this topic, I use the varying effect sizes to help determine which forms of feedback we should prioritize. In chapter 3, section 3.6 (page 109), I begin with the surprising evidence that giving students choice leads to lower-than-usual rates of progress (an effect size of $d = 0.02$). I explain why this is happening and what we can do to offer choices in such a way that the effect size is much greater. Note that you can find the information underlying each of these effect sizes in Hattie (2023).

However, effect sizes are only *part of* the story. Relying on just them would be a bit like checking on just the temperature before deciding what to wear. You wouldn't solely check on forecasts of how warm or cold it will be outside. You would also take note of the likelihood of rain, wind strength, and whether it's going to be sunny or overcast. Similarly, if you received results on your blood pressure or cholesterol levels, you wouldn't assume that these form a complete picture of your health. Effect sizes are the same. They give you useful information, but they don't tell the whole story.

If one intervention has a bigger effect size than another, it means it is *likely* to be better than the other, but not necessarily. The one with a lower effect size might have other benefits that don't show up in the data. It might also be easier or cheaper to implement.

In addition, how effect sizes are calculated is imperfect. More complete guides than this will tell you what effect sizes include and what they ignore; they will also identify—or at least surmise—author bias, inclusion of outliers, and validity of conclusions.

Since this isn't a book about statistics, I won't go into the data in depth. However, the summaries in the next sections should identify some of the pros and cons of effect sizes so that when you see them throughout the book, you will have a sense of their significance.

1.3.1 Why Effect Sizes Are Worthwhile

The following are six reasons why effect sizes are worthwhile to consider.

1. Effect sizes are easy to calculate and understand.

2. They are based on real-life data about what has happened when particular approaches have been used in schools before.

3. They offer a standardized measure of *relative* effectiveness. Interventions with bigger effect sizes are likely to accelerate learning more than those with lower effect sizes.

4. Effect sizes allow us to compare different studies irrespective of the scales used originally. For example, if one group of studies investigates increases in the frequency with which students ask questions, whereas another considers changes in teacher recruitment and retention, these can more readily be considered alongside each other when placed on the same effect size scale.

5. Effect sizes are one of the measures that can support evidence-led practice. They provide high-quality information about what is likely to be beneficial based on existing evidence.

6. When placed alongside Hattie's hinge point (benchmark) of $d = 0.40$ effect size, they can also be used to identify which factors are likely to have a better-than-average or very high impact.

1.3.2 How Effect Sizes Mislead

The following are six reasons why effect sizes can mislead.

1. Education is complex, and it is human. Representing it with a number is a fool's errand.

2. Effect sizes are calculated from biased data. Staff and students adjust their language and actions when being observed. Researchers filter what they notice according to their own interests, expectations, and biases. What is significant to staff (for example, a single word uttered by the most reticent of students) could very well pass unnoticed by data collectors.

3. A common way to investigate impact is to intervene with half of the classes in a school (the treatment group) and then, in the interest of equity, to run the intervention with the other classes (the control group) after the researchers have left. Many teachers, however, choose not to wait. For them, helping *everyone* flourish is much more important than maintaining research integrity!

4. Primary sources of evidence don't usually include effect sizes. Effect sizes are more often calculated by authors of meta-analyses. This distance from the classroom can lead to a loss of nuance and detail.

5. Effect sizes are standardized by dividing a sample by the standard deviation. The results are vulnerable to inflation if the sample contains less variation (for example, a smaller percentage of at-risk students) than the general school population.

6. Effect sizes don't include a cost-benefit analysis. For example, using clickers to gather instant responses from all students has an effect size of 0.24 (Hattie, 2023), whereas classroom discussion has an effect size of 0.82 (Murphy et al., 2009). This indicates that dialogue is the intervention to choose. No equipment is needed, and the impact is four times greater. However, engaging all students in class discussion

is likely to take significantly more time and effort than getting all students to use clickers. So, as a quick win, introducing clickers could be the smart decision.

In this video, James explains some of the key points about using effect sizes.

1.4 Understand Why Some Interventions Are More Equal Than Others

Thinking of effect sizes as a form guide can be useful. How well is one factor likely to perform compared to other factors? It's a bit like betting odds at the races. With one such guide, I turned ten dollars into twenty-five dollars at Caulfield Racecourse in Melbourne (my only trip to the races). A couple of choices were based on the quirkiness of the horses' names, but overall, the form guide helped me—a complete novice at betting on horses—to win a few dollars.

A sport I know more about is football (soccer for our U.S. readers). I don't trust myself enough to place bets with real money, but I do play fantasy football. In the version I play, managers get three transfers per week. To help me make my decisions, I start with the form guides available in-app and online. They give me a good starting point and help me identify players I know little about. I then weigh this advice with my own gut instinct and background knowledge. I think about which players are going up against a former team, which are likely to be rested, which will probably take penalties, and which might form a good differential against other managers. In other words, the form guides are a springboard for me, but they're not my only consideration.

So it is with effect sizes. If you are new to the job or are trying to choose between two relatively unfamiliar initiatives, then an effect size form guide can be very helpful. If, say, you are choosing between clickers and virtual reality headsets, then their relative effect sizes ($d = 0.24$ versus $d = 0.54$) could be the information you need to tip the balance.

However, when you are more experienced in your role or are making choices between familiar contexts, then effect sizes will be one of many factors you consider. For example, if you need to choose between starting the day with an exercise class or adding a broad enrichment program, then the effect sizes of 0.20 and 0.12 could help guide your discussions—*together with* anticipated cost, effort, and expertise required; likely disruption to school transport; students' and parents' preferences; and so on.

1.5 Use a Benchmark

When using effect sizes, it is important to have a benchmark, the most basic of which is to ensure the effects are positive. (You obviously don't want to be using an approach that is likely to have a negative impact on your students' learning!) To ensure effects are positive, you are looking for anything that is greater than zero. So, even an effect size of $d = 0.02$ would be positive—albeit minimally so. As such, it could be worth investing your time and effort in.

Notice that I say it *could be*—rather than *will be*—worth implementing. To say something *will be* worth implementing, I would need to take account of other factors, such as time and cost, as well as understand what it replaces. For example, if an intervention has an effect size of 0.02, then that is positive; but if it replaced something that had an effect size of 0.15, then I ought not to say it is positive. Equally, if I had to invest a lot of time, money, or effort in an intervention and it only resulted in an effect size of 0.02, then I might well be better off looking elsewhere. Yes, its results were more than zero—or in other words, better than nothing—but it didn't take *nothing* to create it.

Researchers Charles E. Moon, Gary F. Render, and Darrell W. Pendley (1985) find that teaching students some relaxation techniques leads to an effect size of 0.16. This is a positive effect and a good one at that. However, we should consider the time needed to teach the techniques and to use them frequently enough to have an impact. Also, consider the activity replaced by teaching relaxation techniques. Time in school is finite, so the addition of relaxation techniques will necessarily require something else to drop from the schedule.

An influence that I might more readily say *will be* positive is playing background music. Researcher Lois Hetland (2000) examined thirty-six studies looking for evidence of the *Mozart Effect* in which playing background music was found to decrease pulse rate, improve classroom behavior, and improve performance on learning tasks. She calculated an effect size of $d = 0.23$, the equivalent of a 50 percent gain in learning progress. This impact seems remarkable given the low cost and minimal effort required and, therefore, will be (rather than *could be*) positive.

Before we all rush to download Mozart music to play for our students, a more recent meta-analysis by researchers Juliane Kämpfe, Peter Sedlmeier, and Frank Rankewitz (2011) shows a negative effect when music is played in the background for adult learners! And when the two studies making the biggest claims were removed from the Hetland meta-analysis, the effects shown in the other thirty-four studies showed minimal impact. So, perhaps playing background music *might* be useful. Some of the time. For some of your students.

But then, couldn't that be said of most interventions? So long as an intervention is likely to have a positive—rather than negative—effect on student learning, then shouldn't it be considered? Well, yes, except we can't simply try everything and hope for the best. We must be discerning about our choices. We have finite resources and time.

Would it be right to cut down the five hours per week devoted to literacy to four if that would allow us to use the *spare* hour for much-needed exercise? Perhaps. But why exercise? Why not introduce road-safety courses in school? Or study taxes? What about first aid? Mindfulness? Care for pets? Bible study? Sailing? Every single one of these has its merits, at least in the eyes of one group or another.

Indeed, most interventions currently trialed in schools have a positive effect on student learning. Of the 322 factors listed in the Visible Learning Metax (n.d.) database (www.visiblelearningmetax.com), 91 percent of them show a positive effect. There are negatives, of course, but the overwhelming majority are likely to improve learning in one way, shape, or form. Presumably, that's why they were introduced in the first place: to improve learning.

These statistics are reassuring. They suggest it doesn't really matter what you choose. So long as you invest yourself in an intervention, believe in it, and introduce it with passion and expertise, then whatever you choose should lead to a positive impact.

However, there simply isn't enough time in the school week to try everything. Students themselves don't have enough formative years for our choices to be random. We must be discerning. We must choose the factors that will help us best.

As discussed in section 1.3 (page 8), Hattie's work was seminal. Before he proposed the benchmark of 0.40 effect size, too many decisions relied on whether a new approach to pedagogy or curriculum was likely to have a positive effect. With this new hinge point, discussions began to center on significance: "Will this intervention have a better-than-average—or more significant—impact than others?"

A good example arose during a meeting I attended. The staff from a group of primary schools were trying to decide if it was a good idea to invest in *Read Write Inc.*, a popular phonics program (Miskin, 2006). The main justification was it would help teach students how to read and write. When asked for advice, I suggested—as gently as I could—that the staff were asking the wrong question. Instead of asking, "Will this help teach our pupils how to read and write?" they should have been asking if *Read Write Inc.* would teach reading and writing *better* than the approaches they were currently using. They were already teaching reading and writing, so instead of looking for something to *start* the process, they should have been looking for something to *improve* the process. Don't compare a proposed change to *nothing*; compare it to *the norm*.

Hattie's hinge point, or benchmark, was useful in this situation. Knowing the average $d = 0.40$ effect size gave us the opportunity to lift the bar from finding something that is better than nothing to finding something that is better than normal.

Of course, one problem is that most schools don't know the effect size data for their normal approaches. They know the grades their students get at the end of the year; they know some students are achieving brilliantly and others are not. But rarely do they know the effect sizes for their own endeavors. In the absence of local data, however, we can use Hattie's benchmark. Indeed, it might be the only one readily available.

Other researchers use different ways to report on effect sizes. A particularly clear one is used by the Education Endowment Foundation in England. It reports in terms of the number of additional months' progress across a twelve-month period. For example, improving parental engagement shows a positive impact of four months' additional progress; providing social-emotional learning interventions is likely to produce equivalent gains; and engaging students in physical activity is shown to add one additional month's progress to academic achievement. But students' repeating a year after they have failed to demonstrate the standard required is likely to lead to a negative impact of minus three months.

There have been criticisms of Hattie's hinge point. Early adopters of his work used the $d = 0.40$ effect size as a cutoff point, below which effect sizes less than 0.40 were regarded disdainfully, as if they weren't worth considering. This is *not* what Hattie intended, a point he makes in *Visible Learning: The Sequel* (Hattie, 2023).

For clarity, any effect size of more than zero indicates a positive gain in student learning. For example, a meta-analysis by Jeni L. Burnette and colleagues (2013) shows the impact of students' having a growth mindset (as opposed to having a fixed mindset) is $d = 0.19$. This is a positive gain, equivalent to improving learning by almost 50 percent, and it is strong evidence that it is better to be in a growth mindset than not. However, since $d = 0.19$ is only halfway toward Hattie's hinge point of $d = 0.40$, some people suppose (or even assert) that a growth mindset is not worth investing in. They believe that only factors above $d = 0.40$ effect size are worth considering. Unfortunately, this is a simplistic conclusion and, as such, a misleading one.

The three intended purposes for Hattie's hinge point of $d = 0.40$ are as follows.

1. **"One year's growth for one year's schooling" is Hattie's mantra:** Having spent many happy hours traveling and presenting with Hattie between 2013 and 2018, I heard this phrase again and again (J. Hattie, personal conversation, April 2013). What he means is every student deserves to make progress of at least $d = 0.40$ effect size every year. If they are making progress of less than $d = 0.40$, then we ought to intervene (for example, adapt our instruction, change expectations, or challenge or support students more). However, if students are making progress of more than $d = 0.40$, then we should celebrate this *and* find out why so that we can replicate their success.

    Perhaps unintentionally, this mantra has political as well as educational implications. Many educational systems around the world determine which schools are working well by the grades their students achieve. A school where most students achieve top grades is successful; those where very few achieve the best grades are considered less successful. What isn't receiving enough weighting is the starting point for students. Selective schools only admit students who have already achieved top grades, whereas others serve communities with high numbers of students with risk factors that lower graduation rates. In effect, some schools begin "the race" with students just a few meters from the finish line, whereas others need to explain to students how the race works and why it is worth entering even though there are many obstacles in their way. In many cases, there are students who start some distance back of the starting line.

    A fairer system would be to consider how much progress students make *as well as* the grades and qualifications they achieve. Hattie's benchmark of $d = 0.40$ effect size can be a strong indicator for this. It is intended not to be used as a "big stick" but to help identify what works best so that successful approaches to learning can be scaled up and replicated.

2. **Look for interventions that improve learning beyond normal:** As Hattie synthesized so many meta-analyses into his database, he noticed that almost everything tried and tested in schools improves learning in one way, shape, or form. As shared earlier, 91 percent of the 350-plus factors in *Visible Learning: The Sequel*

(Hattie, 2023) are positive. This is good news, but it is also a double-edged sword. Whatever intervention I pick is likely to help my students learn, but that could also mean I can do whatever I like. Why teach my students how to read when I could teach them how to juggle instead? After all, juggling has been shown to improve hand-eye coordination. Forget numeracy lessons; let's do yoga instead, because relaxation techniques lead to better learning. Granted, I'm being facetious with these examples, but the point still stands. If my benchmark is zero (do anything that is positive), then I am less discerning than if I lift the benchmark to $d = 0.40$.

3. **The $d = 0.40$ benchmark invites more discussion:** Rather than looking through an alphabetical list of 294 factors showing positive effects, and 28 factors showing negative effects (all shown on www.visiblelearningmetax.com), we should question why some factors are lower than average and why some are much higher. For example, why does being in a growth mindset lead to *only* a $d = 0.19$ effect size when the associated behaviors and attitudes are all so positive? Or why is the jigsaw method (page 295) not commonly used in schools when the $d = 1.20$ effect size is the highest of any teaching method included in a meta-analysis? These discussions could take place without a benchmark, but knowing the average effect adds another dimension to the conversation.

1.6 Check the Reliability of Your Choices

As well as noticing the relative size of the effect, note that not all effect sizes are created equal. Some are calculated from insufficient or weak evidence, whereas others come from extensive research.

When publishing their findings, researchers give a sense of the robustness of evidence available. For example, the Education Endowment Foundation (n.d.b) notes in its examination of *learning styles* "unclear impact for very low cost based on insufficient evidence," whereas for the impact of *feedback*, it states "very high impact for very low cost based on extensive evidence."

Similarly, Hattie includes confidence ratings—or as he calls it, a robustness index—with his data. These represent the quantity of meta-analyses included in the Visible Learning Metax (n.d.) database, the number of studies and students involved in those meta-analyses, and the number of different effects noted. *Effects* are types of impact noted. For example, the following are four different effects: (1) students asking more questions, (2) students talking for longer, (3) students taking more attempts to complete a task, and (4) students showing improvements in their reasoning abilities.

In section 1.5 (page 10), I mentioned the use of background music to help with students' concentration. The Visible Learning Metax (n.d.) database includes two meta-analyses on this topic, which include 79 studies, 3,104 students, and 79 effects. Hattie gives confidence scores of 2 for the number of meta-analyses, 3 for the number of studies, 2 for the number of students, and 1 for the number of effects, and then an overall confidence score of 2. All these scores are out of a maximum of 5. Therefore, the data as they stand now are insufficient to be relied on heavily. But the confidence scores for setting challenging goals for students are 3 for the number of meta-analyses, 4 for the number of studies, 4 for the number of students, and 3 for the number of effects with an overall score of 4 out of 5, which means these data are more robust.

1.7 Learn About Effect Sizes: To Use or Not to Use

 *Not everything that can be counted counts, and not everything that counts can be counted.*

—William Bruce Cameron

The following are five considerations for using or not using effect sizes.

1. **Effect sizes do not provide definitive answers:** They should not be used in isolation. They can help to form a picture of best bets, but they shouldn't be the sole justification. They are calculated from meta-analyses about what worked rather than what will work.

2. **Effect sizes give useful but incomplete information:** For example, if you wanted to know if I drove safely to work today, then information about the speed I was traveling relative to other road users would help you answer that question. But presumably, you would also want to know if I anticipated potential problems, remained alert, kept my eyes on the road, kept a safe distance from other cars, and avoided erratic moves or braking. My relative speed would help you, but it wouldn't give you everything you'd need to know to answer the question confidently. It is the same with effect sizes. They are a very good starting point but are incomplete, nonetheless.

3. **Look beyond the headline:** Don't dismiss a low effect size or accept a high effect size without first exploring the factors behind the statistics. For example, boosting teacher subject knowledge leads to a d = 0.19 effect size (Hattie, 2023). This is lower than most staff would anticipate, particularly given the emphasis on content within the curriculum. If you look beyond the headline, you will find that improved staff knowledge isn't enough to improve student learning; staff also require pedagogical abilities. An expert teacher can cover a lesson outside their subject area more effectively than a novice can teach their *own* subject. The optimum is to have both improved subject knowledge and pedagogical expertise. Improving one in the absence of the other is likely to lead to moderate rather than excellent gains.

    Another example, and one that is controversial, is that reducing the number of students in each class is likely to have a small positive effect rather than the large impact that most staff would anticipate. It has an effect size of d = 0.18. There are many reasons for this, including the following three reasons.

    a. Having fewer students reduces our workload, but there is little evidence that it changes the way we teach.

    b. Reducing quantity is not the same as improving quality, because most teachers would anticipate making more progress with a motivated, engaged class of thirty than they would with a disengaged, disruptive class of twenty.

c. Perhaps most significantly, given the choice between removing ten students at random and being able to choose which two students to remove from a class, almost every teacher would go for the second option!

4. **A gain is a gain:** Don't be too quick to dismiss small effect sizes. The two examples I use in point 3 show effect sizes of $d = 0.19$ and $d = 0.18$, respectively. These are the equivalent of improving learning by 50 percent (when compared to making no changes at all). They are both less than the average effect across all 322 factors in the Visible Learning Meta[x] (n.d.) database, but neither is insignificant. Who wouldn't wish to improve learning by as much as 50 percent? Unfortunately, other factors run contrary to recommending them for implementation—most notably, in the case of reducing class size, the enormous cost associated with hiring so many extra staff to cover the additional classes.

5. **Effect sizes are one more piece of evidence to help you decide what to invest your time, effort, and money in:** If you work with middle or high school students, then you probably already use exam scores, graded assignments, and the percentage of students who secure a place at their first-choice college or university as indicators of good learning. Effect sizes can sit alongside these. However, if you work with younger students, then effect sizes might be one of the few measurements available to you.

Of course, no matter what age of students we teach, we would *also* want to investigate qualitative measures of engagement, participation, and passion; these include students' curiosity and their ability to make connections, apply their learning, collaborate with others, and adapt to new circumstances. Also, we'd probably want to look at attendance rates. Effect sizes can *add to* our collection of evidence.

1.8 Glossary of Terms

The following offers a glossary of terms used in this chapter.

- **Black box:** In this chapter, *black box* refers to a term used by professors Black and Wiliam (2002) to indicate how hidden from view the classroom often is. Their contention is that policymakers feed new inputs such as rules, requirements, and resources into schools and expect successful outputs to follow. What happens between inputs and outputs is whatever teachers do inside this black box.

- **Effect size:** An *effect size* is a statistical calculation that can be used to compare the relative merits of different interventions. There are many conventions for calculating these, though the most common one is Cohen's *d*, used in this book and favored by Hattie. The mean of a control group is subtracted from the mean of an experimental group, and this result is divided by the standard deviation of the entire sample (Colman, 2015). There are many arguments against using effect sizes, many of which are covered in this chapter. However, effect sizes can be useful indicators of the relative impact of one intervention compared with another. Any effect size greater than zero indicates a positive effect on the experimental group compared to a control group. Generally speaking, values between zero and $d = 0.20$ are small but positive; $d = 0.40$ is a medium effect; and $d = 0.80$ is a large positive effect.

- **Hinge point:** John Hattie has been synthesizing the results of hundreds of meta-analyses into one database, Visible Learning Meta^x (n.d.). By placing all 2,100-plus meta-analyses onto the same effect size scale, he has calculated that the average effect size is $d = 0.40$. He calls this the hinge point. Any influence with an effect size greater than $d = 0.40$ is better than average; anything below that is worse than average. In the absence of more contextualized data, this world average is a better benchmark than most. Of the 350-plus influences that Hattie has identified, 91 percent of them show a positive effect. This is good news because when we try to improve student achievement, we normally succeed. What a stunningly successful profession we work in.

  However, if our justification for investing resources in a strategy is "because it is positive," that is a low bar, particularly when we consider almost everything is in that category. Better to lift the hinge point to more than average because that at least exceeds looking for something that is simply better than nothing!

- **Meta-analysis:** A meta-analysis is a systematic search that attempts to identify all the studies that meet a particular set of eligibility criteria (for example, all studies about peer-to-peer feedback in middle schools that include control group data). The meta-analyses included in Hattie's Visible Learning Meta^x (n.d.) database are all based on real-life data about what has happened when particular approaches have been used in schools. By combining information, meta-analyses can provide more precise estimates of the effects than those derived from individual studies.

- **Visible Learning:** Hattie uses this name to refer to his synthesis of studies relating to student achievement. To date, he has included 2,103 meta-analyses in his database. Hattie asserts that teachers should be evaluators of their own impact. So, rather than thinking primarily about what they taught, teachers should shift their emphasis to what students learned.

1.9 Next Steps

There is clear evidence that expert teachers have a greater insight into current research findings than novices do. Even though it's a correlation, not causation, being well versed in empirical evidence is an important characteristic of professional growth.

As researchers Johanna Fleckenstein, Friederike Zimmermann, Olaf Köller, and Jens Möller (2015) report in *Frontline Learning Research:*

Expert and novice teachers' beliefs differ substantially from each other. . . . Expert teachers showed a stronger overall congruence with empirical evidence, scoring higher in achievement-related variables and lower in variables concerning surface and infrastructural conditions of schooling as well as student-internal factors. [It is important, therefore, that teacher-education practices] emphasize research findings and challenge existing beliefs of (prospective) teachers. (p. 27)

This book aims at giving insights into achievement-related variables and current research findings. Throughout the book, I use effect sizes and meta-analyses to inform your decision making. Beyond this chapter, I recommend that you check out the following resources.

Durham University professor Robert Coe was one of the first academics in the United Kingdom to argue for evidence-based policies. He is highly regarded in schools as well as in the world of academia. He has written a thoughtful and well-balanced blog post (Coe, 2018b) about meta-analysis and effect size that he finishes with, "Systematic review based on effect sizes . . . isn't perfect; we do need to understand the limitations; ideally, we need better studies and better reviews. But given where we are, it's the best we have."

Visible Learning Meta^x (n.d.), the research database built by John Hattie's team, allows users to sort factors by a range of criteria from effect size scope (for example, from d = 0.20 to d = 0.40) to domains such as those relating to teachers, students, or home. Every factor includes a link to its underlying research. It is worth noting that some of the effect sizes differ from those published elsewhere because this online database is frequently updated as more and more meta-analyses are added.

1.10 *Teach Brilliantly* Top Ten: *Learning*

The central function of education is to help students learn. Other goals exist, with some more important than others, but when it comes down to it, the central focus is learning. So, what can we do to ensure that all students learn as well as they might?

1. **Learning is driven by what teachers and students do together.** Other people have an influence, but by far, the biggest influence is what takes place between teachers and their students.

2. ***Why* do we want students to learn?** Do we want them to become better citizens, do we want to prepare them for work, do we want to encourage self-development, do we want to broaden their horizons, or is our reason simply, *Why not?*

3. This also provokes the question, ***What* do we want students to learn?** Do we want them to learn literacy and numeracy; what it means to be a good person; how to be happy, engaged, or fulfilled; or what tradition and respect mean within their culture?

4. Whichever way we answer these questions, it brings us to the question, ***How* do we make learning more effective?**

5. A respected, albeit imperfect, way to understand the outcomes of learning is with **effect sizes.** These **offer insights into the relative magnitudes of different influences.**

6. As a general rule, **interventions that show high effect sizes are worth repeating**, whereas those with low or negative effect sizes should be treated with caution.

7. John Hattie's synthesis of 2,100-plus meta-analyses shows that **the average improvement students make in one year has an effect size of d = 0.40. This can**

be regarded as a benchmark such that measures between zero and $d = 0.20$ are considered low effects; outcomes of $d = 0.20$ to $d = 0.40$ are medium effects; and outcomes beyond $d = 0.40$ are high effects.

8. **Other factors should be considered as well as effect sizes.** These factors include desirability of outcome, cost and time to implement, availability of expertise to implement with great quality, and so on.

9. **Low effect sizes should not be quickly dismissed.** A gain is a gain! If the gain is minimal but took very little effort to achieve and has a positive influence elsewhere, then it is likely to be worthwhile. Growth mindset is a good example of this.

10. **Education is complex, and it is human. We will never know for sure which is the best approach to learning.** That said, using data such as those provided by effect sizes can at least take some of the guesswork out of the equation.

CHAPTER 2

When You *Engage* Your Students, Their Learning Gains *Purpose*

 *Students are engaged in learning when their thinking is focused on the topic, action, or meaning that is relevant to the progress you wish them to make. With engagement, the chances of progress are high, but without it, learning will be limited.*

When your students are engaged, chances are good they will make progress. If they are not engaged, then who knows? They might still learn *something*, but it is unlikely to be the thing you want them to learn! So, how better to start this chapter than by looking at some of the best ways to engage more of your students more of the time?

The two strategies I go into the most depth about are (1) questioning and (2) dialogue. Both are relevant to every phase of education and every curriculum area. The first is common in classrooms; the second is less so. Their *effective* use, however, is all too rare. So, I will help you to put that right.

THE BLUEPRINT

Purpose

The following are vital concepts about the purposes of engagement that you will learn about later in this chapter.

- Engagement matters. The more that students feel active and interested in their learning, the more that they fulfill their potential.

- When students are engaged in their learning, they think about and process the information they must attend to in order to make good progress.

- Researcher Amy Berry (2022) finds that teachers' beliefs about engagement have more to do with students' doing of the work and their display of the signs of attentiveness than with the focus of their thinking.

- Students are more likely to engage when classroom activities are authentic, allow for freedom of exploration, and demand effort, concentration, and skill.
- Two strategies in this chapter that are relevant to all curriculum areas and cause students to think more and, therefore, engage more are *questioning* and *dialogue*.

What to Notice

The following lists what is important to notice about engagement.

- **Notice who engages:** Students engage for approximately 50 percent of a lesson (Yair, 2000). One-third of students focus more than that, answering questions and attending to their learning. Alas, an equal proportion of students do the exact opposite.
- **Look beyond the facade:** Many students give the illusion of engagement. They nod, smile, and stick their hand in the air (only to drop it when you look their way). Other students are too busy thinking about their learning to pay attention to classroom etiquette. If we want to boost engagement, we need to pay attention to what our students are thinking about.
- **Notice your sample size:** Trying to identify how well a group of students are engaging by taking responses from just a handful of students is a poor way to make decisions. Forget raised hands and cold calling. There are far better ways to determine student engagement.
- **Notice your pace:** The rate of questioning and the short wait times in a typical classroom are not conducive to thinking. If we want our students to engage, we need to slow down!
- **Notice peer-to-peer talk:** Students rarely know how to talk and think together effectively (Wegerif & Scrimshaw, 1997). Some engage in cumulative talk (full of platitudes but little critical thought), and others in disputational talk (competitive browbeating). But if students are taught to engage in exploratory talk (using critical and collaborative thinking), their social, emotional, and intellectual development improves, and their engagement rises.

Timing

Strategies such as effective questioning and exploratory talk will boost student engagement, but they shouldn't be used all the time. Questioning is best used when you want to understand what your students are thinking about and, therefore, what they are engaging in. Dialogue, on the other hand, is more appropriate when you are ready to hand over responsibility to your students for monitoring and encouraging their own and each other's engagement.

2.0 Understand Student Engagement

Student engagement means whatever students are thinking about. Reading without thinking about what they're reading is not engagement. The same goes for listening, watching, and doing. Engagement, in effect, is thinking about something.

While writing this book, I took my eldest daughter to a hospital appointment. On the way home, I suggested that she drive so that she could get some more practice before her forthcoming test. The route we took went past the village where she spent her first eleven years, yet she didn't know the road at all. Every turn and roundabout was as much a surprise to her as if she were driving at the other end of the country. We must have walked, cycled, or otherwise traveled those same bends hundreds of times, but she just didn't recognize them at all. The moment we stopped, she remembered the surroundings very well—but the road, to her mind, was uncharted.

Then again, why would she remember the road *as a driver*? She had never had to drive it before! She had only ever been a passenger. She could remember where her friends lived, where the park was, and which route she used to walk to school. She had fond memories of riding the adjacent cycle path and remarked knowingly about the new buildings that hadn't existed a few years ago. As for the road, however, it was totally unfamiliar to her, not because it was new to her but because she had never had to think about it before. As a passenger—and a child passenger at that—she had been able to travel the road without thinking. She had never had to engage with the road in the way she needed to that day.

Engagement, then, means thinking about the thought processes that occur during meaning making, determination of next steps, and determination of what is important, relevant, or urgent. Engagement is also making connections, formulating questions, trying to make sense of things that don't make sense, wondering what others are making of it all, and worrying about what is expected of you. All of this is engagement.

So, what is *student engagement*? Actually, the research is mixed. It's not mixed because researchers can't agree on engagement's importance—they all agree engagement *is* vital for students to make good progress in their studies. What they don't seem to agree on is the *definition* of engagement. Some talk in terms of engaging in school life, some in terms of engaging academically, and others in terms of engaging in the completion of assignments and the earning of credits. Many researchers propose a two-dimensional model that includes behavior (for example, active participation, effort, and positive conduct) and emotion (for example, feeling positive toward schooling). Some add a cognitive dimension that includes self-regulation, investment in learning, and deliberate use of strategies (Archambault, Janosz, Fallu, & Pagani, 2009).

Since this book is for teachers, I focus on ways to engage students in classroom activities in this chapter. When I work with leaders, I take a broader approach by looking at students' engagement in the life of the school within and beyond the school gates. Here, I recommend ways to boost your students' engagement in terms of class participation, investment in learning, effort, self-regulation, and use of strategy. Then, in chapter 5 (page 215), I add ways to foster engagement in terms of self-belief, self-efficacy, a sense of belonging, and a belief in the value of learning.

In a 2023 study (Hecht, Bryan, & Yeager, 2023) involving 319 high school teachers from across a southern U.S. state, participants were asked to rank the importance of seven characteristics affecting the professional respect of their colleagues: (1) having high student test scores, (2) having students go on to prestigious colleges, (3) being popular with students, (4) having an advanced degree or qualification in their subject, (5) having an advanced degree or qualification in education, (6) being well organized, and (7) inspiring enthusiasm. Overwhelmingly and consistently, the teachers ranked inspiring enthusiasm for learning far higher than the other characteristics. Ninety-seven percent placed it in the top three, and 81 percent ranked it as the highest priority of all (Hecht et al., 2023).

2.0.1 Looks Can Be Deceptive

If engagement is a continuum, then it's quite obvious when someone is at either end of the scale: when they are super engaged or totally disengaged. What might we notice if someone's engagement is in the middle, when engagement is at a normal level?

There are exceptions, but this is where lessons tend to be: in the middle band of engagement. When I was about eight or nine years old, three of my teachers burst into the room unannounced and acted out a bank robbery. My classmates and I were absolutely rapt, so much so that I can still remember the surprise and fascination more than forty years later. However, that improv lasted only five minutes, after which we all had to write creative stories about—yes, you guessed it—a bank robbery. I'm pretty sure our engagement waned at that point! And can you imagine if the teachers did the same thing repeatedly? Very soon, we would have consigned their improvs to our minds' elephants' graveyard of engagement.

So, yes, the harsh reality is that school lessons tend not to be super engaging (the lessons *you* teach being the exception, of course). Therefore, it is important that we have a sense of what engagement is like when it is normal and what we can do to boost it just a little bit. (Of course, this assumes that no lessons are turgid, because if they are, then engagement needs a whole lot more than a little boost!)

When we think about normal engagement, one problem we face is that looks can be deceiving. Many teachers I meet assume they know which students are engaging with the lesson and which are not, but are their judgments reliable? For example, how many times have you given the impression of engaging with someone only to realize you haven't taken in a word they've said? How often have you had to retrace several pages of a book because your eyes followed the words but your mind wandered elsewhere? (Please tell me you're not doing that right now.) Or how often have you stared at a screen for ages without processing even a fraction of the information on it, no matter how beautifully presented or high octane it is?

So, what can we look for? And, maybe even more importantly, what can we ask for from our students? Appealing to them to "engage, please!" is probably not enough. The following discusses what the research is telling us.

2.0.2 Please Pay Attention

The absolutely classic petition in every classroom is, "Pay attention!" If your students don't pay attention, they won't learn. It's as simple as that.

Something interesting, surprising, thought-provoking, or odd can help grab students' attention. The same, of course, could be said of threats (perceived or otherwise), but we don't want to encourage that kind of provocation, because a fight-or-flight reaction will *prevent* learning rather than stimulate it.

So, using the formula of "do something positive to provoke attention so that students will learn" is the way to go, right? Well, not exactly, because there is considerable evidence that attention *sometimes* leads to learning and *sometimes* doesn't (Keller, Davidesco, & Tanner, 2020). Learning depends on where your students direct their attention.

A classic example is asking students to draw, color, and label a diagram of the eye. When you ask your students what they have learned about the eye, many of their memories will be vague because their attention was on their artwork, not on the biology or terminology. So, an edited formula of "do something positive to provoke attention on the *thing* that you want students to learn" is more accurate. Involving an element of creativity, active participation, or quirkiness is likely to boost engagement, but make sure the students' attention is aroused toward the thing you want them to learn.

2.0.3 It's Been Emotional

Our memories are most vivid when they connect to emotional reactions. My clearest memories of childhood are trapping my thumb in the swing gate on the first day of school, experiencing the thrill of making my whole class laugh, and feeling the pure escapism of leaving behind the mourning adults at my mother's funeral so my cousins and I could throw spinning jennies into the air. Of course, I wasn't trying to learn during any of these events; in fact, I've tried as hard as I can to forget some of them. In school, though, the main purpose *is* learning, so in what ways can emotions support our students' learning?

Staff-student relationships play an enormous role in this regard. Making our students feel welcome and valued in class will go a long way toward attaching positive emotions to their learning. The same can be said of the feelings involved in succeeding, particularly if students succeed against the odds (see my explanation of the eureka moment in section 3.8.3.8, page 142).

Before I lose any old-school mathematicians reading this section, don't worry; learning doesn't *have* to make our students feel warm and fuzzy. It's nice when it does (remember how excited you got when you first came across Euler's identity!), but it's not strictly necessary. As Daniel T. Willingham (2021b), professor of psychology at the University of Virginia, writes:

> If memory depended on emotion, we would remember little of what we encounter in school. So, the answer *Things go into long-term memory if they create an emotional reaction* is not quite right. It's more accurate to say, *Things that create an emotional reaction will be better remembered, but emotion is not necessary for learning.*

2.0.4 Familiarity Can Be Engaging

When students recognize a topic, they are likely to engage more (Willms, 2003). This familiarity helps them know what to pay attention to, what is relevant, and what is (probably) coming next. These are some of the reasons why I highly recommend using preview strategies, as described in section 6.1 (page 272). Of course, there is the proverb, "Familiarity breeds contempt," but I suggest it is more precise to say, "Overfamiliarity breeds contempt." If your students think, "Oh no, here we go again," then that is likely to disengage them. But if they think, "Oh, hang on, I know a bit about this," then that should lift engagement.

We do have to be careful, nonetheless, that we don't mistake familiarity for knowledge. I make a similar point in section 3.4.2 (page 103) when warning of the false sense of security that comes from students' reading over their course notes multiple times before an exam. A good example of this involves flags. Personally, I enjoy a school hall decorated with multiple flags representing the diversity of the students enrolled. Any celebration of, and respect for, multiculturalism is fabulous as far as I'm concerned. However, I have an embarrassing admission to make.

Years ago, after working closely with every school, preschool, and public sector organization in Florø, Norway, I was invited to a staff party. During proceedings, they held a quiz, and one question was, Which of these ten flags is the Union Jack? Sounds like an easy question to answer for this British citizen, particularly as I was the only one among four hundred Norwegians. The problem was the ten flags all looked almost identical. There weren't ten flags from ten different nations; there was one UK flag and then nine slightly amended versions! Some had the Saint Patrick's Cross from Northern Ireland running high from top right to center and then low from center to bottom left; others had the red line on the white background positioned differently. The same applied for the line that runs from top left to bottom right.

Now, it would be fair to say that the United Kingdom isn't a flag-waving nation—at least not compared to some of the other countries I work in—but I must have seen the Union Jack a thousand times. Yet, I still couldn't pick the correct one out of a lineup. Most of the locals could, but this solitary son of England failed miserably. It's similar to the opening story of my eldest daughter driving on a road she'd traveled a hundred times. She had never before needed to engage with the road for that purpose, so her engagement wasn't the right type of engagement. So, it turns out, there is engagement (*falsetto*) and engagement (*dramatic voice*). The question is, What sort of engagement do you want your students to engage in?

Let's return to the example of asking students to draw, color, and label a diagram of the eye. This is a worthwhile assignment *if* you want your students to engage in elements of art, such as color, form, line, and shape—less so if you want them to engage in the names of and relationships among the twelve parts of the eye.

If the latter is your goal, then I would suggest something more like the following.

1. Give each group a plain picture of the eye (without labels).

2. Provide a set of fifteen cards for each group. Twelve cards should each have a part of the eye written on them (for example, the first three cards could say *cornea*, *iris*, and *lens*). The three spare cards could feature spurious terms such as *glasses*, *in the public eye*, and *a bird's-eye view*.

3. Ask the groups to place the labels wherever they think they should go on the blank diagram (using their prior knowledge and guesswork).

4. Pause the groups every so often, and ask them to share their ideas about one of the labels. After taking some responses, confirm which answer is correct, and have each group lock that answer in. This will help the groups place the other labels by a process of elimination.

5. Make this enjoyably competitive so as to add to the students' engagement.

6. Reveal the correct version. Afterward, show some weird, wonderful, and funny images of different species' eyes on the board. Ask the students to spot which parts of the eyes are visible, enlarged, hidden, and so on. Doing this *after* the quiz serves two purposes.

   a. Having the terminology in their minds before they look at the different examples will help students consolidate their new knowledge rather than simply marvel at the strangeness of the eyes.

   b. Engagement is most likely to wane in the middle of a lesson, so rather than starting with the weird and wonderful, keep it up your sleeve until concentration levels are at their lowest.

As Willingham (2009) writes:

> Teachers often seek to draw students in to a lesson by presenting a problem that they believe interests students, or by conducting a demonstration or presenting a fact that they think students will find surprising. In either case, the goal is to puzzle students, to make them curious. This is a useful technique, but it's worth considering whether these strategies might be used not at the beginning of a lesson, but after the basic concepts have been learned. For example, a classic science demonstration is to put a burning piece of paper in a milk bottle and then put a boiled egg over the bottle opening. After the paper burns, the egg is sucked into the bottle. Students will no doubt be astonished, but if they don't know the principle behind it, the demonstration is like a magic trick—it's a momentary thrill, but one's curiosity to understand may not be long lasting. Another strategy would be to conduct the demonstration after students know that warm air expands and that cooling air contracts, potentially forming a vacuum. That way they can use their new knowledge to think about the demonstration, which is no longer just a magic trick. (p. 12)

2.0.5 Story Has Power

There is one way to boost engagement that stands above all others, and that is storytelling. It boosts engagement so much that psychologists sometimes refer to stories as *psychologically privileged*. Our minds seem to much more effectively engage with and remember stories than any other type of information we come across.

In my second year of teaching, I was invited to a leaders' conference. I don't know why I got to go so early in my career; maybe everyone else had a hair appointment. Our wonderful after-dinner speaker, Gervase Phinn, began with a story from his school inspection days. Back then, inspectors were supportive, kindly folk who thought it more illuminative to mix in with the students than to peer over the top of a clipboard from the back of a classroom. One morning, Phinn had offered to read a story to some of the five-year-old students. Seeing as this school was in Cumbria, England, he thought it a nice touch to read a story from the region's most famous daughter, Beatrix Potter. As he reached the point where Peter Rabbit gets himself stuck in Mr. McGregor's field, he asked the students what ought to happen next. "Shoot it!" the students cried. "Yeah, kill him! Rabbits are pests. They should be shot."

I'm still laughing about that story today, and I remember its point: know your audience! Phinn was from Rotherham, an industrial town, whereas his audience was farmers' kids living on the outskirts of the Lake District National Park. One or two of them might even have been descendants of miserly old McGregor! Know your audience, indeed!

Story has the power to connect; it creates the opportunity to weave information and ideas into a narrative that engages the listener's emotions and energy. If I meet someone who has read one of my earlier books, 8 times out of 10, they will mention one of the stories I've included. If they've heard me give a presentation, those chances increase to 9.5 times out of 10. Ironically, I haven't included as many stories in this book, with the exception of this section. This is not because I've fallen out of love with the power of story, nor because I have run out of tales to tell (as my kids will surely testify). It's mainly down to two reasons.

1. This manuscript is already more than 100,000 words, so I need to cut something somewhere!

2. I see this book as the accompanying footnotes to my presentations, offering details of research and lots more cross-curricular examples to add to the strategies I recommend.

Besides, too much of a good thing becomes a bad thing. I've thoroughly enjoyed story-heavy books and presentations from well-known author-consultants, but I'm never really sure what the audience is supposed to take away from an edutainer pitch that is story after story after story. If they're offering the after-dinner speech, then great; entertain us! But if the presentation is part of the main program, then surely a key goal is to lift our gaze from the day-to-day of teaching to consider how we might be even more effective. Yes, please give us a collective pat on the back and a sense of encouragement, but also share some up-to-date and impressive research that might cause us greater gains for less stress. Weave some stories into this, and we'll all remember it more. I think the same can be said for classroom teaching. We should certainly use stories to engage and connect, but don't only tell stories.

Most stories follow five steps. All the following steps include a description of the ways in which I see these fitting into the structure of a lesson.

1. **Scene setting:** Stories typically begin by setting the scene, situating it in a time and space. In the context of a lesson, this can connect to a big question or overarching topic. It can also include the basic information students will need (see my earlier suggestion about teaching the parts of an eye). If you are following the Learning Pit structure, then this relates to stage 1 on sharing first thoughts about the central concept (see section 3.8.1, page 126).

2. **The incident:** In a story, something happens that causes significant change. In a lesson, this should be something thought-provoking that causes your students to

question their assumptions or think differently about the topic. Get this right, and you will notice a significant boost to levels of engagement. In terms of the Learning Pit, this is when cognitive conflict is created to take your students into the pit.

3. **Rising action or crises:** Following the incident, events occur in a story that increase the tension; further details about the setting and characters are revealed. In a lesson, this is the perfect time to use questioning to provoke your students into thinking about the problems, their causes, their effects, personal responses to these things, and so on. This relates to deepening the inquiry and taking your students further into the Learning Pit.

4. **The climax of the story:** This is the big event or payoff in a story; it's what we've all been waiting for. In a lesson, it should be the point at which everything becomes clear—when students have their eureka moment (see section 3.8.3.8, page 142). They should now know why the effort was worth it and be better able to articulate their learning. The dialogue strategies that I share in sections 2.4 to 2.7 (pages 58 to 80) lend themselves brilliantly to this part of a lesson.

5. **The resolution:** In a story, this covers the aftermath. In a lesson, it should include metacognition (how and why we thought the way we thought, and what would work well next time) plus connections to the next steps in your students' learning. With the Learning Pit structure, this is stage 4: reflecting, applying, and adapting.

I don't pretend for a moment that this structure covers all eventualities. Some lessons more obviously lend themselves to the power of narrative than others do. However, the principle still stands: the more you are able to structure the lessons you teach like a narrative, the more likely your students are to engage and therefore remember their learning far into the future.

A similar summary can be offered for this whole section. What I've covered doesn't do much more than scratch the surface of engagement. Classrooms are too complex for there to be one approach, and staff-student relationships are too pivotal for research to provide all the answers for how to engage students. However, what we do know is that the characteristics I've described have been shown time and again to boost engagement in most contexts much of the time. That's not all contexts all the time, but it's a pretty good starting point.

Before I go more deeply into the two engagement strategies that are most generalizable across the curriculum (questioning and dialogue), I think it's worth giving a short summary of the reasons why students do *not* engage in learning. After all, reminding ourselves what we're up against can be a useful springboard for imagining what we might do to improve matters.

2.0.6 Some Factors Get in the Way of Student Engagement

Never underestimate a teacher's ability to engage their learners, for they do so against the odds. The forces of distraction affect and seduce students at every turn.

Engaging your students is one of the most challenging tasks of being a teacher. So many influences compete for their attention. Involvement in leisure and peer-group activities, preoccupations with social media, and commitments outside school are the distractions most frequently mentioned by teachers. But there are many others.

These factors can be grouped into four broad categories.

1. **External concerns:** This is a broad and diverse category covering all non-classroom issues. These include family issues, responsibilities as carers, work obligations, training schedules, and social lives. For example, students wonder what's going on—and what they need to take care of—outside the classroom.

2. **Self-consciousness:** This covers students' focus on themselves rather than on instructional activities. Examples include focusing on health (including mental health) concerns, concentrating on their appearance, and being deliberate about the impression they're giving others. For example, students think, "What am I doing, and what impression am I giving others?"

3. **Surroundings:** This covers the wide range of distractions created by peers, aural and visual stimulants, social hierarchies and conventions, and classroom visitors. For example, students consider who and what else is in the room and how they should respond.

4. **Interactions:** This covers the times when students are observers of interactions without being involved in them directly. It includes taking notice of how you interact with others, how their peers respond to each other, what group dynamics are like, and so on. For example, students observe the ways in which other people in the room respond to one another.

No wonder it is so difficult to engage students! In many ways, it's a minor miracle that we ever manage to.

In fact, not only will all the preceding examples get in the way of attentiveness, but many students will *also* be dealing with processing issues. Those with additional learning or language needs are the most evident, perhaps, but anyone who is unfamiliar with your classroom conventions or is having an off day will face additional obstacles that require extra effort to overcome before they can pay attention.

So, don't be too hard on yourself when your students appear not to be concentrating. Don't be too hard on them, either. However, I don't mean to suggest taking a nonchalant approach. After all, we *want* our students to engage, and we need to do what we can to increase the likelihood that they will. But know that creating sustainable experiences that engage all your students all the time is a Sisyphean task.

Results from the Gallup Student Poll bear this out. To date, this poll has comprised more than 6 million students in grades 5–12 from 8,000 schools across 1,400 districts. Tim Hodges (2018), a senior consultant with Gallup, describes the following.

- Less than half (47 percent) of the students polled are engaged with school.
- Less than one-third (29 percent) are not engaged.
- Almost a quarter (24 percent) are actively disengaged.
- Engagement is highest among fifth graders (74 percent). By middle school, engagement drops to one-half, and by tenth grade, one-third of students are engaged.

These statistics at first seem discouraging, but it is worth remembering that most of us work with students who, in general, are required by law to attend school. Many would not attend school—or would not stay in school later—if they didn't have to. So, to have even one-half of our students engaging at any one time is a good start. We would like it to be better, of course, but it's not a terrible start (even if the enfants are terrible).

Hodges (2018) explains:

> Gallup discovered two items that had a powerful connection to engagement. Students who were able to "strongly agree" with the statements "My school is committed to building the strengths of each student" and "I have at least one teacher who makes me excited about the future" were 30 times as likely to be engaged at school when compared with students who strongly disagreed with the same items.

Returning to the Gallup survey for a moment, I found two connections particularly interesting. The first is that engaged students are 4.5 times more likely to be hopeful about their future than their actively disengaged peers. So, for those who think engagement is fleeting and rather mood based, this doesn't disprove that theory, but it at least says engagement exerts *some* influence later.

Second, although we have every right to worry about the general lack of student engagement shown in Gallup's findings, it seems adult engagement is even worse! Only one-third of staff (33 percent) report being engaged, half (51 percent) report not being engaged, and most worrying of all, a resistant 16 percent are actively disengaged (Hodges, 2018)!

That is a can of worms I am not going to open in this book! So, moving on, then . . .

2.0.7 What Next?

Engaging students is not straightforward. There are just so many influences competing for their attention. It's not impossible, of course. In most classrooms, most of the time, a significant number of students are already engaged. It would be fabulous, though, if more students engaged more of the time, and if this engagement were in their learning rather than in other things. So, that's what the rest of this chapter is about.

I have chosen to focus on two strategies for engagement: (1) questioning and (2) dialogue. According to the research I share later in this chapter, these two approaches are among the most effective ways to boost students' attention and subsequent thinking about their learning.

Questioning has two main purposes. The first is to call on students to be more cognitively active. The second is to determine when to move on to the next part of the lesson. Both are central functions of engaging students.

Dialogue teaches students how to think together, how to collaborate effectively on tasks, and how to make connections within and across subjects. It is one of the best ways to encourage intrinsic motivation.

In this video, James offers some additional examples about engagement.

2.1 Use Questioning to Boost Engagement

 *Questioning is among the best ways to direct thinking and boost engagement. Your students' responses offer insights that allow you to adjust subsequent instruction to better meet their needs. As such, it is one of the most important pedagogical techniques.*

Questioning can be likened to the dynamic flow of a river where the exchange of ideas and perspectives is fluid, continuous, and rich with possibilities. When used effectively, questioning can draw attention to whatever you want your students to think about. This, in turn, engages them in the right thing, whether that is a key concept, a significant meaning, cause and effect, or a technique that you wish them to learn. However, the most common approach to questioning isn't very effective at all! Indeed, it tends to engage only one-third of students (Cazden, 2001). That is not a great return for any strategy, much less one with a primary function to engage students!

Referred to as the *I-R-E pattern* (Mehan, 1979) or *IR-Evaluate approach*, the most common form of questioning in education follows this three-part sequence.

1. **Initiate:** The teacher asks a question.
2. **Respond:** A student answers.
3. **Evaluate:** The teacher confirms the student has answered correctly or, if not, asks a second student to answer.

This approach can be useful for checking factual knowledge or recall, but that's about it.

The one-third of students who pay attention and offer answers are confident in their own abilities, confident in the current subject matter, or confident among their peers. They are willing to engage because the odds are in their favor. Either they answer correctly and teachers praise that, or they get it wrong and they still receive a favorable response for trying. The other two-thirds of students keep their heads down or employ strategies to avoid being asked. Giving an answer in front of everyone else is just too risky for their egos.

This IR-Evaluate approach tends to be accompanied by a lot of teacher talk. Harvard University professor emerita Courtney B. Cazden (2001) finds that teachers fill as much as two-thirds of any questioning sequence when using this approach. Thus, the one-third of students who are likely to offer an answer have just one-third of the discussion time in which to do so. I'm no mathematician, but even I know that's a very low rate of engagement!

The good news is that other studies show student engagement increases dramatically if interactions are more *dialogic* (Gibbons, 2002; Mercer & Wegerif, 2002; Nystrand, 1997; Wegerif, 2013; Yang & Brindley, 2023), which is when students are actively involved in the co-construction of meaning. This demonstrates the need to turn the classic IR-Evaluate into a more dialogic Initiate-Respond-Explore (IR-Explore).

2.1.1 Exploring Instead of Evaluating

 *When questioning your students, use an IR-Explore approach. Do not (publicly) evaluate their answers.*

When you are moving to the more effective IR-Explore approach, the first principle is to neither validate, confirm, nor refute students' answers. This comes with the caveat *insofar as possible* because there might be occasions when it is disingenuous not to do these things. But, in principle, you should avoid giving students the impression that their answers will be publicly evaluated.

I find the best response is to begin with, "Interesting," and then to follow it up with one or more of these questions.

- Can you tell us more?
- Could you elaborate?
- Could you give us an example?
- Could you offer a supporting reason?
- Can you explain your thinking?
- Are there any other terms or phrases you could use?
- Do you think that would always be the case?
- When might that work or not work?
- Are there any exceptions?
- How about if . . . ?

These are *not* probes for cross-examination! They are invitations to explore. Your purpose is to encourage elaboration and wonder, not to fluster or confront. Therefore, tone of voice and body language are also important. Give the impression you are genuinely interested in what your students have to say and the reasons they have for the way in which they think.

At times, you might not want to ask a follow-up question. Instead, you might use encouragers such as, "Uh-huh" or "Go on." Whatever helps elicit more thought, more openness, and more inquiry from your students will be a good thing.

Also, look for ways to invite others into the dialogue. Seek out supporting ideas, questions, and connections by asking these sorts of questions.

- Can anyone think of a counterexample?
- Did anyone else think something similar? Could you explain?
- Is there anyone who thought something different? Could you draw comparisons?

- Who would like to add to what [student] said?
- Could anyone offer a counterexample for what [student] suggested?

Don't be discouraged if some of these questions don't work straight away. Although IR-Explore will have a better impact on student engagement than the more traditional IR-Evaluate, it still won't engage all your students on every occasion. Outcomes are likely to be much better than the one-third of students engaging one-third of the time that Cazden (2001) finds, but you still won't see 100 percent of students engaging 100 percent of the time. The IR-Explore approach is better, but it is not perfect.

As an author-consultant, I often demonstrate IR-Explore in classrooms. I think this is an important walk-the-talk offer to make. Give me any class of students at any age studying any subject, and I'll show you some ways to boost engagement and deepen learning. Staff watch how their students interact, and then we talk about the learning opportunities afterward.

Having run these sorts of demonstration lessons many hundreds of times with students three to nineteen years old, I have been asked lots of questions about the approach. Some of the most frequently asked ones, together with my answers, are as follows.

- **Is Initiate-Respond-Explore suitable for all students?** Generally speaking, yes. But there are exceptions; those who find large-group situations stressful are likely to struggle, as are those who need or prefer more processing time. There are ways to mitigate these circumstances, though, as shown in sections 6.3.1 and 6.4.1 (pages 282 and 291).

- **How long should an IR-Explore sequence last?** However long suits the occasion. When I run a demonstration lesson, the IR-Explore sequence lasts for the whole session, but that is more for the benefit of the observers than for the students. In more usual circumstances, I use IR-Explore as part of a range of strategies to engage my students in their learning. For example, I might spend fifteen minutes at the start of a lesson using IR-Explore to encourage my students to connect to their prior learning; then, later in the topic, I might spend twenty to thirty minutes digging deeply into the significance of key concepts. In between times, I use the approach when I want to engage smaller groups of students in need of chivvying along. As with all pedagogical strategies, one size never fits all.

- **Is IR-Explore always the best strategy?** No. But then again, no strategy is always the right strategy! Classrooms are too complex and students too diverse to think of one strategy that will work every single time. You couldn't even say that IR-Explore is *always* better than IR-Evaluate. It is most of the time, but not always. The IR-Evaluate approach is like the quick-fire questions used at the beginning of a test. Those questions give us a quick sense of what our students know and don't know, but they don't allow for nuance. They don't tell us what else our students think, what their assumptions and reasons are, or which connections they can make, nor do they give us insights into our students' understanding. We just get a quick yes-or-no, right-or-wrong checkup. That might be quite useful at times, but remember that the public nature of IR-Evaluate sequences is stressful for many students, which is why so many disengage from them. It is much better to take the more inclusive, more insightful, and less stressful IR-Explore approach.

- **If I use IR-Explore, does that mean I have to avoid teaching content?** No, not at all! You need *something* to ask questions about, so it might as well be the topic or content you want your students to engage with. If you think it would be reassuring, then you could include facts or truths as a preface to your IR-Explore questioning. This might include confirming A and B are true before asking your students for thoughts about C. Here are two examples: "We know Hamlet is the prince of Denmark and that the ghost of his father tells him to seek revenge, so can anyone add detail to this?" and "We know that all whole numbers are integers, so how many numbers can we think of that are integers but not whole numbers?"

- **Does IR-Explore run contrary to facts and truths?** I get that some people have misgivings about the first rule of IR-Explore being to avoid confirmation or rebuttal of students' answers. However, that is not the same as saying we should take a laissez-faire attitude by allowing anything and everything to go unchecked. For example, if a student were to make a racist, sexist, or otherwise socially unacceptable comment, then I wouldn't hesitate to evaluate it publicly. But when it comes to content-focused answers, there are many ways to avoid the usual evaluation approach. For example, you could ask others if they agree or have different ideas, you could ask for a rationale behind the answer (which normally results in the fault being identified, albeit in a periphrastic way), or you could ask for further explanation so that you provoke reflection and correction.

- **Will IR-Explore work with *my* students?** I expect so, yes. Unless you work with classes of students with no formal means of communication, then I would proffer that IR-Explore will work. It won't work perfectly, because no approach to engaging students does; but certainly, it's better than the more traditional IR-Evaluate. There are caveats to this, and aspects of student needs that should be provided for (as described in the next section), but I'd be willing to wager that it will work. In fact, if you have the opportunity, invite me into your classroom, and let's see if it will work with your students!

- **Does IR-Explore work in every subject area?** Does questioning work in every subject? If your answer is the same as mine—"yes, of course"—then I would recommend thinking the same about IR-Explore. It lends itself more obviously to open-ended aspects of the curriculum—for example, appreciating art, discussing literature, making arguments about ethics in science, or hypothesizing about cause and effect in history or geography. But even in the subjects thought to be more certain, it can engage students more effectively than the traditional IR-Evaluate.

To elaborate on that final question, you probably won't be surprised to know that the subject most cited by teachers as the least compatible with IR-Explore is mathematics. I happen to disagree. I think mathematics lends itself brilliantly to exploration, but I understand why people think this. So, here are a couple of examples that I hope will help.

Example 1:

- **Initiate:** What is 25 × 9?
- **Response:** 225

- **Explore (example questions):**
  - How did you solve that?
  - Did anyone solve it in a different way?
  - How many ways could we solve it?
  - Which strategies are quickest? Easiest? Most reliable? Explain why.
  - How could you explain what to do to someone who doesn't understand multiplication?
  - Could anyone show us how this could be drawn?

Example 2:
- **Initiate:** Using a calculator, what is 25 percent of 30?
- **Respond:** 7.5
- **Explore (example questions):**
  - What buttons did you press to get your answer?
  - Did anyone solve it in a different way?
  - How could you solve the same problem without a calculator?
  - What do you notice about 25 percent as a proportion of the whole?
  - How else could we write this?
  - If I gave you some graph paper, could you solve it without the use of any numbers?

In this video, James summarizes the key points about moving from IR-Evaluate to IR-Explore.

2.1.2 Asking the Right Types of Questions

What sorts of questions should we ask in class, and are some better than others? In 1912, researcher Romiett Stevens (1912) observed teachers in one hundred high school classrooms in six subject areas and found that at least two-thirds of the questions teachers asked focused on recall of facts. Was this necessarily a bad thing, and has much changed since?

Dylan Wiliam (2014) writes about this:

> The whole idea that students should always answer teachers' questions correctly is actually rather odd. If the students are answering every one of the teacher's questions correctly, the teacher is surely wasting the students' time. If

the questions are not causing students to struggle and think, they are probably not worth asking. (p. 16)

Questions are typically classified by the level of cognitive demand required to answer them. The two best-known systems for categorizing questions are (1) open or closed and (2) higher or lower order; the latter is more important and is generally explained in connection with Bloom's (1956) taxonomy. This is explored in detail in the next section.

Although categories of questions are worth thinking about, it is perhaps even more important to think about the process of questioning. After all, giving a quizzical look or an encourager such as, "Uh-huh" or "Go on," could more effectively tease out your students' thinking than asking a perfectly formed, well-timed question.

Early in my career, I cared a lot about the differences between open and closed questions. The professional development of the day led my colleagues and me to believe it was better to ask open questions than closed. *Open questions* are ones that seek long answers, cause reflection, and elicit opinions or feelings, whereas *closed questions* are quick and easy to answer, dealing in facts and often resulting in a yes-or-no answer.

Sounds straightforward enough, but the more I cared about this, the more exceptions to the rule I found. For example, "Is democracy a good way to govern?" sounds like an open question that is seeking a long answer supported by reasons. However, it can just as easily result in a yes-or-no answer. "Where are you from?" has the form of a closed question but could draw out a longer answer. Depending on who is asking it and how much knowledge I suppose they have about my locality, I might answer in terms of the country I am from or the region, town, or neighborhood where I live. I might add something about where I was born and raised compared to where I live now or give an insight into where I most identify with (along the lines of the Māori concept of *tūrangawaewae* [Tūrangawaewae, 2007], which are places where we feel especially empowered and connected). I could even add a description such as *rural, by the coast, on the edge of, halfway between,* or *closest to*. In other words, if I was so inclined, I could give a long answer to a seemingly closed question, and I could give a yes-or-no answer to most open questions.

Ultimately, I still think there are some questions that are better than others for beginning an IR-Explore sequence (as covered in sections 2.1.5.1 and 3.8.2, pages 45 and 129), but I also know it's best to ask multiple questions to bring out the best in students, and these will probably be a mix of both open and closed questions. Added to that, a gesture or single word of encouragement can sometimes be more productive than even the most perfectly formed open-ended question that Socrates himself would have been proud of. Don't you agree?

2.1.2.1 Types of Questions

Questioning that provokes higher-order thinking leads to better learning outcomes. This type of questioning engages critical-thinking and problem-solving strategies and increases the likelihood that students will transfer ideas from one context to another.

Questions serve a range of functions in education. They can be used to test knowledge or understanding ("Can anyone say what photosynthesis is?"), to manage classroom activity ("Are you all ready now?"), and to find out more about what students are doing ("How did you decide the roles each of you would take?"). They can also serve multiple functions at once, finding out what your students know while also refocusing their attention.

When it comes to their form (rather than their function), Lorin W. Anderson and David R. Krathwohl (2001) categorize questions as either productive or reproductive. These match with the terms *higher order* and *lower order*, which are related to Bloom's (1956) taxonomy.

2.1.2.2 Why Higher-Order Questions Are Best

The most important distinction between higher-order and lower-order questions is that those requiring higher-order-thinking skills, such as the following, lead to better learning outcomes. They engage students in critical thinking and problem solving and increase the likelihood that students will transfer ideas from one context to another.

- **Critical thinking:** Requiring reasons, decision making, generalizations, reflection, and evaluation
- **Problem solving:** Meeting a goal that cannot be met using a memorized solution
- **Creative thinking:** Thinking of alternatives, making different assumptions, seeking novel interpretations, and looking for unusual connections
- **Transfer:** Applying knowledge and skills learned in one context to another (For example, learning how to use a Venn diagram in mathematics and then applying this understanding to distinguish between metaphors and analogies in a literacy lesson)

A meta-analysis of fourteen studies found a positive relationship between the use of higher-level questioning during instruction and student gains on tests of both factual recall and application of thinking skills (Redfield & Rousseau, 1981). Hattie has included this meta-analysis in his database and calculated an effect size of $d = 0.73$. The seven other meta-analyses in the same category bring the overall effect size down to $d = 0.49$ (Visible Learning Metax, n.d.).

This is a significant effect.

The bad news is that the research unequivocally shows students are asked many more lower-order questions than higher-order ones, even though students learn significantly more from questions that stimulate higher-order thinking.

In the 1910s, Romiett Stevens (1912) conducted the first systematic study of teacher questioning in the United States. As stated earlier, Stevens found that at least two-thirds of the questions teachers asked focused on recall of facts. More recent studies, including those by researchers Kenneth A. Sirotnik (1983), Hans Gerhard Klinzing and Gisela Klinzing-Eurich (1988), and Martin Nystrand (1997) as well as the 2021 meta-analysis of twenty-nine studies by researchers Robbie J. Marsh, Therese M. Cumming, Justus J. Randolph, and Stephen Michaels (2021), show very little has changed since.

Nystrand (1997) observed fifty-eight eighth-grade and fifty-four ninth-grade English language arts classes in eight Midwestern communities in the United States. He reported that 64 percent of questions in the eighth-grade classes involved recall of facts, with the remaining 36 percent focusing on higher-order thinking such as analysis, generalization, and speculation.

The balance was better in the ninth-grade classes, with 46 percent of questions provoking higher-order thinking.

Questioning that is most likely to engage your students' higher-order-thinking skills includes the following three approaches.

1. **Problems:** Posing problems that have no single solution or that have multiple pathways toward a solution requiring students to define, generate, select, hypothesize, implement, and evaluate
2. **Provocations:** Posing provocative questions, statements, or scenarios requiring students to consider, wonder, compare and contrast, explore, and persist (These start with, "What if . . . ?" or "How about . . . ?")
3. **Parallels:** Asking questions that require your students to explain concepts using analogies, similes, and metaphors

2.1.2.3 Rate of Questioning

Researchers Tamar Levin and Ruth Long (1981) estimated that teachers ask between 300 and 400 questions in a typical school day. More recently, associate professor Christopher Tienken and his colleagues from Seton Hall University published similar findings (Tienken, Goldberg, & Dirocco, 2009), although professors Janet Clinton and Georgia Dawson (2018) put the estimate at 100 to 350 questions per day.

If we ask that many questions in a day, just think how many we ask in a year! Of course, the number of days in a school year varies from country to country, but we can still calculate a range. Of the countries I work in, the United States has the fewest school days (ranging from 172 to 184 depending on the state), and Japan has the most (210 days). If teachers in those countries ask a similar number of questions per day (and that's a big *if*), then we are looking at between 17,200 and 73,500 questions per teacher per year. That hardly seems believable, although a day working with kindergarten children would have you suspecting four-year-olds ask even more every single month!

The point is that teachers ask a lot of questions! Since these questions are typically used for two main purposes—(1) to find out if students are ready to move on to the next part of the lesson and (2) to stimulate more active participation—it is essential that we make our questioning strategies as effective as they can be. Questioning's role is such a pivotal one that it can't be left to providence.

If I scale down to the number of questions per lesson rather than scale up to the number of questions per year, the stats become no less incredible. According to the Organisation for Economic Co-operation and Development's data, the typical number of hours students spend in lessons each day is five hours. So, if we take the most recent estimate (Clinton & Dawson, 2018) that teachers ask 100 to 350 questions per day, then we're looking at 20 to 70 questions per hour!

By far, the best-known and most cited research in this area comes from education researcher Mary Budd Rowe (1986). She documents the astonishing speed at which teacher and student exchanges take place. By feeding hundreds of hours of in-classroom sound recordings into a servo-chart plotter, she discovered that when teachers ask questions, they typically wait 0.9 seconds for students to start a reply (wait time one). If no reply is forthcoming, they repeat or rephrase the question. Then, after a student stops speaking, teachers begin to react or ask the next question less than one second later (wait time two).

This pace has nothing to do with learning and everything to do with exhibition! No one can think at that pace. The most quick-witted people can recall previously learned answers, but even then, how many times have you watched a quick-fire game show and been frustrated by someone else in the room or a contestant on the television beating you to it? More importantly, this pace cannot possibly encourage higher-order thinking. How can you consider meaning or interpretation, much less synthesize or evaluate alternatives, if you have less than one second to do so?

Rowe (1986) recommends a different approach, as she explains:

> If teachers can increase the average length of the pauses at both points, namely, after a question (wait time one) and, even more importantly, after a student response (wait time two) to 3 seconds or more, there are pronounced changes (usually regarded as improvements) in student use of language and logic as well as in student and teacher attitudes and expectations. There is a threshold value below which changes in wait time produce little effect and above which (2.7 seconds) there are marked consequences for both teachers and students. (p. 43)

2.1.3 Finding Too Many Questions and Not Enough Time

Teachers ask sixty to eighty questions per hour (Tienken et al., 2009) and allow an average of 0.9 seconds for students to think before answering each one (Rowe, 1986).

Rowe's (1986) seminal work led to a recommendation to increase wait time—or thinking time—to a minimum of three seconds. Doing this, she notes, leads to significant effects, including the following.

- **The length of student responses increases** between 300 percent and 700 percent, even more in the case of at-risk students:

  > Under the usual 1-second average wait times, responses tend to consist of short phrases and rarely involve explanations of any complexity. Wait time two is particularly powerful for increasing probability of elaboration. (Rowe, 1986, p. 44)

- More responses are **supported by evidence**, explanation, logical argument, and complexity:

  > Under 1-second wait times, the incidence of qualified inferences is extremely low, but it becomes quite common at the 3-second wait time threshold. (Rowe, 1986, p. 44)

- The incidence of **speculative thinking** (*what about* and *what if*) increases:

    Speculative thinking encourages students to imagine past or future possibilities. It often includes pre-factual thinking by allowing students to engage in a topic before they are knowledgeable about the content. In this sense, it is inclusive and creative. (Wegerif, 2015, p. 429)

- The number of **questions students ask**, and the number of experiments they propose, increases:

    As a rule, students ask questions infrequently, and when they do, their questions are usually to clarify procedures and are rarely directed to other students. This situation changes dramatically under the 3-second regimen. (Rowe, 1986, p. 44)

- **Student-to-student exchanges** increase, and the prevalence of speaking via the teacher decreases:

    Under very short wait times, students compete for turns to perform for the teacher. There is little indication that they listen to each other. Under the 3-second regimen, however, they show more evidence of attending to each other as well as to the teacher, and as a result, the discourse begins to show more coherence. (Rowe, 1986, p. 44)

- **Failures to respond decrease:**

    "I don't know" or no responses are often as high as 30 percent in classrooms with mean wait times 1 and 2 of 1 second, which is the most common pace. Increasing wait time 1 to 3 seconds is particularly important for [reducing this effect]. (Rowe, 1986, p. 44)

- **Disciplinary moves decrease:**

    Students maintained on a rapid recitation pattern show signs of restlessness and inattentiveness sooner than do students on the longer wait time treatment plan. At first this seems counter-intuitive to teachers.... [However,] protracted wait time appears to influence motivation, and that in turn may be a factor in attention and cooperation. (Rowe, 1986, p. 44)

- The **variety of students participating** voluntarily in discussions increases, and the number of unsolicited but appropriate contributions increases:

    Typically, six or seven students capture more than half of the recitation time. Under the 3-second regimen, the number of students usually rated as poor performers who become active participants increases. Interestingly, this change in verbal activity gradually influences teacher expectations . . . (Verbal competence appears to be a salient factor in teacher judgments concerning a student's capabilities.) (Rowe, 1986, p. 44)

- **Student confidence** shown by less approval seeking increases:

    Student responses are often inflected as though a tacit question such as "Is that what you want?" were attached to their statements.... This reduces significantly when wait time is increased. (Rowe, 1986, pp. 44–45)

- **Achievement improves** on written measures where the items are cognitively complex (Tobin, 1987).

In addition to these very impressive outcomes, Rowe (1986) notes positive effects on teachers.

- Teachers' responses exhibit **greater flexibility and improved continuity** in the development of ideas as the questioning sequence progresses.
- Teachers ask fewer questions overall, but the quality increases with **more invitations to clarify, elaborate, or find counterexamples**.
- **Expectations improve** for the performance of certain students:

    Previously "invisible" people become visible. Expectations change gradually, often signaled by remarks such as "He never contributed like that before. Maybe he has a special 'thing' for this topic." This effect was particularly pronounced where minority students were concerned. They did more task relevant talking and took a more active part in discussions. (Rowe, 1986, p. 45)

Reading through the rest of Rowe's study, together with subsequent studies by researchers Ken Tobin (1987), Robert J. Stahl (1994), and Dan Rothstein and Luz Santana (2011), provides the following useful annotations.

- Rowe (1987) wrote about two key wait times: (1) after a teacher asks a question (wait time one) and (2) after a student answers a question (wait time two). All the research cited earlier notes that the impact of extending wait time two is particularly powerful.
- The gains are even more significant for at-risk and minority students. For example, educator Wayne A. Winterton (1977) found that Native American students from the Pueblo tribe, who were previously described by teachers as nonverbal, contributed spontaneously twice as often during the longer-wait-time classes as their counterparts in other, more typical science classes did.
- All the researchers mentioned note a threshold of 2.7 seconds, beyond which the effects are marked. Modifications to wait time beyond the normal 0.9 seconds, but less than 2.7 seconds, show little change in the language and logic used by students.
- Professor Robert J. Stahl (1994) recommends switching the term *wait time* to *think time* so as to emphasize the purpose of the increased pause between one person speaking and another.

2.1.3.1 Five Steps Toward Improving Thinking Time

Extending wait time two (after a student has responded) is by far the most effective way to improve student engagement during questioning sequences.

To ease the transition from short wait times (less than a second) to optimum wait times (three seconds or more), I recommend the following five steps.

1. **Arrange the room so that everyone can make eye contact with everyone else:** This is easier said than done in many classrooms, but doing so can lead to many benefits. In a typical classroom talk situation, students address their teacher even

when responding to an idea offered by another student. When it's easier to make eye contact with anyone in the room, student interactions become more authentic.

2. **Create an expectation for thinking time:** Whenever I run a demonstration lesson, I begin with an introduction along these lines: "I expect everyone to listen to each other and to think. Notice that I didn't say, 'Listen and talk.' Of course, I hope that some people will speak, but by far, the most important aspect of this lesson is thinking. So, please think about the similarities and differences between the ideas someone is sharing and what you believe. Consider their point of view. Think about their reasons—and yours. Try to identify examples and counterexamples. Wonder, 'What if?' Take time in this lesson to think deeply.

"To help us do all of this, we need to slow things down a bit. Give people thinking time. Unfortunately, most discussions tend to be quick-fire with one person starting to speak the moment someone else has finished; sometimes, they don't even wait for them to finish, which is hardly conducive to thinking! That's about showing off rather than considering ideas deeply. So, we're going to try to do better than that by giving people time to think. After someone has spoken, please wait three or more seconds before saying something. I don't want this to become a distraction; let's not count out loud or look at our watches! But please do be mindful of giving each other thinking time. You might find the silences a little awkward to begin with, but as time goes on, we'll all get used to it, and when we do, we'll do much better thinking together."

3. **Avoid raised hands:** Whenever possible, go for something much subtler than putting hands up. My preference is to have students give me a thumbs-up with their hand resting on their table or lap. Raised hands are just too distracting. This is particularly true if hands shoot up the moment someone has finished speaking; worse still is if the hands hang in the air when someone is talking. The imploring grunts that younger students use to accompany their raised hands plumb even further depths of distraction!

4a. **Ask good questions:** This sounds obvious, but make sure the questions you ask are worth thinking about! There's little point in giving your students thinking time if your questions require simple, repeated answers. The term mentioned in the research is *authentic questions*. In every study and meta-analysis I've read, questions that are authentic lead to better learning outcomes. These questions are defined as those that evoke a variety of responses from students (because there is no prespecified answer) and that allow teachers to demonstrate they are genuinely interested in exploring students' ideas.

Also, aim for *uptake*, which is another term frequently mentioned in the research about questioning that effectively engages students. *Uptake* is when questions incorporate earlier responses from students. Consider these examples: "Thinking back to [student A's] idea about this, together with [student B's] alternative suggestion, can anyone think of a time when these might . . . ?" and "What [student C] said was really interesting; let's all take some time to think about it, and then in a few moments, I will invite someone to respond to their ideas."

4b. **Ask good questions that are authentic:** It all sounds straightforward—ask authentic questions that connect with your students' lives, show a keen interest in your students' reasons and examples, and build their earlier ideas into your questions, and you will be much more likely to engage your students and deepen their learning.

However, researchers Arthur N. Applebee, Judith A. Langer, Martin Nystrand, and Adam Gamoran (2003) investigated the prevalence of authentic questions and the use of uptake in English language arts classes across middle and high schools in the United States. And in the eighth-grade classes, they found that only 10 percent of teacher questions were authentic and that 11 percent exhibited uptake. In the ninth-grade classes, 27 percent of teacher questions were authentic and 26 percent exhibited uptake. Applebee and colleagues (2003) collected data in grades 7, 8, 10, and 11 and showed that 19 percent of teacher questions were authentic and 31 percent exhibited uptake.

Although authentic questions are generally better than inauthentic ones (because they signal to students that their ideas are important), there is a strong caveat to mention. The correlation with improved academic performance occurs *only when* the questions are related to the subject matter. If they wander off track and focus only on the students' lives or current affairs without any clear link to the curriculum topic, then the improvements in achievement outcomes disappear. The students still appreciate the questions, but their studies don't improve (at least not the ones that are tested).

5. **Quiet the monopolizers:** There are always some individuals who dominate discussions if given half a chance. Most groups have monopolizers. Certainly, every class does. Now and again, we quite like having a monopolizer—it's better than having absolutely no one willing to speak. But most of the time, quieting the monopolizer and inviting responses from a broader range of students is preferable.

Three of the best ways to achieve this are the following.

 a. Introduce *thinking rounds*. Don't signal this ahead of time, but once the usual suspects have offered their first ideas, announce the end of round one. Those who spoke in round one should now take a listening and thinking role. It's fascinating what happens when you get to round three or four and the quietest students speak because they know there's no more competition waiting to silence them!

 b. Use the well-known think-pair-share routine, in which students take time to think by themselves (think) before sharing their ideas with the person sitting next to them (pair) and then sharing the ideas with the whole class (share). This could be adapted so that talk partners represent each other's ideas rather than their own.

 c. Eavesdrop on pair or small-group discussions, identify ideas you think will extend other people's thinking, and then encourage one of the quieter students to communicate these ideas to the whole class.

2.1.4 Increasing the Sample Size

Gathering responses from a few usual suspects is a poor way to judge the competence of the many. There are, however, routines that can be established to improve sampling reliability.

One of the most significant decisions to make in the classroom is when to move on to the next part of the lesson. By far, the most common way to judge this is to ask a question of the whole class and decide whether the responder is accurate. If they are, move on. If not, then ask another student. If the second student provides the right answer, then move on. If not, then ask another. If three students in a row get the answer wrong, then maybe it's time to repeat or clarify.

The problem is that the most confident, most articulate, or most advanced students are almost always the ones who offer answers. Everyone else keeps their heads down. To judge the competence of the many by the answers of these few is a poor way to make decisions.

Imagine that I read a passage of text displayed on the board to a class of students. The text includes the words *guerrilla*, *plaza*, and *incommunicado*. I ask about the meanings of those words. The one student in the class who speaks Spanish at home answers correctly. The other twenty-nine students who know little or no Spanish do not answer. Is this a reliable test? I'm assuming you would say no. Yet, it happens so often when teachers ask a question, the few students with an advantage over the others answer it correctly, and the teacher moves on as if the minority represents the majority.

A popular alternative to this is *cold calling*, when a teacher calls on a student to answer without having volunteered. There are better options, but cold calling is frequently used. Sometimes, this approach is randomized; other times, the teacher makes strategic selections. The hackneyed version involves writing students' names on a set of lollipop sticks and selecting one at random. Random-selection phone apps have now become digital lollipops.

The problem with both of these approaches is that neither increases the sample size. Whether you are choosing students at random or making more calculated choices, you are still only gaining insight into the thinking of a few. I call this *tourist teaching*. Tourists often tell stories about the quirks of an entire nation based on a short visit to the capital city: "We took a trip to see the pyramids in Cairo. I think it's so strange that *Egyptians* will . . ." or "We loved New York, but I found it so exhausting. *Americans* are always . . . ."

An approach that is better than cold calling is making use of mini-whiteboards. These whiteboards can be a distraction, but the benefits far outweigh the problems. Asking a question and having your students write their first thoughts on the whiteboards affords you far more accurate insight into general levels of understanding than you can ever achieve by asking for verbal responses from one or two students. Not that these short written responses are enough by themselves—further questioning is needed for you to understand the thinking behind them. But, as a starting point, they are certainly better than the regular hands-up approach from the few eager beavers.

Another issue with cold calling is that many students offer the illusion of engagement. They turn their heads toward you, distance themselves from disruption, and raise their hands when you ask a question, only to drop their hands if you look toward them, a theatrical groan added for emphasis. "I'm with you," they say, but their inner thoughts say otherwise.

The opposite can also be true. There are students who are careless—or couldn't care less—about outward impressions. They are too busy pondering to worry about politeness. Or they are too busy blocking out the bustle to wonder and puzzle. "Why are you staring out the window?" they're asked. "I'm thinking, Miss," they reply. "Well, stop thinking and get on with your work!" is the satirized reply.

Leaders on learning walks look for levels of engagement. They see students sitting in class, looking attentive, taking notes, and nodding in agreement. Yet, upon deeper scrutiny, those students are found to have been daydreaming, scribbling their names, or writing irrelevant notes. No wonder there is growing disquiet about the robustness and reliability of classroom observations. Are we really able to observe learning, or are we simply taking note of levels of compliance?

As the research psychologists Robert and Elizabeth Bjork point out, distinctions must be made between *performance* and *learning*:

> Performance is what we can observe and measure during instruction or training. Learning—that is, the more or less permanent change in knowledge or understanding that is the target of instruction—is something we must try to infer, and current performance can be a highly unreliable index of whether learning has occurred. (Bjork & Bjork, 2011, p. 57)

"What can I do about the students who won't engage?" is a question I'm frequently asked following a demonstration lesson. As sympathetically as I can, I encourage the questioner to describe how they know when someone is engaging. Invariably, they talk only of outward signs of attentiveness and never of depths of thinking.

So again, I would say mini-whiteboards are a big step up from this. In fact, at the risk of sounding like I have shares in a mini-whiteboard company, I would say these boards—plus a document camera for projecting students' work onto the main whiteboard—are among the most effective pieces of equipment in classrooms.

2.1.5 Using Ten Principles for Effective Instruction

Professor Barak Rosenshine (2012) summarized at least forty years of research on effective instruction, taking evidence from cognitive science, observations of excellent teaching, and research on cognitive supports. To be included in his analysis, every behavior had to correlate with higher student outcomes. From there, he created a set of ten principles for actions that can result in improved learning. In view of the topics of this chapter, I invite you to pay particular attention to principles 3 and 6 (in bold), both of which are further explained after the list of principles (Rosenshine, 2012).

1. Begin a lesson with a short review of previous learning.
2. Present new material in small steps with student practice after each step.
3. **Ask many questions and check the responses of *all* students.**
4. Provide models for problem solving and worked examples.

5. Guide student practice.
6. **Check for student understanding.**
7. Obtain a high success rate.
8. Provide scaffolds for difficult tasks.
9. Require and monitor independent practice.
10. Engage students in weekly and monthly review.

Let's explore the two bolded principles in more detail.

2.1.5.1 Principle 3: Ask Many Questions and Check the Responses of *All* Students

Rosenshine (2012) found that the most effective teachers ask lots of questions and use many different strategies to harvest answers from all students rather than from a few. They also ask students to explain the process they used to answer the questions. Less successful teachers, on the other hand, ask fewer questions and almost no process questions. The ways in which teachers gather answers from many students rather than from a few include the following.

- Students write their first thoughts on a card or mini-whiteboard and show them to the teacher (and to others).
- Students tell the answer to a neighbor, and then the pairs report back.
- Students summarize the main idea in one or two sentences, write this summary on a card, and share it with someone else; this is often done as a paired activity.
- Students raise their hands to indicate a level of understanding. For example, tell them, "Raise your hand if you are confident that you know a good solution," "Raise your hand if you have an idea but are not totally sure it's the right one," or "Raise your hand if you have questions that need answering before you can answer my question."
- Students raise their hands if they agree or disagree with someone else's response or if they have a question or reason to add.

The questions that Rosenshine (2012) discovered were most productive were these.

- How are [this] and [that] alike?
- What is the main idea of . . . ?
- What are the strengths and weaknesses of . . . ?
- In what way is [this] related to [that]?
- Compare [this] and [that] with regard to . . .
- What do you think causes . . . ?
- How does [this] tie in with what we have learned before?
- Which one is the best—[this] or [that]—and why?
- What are some possible solutions for the problem of . . . ?
- Do you agree or disagree with this statement: . . . ?
- What do you still not understand about . . . ?

2.1.5.2 Principle 6: Check for Student Understanding

Rosenshine (2012) showed that effective teachers check for student understanding by:

- Asking questions
- Asking students to summarize the key learning points
- Asking students whether they agreed or disagreed with other students' answers
- Asking students to elaborate on the material
- Finding connections between the material studied and other lessons or contexts
- Asking students to think aloud when solving problems

In contrast, the less effective teachers simply ask, "Are there any questions?" and, if there are none, they assume students have learned the material and proceed to pass out worksheets for students to complete on their own.

2.1.6 Teaching Your Students How to Ask (Better) Questions

Many moons ago, at the beginning of a school year, I told my students that I was going to challenge myself to ask more frequent—and better-quality—questions during lessons. No longer would the students be listening, doing, listening, doing; they were also going to be thinking, answering, wondering, and responding to questions. Lots of lovely questions.

To help me with this, I prepared a crib sheet. At university, I was trained in philosophy for children (Lipman, 1987), so I dug out a list of Socratic questions from my course notes. Partway through a lesson, I'd make a beeline for a group of students, whip out my prepared list, and initiate a questioning sequence: "Could you tell me what . . . ?" "How do you know if . . . ?" and "When might that work more effectively?"

It wasn't long before my students asked if they could have a copy of my Socratic questions. Of course, I obliged. No sooner did they have a copy in their hands than they were asking one another all sorts of inventive, thought-provoking questions. Most of the students at this school experienced risk factors. Their home language was coarse, to say the least. However, here they were, quizzing each other with open, high-quality questions; listening carefully; checking for assumptions; making suggestions; and giving encouragement. This didn't happen overnight, of course, but it was the direction they traveled, and within a few months, their interactions were characterized entirely differently than at the start of the year.

The following year, I created a questioning wall titled "Thinking CAP?" This stood for "Thinking Children Asking Philosophical Questions." The year after that, with the rock band Oasis at its peak, I renamed it "Wonder Wall." I split the display into two sections. On the left, we had lots of question stems. On the right, we placed some of our favorite examples that had been asked by students during their lessons.

Figure 2.1 (page 47) shows the stems we used together with some examples I have remembered through the fog of time.

Question Stems	Our Examples
What is . . . ?	What is value?
What makes . . . ?	What makes something worthwhile?
Would you . . . ?	Would you rather have one million Japanese yen, one million U.S. dollars, or one million Norwegian kroner (and what would you do with it)?
How do we know . . . ?	How do we know if facts are correct?
. . . always (or never) . . . ?	Is proof always a good thing?
What if . . . ?	What if Hitler had won World War II?
Is it possible to . . . ?	Is it possible to be right and wrong at the same time?
When . . . ?	When is it OK to say no?
Who . . . ?	Who decides what makes art *art*?
Can we . . . ?	Can we think without words?
Why do people say . . . ?	Why do people say there is a pot of gold at the end of the rainbow?
What is the difference between . . . ?	What is the difference between sports and games?
Should we . . . ?	Should we obey all rules?
What would you do if . . . ?	What would you do if you couldn't use a calculator?
Are you saying that . . . ?	Are you saying that zero is the same as nothing?

Figure 2.1: Question stems for students to use.

Depending on the students you work with, you might want to offer just two or three question stems and then add to them bit by bit. Sometimes too much choice is overwhelming (see section 6.4, page 287, about cognitive load theory).

2.1.7 Summarizing the Questioning Process

Questioning is the process of directing questions toward learners. As stated earlier, meta-analysis of fourteen studies found a positive relationship between the use of higher-level questioning during instruction and student gains on tests of both factual recall and application of thinking skills (Redfield & Rousseau, 1981). Hattie has included this meta-analysis in his Visible Learning Metax (n.d.) database and calculated an effect size of $d = 0.73$. The seven other meta-analyses in the same category bring the overall effect size to $d = 0.49$. This is a significant effect.

A range of topics have been investigated within these meta-analyses. These include the following.

- The types of questions teachers ask
- The sources of teacher questions
- The effect of teacher questions compared with other instructional methods
- The effects of different types of questions
- The effects of waiting for students to respond after asking questions

- Training teachers to use certain types of questions
- Teaching students how to answer questions
- Teaching students to generate their own questions
- The psychology of question asking and answering

This considerable volume of research has shed light on several issues. For example, the following are known.

- The incidence of higher-order and authentic questions is scarce relative to lower-order and known-answer questions.
- Waiting for students to respond to questions leads to enhanced response quality and improved student achievement.
- Teachers can learn to ask certain types of questions, and students can be taught how to answer questions in a more open-minded, curious way.
- Promoting student-generated questions has positive effects on learning.

Get it right and questioning is one of the best ways to engage your students. By asking questions that provoke higher-order thinking, giving your students time to think, and taking an authentic interest in their answers, you will likely increase their active engagement and boost their learning outcomes.

2.1.7.1 Three Starting Points for IR-Explore Questioning

Earlier, I mentioned that an "uh-huh" or a "go on" might be more effective in certain circumstances than any type of question. Thus, the process of questioning is as significant as, perhaps even more significant than, the actual questions you ask. That said, questions are the building blocks of questioning, and you have to start somewhere. So, in addition to the examples I shared in section 2.1.1 (page 31), here are three ways to make a start with questioning.

1. **"What do you notice?"** If I was limited to one opening line for every questioning sequence, this would be the one I'd choose: "What do you notice?" It is so flexible and productive. It gives the air of being open-ended (tone of voice dependent) and can be applied in any subject area. It invites your students to draw distinctions, make suggestions, ask questions, and suggest alternatives. You could, for example, show one or more calculations on the board and ask, "What do you notice?" You could just as easily share a text, image, diagram, or pose. The answers the question elicits will give you a good sense of where your students' understanding is, what their concepts are, and just as importantly, what misconceptions they might be harboring.

2. **"How do we know?"** This question lends itself brilliantly to drawing out the thinking behind an answer. It is particularly useful when your students are confident in their answer and you're wondering what avenues there are for exploration. For example, having established that a calculation is correct, we can ask, "How can we know (for sure) that this is correct?" Or when studying biodiversity, and having established that an image on the board represents the Amazon rainforest, we can ask, "How do we know it is a tropical rainforest?" Students can then respond in terms of latitude, rainfall, atmosphere, soil fertility,

and so on. Or when studying Wilfred Owen's poem "Dulce et Decorum Est," we can ask, "How do we know the poet was involved in World War I?"

3. **"What's the same and what's different?"** This is a similar type of question to "What do you notice?" but it directs students to comparing and contrasting. So, getting your students to look at two calculations, images, problems, statements, models, approaches, designs, explanations, and so on and then asking them to spot what is similar and what is different is a very strong way to begin an IR-Explore sequence.

You will see in sections 2.4 and 2.5.3 (pages 58 and 73) that many of the dialogue strategies I recommend next are based on this central question.

2.2 Use Dialogue to Build Engagement

Dialogue is one of the most effective ways to boost student learning. It develops language skills and knowledge far more effectively than any other form of classroom interaction does.

Questioning is one of the most common ways to engage students. The problem is it typically relies on the direct involvement of the teacher. It doesn't have to, but it generally does. Dialogue, on the other hand, is a way to engage students without needing a teacher to be involved all the time.

I mentioned earlier in this book that John Hattie and I have worked together many times. During our last speaking tour before the COVID-19 pandemic, I recorded a series of interviews with him. The John Hattie Interviews (The Learning Pit, n.d.) can be viewed at the Learning Pit website (https://learningpit.org/John-Hattie). The video "HATTIE: The Impact of Dialogue" begins with Hattie answering my first question, "Of all the factors influencing student learning that you've included in your database, which effect sizes surprised you the most?" He answers without hesitation: the impact of classroom discussion (The Learning Pit, n.d.).

This QR code leads to the Hattie video
mentioned in the preceding paragraph.

He goes on to say:

> I knew feedback was powerful; I knew about peer effects and student-teacher relationships; I also knew that the jury was still out on the so-called technological revolution—the revolution that has been going on for decades. But the one factor that stood out more than most was classroom discussion. With an effect size of $d = 0.82$, this approach to teaching has the potential to double the rate of learning. (The Learning Pit, n.d.)

Now, there is a caveat to this. Thus far, Hattie has included only one meta-analysis on classroom discussion in his database, covering the outcomes of forty-two studies. So, although the effect size of $d = 0.82$ is considerable, the reliability of these data is weaker than, say, the evidence he has included on feedback, with seven meta-analyses covering 798 separate studies.

That said, other databases, including the one built by the Education Endowment Foundation (n.d.a) in England, have synthesized many more meta-analyses and concluded that *oral language interventions* (classroom discussion, also called *oracy*) have a "very high impact for very low cost based on extensive evidence." They quote six months' additional gain in a school year when using dialogic activities in the classroom. Researcher Catherine E. Snow (2014) shows that classroom dialogue creates opportunities for extended discourse and, consequently, develops language skills far more effectively than non-dialogic interactions.

The meta-analysis that Hattie includes in his database by researchers P. Karen Murphy and colleagues (2009) shows the following.

- Substantial improvements in text comprehension
- Moderate improvements in inference, comprehension, critical thinking, and reasoning

So, it is fair to say that dialogue has the potential to significantly boost student learning. Strong and extensive evidence confirms this. There are also strong links between high-quality dialogue and the IR-Explore approach to questioning that I mentioned earlier. Here's the bad news: dialogue is not yet strongly rooted in daily classroom practice.

2.2.1 Barriers to Dialogue

Dialogic approaches to teaching and learning still encounter many barriers in the school setting, most notably teachers using a monologic approach (a polite way of saying that teachers use a lecture style of teaching) too often. Other barriers include a tension between giving students freedom to interact with each other and delivering curriculum goals (Howe & Abedin, 2013; Lyle, 2008), traditional classroom rules favoring teacher talk (Mercer & Howe, 2012), and seating plans directing students' attention toward the teacher rather than favoring interactions with everyone else in the room. (See section 2.1.3.1, page 40, for notes about arranging the room to encourage eye contact.)

Graham Nuthall (2002), whose research I draw on in this book, gave the Herbison Lecture in 2001 on the cultural myths and the realities of teaching and learning. Referring to his findings from the longest-ever series of studies on teaching and learning, Nuthall (2002) says this:

> What was immediately apparent was that teachers do not talk to students about learning or thinking. They talk about paying attention and not annoying others. They talk about the resources the students will need to use, about how long the activity should take and what will happen if it is not finished on time.
>
> When you listen to students they talk about the same things. They are constantly comparing how much have they done. How long will it take, do the headings have to be underlined, where did you find that answer, do you have to write it all out, does it have to be finished for homework? (p. 19)

Professor Gad Yair's (2000) research makes for equally sobering reading. Yair asked 865 students in grades 6, 8, 10, and 12 to wear digital wristwatches that emitted signals eight times a day. He asked them to note, "Where were you at the time of the beep?" and "What was on your mind?" Of the 28,193 responses, a little under 12,000 took place in school and just over 4,000 took place during learning experiences. Analysis showed the following.

- Students were engaged in their lessons only 54 percent of the time. There was very little variation relative to student ability or curriculum subject.
- Students in grade 6 engaged 62 percent of the time; by grade 12, this engagement dropped to 49 percent of the time.
- External preoccupations encroached on the students' attention 36 percent of the time. For students with risk factors that negatively impact graduation rates, this preoccupation increased to 42 percent of the time.
- Teachers talked for 70 percent to 80 percent of class time. Student engagement was at its lowest during these times.
- Teachers spoke even more to older classes and smaller classes (one of the reasons why reducing the number of students in a class doesn't necessarily boost learning outcomes).

The few bits of good news are that students' engagement improved significantly when working in laboratory classrooms (73 percent engagement) or taking part in group activities (also 73 percent engagement), group presentations (67 percent), and discussions (63 percent). Perhaps most importantly of all, the biggest upswings were experienced by students with risk factors (see chapter 6, page 269, for more about this). So, the biggest barrier to engaging students in dialogue is us teachers talking too much!

Of course, that is not to say we should all become mime artists like the famous Marcel Marceau! Nor should we replace our talk with students completing worksheets in silence. The best way forward is to teach our students how to engage in high-quality dialogue with each other and with us. And a lot of research shows it's not only possible but also very beneficial. The main research I will draw on is by professor Robin Alexander (2001, 2006, 2018) and the Oracy Cambridge team led by professors Neil Mercer and Rupert Wegerif (2002). For now, here are some useful insights from two other meta-analyses.

Engaging students in dialogue about texts (literature or subject-based texts) leads to significant gains in reading comprehension when teachers (Wolf, Crosson, & Resnick, 2005):

- Reformulate and summarize what their students say
- Provide an opportunity for other students to build on these ideas
- Encourage students to put the main idea into their own words
- Press students to elaborate (for example, "How did you know that?" and "Why?")

As students engage in group work during science lessons, the best learning gains are noted when (Howe & Abedin, 2013):

- Groups are asked to seek agreement
- Students are prompted to express contrasting explanations and opinions
- Teachers take a listening role during group activities

2.2.2 Teaching Students How to Engage in Dialogue

 *The object of teaching a child is to enable him to get along without a teacher.*

—Elbert Hubbard

Most peer-to-peer talk is unproductive. Many observational studies confirm this (Blatchford & Kutnick, 2003; Galton, Hargreaves, Comber, & Wall, 1999). Lack of opportunity to engage in dialogue is one barrier, as shown in the previous section. The other obstacle is that students don't typically know how to talk and think together effectively, even though their teachers often assume they do (Wegerif & Scrimshaw, 1997).

The first step to improving dialogue is properly defining it. Dialogue is a specific type of talk, distinct from others more commonly heard in classrooms. It involves teachers and students commenting and cumulatively building on each other's ideas, posing questions, and constructing interpretations together. Key characteristics include:

- Students articulating ideas seen from someone else's perspective
- Sequences of primarily open questions
- Knowledge being co-constructed (for example, "Picking up on what students A and B said, and adding my thoughts, I'm wondering if that means . . .")
- Reasons being offered in support of ideas and opinions
- Students expecting their ideas to be critiqued and improved by others

Unfortunately, the term *dialogue* is often used interchangeably with *discussion*, even though many researchers make important distinctions between the two. Dialogue should have a sense of direction. It should seek a clearer understanding of the truth or move toward a more sophisticated, nuanced solution to a problem. Discussion, on the other hand, doesn't have to stick to the point. It can go in any direction and be entirely responsive to participants' interests and stories.

Dialogue will be as if participants are sailing into the wind; they will take tangents but will always maintain a focus on their intended direction, tacking back and forth across a central line. In contrast, discussion will be about the experience itself, with participants never worrying about a sense of direction or reaching an intended destination.

Rather than continually emphasizing the differences between dialogue and discussion, I tend to use the term *exploratory talk* instead. Staff relate to this well, and often, students do too.

2.2.3 Focusing On the Right Type of Talk

The terms *cumulative talk*, *disputational talk*, and *exploratory talk* were coined by Neil Mercer, professor emeritus of education and director of the Oracy Cambridge project. The way in which he distinguishes among these three types of talk reminds me of Goldilocks's porridge. Cumulative talk is just a little too warm, disputational talk is a little too cold, and exploratory talk is just right.

- *Cumulative talk* is characterized by repetitions, confirmations, and elaborations. It is typically heard when friendship groups work together or when an unfamiliar group is getting to know one another. The talk is positive and affirming, making everyone feel included and welcome. The participants rarely criticize each other, and they don't critique others' ideas. Not everyone in the group takes part, nor are they expected to. The group accepts first ideas and does not try to go beyond these. This leads to an accumulation of common knowledge and a sense of harmony in the group.

- *Disputational talk* is characterized by short interactions and individual decision making. Students make little attempt to listen to each other or to pool resources. The talk is dominated by assertions and counter-assertions. This type of talk is less prevalent than you might think and is actually quite hard to spot because it can occur under the radar. It is much more negative than cumulative talk. Disputational talk is critical of individuals (and their ideas), focuses on differences, is competitive, and is all about being seen to win. Individuals within the group dominate. Mistakes are criticized and perhaps even ridiculed. Disputational talk is similar in outcome to the IR-Evaluate approach to questioning that I described in section 2.1 (page 30).

- *Exploratory talk* is characterized by longer exchanges and the use of questions, reflection, explanation, and speculation. It makes use of critical thinking and can also be very creative. As Mercer (2000) explains, exploratory talk is:

    that in which partners engage critically but constructively with each other's ideas. Relevant information is offered for joint consideration. Proposals may be challenged and counter-challenged, but if so, reasons are given, and alternatives are offered. Agreement is sought as a basis for joint progress. Knowledge is made publicly accountable, and reasoning is visible in the talk. (p. 98)

    Exploratory talk has much in common with the IR-Explore approach to questioning I described in section 2.1.1 (page 31).

Mercer and his team at the University of Cambridge have conducted many studies on the impact of exploratory talk. In one such intervention reported on for the Esmée Fairbairn Foundation in March 2004, they showed teachers how to explain and model exploratory talk with seven hundred pupils, ages six to fourteen (Wegerif, Littleton, Dawes, Mercer, & Rowe, 2004). In the first five lessons, teachers modeled the approach as part of teacher-led activities. In the second five lessons, pupils engaged in group activities that gave them the opportunity to lead their own exploratory talk.

The gains made by the students were impressive. Compared with control classes (Mercer & Littleton, 2007):

- Students began to use much more exploratory talk
- Students pursued group activities more cooperatively and in more depth
- Students became better at solving problems together
- Students became better at solving problems independently (as assessed by scores on Raven's Progressive Matrices)
- Students achieved significantly better scores in tests of science and mathematics
- The number of questions students asked each other increased from seventeen to eighty-six

- The number of reasons given more than doubled
- The number of speculations (what-ifs) rose from two to thirty-five
- The number of words used by the groups almost doubled

The researchers identified two main reasons for these beneficial outcomes. First, the participants appropriated successful problem-solving strategies and explanatory accounts from each other; and second, students learned how to co-construct new, robust, and generalizable explanations. These suggest a *strong connection* between social interaction (thinking together) and improved cognitive development.

This theory is nothing new, of course. Psychologist Lev Vygotsky (1896–1934) wrote at length about sociocultural theory. He suggested that higher mental functions are learned through social interaction before becoming features of the internal thinking of an individual. He described language as both a cultural tool (for developing and sharing knowledge among members of a community) and a psychological tool (for structuring the processes and content of individual thought). He also proposed that there is a close relationship between these two functions of language, which can be summed up in the claim that intermental (social, interactional) activity stimulates some of the most important intramental (individual, cognitive) capabilities (Vygotsky, 1978).

In this video, James explains the purpose of exploratory talk that can be used with middle or high school students.

2.2.4 Exploratory Talk

Exploratory talk is the most effective form of dialogue. It is characterized by longer exchanges and the use of questions, reflection, explanation, and speculation.

The three steps to making exploratory talk the style of interaction for your students are as follows.

1. **Explain what is expected:** I realize this sounds obvious, but it really is the best starting point. Indeed, it is so effective that on countless occasions when I have led demonstration lessons and included a short introduction about exploratory talk, the observing staff have noticed an immediate change in their students' behavior. When working in primary schools, I use the term *exploration* and say the actions I expect of everyone are the following.

- Allow each other to speak. Don't rush each other. It is important that those who wish to share their ideas can do so in an unhurried, exploratory way. Give encouraging gestures so that whoever is speaking feels valued and listened to.
- Ask questions so you understand each other better. When someone has finished speaking, ask follow-up questions to better understand their point of view. This is one way we can show each other respect—by being interested in what others say rather than looking for ways to promote our own views.
- Listen to learn. See what you can learn by listening carefully. Some people jump in as soon as they think they know what someone means, but giving others the chance to fully air their thoughts can lead to additional insights.
- Don't agree straight away. Listening carefully to others does not mean you have to agree with everything they say. In fact, there is a significant benefit to challenging each other, not in a combative way but in an exploratory, thought-provoking way. Ask for more information, suggest alternatives, and use the phrases, "Ah yes, but what about . . . ?" and "Could it be . . . ?"

If working in high schools, I generally explain exploratory talk in comparison with the other two styles of talk (disputational and cumulative). On one occasion, a student who monopolized the discussion in his group called himself out, apologized to his peers for being disputational, and promised to be more exploratory (which he was for the rest of the lesson).

2. **Draw attention to incidents of exploratory talk:** Watch out for students' engagement in exploratory talk, and when it isn't distracting to do so, draw positive attention toward it. These student behaviors include exploring ideas and offering reasons for their thinking, responding positively to being challenged by others, and being willing to change their minds but also assertive enough to have the courage of their convictions. Students might also encourage others to speak, then build on what the others say by reflecting back the words and ideas used; they might express uncertainty or tentativeness; and they might explore differences of opinion without there being a sense of point scoring or making things personal.

3. **Agree to a set of ground rules:** Notice that I didn't start this list with this one. Too often, so much is made of ground rules at the beginning of a lesson that they come across as commandments rather than encouragements. Therefore, I recommend having an implicit set of high expectations to begin with and then making them more explicit later if you feel the need to do so.

The following are suggestions for possible ground rules for exploratory talk.

- Listen with care, empathy, and an open mind.
- Encourage others to contribute.
- Ask questions to better understand each other's points of view.
- Respect the person, critique the ideas.

- Support your thinking with reasons and examples.
- Refer to other people's ideas when giving your thoughts.
- Take intellectual risks.
- Express tentativeness.

Every teacher has their own approach, so I wouldn't want you to think these suggestions for ground rules are the only way to go. Having said that, I would strongly advise against using the phrase, "There are no right or wrong answers." It is better to phrase it as, "We are open to possibilities" or "We will always seek out the best answers." To say there is no right or wrong is, well, wrong! Right answers (or better answers) do exist most of the time, and wrong answers always exist! There is a cartoon that often does the rounds of two people viewing a digit from opposite ends. One says it is 6, and the other says it is 9. The caption often says that reality is a matter of perspective. That might well be the case, but it is also true to say that lots of wrong answers still exist, even if the right answer is unclear. For example, if someone says the digit represents 143, that is wrong. We want to encourage the continual pursuit of better answers, but this does not mean we have to accept any answer.

2.3 Choose the Right Time to Engage Students in Dialogue

Dialogue strategies work best when you want to move your students from surface knowledge to deep learning. Before that, direct instruction, teacher questioning, and topic research work better.

Dialogue is one of the best ways to engage students and deepen their learning. However, it isn't always the best approach to choose. When your students have no knowledge about a topic, direct instruction and student exploration are more appropriate.

A clear way to think about this is with the help of the Structure of the Observed Learning Outcome (SOLO) Taxonomy (Biggs & Collis, 1982). I make several references to this model in the chapter about feedback (chapter 4, page 147) and the chapter about equity (chapter 6, page 269). In many ways, this model is more central to feedback than it is to dialogue, but because this chapter comes first, I will describe it here.

Figure 2.2 shows an abridged version of the SOLO Taxonomy. Instead of using the original terminology of *prestructural*, *unistructural*, and *multistructural*, I have used the terms *no knowledge*, *some knowledge*, and *lots of knowledge*. I have also added the light bulb images, the characteristics of which I will draw attention to in my descriptions afterward. Going for this everyday language should help with its application. It also makes the model more accessible if you want to share it with your students (which I recommend that you do).

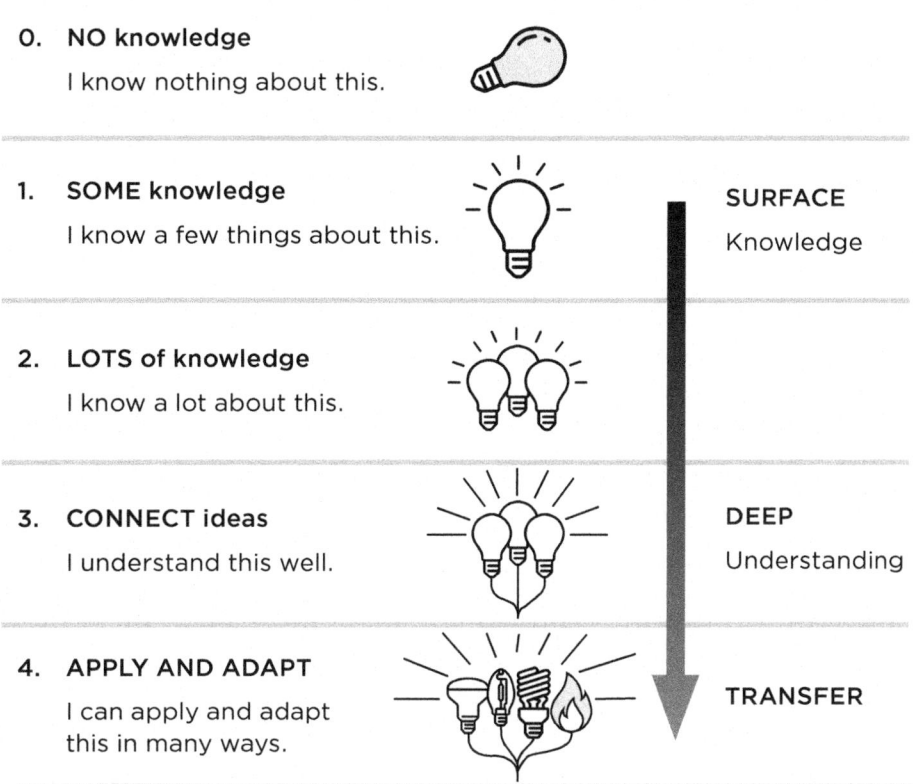

Figure 2.2: The SOLO Taxonomy (abridged).

The diagram in figure 2.2 tracks a learner's progress from knowing nothing (about a particular subject) to knowing something about it, to knowing lots about it, to being able to connect their new knowledge with other ideas within and outside the same domain, to applying and adapting their understanding in different contexts. As the learner moves from one stage to the next, they make progress from surface knowledge to deep learning to an ability to adapt and transfer that learning to different contexts. Surface and deep learning can be accomplished simultaneously, but *ordinarily*, students move from one to the next to the next, as shown in the diagram.

Surface learning includes acquiring new knowledge without paying much attention to the purpose or strategy used, memorizing facts and sequences, repeating routines, and learning ideas or facts without considering their interconnection. *Deep learning* relates to connecting concepts, making meaning, looking for and analyzing patterns and principles, thinking critically and creatively, developing theories, identifying similarities and differences, defining, and analyzing. *Transfer* includes selecting, applying, and evaluating strategies; choosing resources; adapting approaches and ideas to better fit the context; elaborating; creating and synthesizing; and striving toward coherence.

When looking to move students from knowledge to understanding, the first step is to help them make connections. If you look at the different light bulbs I created, you will notice the difference between the three light bulbs at the lots-of-knowledge stage and those at the connect-ideas stage. In the first stage, the power cords are separate; in the second, they are intertwined. This is meant to represent the basic premise for understanding: connecting ideas together to make sense of them. Someone understands when they spot a rule or pattern, when they discern the similarities and differences, and when they can explain the function of one thing *relative to* others. If this is done collaboratively through dialogue and social construction, then understanding can be deepened further still.

Thus, learning should be thought of in terms of moving from knowledge to understanding to application and redesign. So when I write in chapter 4 (page 147), "When giving feedback, make sure that it is good advice that is well used to improve learning and application," this is what I mean: the feedback should help students move from their current stage of learning to their next stage (see section 4.3.3.1, page 158).

Dialogue is one of the best ways to help your students move from stage 2 (lots of knowledge) to stage 3 (connecting ideas) and then to stage 4 (applying and adapting ideas to different contexts). Bear this in mind as you read through the dialogue strategies that I share in the next four sections of this chapter.

2.4 Use Strategies to Help Students Make Connections

When someone moves from knowing something to understanding something, they make connections. In SOLO Taxonomy terms, this is when they move from stage 2 (multistructural) to stage 3 (relational). Here are two strategies to teach your students that will help them make connections.

2.4.1 What's the Difference?

Of all the questions I use to engage students in deeper thought, "What's the difference?" is perhaps the most flexible and productive. Whatever your students are thinking about, if you ask them to compare their main idea or concept with another linked idea or concept, it can lead to some fascinating and thought-provoking dialogue.

Shown in figure 2.3 (page 59) are some examples I used with different student age groups across the curriculum. The italicized words refer to the concepts my students were thinking about. The lowercase words are the concepts I asked them to compare their central concept with. The words in parentheses are some alternatives that I could have used. For example, *acceleration* was the term my year 9 (grade 8 in the United States) students were investigating. So, I asked them, "What's the difference between acceleration and speed?" On reflection, I could have just as productively asked them, "What's the difference between acceleration and velocity?" Or, if I *also* wanted them to make connections with terms used in everyday life (as opposed to keeping the inquiry entirely rooted in science), then I could have asked, "What's the difference between acceleration and momentum, or between acceleration and pace?"

As well as these examples, I have created others to use with the Odd One Out strategy (page 60), so if you look at that section, you will find other sources of inspiration.

What's the difference between . . .

Acceleration and speed (velocity, momentum, pace)?

Artificial and virtual (parallel, apparent, identical)?

Artwork and works of art (painting, the arts, fine art)?

Cause and correlation (connection, association, relationship)?

Change and diversity (variety, difference, otherness, divergence)?

Design and invent (construct, produce, visualize)?

Development and growth (progress, advancement, evolution, improvement)?

Education and learning (studying, knowing, mastering, discovering)?

Energy and power (force, influence, strength)?

Ethics and morals (principles, standards, beliefs)?

Experiment and investigation (exploration, research, testing, examining)?

Facts and information (data, gossip, news, evidence)?

Fair and equal (objective, balanced, equitable, unbiased)?

Family and friends (partners, supporters, peers, associates)?

Famous and infamous (notorious, inglorious, shameful, dishonorable)?

Force and reaction (response, reflex, answer)?

Government and law (constitution, rules, legislation, statutes)?

Health and fitness (stamina, well-being, agility)?

Horizontal and vertical (upright, standing, perpendicular)?

Insects and animals (creatures, pets, livestock)?

Knowing and thinking (reflecting, understanding, remembering)?

Language and communication (contact, speech, rapport)?

Leadership and control (regulation, power, command, protection)?

Listening and hearing (detecting, perceiving, encountering)?

Marketing and advertising (promoting, selling, posting, publicizing)?

Measurement and value (worth, number, significance)?

Metaphor and simile (analogy, euphemism, comparison)?

Mistakes and failure (defeat, disappointment, loss, disaster)?

Nationality and identity (conformity, individuality, personality)?

Number and value (symbol, amount, measure)?

Old and ancient (traditional, archaic, vintage, classic)?

Perspective and viewpoint (opinion, judgment, outlook, interpretation)?

Play and pretend (make believe, imagine, act out, fake)?

Real and living (existing, functioning, surviving, thriving)?

Religion and belief (faith, spirituality, philosophy, dogma)?

Rights and responsibilities (duties, obligations, commitments)?

Risk taking and resilience (strength, persistence, tenacity)?

Science and technology (invention, progress, innovation)?

Shade and perspective (view, slant, position, interpretation)?

Society and culture (values, customs, heritage, lifestyle)?

Stories and movies (films, pictures, drama, theater, television)?

Time and space (capacity, place, range, interval)?

War and conflict (dispute, disunity, disagreement, combat)?

Figure 2.3: Examples of What's the Difference? questions.

A good resource to create and have ready to use is a What's the Difference? table. Some examples are in figure 2.4 (page 61). As you can see, each table has a selection of the main concepts that would usually be included for a topic. If you have these ready, then at the right moments, you can give them as prompts for pairs or groups to engage in dialogue together.

In each case, you should pick two concepts from a table to form a What's the Difference? question. So, for example, the first table is about animals. The options I've provided could lead to any one (or more) of the following questions.

- What's the difference between mammals and birds?
- What's the difference between plants and food?
- What's the difference between amphibians and reptiles?
- What's the difference between carnivores and humans?

2.4.2 Odd One Out

This is the best structure for starting a dialogue in pairs, in groups, or as a whole class. I say this because of its adaptability, lack of preparation time, and suitability for every curriculum area and every topic. What's more, it leads students into higher-order thinking by directing them to spot similarities and differences, give reasons, and make connections. There are so many ways to begin this strategy. I will share the most straightforward approach first and then give options afterward.

Begin by sharing three images, and ask your students to say which is the odd one out and why. If need be, remind them that there are many right answers (but do *not* say there are no right or wrong answers, for the reasons shown in sections 2.2.2 and 4.7, pages 52 and 188). For example, if I am working with a group of middle school students and their topic is health, I could start with three images of food and ask which is the odd one out and why.

Let's imagine the images are of (1) a burger, (2) a salad, and (3) a glass of milk. The routine I use is as follows.

1. Show the images.
2. Ask the whole class which is the odd one out and why.
3. Have the students turn and talk to the person sat next to them for twenty to thirty seconds.
4. Invite a few pairs to share their first thoughts. Check that the students' answers follow the right formula (see page 62). If they don't, then help students reformulate. If they do, then confirm that the answers are legitimate (without giving students any sense that you favor one idea over another) and then move to step 5.
5. Ask the students to split into groups of four and to come up with five reasons why the burger is the odd one out, five reasons why the salad is, and five reasons why the glass of milk is. This means each group comes up with fifteen answers altogether.
6. After a few minutes, invite groups to share their ideas with the whole class. Bring out a range of answers with these sorts of prompts.

Topic: Animals			
Mammals	Birds	Amphibians	Plants
Reptiles	Food	Carnivore	Humans
Topic: Characterization			
Character	Characterization	Dialogue	Narrative
Voice	Sociable	Solitary	Predators
Cast	First person	Second person	Third person
Perspective	Narrator	Third person omniscient	
Topic: Control Technology			
Systems	Actions	Operations	Controls
Programming	Errors	Robotics	CAD
Topic: Fractions			
Fractions	Denominator	Numerator	Percentage
Value	Ratio	Multiply	Decimal
Topic: Materials			
Composite	Synthetic	Polymers	Properties
Construction	CFRP	MDF	Petrochemical
Topic: Meals (French)			
Petit déjeuner	Déjeuner	Je mange toujours	Tous les jours
J'adore	Je voudrais	Nous préférons	Ma viande préférée
Chaque jour	Je suis végétalien	Je l'ai aimé	Je mange sainement
Topic: Music Theory			
Melody	Harmony	Tonality	Tempo
Meter	Rhythm	Timbre	Notation
Texture	Articulation	Dynamics	Structure
Topic: People Who Help Me (for early years students)			
(Images of . . .) Parent	Grandparent	Nurse	Hard hat
Teacher	Police officer	Fire hose	Police helmet
Bandage	Teddy bear	Guide dog	Wheelchair
Topic: Prefixes and Suffixes			
Prefix	Suffix	Root	Meaning
-able	-ship	-ate	Un-
Topic: Theater Design			
Costume	Set	Lighting	Sound
Setting	Period	Themes	Symbols

Figure 2.4: Examples of What's the Difference? tables.

- Could you give us your favorite answer?
- Give us your quirkiest answer.
- Any answers that you think no one else will have thought of?
- Any ideas for this one being the odd one out? (Choose the food that the fewest groups have given answers for.)

7. If you have a particular content objective, you can give students a steer at this point or at step 5 (for example, "Our topic is health, so please relate your answers to this topic. For example, this one is unhealthy because . . . , or these two are processed foods, and this one isn't").

In step 4, I mentioned checking that your students' answers follow the right formula. By that, I mean your students should say something along the lines of, "This one is the odd one out because the other two have [this characteristic], whereas this one does not" or "This one can be used for [this purpose], but these two cannot."

If your students have not followed the formula, then help them reformulate their answer. For example, if they say, "We like this one the best," then you could respond by saying, "So are you saying that this one is the odd one out because you like its taste, whereas you do not like the taste of the other two?"

Odd One Out Options

There are so many options when it comes to the Odd One Out strategy. Here are a few to consider.

- Start with four examples rather than three. In fact, in a sense, you could start with any number of examples, but pay attention to cognitive load (see section 6.4, page 287).
- State a theme or learning intention at the outset so your students know which sorts of characteristics to distinguish between. For example, you could say, "Thinking about our topic of energy, have a look at these images of a plant, a moving object, and a bowl of pasta, and identify as many Odd One Out characteristics connected to energy as you can."
- Split your students into groups, and give each group a different set of examples to review.
- Start a topic with an Odd One Out; then revisit it a few times throughout the topic, adding extra ideas as your students' understanding deepens. This fits nicely with the idea of drawing attention to progress that I write about in section 5.5 (page 240).
- Use the format shown in figure 2.5 (page 63).

One way to help your students organize their thinking is with the use of the diagram shown in figure 2.5. Place an image, word, or concept into each of the three circles. Then, using the letters A, B, C, and so on as references, ask the following questions.

- **Point A:** What makes the [image, word, or concept] in the top circle different from the other two?
- **Point B:** What connects the [images, words, or concepts] in the top and bottom right circles but not the [image, word, or concept] in the bottom left circle?

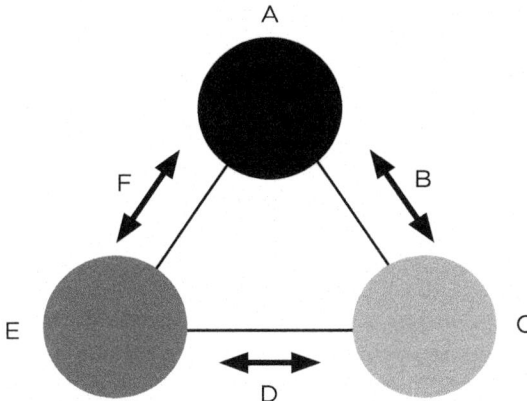

Figure 2.5: Odd One Out structure.

- **Point C:** What makes the [image, word, or concept] in the bottom right circle different from the other two?
- **And so on:** For example, if I put *river* in the top circle, *lake* in the bottom right circle, and *ocean* in the bottom left circle, then the questions I would ask are:
  - *Point D*—What do lakes and oceans but not rivers have in common?
  - *Point E*—What makes oceans different from lakes and rivers?
  - *Point F*—What do oceans and rivers but not lakes have in common?

You might say that the question at point A (What makes rivers different from lakes and oceans?) is almost the same question as the one at point D (What connects lakes and oceans but not rivers?), but by changing the starting point, I have seen groups come up with quite different answers. So, for that reason, I don't think it's worth worrying too much about the repetition.

Odd One Out Examples

The variety of examples you could use for Odd One Out exercises are almost limitless. To give you some inspiration, though, some possibilities are shown in figure 2.6 (page 64).

Here are a few things to note when designing and running Odd One Out exercises.

- Remind your students that the process of thinking together is more important than finishing first or getting as many answers as possible. As described in section 2.2.2 (page 52), their responsibility is to encourage each other to think more; it is not to simply agree with each other. They should be questioning each other, asking for reasons, offering countersuggestions, and so on.

- Be clear about your expectations. You want your students to identify Odd One Out answers rather than simply say what they like or describe one of the options without comparison to the others. For example, a response of, "That one is the best," should be reframed before being accepted.

- Emphasize the principle that many answers are possible with Odd One Out exercises. However, do not use the phrase, "There are no right or wrong answers." I shared some reasons for this in section 2.2.2 (page 52).

Odd One Out Examples

Art and Design

Artists: Picasso, Dalí, Cézanne, Hockney, Banksy, Höch, Westwood, Klint

Painting: Color, primary color, secondary color, palette, shade, brush, sponge, fingers, easel

Styles: Collage, cave art, cubism, graffiti, surrealism, photography, self-portraits, still life

Citizenship and Social-Emotional Learning

Rights: Right to vote, right to speak freely, right to privacy, right to education, right to free movement, right to health care, right to a fair trial, right to life, right to work, right to asylum

Democracy: Types—Athenian, direct, representative, parliamentary
Countries—Norway, Italy, United States, China, Pakistan

Leadership: Coach, visionary, inspirational, strategic, autocratic, democratic, transformational

Relationships: Behaviors—Assertive, passive, aggressive, defensive, inclusive, prejudiced
Status—Independent, social, popular, shy, intimidating, bully, loner

Computing and Information and Communication Technologies

Search engines: Index, URL, algorithms, title, key words, internet, program, webpage, security

Social media: Platform, X (formerly Twitter), Facebook, Instagram, Snapchat, friends, likes, shares, networks, search, block, mute, cyberbullying, phishing, trolling

Programming: Variables, information, value, data, characters, string, code, input, output, software, hardware

Drama

Costume design: Character, context, style, audience, color, symbolism, accessories, hair and makeup

Genre: Tragedy, comedy, history, melodrama, epic theater, improvisation, physical theater

Performance: Posture, mannerisms, movement, accent, gait, gestures, eye contact, audience engagement, rehearsal

Geography

Human geography: Population, migration, urbanization, globalization, tourism, conflict, culture, asylum, poverty, resource management

Physical geography: Volcanoes, earthquakes, tsunami, storm, hurricane, rivers, seas, oceans, glaciers, streams, valleys, scale

Mapping skills: Atlas, globe, scale, physical features, human features, political features, latitude, longitude, the equator, Ordnance Survey maps, grid reference, contours, sketch maps, photographs, satellite images, aerial photographs, ground photographs

History

Elizabeth I: Act of Supremacy, Act of Uniformity, Religious Settlement, Church of England, Protestants, Catholics, Puritans, Privy Council, William Cecil, Robert Dudley, Francis Walsingham, monopoly licenses

Life under the Nazis: Treaty of Versailles, economic depression, high unemployment, rearmament, Law for the Encouragement of Marriage, Mother's Cross, Hitler Youth, League of German Maidens, SS, Gestapo, SD, SA, censorship of the press, control of the radio, mass rallies (Nuremberg), swastika, party flags, arm salute, anti-Semitism, eugenics, Aryan race, sterilization, euthanasia, persecution of Jews

Ancient Greece: Delphi, Athens, Olympus, Sparta, Knossos, Zeus, Athena, Hades, Heracles, Perseus, Theseus, Achilles, Medusa, Minotaur, Minos, myth, legend, story, chronicle

Literacy and English Language Arts

Characters: Pick three characters from the novel or play your students are studying.

Genres: Fiction, poetry, novel, drama, narrative, prose, nonfiction, science fiction

Grammar: Verb, noun, preposition, determiner, tense, possessive, infinitive

Modern Foreign Language

Celebrations: Spanish—el Año Nuevo, el árbol de Navidad, los fuegos artificiales, el día festivo, la Navidad, el villancico, la Nochebuena

Food and drink: Gaelic—lòn, stòr-bìdh, deoch, òl deoch-slàinte, cuirm-dhighe, companach òil, co-òl, neach-òil

Verbs: French—danser, jouer, manger, nager, regarder, chanter, dessiner, jouer au foot, regarder la télévision

Modern Studies

Children's rights: Education, freedom of speech, poverty, inequality, standard of living, democracy, censorship

Media: Free press, balance, bias, print, broadcast, online, quality, accuracy, impartiality, trustworthiness, fake news

Causes of inequality: Unemployment, low pay, long-term illness, gender, race, social mobility, education, economic poverty, aspirational poverty

Music

Songwriting: Subject, melody, rhyme, repetition, message, emotion, hook, verse, chorus, lyrics, notes (Compare lyrics from three different songs.)

Genre: Pop, rock, jazz, classical, electronic, acoustic, country, hip-hop, heavy metal, folk, R&B, dance, punk

Numeracy and Mathematics

Fractions: Whole, decimal, percentage, equivalent fraction, denominator, numerator

Place value: Place value, number, value, numerals, digits, partition, decimals, tens, ones

Roots: Square root, cube root, squares, indices, integer, digits, decimal place, multiply

Physical Education

Athletics: Walking, jogging, running, sprinting, hurdling, relays, jumping for height, jumping for distance, takeoff, landing, throwing underarm, throwing overarm, throwing at a target, throwing for distance, throwing for height

Dance: Performance, communication, presentation, rhythm, melody, movement, poise, balance, coordination

Games: Kicking, striking, handling, dribbling, carrying, controlling, throwing, bouncing, rolling, receiving, catching

Science

Planning for an experiment: Method, diagram, apparatus, variables, data, instructions, hypothesis, prediction, results, observations, measurements, conclusion, evaluation (Compare three or more different plans or reports.)

Electricity: Particles, electrons, circuit, conductors, insulators, static, wires, flow (Three or more different circuit types can be compared.)

Solids, liquids, and gases: Melting, evaporation, condensation, hardening, pouring, floating, expansion, heat movement, freezing, steaming, water, oil, sand, helium, smoke, wood, syrup

Figure 2.6: Examples of categories to use for the Odd One Out strategy.

- When designing an Odd One Out exercise, select examples that are accessible to all students. For example, if I want my students to compare properties of materials, there are likely to be some who don't know what polymers, composites, or ceramics are. Accompanying images of these materials being used in everyday objects will help students engage more.

- Connected to the previous point, also be willing to accept answers at different levels of complexity. For example, a student operating at the surface level of knowledge might suggest that a polymer is the odd one out because it is the only one that begins with a *p*, whereas composites and ceramics begin with a *c*. At the other end of the scale, a student in the same class working at a much deeper level of understanding can still challenge themselves to think of answers that others won't know (for example, some composites will conduct electricity, whereas ceramics and polymers won't).

Odd One Out Extension

Figure 2.7 shows an example of one way to extend the use of Odd One Out. When I am classroom based, I create a three-by-three grid such as this on a wall or in a corner of the whiteboard. I can then add nine examples to allow some flexibility and choice for my students.

	A	B	C
1	△	½	50%
2	4	IV	□
3	8	○	5

Figure 2.7: Odd One Out extension.

A grid like this allows me to set up learning in lots of ways, including these options.

- Give each group a set of three to begin an Odd One Out dialogue. For example, one group could take the three items listed in column A, another group could take column B, another group could take row 1, and so on.

- Groups could choose their own set of three (or four) to begin an Odd One Out dialogue.

- Put some new examples on the board before you head home at the end of the day. Then, ask your students to engage in an Odd One Out dialogue as soon as they get to class the following morning.

- Share just three or four examples; then ask your students to complete the grid of nine. Then ask them to select the three that they like the look of and begin their Odd One Out dialogue.

2.5 Use Strategies to Help Students Sort and Classify

Sorting and classifying activities can help students develop a range of thinking skills. These include being able to identify patterns, relationships, similarities and differences, and matching. When students do this sorting and classifying as part of a group activity, it can also help improve the quality of the dialogue that follows.

Of the broad range of strategies you could use, my favorites include ranking, Is–Could Be–Never Would Be, and Venn diagrams.

2.5.1 Ranking

A strategy that lends itself brilliantly to dialogue is ranking. When used effectively, it causes students to explore viewpoints, give reasons, question each other, observe, describe connections, compare and contrast, and reflect and judge. All of these are higher-order-thinking skills. The three structures for ranking that I've included here are (1) diamond ranking, (2) pyramid ranking, and (3) line ranking. Any structure will work so long as teachers use it to rank options relative to each other and to the central concept or question.

Beware of students' trying to avoid thinking too hard by sorting the options into alphabetical order! I've seen this happen many times in classrooms and sometimes even in staffrooms! If your students do this, gently remind them that the task is *not* to sort but to rank and that alphabetical order is not a rank.

The following are some of the best structures for ranking.

- **Diamond ranking:** A *diamond rank* has the structure shown in figure 2.8 (page 68). It places one option at the top, two options as second equal, three options as third equal, two as fourth equal, and then a single item at the bottom.

- **Pyramid ranking:** *Pyramid ranking* is similar to diamond ranking except that it is in the shape of a pyramid or triangle, as shown in figure 2.9 (page 68). This allows for a different number of ideas to be ranked. It also means that students don't have to place one of the ideas at the bottom, which might, on occasion, better suit your intentions. For preK to grade 3 students, you could reduce the number of positions to three: a top factor plus two factors in equal second place. Or for high school students, you could increase the number to ten or fifteen.

- **Line ranking:** A *line rank* often leads to more deliberation than the other two styles of ranking because there are no equal spots. Instead, each characteristic should be given a position that is different from any other. As with all the other ranks, this position could be based on importance, relevance, significance, or any other agreed-on quality. The structure is shown in figure 2.10 (page 68).

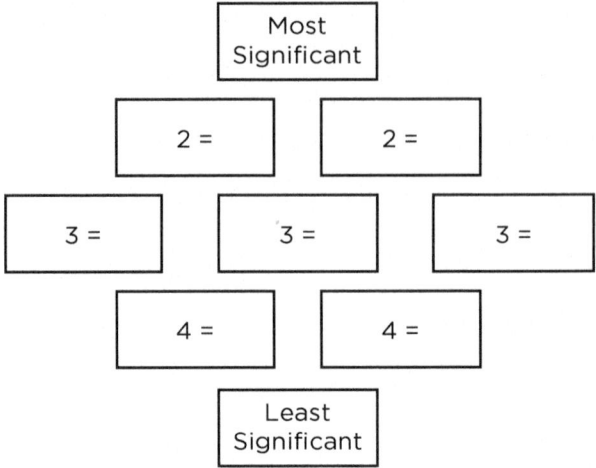

Figure 2.8: Diamond rank.

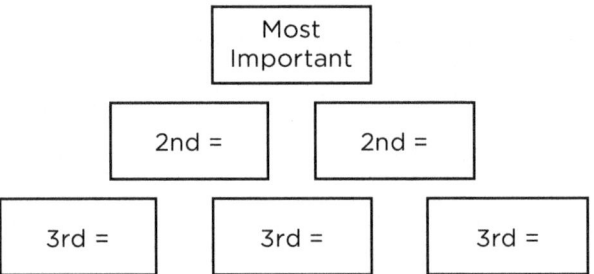

Figure 2.9: Pyramid rank.

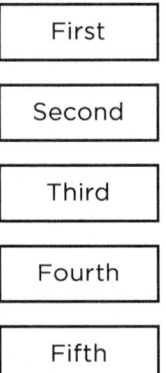

Figure 2.10: Line rank.

As with all dialogue strategies, the process is more important than the structure or the outcome. So, if one group switches from a line rank to a pyramid rank, that is fine. Similarly, if one group doesn't complete their ranking by the end of the time slot, that is fine too. So long as they are questioning each other, seeking alternative explanations, giving reasons, being willing to change their minds, and so on, encourage them to continue.

Ideas for Ranking

Some sample contexts to spur ideas for ranking are shown in figure 2.11. In each case, I have given nine items per category so that you could use any of the three structures shown in figures 2.8 (page 68), 2.9 (page 68), and 2.10 (page 68). However, for the purposes of differentiation, you could give different content to different groups.

Chemical elements: Carbon, copper, gold, hydrogen, nitrogen, oxygen, potassium, silicon, sodium

Events in history: Apartheid (end of); Berlin Wall (fall of); COVID-19 (pandemic); Falklands War; Hiroshima (atomic bomb dropped); Maoist China (establishment of); moon landing (first one); pyramids (building of Egyptian pyramids); 9/11

Festivals: Cannes Film Festival, Carnival (Rio de Janeiro), Día de los Muertos, Diwali, Edinburgh Fringe, Gion Matsuri, Mardi Gras, Saint Patrick's Day, Songkran

Food and drink: Carbonated drinks, dairy, fruits, grains, nuts, protein, sugar, vegetables, water

Forces: Drag, electricity, friction, gravity, magnetism, muscular, nuclear, spring, tension

Fuels: Alcohol, biodiesel, coal, diesel, electricity, gas, oil, petrol, wood

Languages: Arabic, Bengali, Chinese, French, Icelandic, Māori, sign, Swahili, Tagalog

Literary characters: Atticus Finch, Catherine Earnshaw, Elizabeth Bennet, Fitzwilliam Darcy, Gandalf, Hermione Granger, Jane Eyre, Jay Gatsby, Sherlock Holmes

Parts of the body: Chest, eyes, foot, hand, mouth, nose, stomach, teeth, tongue

Planets: Earth, Jupiter, Mars, Mercury, Neptune, Pluto, Saturn, Uranus, Venus

Sources of light: Anglerfish, candle, fire, glowworms, lasers, light bulb, lightning, stars, sun

Sports: Boxing, curling, cycling, football, hockey, horse racing, pickleball, sumo wrestling, tennis

U.S. presidents: John Adams, Thomas Jefferson, John F. Kennedy, Abraham Lincoln, Richard Nixon, Barack Obama, Franklin D. Roosevelt, Harry S. Truman, George Washington

Works of art: *A Sunday Afternoon on the Island of La Grande Jatte*, Georges Seurat; *Arnolfini Portrait*, Jan van Eyck; *Arrangement in Grey and Black No. 1*, James Abbott McNeill Whistler; *The Birth of Venus*, Sandro Botticelli; *Girl With a Pearl Earring*, Johannes Vermeer; *Les Demoiselles d'Avignon*, Pablo Picasso; *Mona Lisa*, Leonardo da Vinci; *The Starry Night*, Vincent van Gogh; *The Kiss*, Gustav Klimt

---

Figure 2.11: Ideas for ranking.

Approaches to Ranking

Here are a few things to note when using ranking to engage your students in dialogue. These are *in addition to* the notes shared at the end of section 2.4.2 (page 60), where I wrote about running the Odd One Out strategy.

- Do *not* give your students the criteria to use when ranking. Let that decision be part of their dialogue. As noted in the chapter about challenge (section 3.0.2, page 94), we too often give students a puzzle with only one dimension to solve. This can help with cognitive load, but it can also make the task too easy. So, at times, it is better to give your students more elements to consider. Generally speaking, ranking is one of those times!

- If your students ask you, "How should we rank these things?" then respond with something like, "That's a good question! What options have you thought of so far?" If they look blankly at you, then perhaps give them one or two ideas, but don't solve that part of the puzzle for them. For example, if I give my students a set of countries and ask them to rank them, they invariably ask me how they are supposed to do it. I respond by repeating the structure (for example, a diamond rank) and then asking them for ideas for criteria they could use. For example:
    - **Countries to rank:** Argentina, Australia, Denmark, Ireland, Japan, Norway, South Africa, Sweden, and United Arab Emirates
    - **Possible criteria (do not give these to your students; let them come up with possibilities):** Quality of life, tourist attractions we can name, Olympic success, frequency of being mentioned in our country's news, most celebrities we can name, distance from our classroom, population size, gross domestic product, distance from the equator, and so on
- Notice that some of these criteria are more subjective than others. Depending on your purpose, you might want to limit your students' choice to only those that can (or can't) be settled objectively.
- It is always best to get your students to write the items they are ranking onto pieces of paper or sticky notes. Everyone in a group should then be able to rearrange the order of them to demonstrate their thinking to their peers. If your students are not using the items in this way, remind them to do so. And keep reminding them (as noted in sections 2.2.2 and 3.8.3.1, pages 52 and 137) that their job is not to agree with each other. They should be challenging each other, coming up with problems and possibilities, suggesting alternatives, giving reasons, and so on.
- If some groups finish early, encourage them to share their rankings with each other and to challenge the thinking of other groups.

2.5.2 Is–Could Be–Never Would Be

This strategy is a favorite of mine for getting my students into the Learning Pit. I call it *Is–Could Be–Never Would Be* because it involves asking your students to identify examples that represent a concept or definition (Is); those that *might* represent it, depending on the circumstance (Could Be); and those that definitely would not represent it (Never Would Be).

So, for example, if you showed images of the following items, you could ask your students to decide which of them *is* a pet, which of them *could be* a pet, and which of them should *never be* a pet: any animal, a book, a cat (wild), dinosaur bones, an eagle, a football, a ghost, a hedgehog, an insect, a jellyfish, a keyboard, a lettuce, a mouse (wild), nightmares, an ornament, a project, the queen of hearts (playing card), a rabbit, a spider, a theory, a unicorn, water, an Xbox, a yak, and zoo animals.

When creating your own set of examples, make sure that you include:

- Examples that are easily accessible for your students as well as examples that are beyond them (so that they need to look online or ask others to explain)

- Examples straight from the curriculum as well as examples from everyday life
- Examples that quite easily fall into one of the categories (Is–Could Be–Never Would Be) as well as those that are much more ambiguous
- Opportunities for your students to add extra examples for their peers to categorize (extra points for the most disputable examples)

In figure 2.12, I have given you some examples to begin with. Where possible, I recommend that you display images for your students. Thus, the words I've shared are intended as suggestions for the search terms you might use.

What Is Competition?
1. Sport
2. Something that has winners and losers
3. Something in which the winners are awarded medals
4. Rivalry for supremacy
5. Two groups each wanting the same thing
6. An important force in biology
7. A system to showcase superiority
8. The promotion of egotism and individualism
9. An essential element of progression and success
10. An exciting aspect of a game
11. The opposite of cooperation
12. An essential component of evolution
13. A healthy activity that benefits everyone
14. A discipline that builds character and self-esteem
15. A means of measuring levels of performance
16. A team-building activity
17. A recipe to create hostility
18. A contest to see who is best and who is worst
19. A human construct
20. Something present across the animal kingdom

What Is Courage?
1. Trying a new activity
2. Sticking to what you know you're good at
3. Singing in the shower
4. Singing in front of the whole school
5. Standing up to a bully
6. Bullying someone who is a bully
7. Telling the truth when it will get you into trouble
8. Taking students through the Learning Pit
9. Telling a lie to get a friend out of trouble
10. A wheelchair user taking part in sports day
11. Taking part in sports day knowing you'll come last
12. Going to school when you don't feel very well
13. Saying no to a teacher
14. Standing up for what you believe in
15. Keeping quiet when you feel like shouting
16. Moving to a new country
17. Learning a new language

What Is Democracy?
1. Laws
2. Having choices
3. Enjoying freedom
4. Elections influenced by social media
5. Being forced to vote—by law

Figure 2.12: Example for the Is–Could Be–Never Would Be strategy.

Continued →

6. Being forced to vote—by intimidation
7. Media backing one candidate
8. A lottery
9. Live TV debate
10. A politician voting against their conscience
11. A politician doing what the electorate wants
12. A politician going against what the electorate wants
13. One candidate having a lot more funding than all others
14. A one-party state
15. Having the prom king and queen chosen by students
16. Having the prom king and queen chosen by teachers
17. Any decision decided by a vote

What Is Energy?
1. A battery
2. A plug
3. Being able to do something
4. Feeling excited
5. Being nervous
6. Not being able to sit still
7. The ability to do work
8. The reason why things change and move
9. Something that cannot be created or destroyed
10. A process that can be measured using joules

11. A word with a Greek origin meaning *activity*
12. Power
13. A scientific term
14. Something bad for the environment
15. Something that can't be destroyed
16. Something that is all around us and takes many forms
17. A resource that once used cannot be replenished
18. A property that exists in ten common forms
19. $KE = \frac{1}{2}mv^2$
20. The movement of atoms and molecules

What Is Poetry?
1. Nursery rhymes
2. A song
3. A short story
4. A piece of writing using silly words
5. Something to read aloud
6. A joke
7. Repeating words in a pattern
8. A letter
9. Words written in a shape
10. Sentences that rhyme
11. Words organized into verses
12. A problem to solve
13. A piece of clothing
14. Something to eat
15. Something beautiful

Some questions you could ask to encourage your students to reflect on the process include the following.

- Which examples most easily fit into one of the categories (Is–Could Be–Never Would Be) and why?
- Did any group have those examples in a different category? Why?
- Can anyone think of a good reason why one of those examples should not (or could not) fit into that category now?
- Which examples were the hardest to place into a category and why?
- What was the best challenge you heard (that perhaps caused you to change your mind)?

- What characteristics do the objects in the Is category share?
- What characteristics do the objects in the Never Would Be category share?
- What are the main characteristics that are different between the objects in these two categories (Is and Never Would Be)?

2.5.3 Venn Diagrams

When leading demonstration lessons, I often use a Venn diagram to help students deepen their thinking during a dialogue. Figures 2.13 and 2.14 show examples of using a Venn diagram to compare the similarities and differences between two concepts. Subsequent figures in this section show how to use the diagrams to determine the relationship between the two concepts.

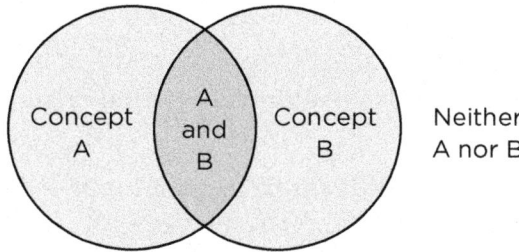

Figure 2.13: Venn diagram template.

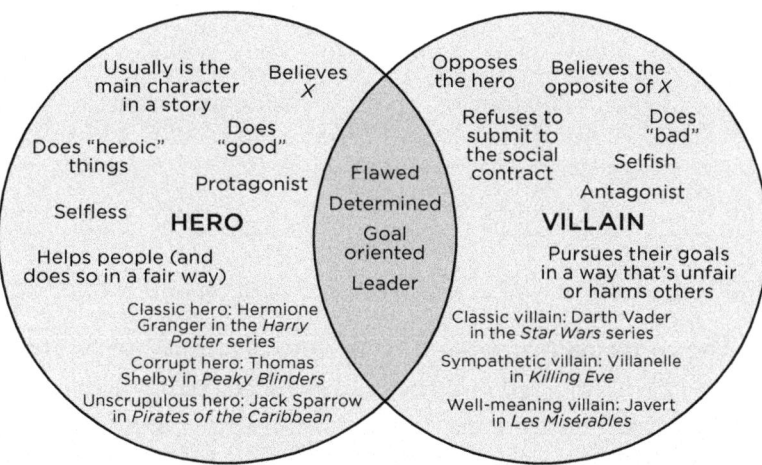

Figure 2.14: Venn diagram comparing heroes and villains.

When introducing Venn diagrams to your students, you might begin with two separate circles. This helps those students who find the overlap too abstract to begin with. Then use questioning to identify characteristics that neatly fit into one or the other category (in the case of figure 2.14). After that, you can bring in examples that fit into both categories so that your students come to realize an overlap is needed.

As with all the strategies I've included in this chapter, pairs, groups, or the whole class can create Venn diagrams. Of course, individuals can also complete the diagrams, but I am recommending the approach as a focus for dialogue.

It helps if you can give your students hoops and ask them to write their ideas onto sticky notes before placing them in the right area of the diagram. This means they can more easily move their ideas around if, through dialogue, they think of alternative reasons and explanations (which we hope they will). If a few of the pairs or groups find the task undemanding, you could add challenge by (1) adding a third (or even fourth) category or (2) asking your students to place the characteristics according to the degree to which they fit the category. For example, if they think opposing the hero is an essential quality of being a villain, then they could place this example in the villain circle but as far away from the hero circle as possible. Or if they think taking risks is something more connected with being a hero but villains also do this at times, then they could place this characteristic in the hero category but close to the villain circle (although not in the overlap).

2.5.3.1 Relationship Between Two Concepts

Sometimes, you might want to ask your students how ideas relate to each other. Present the following four options to them.

- **Option 1: The concepts are different from each other**—Figure 2.15 is a diagram that represents this situation, in which two concepts are entirely different from each other. For example, sharks and furniture are entirely different from each other; there is no overlap.

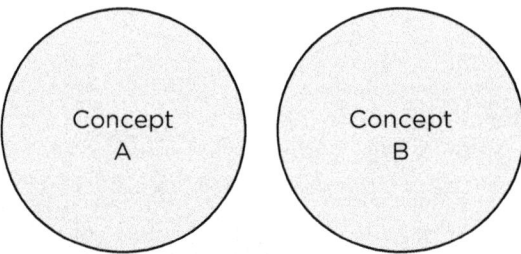

Figure 2.15: Venn diagram option 1.

- **Option 2: The concepts overlap**—This option, illustrated in figure 2.16, is a classic Venn diagram in which two concepts share some characteristics in common but are, nonetheless, different from each other. For example, sharks and crocodiles both belong to the animal kingdom, are carnivorous, and hunt in water. However, one is a fish, the other a reptile; one is aquatic, the other amphibious. Sharks breathe through gills, and crocodiles hold their breath; sharks don't have bones, and crocodiles do.

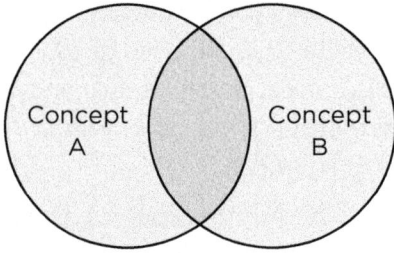

Figure 2.16: Venn diagram option 2.

- **Option 3: All of one concept is a subset of the other concept**—A classic example is all cats (concept B) are animals (concept A) but not all animals (concept A) are cats (concept B). However, the categorizing relationship between cats and animals is easily agreed on and, therefore, fairly mundane. This becomes more interesting when the relationship between two concepts is unclear. For example, I remember a fascinating dialogue with some grade 9 students when trying to decide the relationship between justice and revenge. Many of them thought that revenge (concept A) is always a part of justice (concept B) but justice is not always a feature of revenge. Therefore, they used the option 3 diagram to illustrate their thinking. Others thought it is the other way around and justice is always a part of revenge, but revenge doesn't always play a role in justice (at least it shouldn't when it comes to the justice system). Therefore, for them, option 4 was the accurate representation of the relationship between the two concepts.

- **Option 4: The set–subset relationship is the other way around**—Figure 2.17 illustrates the diagrams for both options 3 and 4.

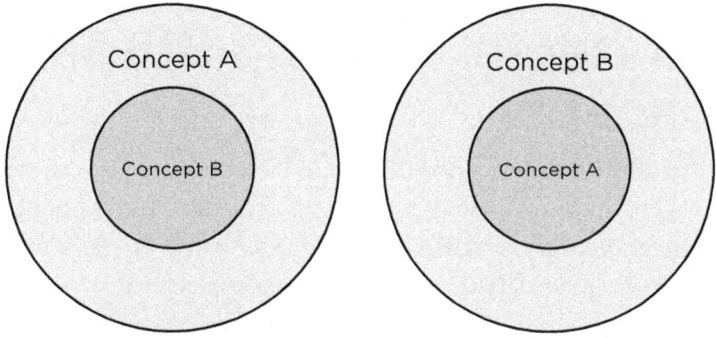

Figure 2.17: Venn diagram options 3 and 4.

Options 3 and 4 show the situation in which one concept is a subset of another. For example, sharks are a subset of animals. All sharks are animals, but not all animals are sharks. Whenever I use option 3 or 4 with students, they often refer to it as the fried-egg relationship (due to the visual resemblance).

If you look back at section 2.4.1 (page 58), you will see the examples I suggested you could use with the question, "What's the difference between . . . ?" So, using those same examples, you could ask your students which of the Venn diagram options, 1 to 4, best represents the relationship between:

- Design and invention
- Development and growth
- Education and learning
- Facts and information
- Government and law
- Knowing and thinking
- Listening and hearing
- Measurement and value
- Real and living

- Religion and belief
- Science and technology
- War and conflict

For example, if concept A is *design* and concept B is *invention*, how would you represent the relationship between these two concepts? Would it be one of the following?

- Option 1, meaning A (design) and B (invention) are entirely separate notions (There is no similarity between them.)
- Option 2, meaning there is some overlap (There are ways in which A [design] and B [invention] share similar characteristics or examples, but they also have a distinctiveness.)
- Option 3, meaning B (invention) is a subset of A (design)
- Option 4, meaning A (design) is a subset of B (invention)

2.6 Use Strategies to Help Students Think About Concepts

Having a concept of something means being able to recognize that thing and being able to distinguish it from other things. This makes concepts crucial to psychological processes such as categorization, inference, memory, learning, and decision making. As such, they could—and, in my opinion, should—be placed at the center of student learning.

The strategies I share in this chapter will help your students think deeply about concepts.

2.6.1 Concept Lines

A concept line invites participants to indicate the extent to which each term or characteristic represents or defines a concept. The starting point is to get your students to list the terms they have used with the concept they have been talking about; then have them place these terms on the concept line. The closer your students place a term to the right end of the line, the more they think it is connected to the concept. The closer they place it to the left end, the less they think it is connected. Sometimes it helps students to label the line as if it were a number line, with zero in the middle, ten at the far right, and minus ten at the far left.

The deepest thinking comes from deciding the relationship between very similar terms. For example, figure 2.18 (page 77) shows where my students placed terms connected with *explorers*. They found it straightforward to place *optimism* at one end of the line and *pessimism* at the other. However, when it came to deciding in which order to place *curiosity*, *imagination*, and *courage*, they found it much more complex. This is a good thing, as it leads to more demand for higher-order-thinking skills.

Pessimism	Idleness	Fearfulness	Timidity	Relaxed	Patience	Laid Back	Indecisive	Leadership	Organization	Risk Taking	Focus	Courage	Imagination	Curiosity	Optimism

Figure 2.18: A concept line about explorers.

Figure 2.19 gives examples of items from different curriculum areas that your students could place on concept lines.

> **Belief:** Action, attitude, confusion, delusion, doubt, idea, indifference, mindset, opinion, philosophy, questioning, religion, skepticism, stance, thought, uncertainty, understanding
>
> **Creativity:** Comfort, conservatism, familiarity, fear of failure, imagination, invention, originality, playfulness, problem solving, productivity, resourcefulness, rule breaking
>
> **Equation:** Calculation, expression of equal values, mathematical sentence, numbers, statement of equality, solution, use of = sign, variables, $2 + 2 = 4$, $4y + 2 = 18$, $4 \times 2 + 3y - 28 = 0$, $k + 7$, $10 - 3$, $u + w$, $9t$, 0
>
> **Explore (verb):** Analyze, avoid, discover, disregard, find, hunt, ignore, inquire, inspect, navigate, neglect, overlook, reject, research, search, travel
>
> **Literary devices:** Alliteration, anagram, autobiography, characterization, dialect, dramatic irony, essay, fairy tale, genre, idiom, imagery, metaphor, rhyme, setting, wit
>
> **Love:** Admiration, affection, attachment, attraction, care, companionship, compassion, dislike, egotism, emotion, hatred, infatuation, lust, narcissism, romance, selfishness, vanity
>
> **Poem:** Drama, joke, letter, literature, narrative picture, piece of writing, prose, rhyming verse, song, speech, story, symbolism, verse

Figure 2.19: Example topics to place on a concept line.

2.6.2 Concept Targets

Concept targets usually have three circles: (1) inner, (2) outer, and (3) middle. The inner circle represents the central concept your students are discussing. The outer circle represents things that are only slightly connected. The middle circle represents the half-and-half position.

A concept target follows a similar principle to a concept line, in that where students place a term relative to other terms will show how much or how little they connect it with the concept. Placing a scoring line from ten (out of ten) in the center of the inner circle to zero at the outer limits of the outer circle can help students be more methodical and discerning. Figure 2.20 (page 78) shows a worked example of a concept target.

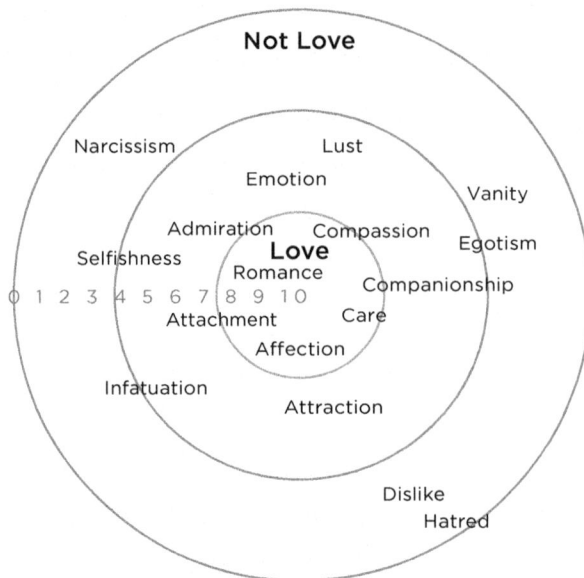

Figure 2.20: A concept target about love.

2.6.3 Concept Tables

Concept tables are generally prepared in advance. They can provide an additional challenge for your students. Equally, educators can use a concept table as an organizing scaffold to help some groups focus their dialogue more effectively. In some concept tables, you could leave some rows blank for your students to add their own suggestions. Figure 2.21 and figure 2.22 show examples.

Examples	Is a Number	Seems Like a Number	Is Not a Number	Reason
Something we count with				
A digit				
Objects				
Quantity				
Money				
A measurement				
Patterns in nature				
Codes				
Pieces of pizza				
Three fingers				
A calculator				
Writing				
An abacus				
Poetry				

A beehive				
VIII				
Four candles				
A century				
A centurion				
A symbol representing the value of something				

Figure 2.21: A concept table about *number*.

Examples of *Just*	*Just* Means *Only*	*Just* Means *Fair*	*Just* Means *Exactly*	Reason
It is only just midday.				
It's not just for me.				
I'm just saying hello.				
He got his just deserts.				
Just $15				
I only just passed the test.				
I've just about had enough of this lesson.				
Can I just have five more minutes, please?				
I'm just going to have my dinner.				
The decision was a just one.				
Just an old coat				
Just the ticket				
Just what the doctor ordered				
Just in time				
Just off the boat				

Figure 2.22: A concept table about *just*.

2.7 Use Strategies to Help Students Examine Opinions

Expressing opinions is a delicate issue in most classrooms. To protect their egos, students will often seek affiliation with others or use displays of humor and uncertainty (Degoumois, Petitjean, & Doehler, 2017). As teachers, we can provide support by shifting the focus away from the students themselves and onto the nuances of the topic. Opinion lines and opinion corners can help frame this more effectively.

2.7.1 Opinion Lines

Opinion lines are useful for exploring ideas using examples, gauging degrees of agreement and disagreement, and understanding preference.

The best way to set them up is as follows.

1. Create a line long enough for all your students to stand along. It might help to mark this with a rope or some string (see figure 2.23).

2. Mark one end with a *Completely Agree* sign and the other with a *Completely Disagree* sign. Talk through the other descriptors shown in figure 2.23 if you think that will help your students understand the degrees of agreement and disagreement.

3. Formulate a statement that expresses a point of view relating to the central concept your students are talking about. Make it bold and contentious to increase the likelihood that everyone will have an opinion. The following are some examples.

    - All bullies should be banned from school.
    - Cheating is always wrong.
    - Everything has value.
    - John Lennon was right that life would be better if there were no countries.
    - King Lear was "more sinned against than sinning."
    - Negative numbers are unnecessary.
    - People should be fined for not recycling.
    - The Battle of the Somme was the greatest battle in history.
    - Women should be allowed to play professional sports on men's teams.
    - Zoos are good for animals.

4. Explain to your students that you are going to give them a contentious statement to think about. Say they will have time to think about it first and you will then ask them to stand on the part of the line that corresponds with how much they agree or disagree with the statement. Give them the statement.

5. Once your students have taken a place on the line, get them to talk with the people around them to compare their reasons for standing where they are. Encourage

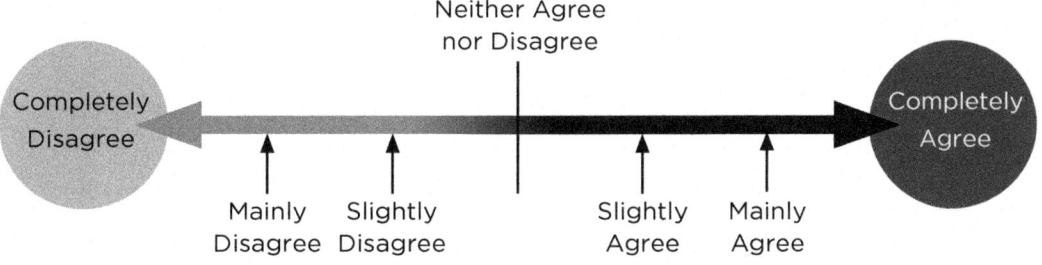

Figure 2.23: Opinion line.

them to use one or more of the following phrases so that their conversations are more exploratory than cumulative.

- What do you think?
- What are your reasons?
- I agree with you because . . .
- I disagree with you because . . .
- Is there another way of looking at this?
- What if . . . ?
- Have we considered all the factors?
- What do you think is the most important reason?
- What have we agreed?

As well as these phrases, encourage your students to use *thinking language*, such as the terms *fact, reason, evidence, convince, assumption, persuade, reliable, opinion, agree, disagree, exception, example, conclusion, argument*, and *if . . . then*.

When using this activity, I always like to have an "Ah, but what about . . . ?" statement or fact to use as a follow-up to each provocation. This really helps deepen students' thinking. For example, if I use the provocation that all mobile phones should be banned in schools, I will follow it up later with the news that France has done exactly that, or I will share statistics about ways that social media can have a negative impact on mental health. Not only does this generally lead students to move their position along the line, but it also causes them to take more notice of complexity.

There are many ways to run an opinion line dialogue. Here are some of my favorite alternatives.

- **Alternative 1:** Read out an item, and ask just a few of your students to decide how they would respond. Once the chosen few have decided where to stand on the line, you can then invite other students to ask them questions about their positions. The questions might explore reasons and alternative ideas. Ask the students on the line to move if, at any point, their opinion changes in response to the comments and questions from their classmates.

- **Alternative 2:** Combine opinion lines with role play. Your students could take the roles of characters and position themselves according to how they think the characters would respond. They could answer questions in character.
- **Alternative 3:** Give different groups different opinion lines. For example, split your students into three groups and give each group one of the three opinion lines in figure 2.24 (page 82).

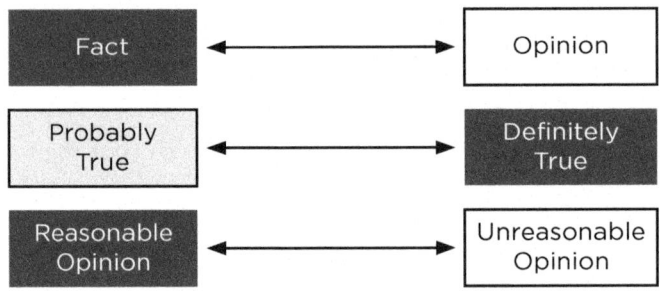

Figure 2.24: Variations of opinion lines.

Now, give the same statement to all three groups, irrespective of which opinion line you are asking them to stand on. For example, you could use the statement, "Stealing is wrong." The first group can then consider if this is a fact or an opinion, the second group can consider if it is probably true or definitely true, and the third group can think about whether it is a reasonable opinion or an unreasonable opinion. Comparing the differences in responses can create an interesting dialogue in itself. Here are some more example statements for you to use.

- Robin Hood was right to steal from the rich to give to the poor.
- Robin Hood was a moral man.
- When a teacher confiscates something from you, this is not stealing.
- Religion has been the root cause of many wars.
- Serial killers should receive the death sentence.

2.7.2 Opinion Corners

Opinion corners have a similar structure to opinion lines, so teachers can introduce them in a similar way. The main difference is that using the opinion corners will prevent your students from sitting on the fence because opinion corners require them to choose from one of four descriptors: (1) strongly agree, (2) agree, (3) disagree, and (4) strongly disagree. Set up opinion corners as shown in figure 2.25.

After you read a statement (examples are given later), your students should stand in the corner that best represents their opinion on the matter. Tell them they have to choose one of the corners. They cannot stand somewhere in the middle. They must decide. They may move if they change their minds, but even then, they should move from one corner to another rather than to the middle or off to a side somewhere.

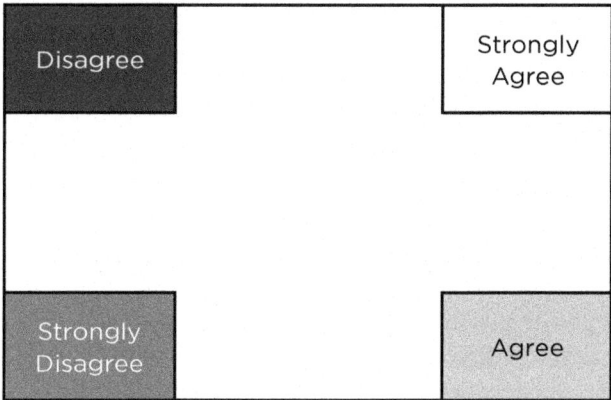

Figure 2.25: Opinion corners.

Once your students have chosen a corner, get them to talk about their choice with the people around them. After that, get a spokesperson from each corner to summarize the reasons why the people in their corner made the choice they did. This will give your students a chance to hear different perspectives on the issue.

Here are some statements to get you started with opinion corners.

- Students should never have to take tests.
- Students should be allowed to listen to their own music during lessons.
- Violent video games are a bad influence on young people and should be banned.
- Footballers are paid too much money.
- "Poverty is the parent of revolution and crime." —Aristotle (Stanford Center on Poverty and Inequality, n.d.)
- "We cannot all succeed when half of us is held back." —Malala Yousafzai (2013)
- "Education is the most powerful weapon which you can use to change the world." —Nelson Mandela (Lib Quotes, n.d.)

When a student moves corners, it is a great opportunity to ask the student what they heard that made them change their mind. This encourages the idea of persuasive language, can add to students' verbal and written vocabulary, and reinforces that reflection is part of successful learning. Written vocabulary can then be built on further by asking questions such as, "How would you encourage other people to come to your corner?"

An additional bonus with opinion corners is that it places the teacher in the direct role of mediator: supporting, prompting, and questioning the process of learning rather than giving answers. As the only person who is allowed to stand in the middle of the room, you are positioning yourself as the only person with no opinion.

2.7.3 Thinking Corners

Thinking corners are almost the same as opinion corners but are set up with four statements rather than one. So, instead of reading one statement to your students and asking if they agree or disagree, this time, you place a different statement in each corner and ask your students to pick the one that most closely matches their thinking. Here are some sample statements to get you started (figure 2.26, page 84).

We should invest more in *renewable energy.*
- Corner One: Renewable energy will not run out.
- Corner Two: Renewable energy has enormous environmental benefits.
- Corner Three: Renewable energy has geographic limitations.
- Corner Four: Renewable energy has limited storage capabilities.

***Art* is an important part of education.**
- Art promotes imagination, creativity, and self-expression, allowing us to develop our individuality.
- Art encourages cultural appreciation and fosters respect and understanding of diversity and history.
- Art has limited career prospects and so is not as important as many other subjects.
- Art is a waste of time for anyone who isn't artistic to begin with.

This is what makes me *who I am.*
- My body and all the physical and biological parts of me
- My actions and behaviors and the choices I make
- My community, my family, and my friends
- My mind, my thoughts, my emotions, and my beliefs

The person I am is *constantly changing*.
- My genetic code never changes and ensures I remain the same person.
- I change with every new moment and experience.
- My soul will always stay the same and is unchangeable.
- My personality grows but does not change.

There are many examples of abusive or *unhealthy relationships* in fiction.
- They normalize dysfunctional relationships and should be banned.
- They are fine for adult fiction but not for young adults or teens.
- These relationships are real and happen, so why not read about them?
- They should be included but only when represented in a negative light.

Nothing is truly *random*.
- No, events that are unpredictable today could be predictable tomorrow.
- Everything has a cause-and-effect relationship, so nothing can be random.
- If something has no pattern, then it is random.
- What we think of as randomness is just chaos.

***Numbers* are real.**
- Numbers are not real because they are not physical and cannot be touched or observed.
- Counting objects is real, but the numbers themselves are concepts and not real.
- Numbers exist and become real when you write them down.
- Numbers found in nature are real as they are observable.

Figure 2.26: Example statements for a thinking corners activity.

2.8 Understand That Not All Those Who Wonder Are Lost

The first novel I chose to read as a child was *The Lord of the Rings* (Tolkien, 1954). In volume one, there is a poem by Bilbo Baggins that begins, "All that is gold does not glitter; Not all those who wander are lost" (Tolkien, 1954, p. 113). I have named this section by adapting the second line to *wonder*. I have done that because I'd like to draw your mind back to section 2.1.4 (page 43), where I wrote about the difference between authentic student engagement and the illusion of student engagement.

Many students know how to play school. They're quiet in class. They nod occasionally. They put their hand up in the air during questioning sequences but drop it again whenever there's the danger of being asked to contribute. They pretend to work diligently on a digital device. They also complete their assignments on time without committing their learning to memory; it was just a hoop to jump through. For them, the original aphorism used, "All that glitters is not gold," is fitting.

However, the opposite is also common in many classrooms—students who never offer an answer, avoid eye contact, and appear inattentive but who are genuinely concentrating. They think about the ramifications of what is said and how it connects to their earlier thoughts. For them, the slight adaptation of Bilbo's poem is more appropriate: "All that is gold does not glitter; not all who wonder are lost."

Thus, if we genuinely want to engage our students (rather than simply seek compliance), we must look beyond the facade. We can't judge engagement by outward appearances; it is too desultory. We know human interaction is essential for learning—particularly in the pandemic age (Toth, 2021)—but that can come in many forms. Extroverted expressions are but one clue exhibited by some.

A fascinating way to frame this is to think about extroverted and introverted thinking. These terms come from the work of educator Katharine Cook Briggs and her daughter, Isabel Briggs Myers. During World War II, they created the Myers–Briggs Type Indicator (MBTI; Conoley & Kramer, 1989) to help women identify the sorts of wartime jobs in which they would be most comfortable and effective. Their work was based on the theories of Carl Jung.

Of the four pairs of preferences proposed in the MBTI assessment tool, one set of opposites focused on the difference between extroversion and introversion. It identified that some people tend to act–reflect–act (extroversion), whereas others reflect–act–reflect (introversion). Or put another way:

- *Introverted* thinking is when someone *thinks to talk*
- *Extroverted* thinking is when someone *talks to think*

The MBTI is a personality test and, therefore, should be taken with a very big pinch of salt. It is also context related: How many of us are introverted when dragged to a party of complete strangers but extroverted when playing host at our own party? Context obviously matters! So, it is simply not true to say that we are either one way or the other all the time.

That said, there is some truth to this concept. There are some students in every class who lean toward extroverted thinking. They need to think aloud if they are going to think effectively. Some students in the same class, however, lean toward introverted thinking; they need lots of time (perhaps more than the lesson will allow) to think deeply before they arrive at an answer that they think is worth sharing.

Incidentally, introverted thinkers are not shy. Some might *also* be shy, but introverted thinking is not about timidity; it is about precision of thought. Introverted thinkers see little value in sharing their thoughts until they are certain that they know what they think! In their mind, opinions should be measured and exact. Because of this, they need time to think things through before stating their position. Adults who are introverted thinkers will often use the phrase, "Let me come back to you on that one," or "I need to think about it first." However, many students in the classroom don't feel in a position to make such requests.

The reason I am writing about this is these divergent systems give very different impressions of engagement. The extroverted thinkers are too busy talking to demonstrate engagement with others; the introverted thinkers are too quiet to prove they're ever engaging at all. So, in many classrooms, out comes the talking stick. "When it's passed to you, it's your turn to talk," advises the teacher, inadvertently sending everyone into a tailspin.

The extroverted worry they won't be able to contain themselves long enough to wait their turn to talk. The introverted look fearfully at the stick, wondering what on earth they can say to pass it along as painlessly and quickly as possible. The pressure builds. Eventually, the extroverted jump the queue and blurt out their thoughts. "Shhhhhhh," admonishes their teacher. The introverted, meanwhile, have long since stopped thinking about the content and are instead rehearsing a stock-in-trade phrase that will get everyone off their back. Crazy, isn't it? A convention designed to encourage everyone to participate actually stops many students from thinking!

A better approach is to be up-front and honest with your students. Tell them you know some of them do their best thinking out loud, whereas others prefer lots of thinking time before saying anything. I typically say something along the lines of this: "It's nigh on impossible to keep everyone happy all the time, but we'll do what we can do. There will be opportunities to share your ideas with the person next to you, and there'll be time for all of us to think. If you'd like to say something, then pop your thumb up. Don't raise your hand—that's far too distracting. Raise your thumb (keeping your hand on your knee or on the desk in front of you), and either the previous speaker or I will invite you to share your thoughts with the whole class when the time is right."

After that introduction, you could use one or more of the following approaches. These are in addition to the guidance I have given in sections 2.1, 2.2, and 2.3 (pages 30, 49, and 56).

- **Reflection time:** Give plenty of reflection time. Don't be frightened of silence! Rowe's (1986) research (see section 2.1.3, page 38) recommends a minimum of three seconds' wait time.

- **Midway pause:** Pause a dialogue halfway through to give some additional thinking time. If you are a class teacher (rather than a subject teacher), you might even pause overnight or for an extended period during the same day before returning to the topic.

- **Inner circle and outer circle:** These work particularly well if you have a group of twenty or more. Split the group and get half of the students to sit in a circle, with the other half sitting around the outside of the circle. The outer group can record the dialogue—with a mind map, concept map, or something similar—as well as jot down their own thoughts. If you swap the groups periodically, perhaps every five to ten minutes or so, then everyone will have a chance to reflect quietly and speak if they want to.

Of course, many teachers might still worry if some students don't speak. However, we don't know that students are concentrating even if they do speak! Many students have learned phrases and tactics designed to give the impression that they are focusing when, actually, their mind is elsewhere. So, whether you are in dialogue with one student or a whole group of students, I recommend implementing the following.

- **Pause and reflect time:** As I mentioned in section 2.1.3 (page 38), there are significant gains to be made by slowing down and giving students time to think. Rowe's (1986) research shows that wait time (or thinking time) should be at least three seconds.
- **Provisional language:** Phrases such as *perhaps*, *maybe*, or *I was wondering* can be particularly helpful for introverted thinkers. This is because, as I mentioned earlier, introverted thinkers will rarely speak until they are absolutely certain of their own beliefs. Therefore, this convention gives them the opportunity to try out their ideas without committing to them.
- **Thinking:** Remind your students that the most important thing is to think about the question. So long as everyone does that, it is up to individuals whether to share their views with others.

Once your students begin to share their first thoughts, guide the others to respond encouragingly and to build on what has been said. This can be done in one or more of the following ways.

- **Repeat–paraphrase–connect:** After a student has expressed their first idea, get others to repeat word for word what they said, paraphrase by saying the same thing in a different way, or connect what was said to an idea of their own.
- **Meaning:** A particularly effective strategy is to respond to a student's contribution by asking if anybody else knows what the student meant. Some of your students will feel certain that they understand, so ask them to explain. If only two of you are in the discussion, then you could try explaining what you think the other person meant. Either way, make sure you then ask the first person if that indeed is what they meant. Usually, the explanation is close to the intended meaning but not exactly accurate, which gives the first person an opportunity to clarify their thoughts even more. This strategy also teaches us there is often a marked difference between what someone says and how others understand it.
- **Agree:** A simple (and effective) convention is to ask everyone taking part in a dialogue to begin their first few responses with, "I agree with . . . because . . . ," as this requires participants to listen carefully to what others say.

2.9 Dialogue Summary

 *Dialogue is one of the very best ways to engage your students. It helps you find out what they think, listen to their emerging ideas, and encourage them to talk through their understanding and misconceptions.*

At its best, dialogue weaves together a rich array of perspectives and questions that nurture critical thinking and intellectual growth. This dynamic classroom strategy has been shown to encourage deeper thinking and promote a positive impact on academic outcomes. As I mentioned in section 2.2 (page 49), when I recorded a series of videos with John Hattie in 2019, he identified dialogue as the most surprisingly effective approach to boosting student learning.

Professor Robin Alexander (2018) and his colleagues at the University of Cambridge led an independent evaluation of a dialogue intervention involving 5,000 nine- and ten-year-olds and 208 teachers in England. They calculated that after twenty weeks, students in the intervention group were two months ahead of their control group peers in English, mathematics, and science tests. Coded video data also showed that the changes in both teacher and student talk were significant (Alexander, 2018).

Effective dialogue is recognizable when:

- The focus is on common interests, not divisive ones (Dialogue is not debate!)
- Decision-making processes are kept separate from the dialogue (This is not about making decisions but about understanding each other more.)
- Assumptions that can lead to distortions of certain points of view are clarified and brought into the open
- Students are encouraged to reveal their own insights and assumptions before speculating on those of others
- Concrete examples are used to raise general issues

Dialogue contrasts with *monologic* talk, which tends to be dominated by the teacher and follows the Initiate-Respond-Evaluate (IR-Evaluate) sequence. This pattern is typified by the teacher asking a closed question (Initiate), a student answering (Respond), and the teacher confirming or refuting that answer (Evaluate). Such an approach is common in classrooms (Howe & Abedin, 2013) but has been criticized for limiting the meaningful engagement of students (Mercer, 1995).

Dialogue—or dialogic talk—takes a more conversational approach, trying to consider several points of view (Howe & Abedin, 2013). It encompasses encouraging, nonevaluative feedback (Chin, 2006) and refocuses the conversation away from the teacher's initiating moves toward students' responses (Wolfe & Alexander, 2008).

It is useful to think of dialogue as *exploratory talk*. This term, coined by University of Cambridge professor emeritus Neil Mercer (2000), is characterized by longer exchanges and the use of questions, reflection, explanation, and speculation.

The benefits of exploratory talk include the following.

- Encouraging active student participation (because students develop a sense of ownership of their learning journey)

- Developing critical-thinking and problem-solving skills (because students are challenged to analyze, evaluate, and synthesize information)
- Building stronger communication skills (because students learn to articulate their thoughts and ideas effectively)
- Creating a positive attitude toward learning (because students experience the joy of discovery and intellectual curiosity)
- Building a sense of community and collaboration in the classroom (because students learn to support each other more effectively)

Despite all these benefits, dialogue is still not used very often in classrooms. So, I'd like to give the last word of this summary to one of the 20th century's greatest advocates of dialogue, Paulo Freire (1970/2000), who in the 1970s proposed a dialogic approach in which students become active agents in their own education. He believed that dialogue is key to learning, and that dialogue has to be based on respect and the coproduction of knowledge. If the structure of education does not involve or permit dialogue, then it should be challenged, he argued.

2.10 *Teach Brilliantly* Top Ten: Engagement

Engaged students learn more. Unfortunately, the forces of distraction are strong and overflowing. So, do what you can to make learning authentic, questioning open and inviting, and dialogue exploratory and inclusive.

1. The **more that students engage in learning, the more that they fulfill their potential** (Csikszentmihalyi, 1990).
2. **Students engage when activities allow for freedom of exploration** and demand effort, concentration, and skill.
3. **In a typical classroom, students engage for approximately 50 percent of a lesson** (Yair, 2000).
4. Clever use of questioning and dialogue can improve this rate dramatically. However, **the most common pattern of Initiate-Respond-Evaluate is relatively ineffective**.
5. **It is better to explore students' answers by asking for further details**, including supporting reasons, examples, and counterexamples.
6. Engagement can be confused with compliance. Better to **emphasize the need to listen and think** than to have every student look to the front and take a turn to speak.
7. **Introverted thinkers engage during periods of quiet reflection. Extroverted thinkers need lots of time to think out loud** (without being shushed for doing so). Good luck providing for these opposite ends of the spectrum—and everyone in between!
8. As an absolute minimum, **the wait time after a student answers and before you invite others to respond should be increased to at least three seconds**. This won't be enough for introverted thinkers, but Rowe's (1986) research shows this is the threshold beyond which outcomes dramatically improve.

9. **When giving your students the opportunity to collaborate in groups, teach them how to engage in exploratory talk.** This includes building on others' ideas, offering reasons to support opinions, and being open to critiques and reformulations of their own ideas.

10. **Questioning sequences and dialogue do not have to arrive at an answer or resolution for them to be of value.** The most significant learning comes from the process of thinking together and exploring ideas deeply.

CHAPTER 3

When *Challenge* Is Just Right, Students' Abilities *Improve*

 *Challenge leads to learning. Applied appropriately, it takes students to their next stage of development. Too much challenge creates cognitive overload. Too little lowers expectations.*

The sweet spot for challenge is when students are out of their comfort zone but not so far out that the task seems impossible.

Think of it in much the same way as when children learn to ride a bicycle. When they wobble on that bike—but make headway—the level of challenge is just right. They feel a certain level of discomfort but are not so far out of their comfort zone that they refuse to even try. Contrast this with a competent rider cycling by, perhaps so confident that they don't even have to hold the handlebars (remember those days?), or a child so fearful that they would rather watch from the sidelines than risk falling off their bike. In these two examples, the riders are *not* learning; they are performing or avoiding, but not learning.

Therefore, the optimum level of challenge should cause your students to wobble. In the bike-riding example, this is a physical wobble. In most school contexts, it will mostly be cognitive. Whichever it is, it is the wobble that we should be trying to create. Not all the time, of course; there are times when we want our students to consolidate or perform. But when our intention is to cause students to learn, we should be designing tasks and praising, encouraging, and directing our students in such a way as to cause them to wobble.

THE BLUEPRINT

Purpose

The following are vital concepts about challenge within the learning process.

- Challenge is a vital and necessary condition in the learning process.

- Challenge makes learning stick. The more that students are required to think through and overcome challenges, the more that they are able to retrieve their learning when they need it.

- Students learn significantly more from teachers who hold high expectations for them. These expectations rely on three core principles: (1) setting aspirational goals for all students, (2) using strategies to better understand how students are thinking and what they need next, and (3) getting the levels of challenge just right.

- The Learning Pit is a framework that can help students prepare for and respond to challenge more effectively. It also improves the fluency with which they articulate their learning.

What to Notice

The following lists what is important to notice about challenge.

- **Challenge needs to be just right:** Students need to perceive that, with enough effort and the right strategy, success is within their grasp. If it seems beyond the realm of their own possibility, they are unlikely to engage.

- **The outcomes of challenge are what is desirable:** The impact on long-term retention and transferability of learning makes challenge advantageous; the success of performance and the rate of progress do not, because both of these tend to drop.

- **Increasing challenge doesn't always mean harder tasks:** Varying the conditions of learning can work just as effectively, often more so. For example, using a different style of pedagogy or an alternative setting, reordering instruction so that topics are interleaved, and creating opportunities for students to generate their own solutions rather than presenting prefabricated resolutions will all add desirable difficulty.

- **Extrinsic rewards and profligate praise deter students from choosing challenge:** Studies have shown that merits and plaudits, once thought to be powerful motivators for learning, inadvertently steer students toward easier options.

- **Students expect learning to be linear even though it rarely is:** Progress typically includes performance dips. These can be discouraging if a student thinks they are the only person suffering these setbacks. A model such as the Learning Pit can forewarn and forearm.

Timing

Challenge is not always appropriate. It ought to be in a symbiotic relationship with success. If students fail, fail, and fail again, then challenge is the last thing they need. Reassurance, scaffolding, and guidance will be far more fitting. If, however, they have tasted success and—even more importantly, feel successful—then

> bring on the challenge! Researchers Robert C. Wilson, Amitai Shenhav, Mark Straccia, and Jonathan D. Cohen (2019) have calculated the optimum balance is 80 percent to 85 percent success, 15 percent to 20 percent challenge. "Succeed, stretch; succeed, stretch" should be the mantra of every classroom.

3.0 Understand That Without Challenge, There Is No Learning

In a profession filled with complexity, it is rare to be certain, but we know for sure that learning begins at the edge of challenge. Centuries of theory and research prove this to be the case (Bruner, 1957; Dewey, 1916; Feuerstein, Feuerstein, Falik, & Rand, 2006; Lipman, 1987; Montessori, 1967; Vygotsky, 1978). Stay in our comfort zone, and we will not learn. We can rehearse, practice, and revise, but we won't learn—at least not if we understand learning to be the process of acquiring *new* knowledge, skills, understanding, behaviors, values, or preferences.

Therefore, challenge is neither just a nice bonus nor something to help students along the way. It is a vital and necessary condition in the learning process. So long as you challenge your students, then everything that is good will follow! Except that it isn't that easy, because too many students avoid challenge, too many teachers reduce challenge (to make tasks more manageable), and too many parents take on challenges by proxy to ensure their progeny succeed.

So, what conditions should we create so that our students willingly step out of their comfort zone more of the time? Let's start with the reasons for challenge and some of the barriers that get in its way.

3.0.1 Why Challenge Is So Important

The following list describes four reasons why challenge is so important for learning.

1. **Challenge is necessary:** Without challenge, there is no learning. Challenge takes us out of our comfort zone. Psychologists Lev Vygotsky and Michael Cole (Vygotsky, 1978) called this stepping into the *zone of proximal development*. I call it going through the Learning Pit. Vygotsky's assertion was that a child's current ability is their yesterday (of development), and what they can do next is their tomorrow (of development). Challenge, therefore, is the vehicle that takes students into their future (Blackburn, 2018).

2. **Challenge provokes thinking:** Contrary to popular opinion, the brain is *not* designed for thinking. It is designed to save us from thinking (Willingham, 2021b). It uses so much of its capacity for other tasks (the most complex of which is seeing) that whenever it can rely on memory and rehearsed responses, it does so. Its nature is to take the path of least resistance, thus conserving energy for functions of living and surviving. A stimulant that provokes a different response is challenge. When we perceive it safe to do so, our brain stops noticing quite as much of the environment around us and begins working on thinking instead. This is when we become lost in thought.

3. **Challenge is good for us:** Overcoming challenge strengthens us; it boosts self-efficacy—one of the qualities most likely to improve a student's approach toward, and their subsequent success with, learning (Çiftçi & Yildiz, 2019). It builds capacity. It enhances flexibility. Even adversity is good for us (once we've come out the other side)—though this is *not* a call for cruelty in the classroom! The term *desirable difficulty* is a more appropriate term and is described later. But no matter the term we use, challenge for the mind is like resistance for our muscles. It provokes more effort and determination than normal. This, in turn, leads to enhanced growth and development.

4. **Challenge makes learning stick:** The adage, "Easy come, easy go," is as applicable to learning as it is to money. When we make tasks easier for our students, they finish quicker and also forget quicker, whereas when we increase levels of challenge—for example, by varying the timing, location, and consistency of tasks—the outcomes improve significantly (Roediger, Agarwal, McDaniel, & McDermott, 2011). A representative study involved eight- and twelve-year-old students engaging in a simple throwing task. One group practiced from the distance that all students would be tested from later. The other group practiced from varying distances. All students were prevented from seeing where their shots landed but were given verbal feedback about their success. At the end of the twelve-week physical education program, those who had been required to throw from varying distances performed significantly better than those who had practiced only from the test distance (Kerr & Booth, 1978). Although this sounds like a fun little experiment, a wide range of experiments in many different contexts show equivalent results; be it in mathematics, language, humanities, or the sciences, increased challenge leads to improved learning outcomes (Bjork & Bjork, 2011; Butler, 2010; Dunlosky, Rawson, Marsh, Nathan, & Willingham, 2013; Rohrer, Dedrick, & Stershic, 2015).

Challenge, therefore, is good for us—not just good in the sense of being preferable but also good in terms of necessity! Without challenge, there is no growth, and there is no learning. Why, then, do we avoid challenge? What gets in the way of it being a positive feature of every lesson and learning experience?

3.0.2 What Gets in the Way of Challenge

The following list describes five attributes of challenges.

1. **Challenge must be just right:** Our curiosity is provoked by puzzles we believe we can solve. If tasks seem too difficult, we rarely engage. If they turn out to be too easy, we quickly grow bored. Puzzles, therefore, have to be just beyond what we can do routinely. How far beyond depends on a range of factors, including self-efficacy, perceived risk to ego or safety, past experiences, and levels of encouragement. But in whatever way these factors are arranged, the core principle remains constant: for interest to be piqued, the existence of challenge is not enough. It must be the right degree of challenge, for the right purpose, at the right time. Only then will challenge provoke positive circumstances.

2. **Challenge requires trust (part 1):** Typically, we do not appreciate the beneficial effects of challenge until much later. This appreciation requires a lot of trust and foresight. Will our future gains be sufficient to overcome the negative experiences of high effort today? What evidence do we have? If, in general, we feel less successful today (because we are attempting something beyond our comfort zone), do we believe the outcomes will be worth it? If yes, then we might persevere. If not, then prevarication and distraction prevail.

3. **Challenge requires trust (part 2):** Engaging in activities that take us out of our comfort zone represents a risk to our ego. This can feel negative in private and worse if it happens in public. If peers unexpectedly outperform or ridicule us, then any consent to engage dissipates further still. Therefore, trust is required to overcome all of this. Trust that the situation, its purpose, and those who surround us are on our side (or at least not against us).

4. **Challenge requires resolve:** Effort and determination are applied toward challenge when there is the resolve to do so. Without it, challenge remains untouched. Even when the conditions are optimal, those who have no resolution will not engage. They might give the impression of trying, they might encourage others, but they will not directly attend to challenging themselves. This resolution can come from different quarters. Being in the habit of taking on challenges and choosing to take on challenges because it is preferable are the most potent. Being encouraged to take on challenges, or even forced to do so by circumstance, can also work, albeit with less sense of ownership.

5. **Challenge slows progress:** Although growth and progress increase in response to challenge, these tend to be longer-term effects. In the moment, progress can feel as if it is slowing down. For students, this often includes finishing a task later than others, missing out on free time because of these prolonged efforts, having to take incomplete work home to finish, or being awarded lower grades if assessments are timed before their task is finished.

In this video, James summarizes the key points about challenge.

3.1 Make Challenge More Desirable

Earlier in my career, I thought making the case for challenge would be enough. If I could demonstrate that challenge improves learning—and offer ways to make it work—then all that is good would follow. My students would willingly step out of their comfort zones, and my colleagues would ratchet up the incidents of challenge in their lesson plans.

It didn't work out that way. It still doesn't. There are just too many factors getting in the way and too many reasons not to engage in challenge. Just as it is with food and drink, knowing what is good for us and acting in accordance with those beliefs are often miles apart.

So, throughout this chapter, I share some of the most up-to-date research on the topic together with the best practical advice I can offer. I'm sorry to say your students will still dodge challenge, and you will still wonder if you're fighting an uphill battle. After all, staying in our comfort zone as teachers is also easier—much easier—than taking on challenges. Ultimately, though, it is worth it. Developing the right strategies and creating optimal conditions for challenge *will* lead your students into building better attitudes and, therefore, enhanced learning outcomes.

The four pillars of challenge are when your students experience the following.

1. **Making the challenge worth it:** Students need to be convinced that a challenge is worth their investment.
2. **Owning the challenge:** Students have a high degree of control.
3. **Having permission to try:** Students have permission to take risks (and potentially fail).
4. **Being in the habit:** It is just what one does (because students are in the habit of it).

To explain these properly, I will relate them to a challenge I engage with often: swimming.

I try to swim at least four times a week, more if I'm home, and as I can fit it in if I'm traveling for work. Whenever I go, it is a challenge for me to do so—a challenge to find an extra ninety minutes in my day and a challenge to swim the distance and speed I aim for. It would be easier if I didn't go. Not better, but easier. The factors influencing my decisions are shown in the next section, together with annotations that connect with the school context.

3.1.1 Making the Challenge Worth It

By far, the most important factor in my decision to swim is that I've decided it's better to do it than not. I know exercise is important, so of the choices readily available to me, this is the one I choose. I don't go because I love it. If medical science one day revealed that it isn't a heart-healthy activity, I would give up on it. The stress on my body and the monotony of counting laps are just not seductive enough. A vacation pool with a swim-up bar would be a completely different proposal, but my swimming means going up and down, up and down, again and again and again. I don't do it for hedonism; I do it for sagacity.

This isn't just about belief; it is also about evidence. I need to see or feel improvements if I am to continue. In my case, I feel fitter. I don't just feel it but know I am. This makes the efforts worthwhile. Indeed, it is sometimes the only reason I haul my aching body to the pool in the first place!

As with my swimming, the single biggest factor in students' taking on challenge is that it is worth it to them. Duping them sometimes works, but on the whole, students need to be convinced that challenge is the better choice if they are to invest anything other than their bare minimum. They have to see or feel the improvements. They need to be able to reflect on the journey they have taken and be able to notice the gains they have made if they are to continue.

The examples of drawing attention to progress that I mention in section 5.5 (page 240) go a long way toward helping with this.

Challenge does not need to represent the nicer option—often it won't—but your students have to believe there is enough benefit in it to make stepping out of their comfort zone worthwhile.

3.1.2 Owning the Challenge

I choose the amount of challenge I engage with in the pool. I set my targets and try to beat them. On a good day, I push myself; on an off day, I do just enough to make the trip worthwhile. Step onto an ice rink, though, and challenge will come at me whether or not I want it to. Staying upright, building momentum, stopping, starting, and avoiding others—all of these will be a challenge. In the pool, I can put in a good shift without really testing myself. I can add a challenge here and there if the mood takes me. When it comes to ice skating, I will spend considerable energy trying to bring myself back from the b(rink).

A sense of control is an important factor when it comes to challenge. If students can add challenge to what they are doing *when they are ready to do so*, then their attitude is likely to be a favorable one. This is the case for me in the pool. However, when students find themselves struggling to wrestle control of the many variables, they may well feel overwhelmed. This would be me on the ice.

It is important to recognize the differences in these two situations—and to be aware of how looks might be deceiving. Students in control will seem as if they are performing effectively—and will typically be praised for it, even though they might *not* be out of their comfort zone. But those who are attempting to wrestle control may seem hesitant or even fearful. In these situations, students are often implored to try harder or have another go, even though they are already a long way out of their comfort zone.

3.1.3 Having Permission to Try

I feel as if I have permission to challenge myself in the pool. This belief comes from many sources. First, I have enough capability that I'm not going to make a fool of myself or get in people's way. Neither of these things would be true on an ice rink. I also know the etiquette of my local pool enough to understand what is acceptable and what is not. For example, I know I can challenge myself by using flippers but not by diving from the shoulders of someone else. Just as importantly, I feel as if I'm among friends—I know many of the lifeguards and fellow swimmers well enough that if I were to challenge myself with a brand-new routine, I'm sure they would show curiosity and encouragement rather than disdain or suspicion. In effect, I belong there. I am welcome there. Therefore, I have tacit permission to try new things.

Do your students feel as if they have permission to take on challenges? You give permission, of course, and encouragement, but do their peers? In every subject area? How about the students who do not think of themselves as creative? Do they have permission to try new techniques in art or music? What about the students who do not believe they are sporty? Can they try new techniques in physical education or on the sports field without risking ridicule? Do your students have permission to ask questions if they think of a connection that they'd like to test out?

Do they have a clear enough understanding of what is allowed or expected? Have your students learned how to encourage and show interest in other students who are trying new things? The research is clear that students who believe they fit in and have permission to experiment will do so (Becker & Luthar, 2002; Maslow, 1968; Pittman & Richmond, 2007). Those who don't, don't.

3.1.4 Being in the Habit

I have developed a habit for swimming. By doing so, I need less mental preparation than I once did. It used to be that I had to convince myself swimming was worth it—worth setting an early alarm, worth going tomorrow even if I wouldn't have another opportunity for another week after that, worth putting a bag together with swim gear, showering gear, and work clothes for afterward. My trips were sporadic, and each visit took effort. Then the pandemic hit; I couldn't travel, but I could swim every day. I did it so much that now it feels odd not to. My fellow swimmers expect to see me and ask where I've been if I don't turn up. My bag sits by the front door, just needing a fresh towel, trunks, and a water bottle. Lavish plans about fitting everything in are no longer needed; it's all part of the routine now. Even if my body says no, my mind says I had better get on with it. The last thing I want to do is lose a habit that took so long to build up.

The importance of getting your students into the habit of taking on challenges shouldn't be underestimated. Indeed, this is the answer to the question I am asked time and again about ways to encourage students who avoid challenge: take one small step after another until they are eventually in the habit of rising to challenges. Don't plan a special day once or twice a year (although these are nice bonuses). Instead, add a little challenge every lesson, every day. Increase adding challenge bit by bit until, eventually, challenge is the norm. Make it such an everyday part of your classroom that its absence would be immediately noticeable, and its return requested.

So, there you have them: the four pillars of challenge that, when developed, will encourage your students to engage in challenge. They don't all have to feature in every challenge, although the more that they do, the more likely your students are to take a positive attitude toward challenge. Don't just take my word for it. Instead, let's take a look at the research evidence.

3.2 Learn What Research Says About Challenge

The different meta-analyses about challenge identify the following four categories.

1. Holding high expectations for all students
2. Creating desirable difficulties
3. Setting appropriately challenging goals
4. Giving students control over their learning

I describe each of these categories across the next four sections. For now, here is a summary of each one, together with their relative effect sizes (represented by $d =$).

1. **Holding high expectations for all students (d = 0.50 to 1.44):** This is the factor that influences student learning the most. This includes students' skills, prior knowledge, background variables, and attitudes and beliefs. After that, the second most influential factor is the teacher. What teachers and students do together is what drives learning, and right at the core of that are the expectations that teachers hold for their students. The differences in impact between a teacher with low expectations and a teacher with high expectations are astonishing. Those with higher expectations set more aspirational goals, use time more effectively to better understand where students are and how to move them on, and get the levels of challenge just right.

2. **Creating desirable difficulties:** The term *desirable difficulties* comes from Robert Bjork (1994), distinguished research professor of cognitive psychology at UCLA (Bjork & Bjork, 2011). His research shows that when learning is made more challenging, it can lead to additional benefits in terms of long-term memory, skill, knowledge retrieval, and transfer from one context to another. Bjork (1994) recommends four approaches to creating desirable difficulties.

    a. Varying the conditions of learning (effect size unavailable)
    b. Spaced (versus massed) learning (d = 0.65)
    c. Interleaving (d = 0.44)
    d. Generation and testing (d = 0.50 to 0.96)

3. **Setting appropriately challenging goals (d = 0.59):** Challenge should be at the edge of competence—not so hard that students are discouraged but not so easy that they grow bored. Researchers Celeste Kidd, Steven T. Piantadosi, and Richard N. Aslin (2012) call this sweet spot the *Goldilocks zone*. Researchers Robert C. Wilson, Amitai Shenhav, Mark Straccia, and Jonathan D. Cohen (2019) estimate that when challenge is optimal, it will lead students to be able to achieve an 80 percent to 85 percent success rate.

4. **Giving students control over their learning (d = 0.02):** This influence is the odd one out due to its low effect size. All the other factors in this section are likely to lead to substantial or very high effect sizes. The conundrum is that although students like choice (and teachers typically like to offer a certain degree of control and ownership), it all too often leads to less learning, not more. This is *not* because choice is a bad thing but because students tend to choose the option that they perceive will be easiest for them to succeed with. In other words, they choose low levels of challenge rather than optimal levels. This doesn't have to be the case—and I share some ways to address this in section 3.1 (page 95)—but nonetheless, research shows that choice typically means less challenge and, therefore, lower levels of learning.

3.3 Hold High Expectations for All Students

In *Visible Learning: The Sequel*, Hattie (2023) begins his summary about the effect of teachers with, "The most critical teacher influences relate to their having high expectations for all students" (p. 240).

This is not some throwaway line in the middle of a 500-page book. It is Hattie's considered opinion based on his synthesis of forty-seven meta-analyses covering 2,238 studies, all of which examine how teachers can best affect student learning. That, in itself, should be enough to emphasize the huge significance of teacher expectations. However, when you drill down to the differences in effect size between teachers with low expectations and teachers with high expectations, it becomes even more astonishing.

The effect sizes range from $d = -0.03$ to 0.20 for those with low expectations and $d = 0.50$ to 1.44 for those with high expectations. That is the difference between slight negative and low impact on the one hand and between high and very high impact on the other. To use the colloquialism: wow. Just wow!

Whatever you do, please, please, please hold high expectations for your students. Everything else will follow after that.

Expectations refer to the "inferences that teachers make about the present and future academic achievement and general classroom behavior of their students" (Good & Brophy, 1997, p. 79). Put simply, the measure has to do with holding expectations that are significantly above or below students' demonstrated level. For example, if I view a student's D grade on their last exam as a challenge to do everything in my power to lift their performance during the next set of lessons so that they achieve a significantly better grade on the next exam (because I believe they are capable of it), that is a strong indicator of holding high expectations. If I view that same grade as a predictor of what to expect from that student in subsequent lessons or exams, that indicates average expectations. And if the D grade surprises me because it is higher than I anticipated (bearing in mind the student's background, condition, label, or behavior), that indicates low expectations. As Shengnan Wang and her doctoral supervisors at the University of Auckland found when reviewing the research about teacher expectations between 1989 and 2018:

> The evidence [suggests] that teachers generally predicted students' ability and performance based on students' previous academic achievement. However, in addition to prior performance, several studies showed that expectations could also be affected by other factors such as information about students' socioeconomic status (SES), ethnicity, gender, physical appearance, and other personal characteristics of students. (Wang, Rubie-Davies, & Meissel, 2018, p. 127)

The expectations we hold for our students' progress are significant in many ways. Not only do they determine how we interact with our students, how much we expect from them, and how much we challenge them, but they also play a significant role in how students view their own capabilities and possibilities. Students tend to be very accurate in observing and interpreting our behaviors. For example, in comparing the changes in the self-perceptions of students who are in classes with high-, average-, and low-expectation teachers across a year, researcher Christine M. Rubie-Davies (2006) finds students' self-perceptions change over the year in line with their teachers' expectations. Researchers Michael E. Woolley, Marilyn E. Strutchens, Melissa C. Gilbert, and W. Gary Martin (2010) further find that teachers' high expectations have significant and positive correlations with students' confidence and interest in their studies, whereas low expectations are significantly and negatively associated with students' anxiety about their studies, particularly in mathematics.

Based on the research evidence shown in figure 3.1, it is clear that we must view ourselves as agents of change. We should not think of ourselves simply as facilitators of student activity or

Low Expectations (d = −0.03 to 0.20)	High Expectations (d = 0.50 to 1.44)
View low performance as understandable, and expect this low performance to continue.	Expect improvements for all students. View current ability as the launchpad, not the predictor.
Hold a fixed view of ability and intelligence (see section 5.4, page 230, for more).	Hold an incremental view of ability and intelligence (see section 5.4, page 230, for more).
Show inappropriate levels of challenge for high-ability and low-ability students.	Challenge is closely matched so that all students go beyond their current ability.
Expect progress for some students, but not all.	Expect all students to make good progress.
Group students by ability. Students rarely change groups—once a middle band, always a middle band.	Group students according to interests and current learning (see section 5.6, page 247). These groups are fluid, changing often.
Set distinctly different tasks for high, middle, and low groups. This includes lots of repetition and lower-level tasks for lower-ability students.	All students engage in similar activities. Differentiation allows for different paths and timings for the successful completion of similar success criteria.
More time is spent with lower-ability students. Higher-ability students are expected to work independently.	Similar amounts of time are spent with all students, encouraging, challenging, questioning, and guiding.
More time is spent on crowd control (patrolling the classroom, giving praise for compliance, giving warnings to those not on task, and reminding students about procedures and routines).	More time is spent on feedback, helping students (1) accurately identify how much progress they've made so far and (2) decide what to do next to make even more progress.
Ask mostly closed questions (see section 2.1.2, page 34, for more).	Ask mostly open, higher-order questions (see section 2.1.2, page 34, for more).
Very few conversations with students to assess and monitor their learning occur.	More time is spent on assessment *for* learning conversations (see section 4.6, page 186, for more).
Reference prior knowledge based on the year group and school calendar (for example, "This class is in the second semester of grade 9; therefore, they will know . . .")	Strategies such as preview (see section 6.1, page 272) are used to identify what students know so that activities connect to, and build from, these points.
Lessons follow earlier planning. Very few adjustments are made.	Lessons are adjusted in response to student need and questions.

Figure 3.1: High expectations versus low expectations.

mediators of behavior. We have to expect every single student to make excellent progress from wherever they are starting.

This does not mean that every student will achieve a top grade; with the norm referencing underpinning most grading systems, that would be impossible. However, it does mean that learning should be accelerated for every single student. The trajectory of progress for everyone should be steep.

To achieve this progress, the challenge must be just right. Identify where your students are right now, connect to their prior knowledge and interests, and set challenges that will take them just out of their comfort zone and into their zone of proximal development (Vygotsky, 1978) or, as I call it, through the Learning Pit (see section 3.7, page 113). Some other helpful terms are *desirable difficulties*, *productive struggle*, and *appropriately challenging goals*.

3.4 Create Desirable Difficulties

Bjork introduced the concept of desirable difficulties in his seminal 1994 work. Since then, it has become a well-known term for many educators. The theory is based on Bjork's concern that many of us believe memory works like a tape or video recorder, with repeated exposure to the same material enabling it to be written into our memory. This belief causes us to go through the same material in the same way many times in the false belief that this will result in effective learning. It doesn't.

I include the term in this section because, all too often, people imagine that challenge equates to increasing the difficulty of content. Generally, this means giving students more information, setting tasks with increased complexity, or removing variables such that students have fewer resources on hand with which to solve a problem. These are all valid. Robert Bjork, however, adds other approaches.

It is important to note that Bjork does *not* promote the idea that everything difficult will be desirable for learning. There are, of course, many difficulties that are undesirable, ones that will create barriers to learning. By "desirable difficulties," he means introducing challenges requiring more effort than normal to "trigger encoding and retrieval processes" (Bjork & Bjork, 2011, p. 58).

From the evidence collected, researchers Bjork and Bjork (2011) recommend four main approaches, which are covered in the next four sections: (1) variations in the conditions of learning, (2) spaced versus massed practice, (3) interleaving, and (4) generation and testing.

3.4.1 Variations in the Conditions of Learning

If all the learning in one domain takes place under standard conditions—for example, same teacher, same teaching style, same classroom, same cadence of lesson structure, and same textbook—then the learning is likely to be fixed in that context. This might not be noticeable if later retrieval takes place under the same conditions, but learning loss is likely to be pronounced when the situation changes. This is often why students struggle to apply learning from one subject to another or from one school to the next.

To mitigate this effect, Bjork and Bjork (2011) recommend varying the conditions at the point of learning. Rather than hoping (or expecting) circumstances to remain constant, we should assume they *will* change. Desirable difficulties therefore mean introducing changes at the point of learning. Add difficulties in now rather than wait until they present themselves uninvited later.

In some ways, this flies in the face of conventional wisdom; we have long assumed that predictability and stability improve learning. We work hard to make the classroom a predictable place with routines, familiarity, and fraternity. This still holds true, which is why Bjork and Bjork (2011) distinguish between ease of learning and *success of retrieval*. These two factors seem to be at odds with each other. As one increases, the other decreases. The easier and more readily accessible the learning is, the less likely students will remember the lessons learned when they need to rely on those memories at a later date. The adage of "Easy come, easy go" that I mentioned earlier is appropriate here.

Varying the conditions of learning can include covering the same material with a teacher whose style is very different. For example, think of a science teacher and a geography teacher swapping classes for a period or two to go over a familiar topic with students from their own vantage points. Or think of a first-grade teacher swapping classes with a fifth-grade teacher for a morning. Other conditions include moving rooms or learning outside rather than inside, solving problems that are presented in divergent and novel ways, changing the emphasis or big question that directs the learning (for example, taking a philosophical approach to a mathematics topic, taking a historical approach to a science experiment, or using drama to explore a content-rich topic), and running revision classes at irregular hours in different settings with other teachers.

3.4.2 Spaced Versus Massed Practice

Covering a topic in depth within consecutive lessons is certainly more convenient and conventional than studying some of it now and some of it later. Yet, what is good for organization is not so good for memory.

Introducing the desirable difficulty of chunking a topic and distributing it across a wider time frame enhances learning. This is one of the most generalizable and robust effects noted in experimental research on learning and memory. Called the *spacing effect*, it has been demonstrated for all types of materials and tasks, including with animals as well as with humans. The phenomenon was first identified by Hermann Ebbinghaus and published in detail in 1885 (makes you wonder why it is still a novel idea for many!). Hattie has included five meta-analyses covering 510 studies about spacing in the Visible Learning Metax (n.d.) database. The effect sizes range from $d = 0.27$ to 0.96, with an overall effect of $d = 0.65$. This has the potential to considerably accelerate student learning.

Spacing versus massed practice looks like this: Take a topic. Let's say you plan to use six lessons to cover it from start to finish. Space this learning by covering two or three lessons now, enough that your students have moved from knowing very little to knowing quite a lot. Then begin teaching a second topic, connecting it to prior learning as you would ordinarily. Then, some weeks later, return to the first topic to revise what was taught initially and to add extra layers. Take a different pedagogical approach with less direct instruction and more problem solving than you used in the first two or three lessons. Ask your students to create a quiz for each other on the content so far. Then press pause again. Return a few more weeks later for the last lesson. Encourage your students to take a similar approach to revision for exams. "Little bits and often" is the mantra. Make sure they engage with the material in different ways with different people, using different types of media at different times. The desirable difficulty of spacing and variety will lead to longer-lasting learning.

One quick caveat: Cramming for exams works! Therefore, the advice in this section should *not* be used to dissuade your students from doing last-minute revision for a single subject. However, cramming supports short-term performance only, not long-term retention. So, if they have four weeks to prepare for exams, then spacing out the topics and circling back to them again and again is the way to go. However, if they have four *hours* before an exam, then cramming as much of the same subject as possible into their brains is far more effective for improving performance (although this learning will likely be lost soon after the exam is finished).

3.4.3 Interleaving

Interleaving takes the spacing effect mentioned earlier one step further. Imagine, for example, you are going to teach three different approaches to solving a problem, analyzing examples, or developing techniques for accomplishing a skill. Instead of teaching A, then B, and then C, you interleave the three such that students study *part* of A, closely followed by *part* of B and *part* of C. Then you return to A to study more of that, followed immediately by another part of B and another part of C, and so on.

It sounds like an organizational nightmare and maybe not so desirable for us, the instructors! However, Bjork and Bjork's (2011) evidence is strong: interleaving improves long-term retention and transfer of skills.

Some of the more interesting experiments are as follows. In a pinball experiment, participants learned three ways to knock down hinged barriers on a pinball-like apparatus in a prescribed order (Shea & Morgan, 1979). Everyone made attempts to successfully complete the task. The blocked group practiced one pattern at a time: six attempts with the first, followed by six attempts with the second, and then six with the third approach. The interleaved group had to practice the patterns in a randomly determined order. Interestingly, the blocked group improved their techniques more rapidly than the interleaved (random) group. However, when both groups were retested ten days later, the interleaved group performed far better.

In a mathematics experiment, participants were asked to learn formulas for calculating the volumes of different solids, such as a truncated cone. The blocked group performed slightly better on a test immediately after the experiment, but the interleaved group performed significantly better on a delayed test. The difference was striking. The interleaved group scored 63 percent on a test one week later compared to just 20 percent for the blocked group (Rohrer & Taylor, 2007).

In an art-based experiment, participants were asked to learn the styles of twelve artists based on a sample of six paintings by each artist (Kornell & Bjork, 2008). The blocked group studied all six paintings of one artist, then moved on to the second artist's paintings, and then the third, and so on. The order in which the interleaved group studied the paintings was randomly generated, with paintings from any of the twelve artists clustered together. The results were surprising because not only did the art teachers involved in the experiment assume it would be easier to note the common characteristics of an artist's paintings by grouping them together, but also the students were more confident following the blocked approach. However, members of the interleaved group were able to far more accurately identify which painting belonged to which artist in a later test. They could also talk in more depth about the similarities and differences between paintings and between artists.

The reason why interleaving improves encoding (and is therefore a desirable difficulty) is still open to interpretation. "One theory suggests that the *interference* caused by studying different things at the same time forces learners to notice similarities and differences" (Bjork & Bjork, 2011, p. 61). This leads to higher-order thinking, which in turn leads to higher-order encoding. Another theory is that interleaving causes reloading. That is to say, instead of studying A and then B and then C, interleaving involves studying part of A, part of B, and part of C, then adding a bit more of A, which causes students to think back to what they've understood so far and reload that information.

3.4.4 Generation and Testing

The final category of desirable difficulties that Bjork and Bjork (2011) recommend is *generation* (generating solutions rather than looking them up) and *testing* (although very few students think of tests as desirable). The evidence is clear that generating an answer, solution, or procedure creates much longer-lasting effects than looking up or being told an answer. Indeed, its effect rivals the spacing effect for generality and significance for learning. When guiding students through the Learning Pit, I call this the *eureka moment* (see section 3.8.3.8, page 142).

Closely related to generation is testing. Although it suffers from a negative reputation due to its use in high-stakes assessment, when tests are used as learning events, they are considerably more effective in the long term than reading material over and over again. Research shows this is true even when no corrective feedback is offered, although with it, testing is even more effective. This is when testing becomes formative (see section 4.6, page 186).

Two other benefits of testing should be noted. First, "tests can have a metacognitive benefit when used to identify what has and has not been understood" (Bjork & Bjork, 2011, p. 62). Rereading a chapter or set of revision notes cannot do this. Tests check understanding much more effectively. Second, tests can (and should) lead to adapted instruction. As I describe in sections 4.6 and 5.5.2 (pages 186 and 244), when the results from testing are used to adjust what is taught next or how it is taught, benefits are intensified. This is when results are viewed as feedback to teachers even more than feedback to students.

With all desirable difficulties, there is a marked difference between what *appears* to be optimal learning and what actually results in improved retention, recall, and transfer. Bjork and Bjork's (2011) research illustrates that good performance during learning episodes tends to be mistaken for good learning when, in fact, later retrieval shows they are not the same. Conditions of learning that make performance improve rapidly often fail to support long-term retention and transfer, whereas conditions that create challenges and slow the rate of apparent learning tend to optimize long-term retention and transfer.

I'd like to finish this section with a clear illustration of the differences between learning confidence and learning outcomes. The left panel in figure 3.2 shows the proportion of participants who selected blocked, interleaved, or same in response to the question, "Under which condition do you believe you learned better?" The right panel shows the actual performance of the participants in blocked learning and interleaved learning. In this graph, *same* represents the participants who scored the same irrespective of whether they learned in a blocked or interleaved manner.

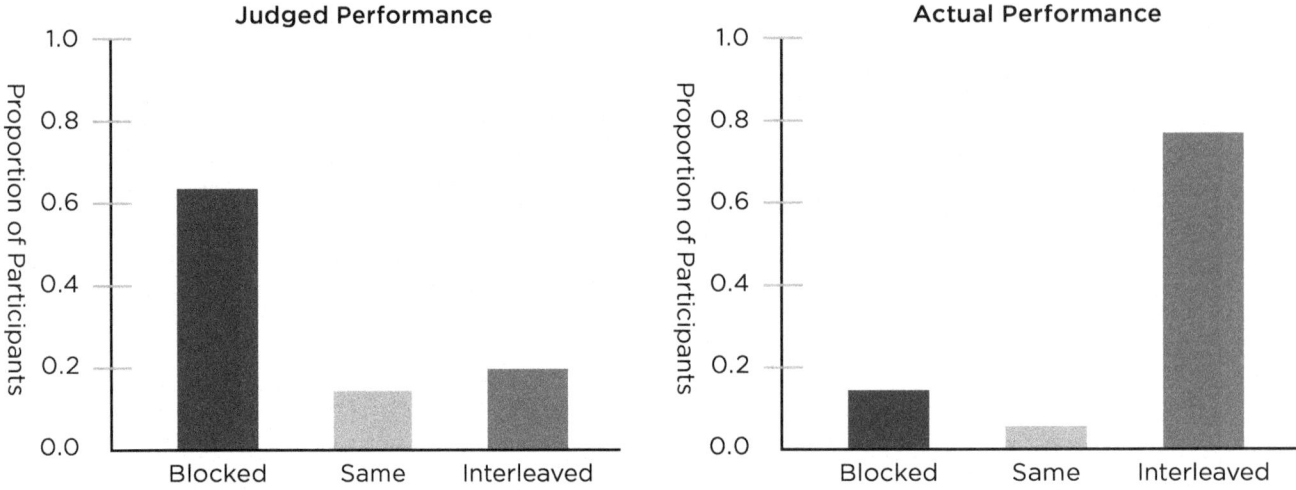

Figure 3.2: Differences in perceived performance compared to actual performance.

3.5 Set Appropriately Challenging Goals

The third way in which challenge is examined in research experiments is through the setting of appropriately challenging goals. As previously noted, challenge should be at the edge of competence: not so hard that students are discouraged, but not so easy that they grow bored. Researchers Celeste Kidd, Steven T. Piantadosi, and Richard N. Aslin (2012) call this sweet spot the *Goldilocks zone*.

An interesting development in this field is that researchers Robert C. Wilson, Amitai Shenhav, Mark Straccia, and Jonathan D. Cohen (2019) calculate the optimal accuracy for training is around 80 percent to 85 percent. They show theoretically that studying at this optimal level can lead to exponential improvements in the rate of learning.

For those of us in the classroom, this can be a useful guide. It means we should be designing learning activities for our students in which, even when they marshal all their personal and intellectual resources, they should only be able to succeed with 80 percent to 85 percent of the task. Thereafter, they should require inspiration or suggestions from others (either you or their peers).

However, I am *not* suggesting that it should be impossible for students to succeed with 100 percent of a task! Context is crucial. In a *learning* situation—one in which you want to stretch your students' capabilities so that they will eventually grow to meet those demands later—the 80/20 split is a very useful guide. When they are taking an assessment or taking part in an observed performance, then it would be delightful if they could score 100 percent.

Here's a story to illustrate the point. The first time I took my son to see our local football team play, he asked about the purpose of the coin toss before the game began. I explained that whoever wins chooses the direction of play in the first half. He asked why this was important, so I drew attention to the slope on the pitch (our local ground has the dubious pleasure of including the steepest slope of any pitch used by professional teams in the United Kingdom). I said, "Son! Look at the pitch. Which way would you want to be kicking in the second half when your legs are tired?" He considered this for a moment and replied, "Uphill, Dad." "Why?" says I. "Because challenge is good, isn't it, Dad?"

This poor boy! He'd suffered my pedagogical theories so much that he was now in danger of brainwashing! So, I explained to him he was absolutely right that *when it comes to training*, challenge is good. But when it comes to match day, our team needs all the advantages they can lay their boots on. Indeed, the very next season, they were relegated out of the football league altogether—so advantage was even more important to them than most.

So, when it comes to training, or learning, situations, the 80/20 principle applies brilliantly. Set challenges such that even when your students—or in this case, your team—put in every skill and effort they can, they still only achieve about 80 percent to 85 percent of their goal. The other 15 percent to 20 percent should come from additional direction, instruction, suggestion, and encouragement. However, in situations where performance has to be at its very best—in exams, during performances, or when playing your local rivals—getting as close to 100 percent as possible should very definitely be the goal. As the saying in sports goes, train hard so that you can play easy.

I would love for every lesson to be challenging enough that taking an assessment in the exam hall feels straightforward, for every practice or dress rehearsal to make performances feel easy by comparison. In section 1.2 (page 5), I shared three examples to show how important context is. These were (1) making mistakes can be instructional (at the right time); (2) going into the Learning Pit can deepen learning (at the right time); and (3) dialogue can significantly improve learning (when used at the right time). I now add a fourth example, which is the appropriate level of challenge is somewhere in the region of 80 percent to 85 percent attainable and 15 percent to 20 percent out of reach, but *only when the time is right*. When your purpose is to stretch your students so that they are out of their comfort zone, the 80/20 split is optimum. However, if your purpose is assessment or performance, then hope your students will remember everything you've taught them so that they ace the test! Now that we've made that important distinction, let's return to the 80/20 guidance.

If you have students getting close to 100 percent on every *learning* task or assignment you set, then there is a good chance it is too easy for them; conversely, if some students never get close to an 80 percent to 85 percent success rate, then the challenge is probably too high. These targets may need adjusting according to context. For example, they are likely to fit well with closed-answer situations (such as spelling or mathematics learning tasks) but less well with open-ended subjects (such as those within humanities and languages). Nonetheless, the principle is sound that a marker of challenge is that students should be able to succeed with most—but not all—of a task. If they are acing it, then there isn't enough challenge for them. If they get nowhere close every time, then it is too challenging.

These figures shouldn't be seen as the target for attempt one. So, for example, if we expect students to make three attempts at a given task, then they should be close to 85 percent accuracy after their second or third attempt. I say three attempts, as it fits with the Seven Steps to Feedback that I share in section 4.9 (page 198), in which we should expect attempt one followed by peer feedback, attempt two followed by teacher feedback, and then attempt three.

Interestingly, interview-based analyses of the enjoyment of intrinsically motivated, goal-directed activities such as chess or rock climbing show that the optimal level of challenge is a 20 percent chance of winning or succeeding (Abuhamdeh & Csikszentmihalyi, 2012). So, perhaps the balance between achievable and challenging is different in every circumstance (and for every student). However, what the ratios have in common is that they are never 100 percent one way and 0 percent the other. Learning tasks should always include demands that students will not be able to achieve. That is not to say they should never attain full marks on a performance task, but on a task designed for the purposes of learning, *appropriately challenging* should include a degree of unachievability. That is to say that right now, at students' current levels of ability, they are unable to succeed with 100 percent accuracy.

When we get these levels right, Hattie (2023) calculates the effect size across six meta-analyses involving 375 studies as $d = 0.60$. Bearing in mind the hinge point (see section 1.8, page 15) of 0.40, this represents 50 percent more learning than normal. Setting appropriately challenging goals is definitely worth it!

3.5.1 Flow Theory

Having referenced psychologist Mihaly Csikszentmihalyi earlier, I think it is worth mentioning his theory of *flow*. He describes flow as a state of deep absorption in an activity that is intrinsically enjoyable—for example, when artists or athletes are focused on their play or performance (Csikszentmihalyi, 1990). Individuals in this state perceive the activity as worth doing for its own sake, even if no further goal is reached (Nakamura & Csikszentmihalyi, 2002). So, although educational research tends to justify challenge as a means to improving learning outcomes, remember that challenge can also be enjoyed for its own sake, not because it will help someone improve but because they enjoy it. In a school context, we see this when students are following their passions and entirely immerse themselves in the experience, not for the purposes of praise or a grade but because it gives them enormous satisfaction.

The flow experience is believed to occur when someone's skills are neither overmatched nor underutilized to meet a given challenge. As Csikszentmihalyi (1997) describes, "the balance of challenge and skill is fragile; when disrupted, apathy (i.e., low challenges, low skills), anxiety (i.e., high challenges, low skills), or relaxation (i.e., low challenges, high skills) are likely to be experienced."

3.6 Give Students Control Over Their Learning

It is a commonly held belief that choice has a positive impact on an individual's feelings, beliefs, and behavior. *Choice* is always used as a positive reference in political slogans and consumer campaigns, and it has been used to attract students to one school instead of another.

Early educational studies showed that choice is a powerful motivator, demonstrating that students are more likely to engage in an activity if they believe they have chosen it (Lewin, 1952). Richard DeCharms (1968) made an even stronger case, claiming that choice is a *necessary* condition for engagement. Later, self-determination theory showed that not only does choice enhance intrinsic motivation, but the opposite is also true; when students perceive conditions are controlling, they disengage (Deci, Connell, & Ryan, 1989).

It's strange, then, that more recent studies have shown choice has little to no effect on student motivation or performance (Carolan, Hutchins, Wickens, & Cumming, 2014; Landers & Reddock, 2017; Overskeid & Svartdal, 1996; Parker & Lepper, 1992; Reeve, Nix, & Hamm, 2003). For example, giving students a choice between working on a crossword puzzle and working on an essay task showed no effect on engagement and task performance (Flowerday & Schraw, 2003).

This effect has concerned me for decades. In 2003, I came across the name John Hattie for the first time. He had just published the paper *Teachers Make a Difference, What Is the Research Evidence?* (Hattie, 2003). I was leading a multimillion-pound social regeneration project at the time. Our budget afforded us many possibilities but brought with it enormous responsibility. No longer could I promote strategies that I thought worked well; I had to find those supported by extensive and reliable evidence.

In following Hattie's work, I came across the meta-analyses about student choice included in his expanding database. Back then, there were just two meta-analyses, and both related to control over learning in information and communication technology. However, in 2008, a third meta-analysis examined forty-one studies about student choice in a variety of subjects. In 2023, there are six meta-analyses covering 226 studies (for example, Carolan et al., 2014). The overall effect size shocked me: $d = 0.02$. *Surely that can't be right!* I thought. *How on earth can choice reduce the effect of learning outcomes?*

Choice enhances intrinsic motivation, effort, task performance, and perceived competence. We know this from our own experiences as well as from experimental evidence. So, how can something so positive have such a diminishing effect on learning? The answer lies in its connection to challenge (or lack thereof), which is why I have included the topic in this chapter.

I often ask students which of these options they would choose: (a) a task they believe they can complete accurately or (b) a task that is likely to take them out of their comfort zone and cause them to think. Almost everyone opts for the easier task. This is not just *my* students answering. One of the best aspects of my job is taking learning walks around lots of schools all around the world. I find it fascinating, inspiring, and thought-provoking in equal measure. Generally speaking, I ask students what they are learning, how much progress they've made, and what they plan to do next. I guess these questions will be very familiar to you, particularly if you've read ahead to sections 4.2, 4.3, and 4.5 (pages, 150, 151, and 179) in the feedback chapter. Another favorite is to ask the question about choice in the previous paragraph.

 *When students are given a choice, they typically choose the easier option. This leads to less challenge and lower learning outcomes. This, however, does not mean we should stop giving students choice!*

Instead of abandoning choice, we should understand what is happening and why. Then adjust the conditions so that choice leads to more learning, not less.

The insights I have gained into why choice leads to less challenge come from two sources: (1) student voice and (2) research. The first of these is the most important. I ask students to tell me which task they would choose—(a) easier or (b) challenging—and then prompt them for their supporting reasons. Figure 3.3 shows a summary of the responses they gave.

Easier Task "I would pick the task I am confident about completing because . . ."	Challenging Task "I would avoid the task that will take me out of my comfort zone because . . ."
"It makes me feel clever when I complete the task easily."	"*I feel frustrated* when I can't work out what to do."
"*Teachers praise* me when I complete tasks easily."	"Teachers tell me to *concentrate more* if I don't finish tasks quick enough."
"*I finish quicker* (which means less homework or more playtime)."	"Challenging tasks might *never end*."
"I want to *keep up* with (or, if possible, outperform) my friends."	"I might get *left behind* or look stupid in front of my friends."
"It is *less effort*."	"I can't be *bothered*."

Figure 3.3: Reasons students give for the choices they make.

In many ways, these answers say as much, if not more, about the learning culture—what's encouraged, praised, or scorned—as they do about the benefits or problems of choice. I recommend ways to change this in the next section. For now, here are five modifiers mentioned in the meta-analyses.

1. Choice has a positive overall effect, which is important to note! Do not stop offering choice to your students!

2. The number of options is important. Too few options lead students to assume that they are being controlled with false choice; too many options are overwhelming. In the research, this draining effect of too many options (and too many choices) is referred to as *ego depletion* (Patall, Cooper, & Robinson, 2008).

3. The number of times that students are invited to choose is also important. Multiple opportunities appear to yield greater benefits than making a single choice. However, after a certain point, being asked to make choices again and again becomes overwhelming and exhausting.

4. When choice is presented in a manner that implies pressure (from teachers or peers) to pick a particular option, benefits are reduced.

5. Perhaps most importantly, the main benefit of choice is to boost intrinsic motivation, so anything that reduces this inner drive will reduce the positive impact of choice. The biggest detractors for intrinsic motivation are extrinsic motivators. I cover the negative effect of praise and reward systems in depth in section 5.7 (page 251).

3.6.1 Making Challenge Interesting

Students typically learn less when they are given a choice of tasks. It's not because choice is a bad thing but because they tend to pick whichever option they perceive to be the most likely to lead to success. In other words, they pick the option with less challenge rather than more. They go low when, ordinarily, we would prefer them to go high. Some of the reasons why students do this are shown in figure 3.3.

This doesn't have to be the case. We can do many things to turn this around and cause students to choose more challenge rather than less. These include the following.

- **Provide no easy options:** In the short term, make sure you offer no easy options. This won't work forever, because students, particularly older ones, will soon notice they are being misled by false choice. However, giving students choices between *spicy*, *hot*, and *too-hot-to-handle* tasks (or whatever terms work for you to ensure the options range from challenging to super challenging) will help your students set off in the right direction.

- **Challenge is interesting:** Most students think challenge equates to difficulty. This is one of the reasons why they find it so unappealing. After all, who likes difficulty? Who wishes for more difficulty in their lives? Certainly not me! I like challenges (the right kind!), but I have no fondness for difficulties.

  If your students think of challenge as difficult, then their mindset ought to be modified. To help with this, I use the term *interesting*. So, rather than giving the impression of challenge equating to difficulty, I do what I can to give the impression that challenge makes life interesting. For example, if I see a student doing something with ease (and I believe it is in their best interests to challenge them some more), I say something along the lines of, "That seems to be too easy for you, so let's try to make it more interesting." The caveat in parentheses is important because there will be times when it is better for your students to be in their comfort zone. For example, if they have been struggling to understand a concept and have at last figured it out, then resting in their comfort zone and consolidating their new learning could be the best option. In such a case, I would say something more along the lines of, "Well done for figuring it out. That took determination and strategy. Now, take time to go over it a few times and make sure you're absolutely happy with your solution before we find something to make it even more interesting for you." Or, when one of my students complains of a task being too hard for them, I respond with, "It is interesting, isn't it? What strategies have you tried so far to figure it out?"

- **Do not praise easy success:** It is counterproductive to praise a student for succeeding with a task that was easy for them. I explore this in more depth in section 5.7 (page 251). The evidence is clear that praising students for doing something that was easy for them implies either you didn't realize how easy it was or you have low expectations of their abilities (Meyer, 1992). Furthermore, since praise is often used to reward what we want, many students make the connection (usually subconsciously) that completing easy tasks is what their teacher wants. This inadvertently steers them toward a preference for easier tasks in the future. "Praise for successful performance on an easy task can be interpreted by a student as evidence that the teacher has a low perception of [the student's] ability. As a consequence, it can actually lower rather than enhance self-confidence" (education professor Deborah J. Stipek as cited in Coe, Aloisi, Higgins & Major, 2014).

  Omitting praise does *not* mean criticizing instead! Rather, we should be confirmatory but neutral in our stance—for example, "It's looking like you're getting that done easily. Would you like something a bit more interesting?"

- **Praise ongoing efforts:** Do not praise your students when they are completing easy tasks, but *do* praise them when they are engaged in more challenging endeavors. When your students are struggling, that is when they need praise most—and when it is most beneficial. Use it to encourage determination, effort, strategy, focus, willingness to try alternatives, thoughtfulness, collaboration, and so on. Make sure you praise what they are doing rather than who they are. This is the difference between process praise and person praise. This topic is covered in more depth in section 5.7.1 (page 253).

- **Do not rescue (yet):** When we rescue our students, we deny them the satisfaction and longer-term memory effects of figuring something out for themselves. That is not to say we should *never* help them! Unfortunately, too many adults (parents in particular) will rush to help children the moment they begin to struggle. Colloquial terms I've heard for this phenomenon include *snowplow parents*, *helicopter parents*, and *bubble wrap parents*. I particularly like the Scandinavian version of *curling parents* and the Japanese idea of *bonsai parents*. Whatever we call this approach to parenting, the effects are worrying; children who are overprotected tend to be more anxious and display lower levels of resilience, independence, and self-efficacy (Gerull & Rapee, 2002).

The rescuing phenomenon, in particular, isn't limited to parenting; it happens in schools too. So, the question is, How do we get the balance right between doing our job of teaching and not overly guiding our students? Fortunately, there are ways to frame our responses.

Think of a child learning to ride a bicycle. Initially, they tend to wobble a lot. When they do that, we encourage them; we don't rescue them. We *don't* do it for them. We cheer them on: "Keep going! You're doing great." We probably mix in a few words of instruction: "Lift your head. Look far ahead of you because that will help you balance." This is exactly what we *should* do in the classroom. We should encourage without rescuing.

Incidentally, the English word *encourage* comes from 15th century French—*en* (meaning "to put in") and *corage* (meaning "heart"). Therefore, to encourage is to give heart. What a lovely notion! Better, I would say, than *praising*, given the problems associated with praise (covered in section 5.7, page 251).

Back to bike riding. If a child falls off their bike, that's when we should rescue them. First, we check that they're OK. If they are, then we put them back on their bike and give them some additional support. This normally means running alongside them, holding the bike frame, and then letting go again at the appropriate moment. It doesn't mean riding on the back of the bike with them. The child continues to be the one attempting to ride, but this time, we give them such extra support. Or, to use the term first coined by Jerome Bruner (Wood, Bruner, & Ross, 1976), we offer them some *scaffolding*.

The scenario of teaching a child to ride a bike can be a useful guide for everyday teaching. If we think of wobbling on a bike as cognitively wobbling in the classroom, and falling off a bike as failing at or giving up on academic tasks, then taking a similar approach to supporting students can be helpful. This means encouraging your students when they are confused or struggling but *not* rescuing them. Then reassure, instruct, and scaffold if a student is making absolutely no progress at all.

I shared earlier (section 3.2, page 98) that researcher Robert Wilson and his colleagues (2019) at the Princeton Neuroscience Institute have calculated an optimal learning level of 80 percent to 85 percent. Above this level of accuracy, tasks are too easy for students, so although performance will increase, learning will decrease. Below this level, the challenge for most students becomes too much. With this as a guide, anything in the range of 65 percent to 85 percent accuracy should attract encouragement only—no rescuing. If accuracy drops further, going below 65 percent, then some instruction might be needed. Below something like 40 percent, scaffolding is very likely going to be required one way or another.

As a rule of thumb, I recommend asking yourself if the challenges your students are engaging with are desirable ones. I realize this is a subjective question, but if your answer is "probably yes," then I'd be inclined to encourage more and instruct less; if, however, the opposite is true, then scaffolding is likely needed sooner than later.

It is worth noting again that desirable doesn't necessarily mean sought after or wished for by your students. As described in section 3.4 (page 102), desirable difficulties often slow progress and cause students to feel as if they are learning less well compared to when they attend to normal (easier) tasks. The term *desirable difficulties*, therefore, relates to the attractiveness of outcomes rather than to the desirability of experiences. Learning should be judged in much the same way as I recommend judging feedback (see section 4.3.3, page 158): by its outcome rather than by its inputs.

3.7 Understand Challenge and the Learning Pit

When students overcome challenges, it has a positive effect on learning results. Extensive evidence shows this, a summary of which appeared in section 3.0.1 (page 93). Unfortunately, research also shows that in normal circumstances, students tend *not* to choose challenge (see section 3.2, page 98). If there is a more straightforward option offering an immediate reward—be that praise, the satisfaction of task completion, or the conservation of effort—then most opt for ease. This leads to the illusion of enhanced performance, but ultimately fewer long-term advantages.

Clearly, the onus to persuade students to step out of their comfort zones rests on us, except such strategies are not very sustainable if we must always be the ones to drag students, point the way out to them, or persuade them. Therefore, a different solution is needed.

At the beginning of this chapter, I described four factors influencing students' decisions of whether to step out of their comfort zones (page 96). These are (1) thinking of challenge as being worth the effort; (2) having a sense of personal control or efficacy during the challenge; (3) feeling as if they have tacit permission to make mistakes or even fail; and (4) being in the habit of taking on challenges. Among the huge volume of research on motivation, one meta-analysis stands out. Based on comprehensive investigations into what motivates students, researchers Cristina D. Zepeda, Rachel S. Martin, and Andrew C. Butler (2020) identify two criteria that stand out above all the others. These match the Goldilocks principle (Kidd et al., 2012) described in section 3.5 (page 106).

1. Students should perceive that achievement is possible and that they will be able to solve the puzzle eventually.
2. Students need to feel a sense of progress toward their goal, and they need to feel as if they are getting better or at least taking steps in the right direction.

In both cases, the Learning Pit can make a worthwhile contribution.

The next four sections cover what the Learning Pit model is, why I created it, how to introduce it to your students, and ways to make it work with all the themes of this book: challenge, feedback, dialogue, growth mindset, and questioning.

3.7.1 Learning Is Not Linear

Too often, learning is described as if it were linear. Start with step 1, then take steps 2, 3, 4, and 5. Pause to reflect and connect. Make sure you are happy with your first five steps, then take steps 6, 7, and 8. Keep going, even if your steps are small or slow. Eventually, you will make it.

It sounds ideal, except that so very often, steps 1 and 2 are *not* followed by 3 and 4. Instead, regression rears its head. What we thought was straightforward enough last week turns out to have lots of exceptions this week. What we could do yesterday isn't working quite as well today. This is normal. Learning tends *not* to look like a set of stairs heading toward excellence. Instead, performance dips will occur along the way.

I think students need to know this, not so they are fearful but so they can prepare better. If they anticipate setbacks, they can recognize them more easily when they occur, acknowledge that they are normal rather than things that only happen to them, and use productive strategies and attitudes to overcome the dips. I call this going through the Learning Pit.

In this video, James introduces the Learning Pit.

3.7.2 The Foundations of the Learning Pit

When I first introduced the Learning Pit to my students, it looked as basic as it does in figure 3.4. I didn't even have a whiteboard back then, so I had to create the original in chalk. Over time, as I shared the idea with colleagues—both in school and at teaching conferences—the model grew in popularity. Eventually, I got around to writing about it, first in an article for the journal *Teaching Thinking and Creativity* (Nottingham, 2007) and then in my first book, *Challenging Learning* (Nottingham, 2010). Now, if you do a search online for the Learning Pit, you will see hundreds of millions of results. So, it would be fair to say my model has become popular.

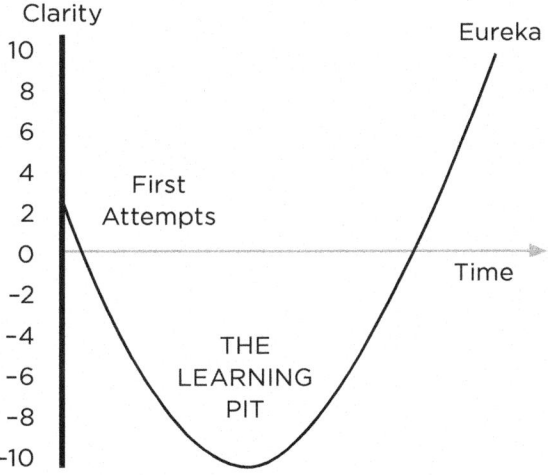

Figure 3.4: The Learning Pit original illustration.

Approval of this model has been helped by mentions in many quarters, including *The New York Times* (Anderson, 2022), the *Financial Times* (Green, 2016), BBC Radio 4 (January 11, 2020, 4:15 p.m.), Cambridge Assessment International Education (Whyte, 2016), and the Finnish Broadcasting Company (November 13, 2018, 6:43 a.m.). The model appears in books by King's College London visiting professor of education Guy Claxton (2017) and Stanford University professor Jo Boaler (2022). It is recommended by Ron Ritchhart (2023) of Harvard University's Graduate School of Education, John Hattie (2017) of the University of Melbourne Graduate School of Education, and Carol Dweck (2016), the Lewis and Virginia Eaton Professor of Psychology at Stanford University.

Since those early days of chalk pits melting on a playground wall, the illustrations have improved markedly. There are now four main types, examples of which are shown in this section.

By far the most popular version shows the thoughts someone is likely to experience as they go through the Learning Pit (figure 3.5). Please note that the Learning Pit is generally a collaborative experience, so this version would be even better if it featured a group of students thinking about their experiences.

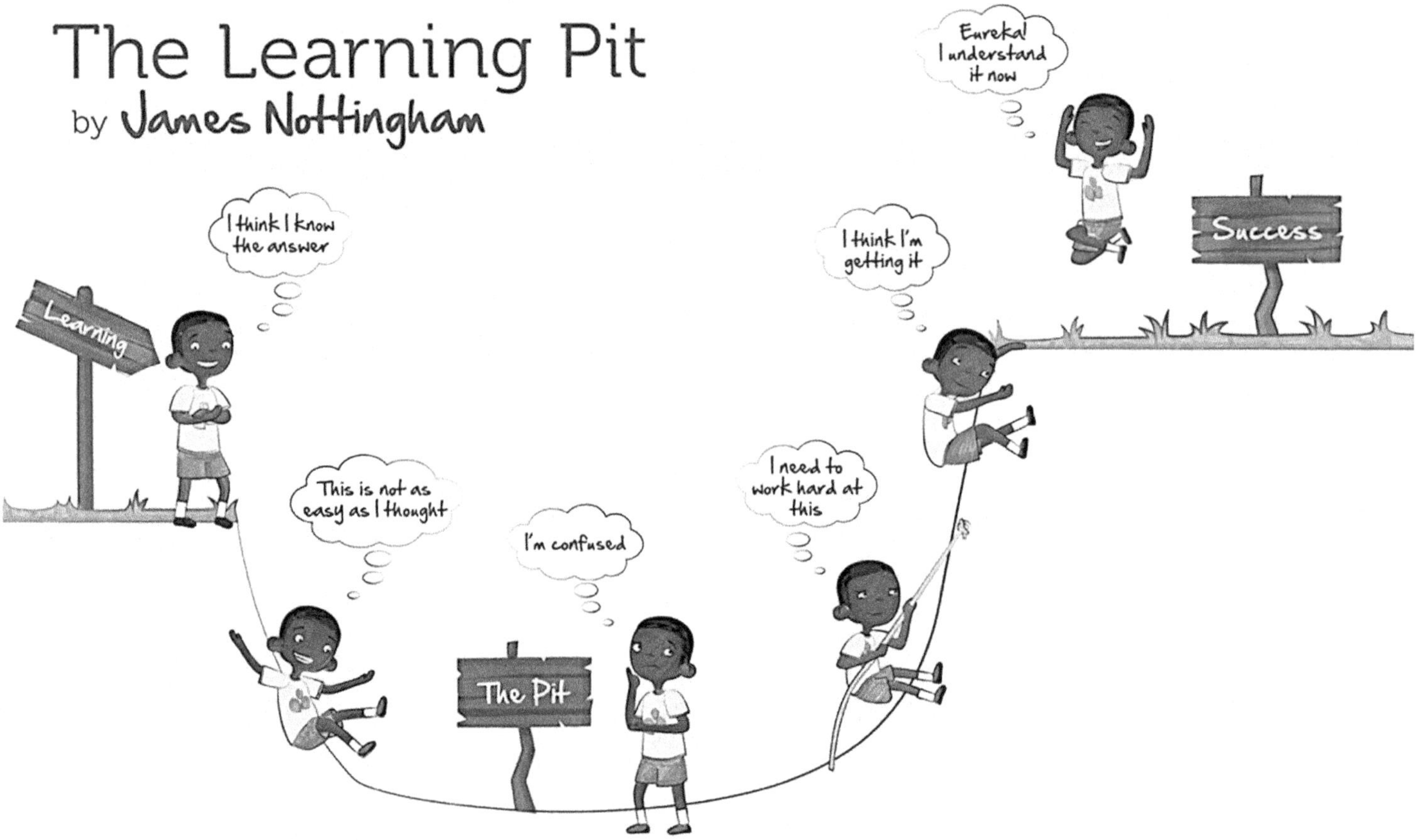

Source: James Nottingham.

Figure 3.5: The Learning Pit, version 1—Thought bubbles.

Use this QR code to download high-resolution color images of figures 3.5 to 3.8 and 4.13.

Another popular version is blank apart from a few labels. Students stick photographs or cartoons of themselves on whichever part of the pit they believe they are in currently. Figure 3.6 shows a template for this approach. You can also find lots of examples of completed versions online.

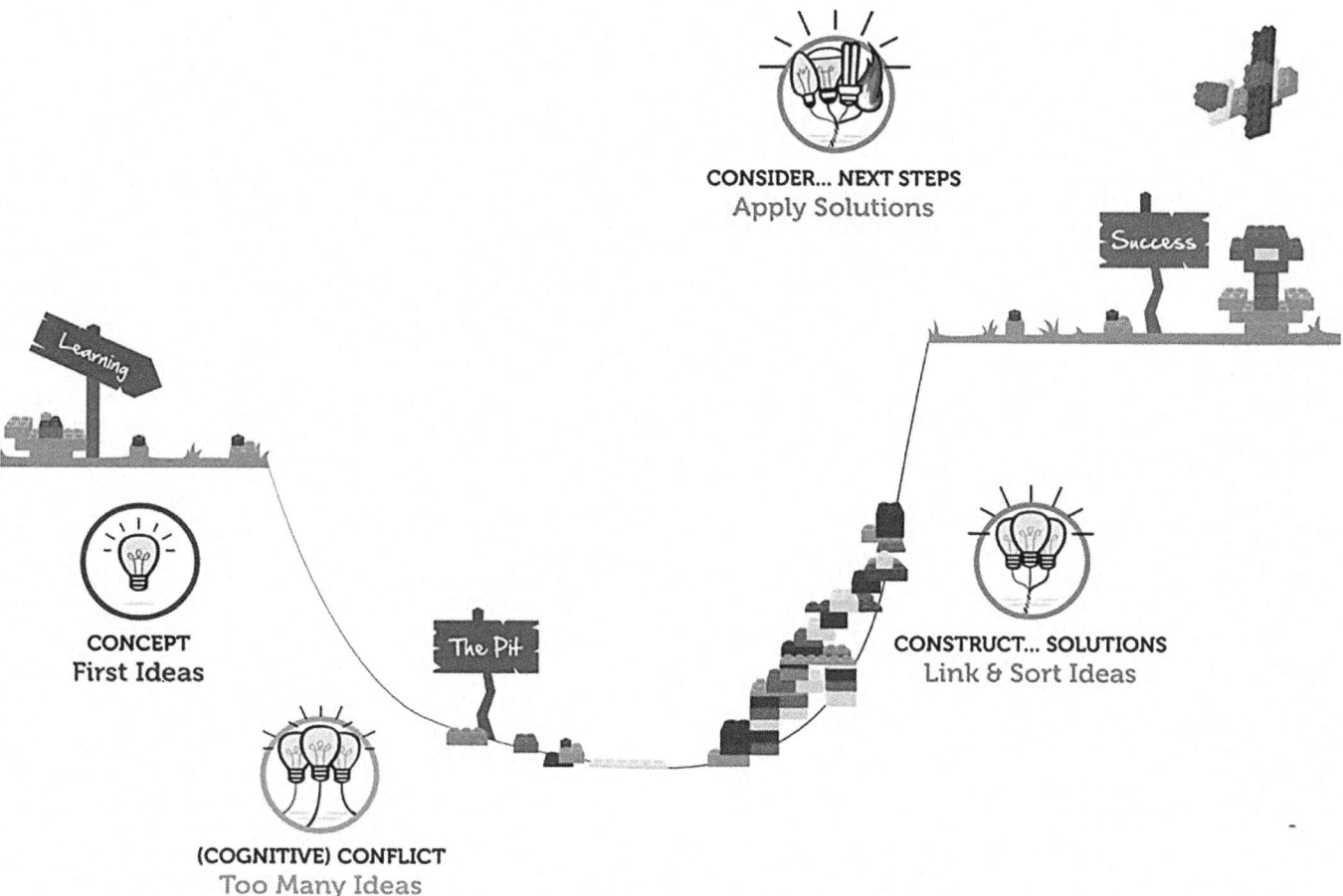

Source: *James Nottingham.*

Figure 3.6: The Learning Pit, version 2—Progress template for students.

The third version includes a lot more detail. Figure 3.7 (page 118) shows an example that I created for a rugby foundation in New Zealand. In section 4.8 (page 195), you will also see a Learning Pit with lots of detail shown.

A category recently added and proving to be very popular is the bilingual version, as in figure 3.8 (page 119). Not only are these bilingual illustrations great resources for language teachers, but they also show respect for context.

All these images are available for download from my website, LearningPit.org (https://learning pit.org). I designed them, then had the fabulous team at https://ideographic.co.uk illustrate them for me. You are very welcome to use them for educational purposes with your students. Use the code ST-JN2024 to gain full, free access. Alternatively, you could design your own version and send it to me so that I can ask Ideographic to turn it into the house style. This approach has been used for all the bilingual versions you can find on my website.

One final category that I should mention includes misleading versions of the Learning Pit. A classic example of this is an illustration that has been reposted thousands of times, although I can't find the original source. It has a brick wall in the middle; I'm not against that per se, but

Source: James Nottingham.

Figure 3.7: The Learning Pit, version 3—Detailed descriptions.

it makes the version I'm talking about easily identifiable. The reason I don't like that illustration, apart from its lack of attribution, is that its finish point is at the same height as its starting point. Some students find this odd. They wonder what the purpose is of going through all the effort to work their way through the pit only to end up at the same level of understanding. They argue it would be better to bypass the pit or skip over it rather than go through it. Granted, only students who are literal in their thinking or have a particular fondness for detail really worry about (or even spot) this inference, but I want the pit to be fully inclusive, so I think the implication is important.

Figure 3.9 (page 120) shows the difference I am describing. The image on the left is similar to versions I see in many classrooms. The one on the right is a more accurate representation of the concept I originally envisaged.

A quick note before we continue: As you may have noted on the phrase's first use in the introduction (page xi), I hold a registered trademark for the Learning Pit (Patent & Trademark, Reg. No. 6,381,157). This seems heavy-handed, particularly in an educational context. If good ideas can help improve learning experiences, then I think they should be

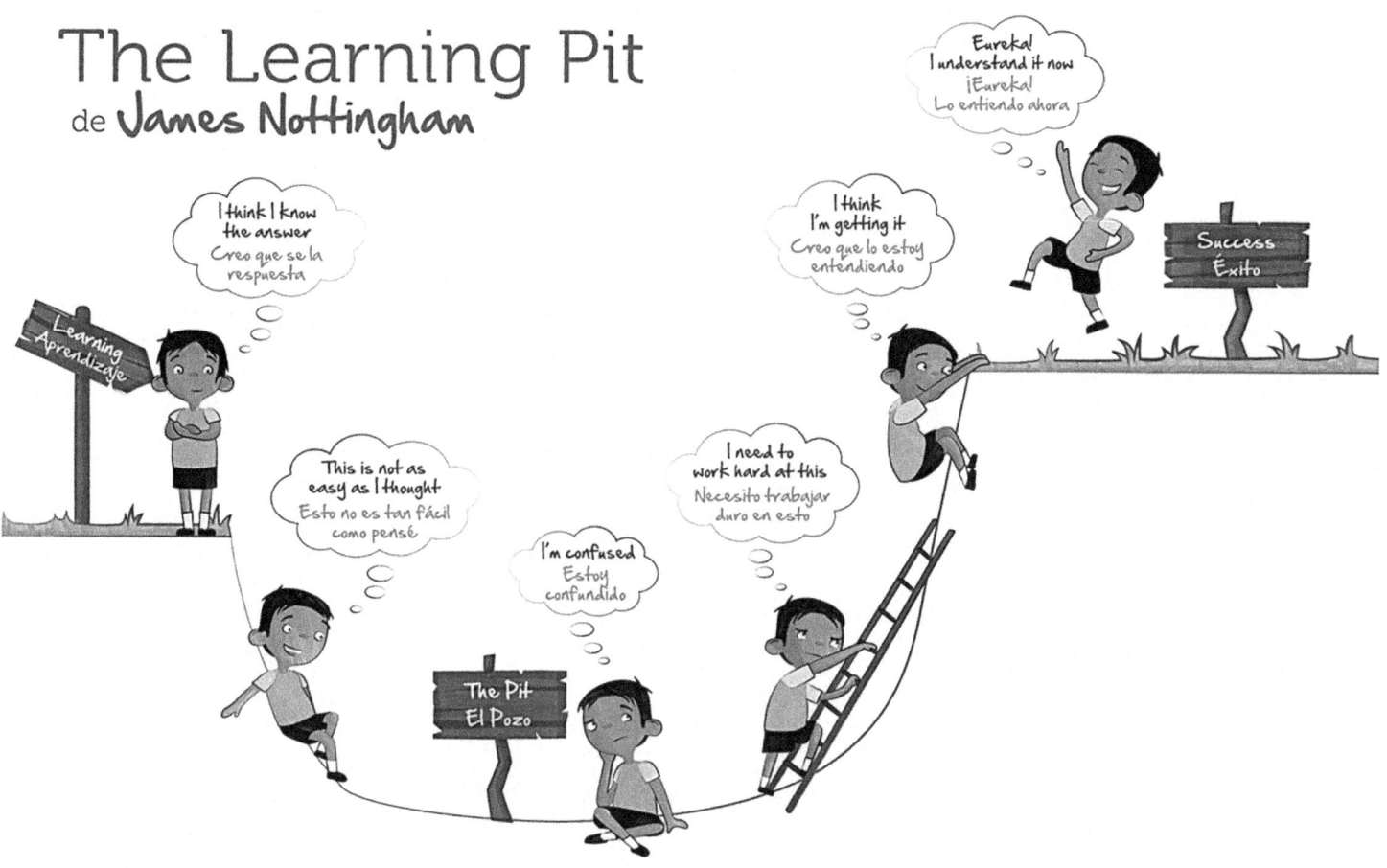

Source: James Nottingham.

Figure 3.8: The Learning Pit, version 4—A bilingual illustration.

made freely available. That said, attribution doesn't go amiss! So, here's some information to help you with that.

- If you are using any of the images downloaded from LearningPit.org, then you should include the following: "© 2021 The Learning Pit by James Nottingham."

- If you or your students create your own illustrations, then any posted online or made into a display should have this message: "Illustrations by [your name or class name] from James Nottingham's Learning Pit."

- If you wish to quote the first time the Learning Pit appeared in print, then you could use "(Nottingham, 2007)" to refer to this source: Nottingham, J. A. (2007). Exploring the Learning Pit. *Teaching Thinking and Creativity, 8:2*(23), 64–68.

However, if you want to refer to my use of the Learning Pit in any of the twelve books I have written, this one included, then you can use the normal referencing convention.

Figure 3.9: The wrong way (left) and right way (right) to draw a Learning Pit.

3.7.3 Students' Introduction to the Learning Pit

There are three ways I recommend introducing the Learning Pit to students. First, if you work with learners in the seven- to thirteen-years-old range, then I'm delighted to say that I have posted an appropriate introduction video online.

In this video, James introduces the Learning Pit.

Second, if you work with students over thirteen years old, then you might want to get them to do some online research first. Reading *The New York Times* article "Learning the Right Way to Struggle" (Anderson, 2022) and comparing some of the different Learning Pit images available on the web would be a good way to start.

Third, over the next few pages, I share some key points that I encourage you to use when introducing the Learning Pit to your students. This is not a script! You do not need to follow it word for word. Sharing *something* like this, however, will help make the starting point an effective one.

Example Narrative To Use When Introducing the Learning Pit to Your Students

I want to introduce you to the Learning Pit. It is an illustration of the path we often take when learning something new.

A lot of people think that learning is a series of steps, each better than the one before. Unfortunately, that's not normally the case. Instead, we tend to take two or three steps forward, and after that, we feel as if we're going backward for a while. This can be really dispiriting if we think we're the only ones suffering these setbacks, but it turns out that everyone experiences this. Think of any of your favorite performers, online personalities, or sports stars. Look hard enough, and you will find they all have stories of struggle—how they had to dig deep to overcome challenges, how they felt like giving up but didn't. And look at where they are now.

In school, these dips happen all the time. For example, I show you a new technique in [subject], and it all seems to make sense. You have a go, and it works. Some people even call this beginner's luck. But then, when you try it again for homework or return to it a few days later, it doesn't seem to work as well. Maybe you've forgotten a crucial aspect of it, or maybe you've gone from the first, simple version to the more accurate (but complicated) version. Whatever the reason, you feel as if you've gone backward rather than forward. This is called going into the Learning Pit.

Being in the Pit Is Good for Us

When you find yourself in the pit, do not worry! Remind yourself that this means you are learning. In fact, there is a lot of research to show that the more you struggle with something, the longer lasting your learning will be. Researchers call this **retrieval**. So, sometime in the future, when you need to retrieve what you've learned, your brain is more likely to remember it if it was a challenge when you first came across it. One of the best-known researchers, Robert Bjork, even calls this **desirable difficulty**! Of course, it doesn't feel very desirable when you're struggling, but what he means is the results are desirable because memories last longer, understanding deepens, and learning habits strengthen.

Being in the Learning Pit is therefore good for us, so good that I'm going to try to get us into it as much as possible. [Add an evil laugh for full kitsch effect.] I'm going to use questioning to get us to think more rather than give hints to make things easier. I will design lessons that purposefully take us out of our comfort zones and into the Learning Pit. I won't make things so hard that we won't know where to start; I will try to get the balance just right.

The best balance for learning is that after lots of trial and error, you succeed with about 80 percent of what you are trying to do. That means 20 percent should be just out of your reach. Of course, we all want to succeed as much as possible—and when it comes to performances that matter (for example, competitions, exams, shows, and so on), acing them is fabulous. But when it comes to learning, we should be engaging in things that are just a little beyond us right now.

Have you noticed that I keep saying "**our** learning" and "get **us** into the Learning Pit"? That is because I plan to go into the pit with you. This will give me insight into your thought processes. It will show me what you understand and what you need more help with. All of this will give me a much better idea about what to teach you next.

So, you're likely to hear me say things such as, "I'm sorry, I don't understand. Could you give me more information? Or an example? Or a reason?"

When I do this, don't worry that you're not making sense. Just think to yourself that what I'm trying to do is get us all to think more.

The Learning Pit Is a Collaborative Endeavor

I mentioned earlier that I'm aiming to get everyone into the Learning Pit. However, you do not need to wait for me to do this. I want you to do it for yourself and for each other. So, if you're finding things easy, look for ways to make things more challenging for yourself. Maybe add or subtract a variable, try it in a different way, use a nondominant strategy, rearrange the sequence, look for exceptions, or find reasons. Find any challenge that will make you think harder. Try not to think of lessons as things to get through just because you have to be here. See them as opportunities to improve your learning abilities, to strengthen your learning muscles. Get yourself into the pit as often as you can.

I also want you to do the same for each other. When you engage in group work, your job will not be to agree with each other. Do not make things easier for your classmates. Instead, you should get them to think more. Ask them questions. Encourage them to give examples, reasons, and meanings. The more you cause them to think, the more they will learn. The better they become as learners, the more they will be able to challenge you—and so everyone's standards of learning will lift.

Next Steps

At the beginning, you will get lots of opportunities to try things out without pressure. So, don't worry—you will have time to explore. Only after you've made a good start will I try to get you into the pit.

When this happens, it will feel as if I'm moving you from straightforward to complex, or from easy to challenging. At least I hope it will because that's what I will be trying to do with and for you all!

Once you're in the Learning Pit, we will find ways to problem-solve. Throughout this school year, I will teach you lots of ways to do this. It will include sorting ideas, ranking things from best to worst (and deciding what **best** means), looking for similarities and differences, identifying cause and effect, hypothesizing, rearranging sequences and noting the effect, and analyzing concepts.

A combination of these strategies will help us find better solutions, which, in turn, will take us out of the Learning Pit. Sometimes, this will best be done by yourself, and other times, it will be a collaborative exercise.

Taking Care of Each Other in the Learning Pit

Everyone can make progress. We know this for sure. Research proves it, and experience shows it time and again. Today, some of us will start further ahead than others, but that's because they have already made lots of progress. They've put in lots of hours, worked at something for longer, thought about it more. Others haven't had those advantages—yet. So, when we all get into the Learning Pit, we will do so from different vantage points.

Some ways in which we will take care of each other as we go through the pit include the following.

- We will encourage each other. There will be no making fun of someone for struggling with or not knowing something. If they are in the pit, we should cheer them on, not poke fun at them. Ever.
- If you find that you're the only one in the pit, ask someone else to join you (notice that I didn't say, "Ask someone to rescue you"). Invite them to examine the conundrum you are working on to see if they can make sense of it. Ask them questions, and look for examples together. What works and what doesn't? What reasons can you both find?
- If you see other people going into the pit, but you haven't gone in yet, look for ways to challenge yourself. Remember that the optimum balance for learning is 80/20, with the 20 percent representing things beyond you right now that cause confusion or frustration. So, ask others to help challenge you. Or look at what is perplexing them to see if they've found something that will help challenge you more. Help each other out—not by giving each other the answers but by challenging each other more!

3.8 Create Challenge With the Learning Pit: A Step-by-Step Guide

I have written four books focused entirely on ways to guide students through the Learning Pit. The most in-depth guide is *The Learning Challenge* (Nottingham, 2017). The pocket guide is *The Learning Pit* (Nottingham, 2020). I have coauthored two books with lesson guides and resources: *Learning Challenge Lessons, Elementary* (Nottingham & Nottingham, 2018) and *Learning Challenge Lessons, Secondary English Language Arts* (Nottingham, Nottingham, & Bollom, 2019). So, if you want a much broader set of resources and examples from across the curriculum, choosing one or more of these books would be the best way to go.

For the purposes of this book, I will show you how to get started with the model and indicate ways in which it helps create optimal levels of challenge for your students. The following guide centers on concepts, but the approach can work just as well in performance-based contexts such as physical education, music, art, and drama. Indeed, wherever there is challenge within learning, being in the pit can be a helpful reference for students.

Originally, I conceived four stages of the Learning Pit. Since then, I have added extra steps within stages 2 and 3 that I will also show you. Figure 3.10 illustrates these stages.

1. **Concept:** The Learning Pit begins with a concept that students are familiar with. This concept should be relevant to their current studies. Examples are shown in section 3.8.1, page 126.

2. **Conflict:** Once students have expressed their early ideas about the chosen concept, questioning is used to create cognitive conflict. This happens when students hold two or more conflicting beliefs about the same thing. The dissonance they experience creates the feelings of being in the pit and provokes the use of higher-order-thinking skills.

3. **Construct:** Experiencing cognitive conflict helps students think deeply about concepts. At some point, though, they need to create a resolution that builds their understanding. This stage is focused on doing just that by connecting, analyzing, sorting, and categorizing and grouping ideas into an arrangement that is accurate and functional.

4. **Consider:** Having constructed a stronger, more nuanced understanding of the concept, students will have emerged from the pit. They can then look for ways to apply their new ideas to different contexts. They should also engage in metacognitive thinking by reflecting on their learning journey and considering what they have learned and how.

In performance-based learning contexts, these four stages can be thought of as the following.

1. Preparation and goal setting
2. New technique (that seems to conflict with well-rehearsed techniques)
3. Trial and error
4. Application and reflection

The four stages of the Learning Pit match these stages in the SOLO Taxonomy (see section 2.3, page 56).

1. Unistructural (few ideas)
2. Multistructural (lots of ideas)
3. Relational (connecting ideas)
4. Extended abstract (transferring ideas)

John B. Biggs and Kevin F. Collis (1982), the creators of the SOLO Taxonomy, showed a role for cognitive dissonance at *every* stage of SOLO, not just at stage 2. I agree with this interpretation—after all, challenge provides the necessary catalyst for movement from *any* stage of learning to the next. So, when I match stage 2 of the Learning Pit with stage 2 of the SOLO Taxonomy, I do so to emphasize the number of ideas available to students at the time. I have heard people use the phrase *being in the pit* to mean that they know nothing, whereas the correct interpretation is that they know lots.

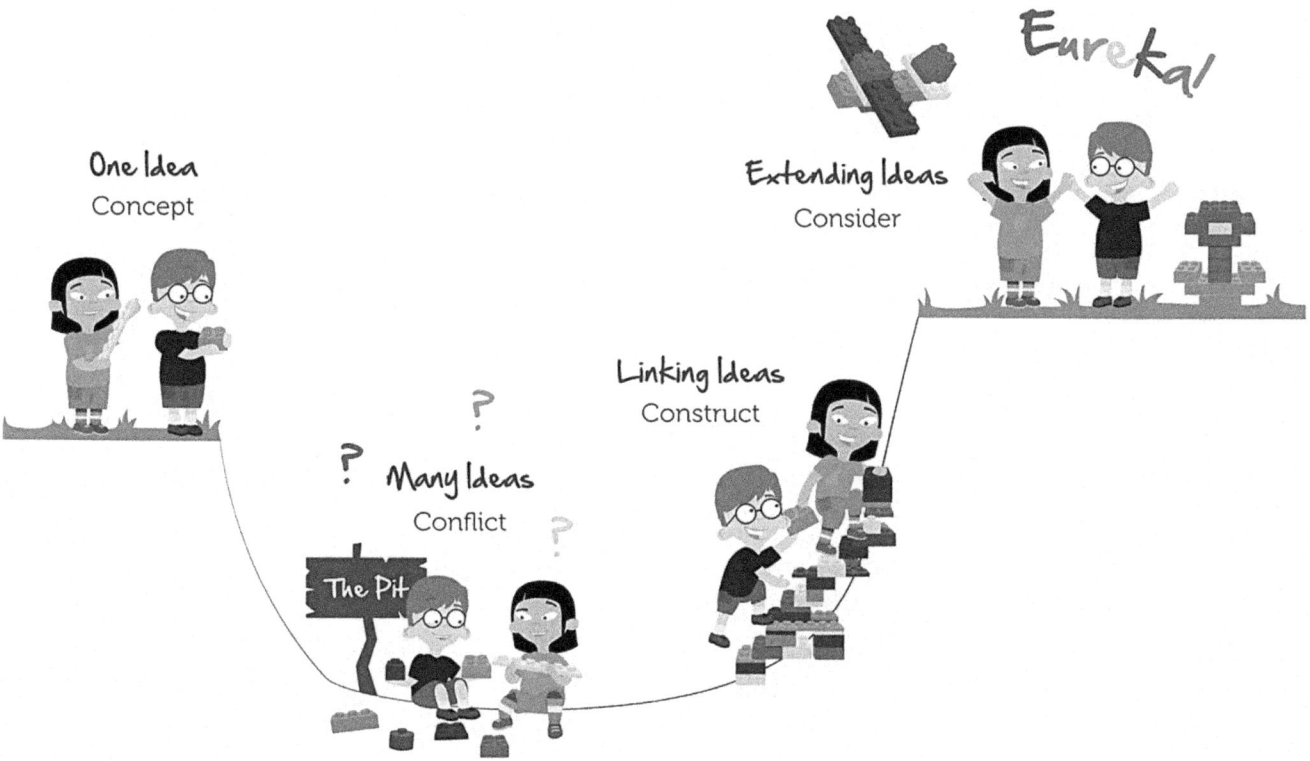

Source: James Nottingham.

Figure 3.10: The four stages of the Learning Pit.

3.8.1 The Learning Pit Stage 1: *Concept*

The Learning Pit typically begins with a concept that your students are familiar with. As I noted earlier, it can just as effectively apply in performance-based contexts such as drama and physical education.

Having a concept of something means being able to recognize that thing and being able to distinguish it from other things. For example, being able to recognize advice when offered it and to distinguish it from instructions or orders could be said to signify having a concept of advice.

There are many different types of concepts. For the purposes of this book, I have focused on two main types: (1) *abstract* and (2) *concrete*, which are often referred to as *theoretical* and *practical*.

- Abstract concepts are most commonly characterized by having no physical or spatial grounding. Examples of abstract concepts include notions of love, truth, conscience, success, goodness, and morality, plus many isms, such as racism, sexism, communism, and feminism.

- Concrete concepts are physical things that can be seen, heard, felt, tasted, or smelled. Examples of concrete concepts include chalk, footballs, books, animals, houses, cities, tables, waves, mountains, and rivers.

Taking students into the Learning Pit is often easier with abstract concepts, but it is possible with concrete concepts. For example, you could ask your students what a *chair* is. They are likely to say, "It's something to sit on." If you wanted to create cognitive conflict and take them into the pit, then you could point out that you can sit on a beach or the floor, but they wouldn't be thought of as a chair. Your students might then improve their answer, saying, "A chair is something to sit on that has four legs," at which point you could remind them that a table has four legs and can be sat on, or that some chairs have fewer than four legs or even no legs at all. So, they might come back with, "A chair is meant for sitting on and normally has a back to it," and you could ask whether stools are chairs even though they don't have backs to them, and so on.

Now, of course, the concept of a chair is unlikely to feature in a curriculum topic, but I think the point still stands; it is possible to get your students into the Learning Pit even with seemingly straightforward, concrete concepts.

The concepts that more obviously lend themselves to taking students into the Learning Pit are abstract notions that are open to interpretation. In section 2.4.1 (page 58), I gave lots of example concepts for asking your students, "What's the difference?" These included *artificial, artwork, change, design, experiment, force,* and so on. In section 2.5.2 (page 70) are other examples to use with the convention Is–Could Be–Never Would Be. These include *competition, energy,* and *poetry*.

A lot of teachers use the Learning Pit in social-emotional learning contexts. Concepts from that area of study that are particularly suitable include those shown in figure 3.11.

Behavior	Emotions	Hatred	Relationships
Bravery	Empathy	Human	Responsibility
Bullying	Enterprise	Humane	Revenge
Community	Equality	Justice	Rights
Conscience	Equity	Life choices	Risk
Consequence	Fairness	Love	Self-awareness
Courage	Fame	Nation	Talent
Culture	Freedom	Neighbor	Truth
Decisions	Friendship	Optimism	Value
Democracy	Growth	Perspective	Welfare
Duty	Growth mindset	Pessimism	Willpower

Figure 3.11: The Learning Pit social-emotional context words.

Every curriculum topic has at least one central concept that can be the focus for taking your students into the Learning Pit. Bear in mind, however, that your students need to be familiar with that concept *before* you try to take them into the pit. After all, you are aiming to create cognitive conflict in their minds (see the next section, page 129), and this is possible only if they already have an idea or two to conflict with. There is little point in trying to take first-grade students into the pit about the concepts of democracy, patriotism, foreshadowing, and the law of opposites, because they simply won't have enough familiarity with any of these topics for cognitive conflict to exist.

That said, there are many topics that students understand even before they study them. For example, even the youngest students in elementary school have a sense of fairness and fair testing, heroism and heroes, friendship and friendliness, and value and worth long before these topics appear as areas of the curriculum.

The guide I use in determining whether a concept is suitable for the purposes of deeper investigation is to ask, "What is [that concept]?" and "What does [that concept] mean?" If either of these questions provokes a first response along the lines of, "It depends," that is a good indication the concept will work for the Learning Pit approach. For example, a first response to the question, "What is power?" is likely to be, "It depends on what sort of power we're talking about, who wields it, and toward what or whom." Similarly, "What is evidence?" can lead to considerations of type (circumstantial, forensic, demonstrative, or anecdotal) and context (science, mathematics, literature, politics, and so on), all of which lend themselves to the creation of cognitive conflict.

Concepts that are central to curriculum topics I have explored with students include those shown in figures 3.12 and 3.13 (page 128).

3.8.1.1 Facts or Concepts

Facts don't lend themselves to taking students into the pit as well as concepts do. They have close relationships with each other, which makes distinguishing between them difficult at times. Nonetheless, the differences are important.

Choice: Does the poem "The Road Not Taken" show us how to make the right choice?

Conflict: Was the California Gold Rush of 1848 the main cause of conflict between Native Americans and European Americans?

Dreams: How are dreams presented in *Jane Eyre*?

Fame: Is fame important?

Foreshadowing: Which example of foreshadowing in *Of Mice and Men* has the most impact on the reader?

Friendship: Was Toto Dorothy's only true friend?

Gender stereotypes: Does Louisa May Alcott's *Little Women* accept or challenge gender stereotypes?

Happiness: Did Anne Frank experience happiness?

Intent: What was the intent of President Reagan's speech at Moscow State University in 1988?

Love: Is Romeo really in love?

Monster: Does Heathcliff become more or less monstrous over the course of *Wuthering Heights*?

Patriotism and pacifism: Was Wilfred Owen a patriot or a pacifist?

Power: Who has the most power in *Romeo and Juliet*?

Responsibility: Who was responsible for the death of William in Mary Shelley's *Frankenstein*?

Rhetoric: For example, why was Winston Churchill's speech effective?

Symbolism: Which is the most important symbol in *The Great Gatsby*?

Sympathy: Do we feel sympathy for Scrooge in stave 1 of *A Christmas Carol*?

Theft: Was it acceptable for Liesel to steal in *The Book Thief*?

Tragic hero: Was Macbeth really a tragic hero?

Victim and villain: Is Tybalt a villain or a victim?

Figure 3.12: Examples of literature and language concepts.

Apologizing (Should you always say sorry?)	Greatest	Responsibility
	Habitats	Risk
Being the best	Help (people who help us)	Rubbish
Choice	Hero	Shape and space
Color	Knowledge	Social media
Cost	Language	Stories and fairy tales
Deforestation	Living things	Time
Exploration	Making decisions	Treasure
Fairness	Metaphor	Xenophobia
Friendship	Original	You (identity)
Good thinking	Proof	Zoos

Figure 3.13: Examples of concepts for elementary school students.

Ordinarily speaking, a concept is an abstract idea generalized from particular evidence, whereas a fact is something that is known to be true or a thing that is indisputably the case. Put a different way, concepts and facts differ in their level of abstraction. Facts can be memorized, whereas concepts require more deduction and reasoning.

A good example of a fact is that the smallest country in the world is Vatican City. This is known to be true and is indisputably the case. However, within that sentence is the term *country*, which is an abstract notion based on several different variables, including area, governance, borders, history, citizenship, and so on. Indeed, there are several entities—including Taiwan, Palestine, and Kosovo—that are recognized as countries by some and not by others. Therefore, this points to the idea that *country* is a concept.

Other examples include the following.

Fact: The number seven can be written as the digit 7.

Concept: The term *number* is a concept.

Fact: Her name is Kamala.

Concept: *Name* is a concept, particularly when we contrast its use with personal names, proper names, general names, nicknames, and so on.

Fact: Your heart pumps blood through your body.

Concept: When we use *heart* to say "take heart" or "think with your heart," then *heart* becomes a concept.

Fact: The leaves of living plants are usually green.

Concept: When we use *living* to ask, "Are you really living or simply just existing?" then living becomes an abstract notion and, as such, is a concept.

In many ways, facts are easier to teach—and learn—than concepts. It's certainly easier to test someone's knowledge of facts than it is to test their understanding of concepts. This probably explains, at least in part, why facts and knowledge dominate so much of what is taught in schools. In fact, we often look at learning standards and try to convert them to a bank of facts to be learned, whereas we might be better served searching for the concepts underlying the written standards.

That is not to say that concepts should be ignored. In fact, quite the opposite! Concepts should be explored so students have the opportunity to make meaning, view perspectives, consider exceptions, and test generalizations. This importance of understanding concepts is one of many justifications for including Learning Pit experiences in everyday teaching.

3.8.2 The Learning Pit Stage 2: *Conflict*

Stage 2 of the Learning Pit concerns creating cognitive conflict in the minds of your students. It is this step that can place the Learning Pit at the heart of a culture of thoughtful, engaging challenge.

Cognitive conflict is the disagreement between two or more ideas or opinions a person holds at the same time. In life, this can lead to unpleasant feelings of unease; but used wisely in an educational context, it can lead to deeper thinking and a greater need for higher-order-thinking skills, such as critical and analytical thinking, problem solving, evaluation, and metacognition.

3.8.2.1 Examples of Cognitive Conflict

When asked to give an example of cognitive conflict that is relevant for students, I tend to offer the idea that stealing is wrong but that Robin Hood is thought of as a moral character. Many people come back with the justification that he stole from the rich and gave to the poor, but when pressed, these same people agree that stealing from banks and giving to homeless people today would be thought of as wrong. Then, there is the consideration of what constitutes stealing. What about, for example, taking a pen from a hotel room or amenities from the bathroom; spotting a good idea on a classroom wall and replicating it in your classroom; taking someone else's parking spot; sharing someone else's exciting news ahead of time, thereby stealing their thunder; hearing an idea and repeating it as if it were your own; or using ChatGPT to "write" an essay?

Examples of cognitive conflict that students might experience include knowing that it is best to tell the truth, but also there are advantages to telling lies; that killing animals is cruel, but eating meat is fine; that body image used in advertising doesn't reflect reality, but nonetheless, they are expected to look as similar to the advertised people as possible; and that pain is the body's way of saying stop, but healthy exercise can cause pain. Students might also know from past experience that the latest phone or device will not add value to their lives, but also think that this latest edition will be different; and they might be told that by spending money, they will save money, but also know that the opposite is true.

There are a great number of situations in literature that offer cognitive conflict. A well-known one—or at least a frequently repeated one—appears in *Animal Farm*: "All animals are equal, but some animals are more equal than others" (Orwell, 1945). Then, there is the interaction between Alice and the Mad Hatter in *Alice's Adventures in Wonderland*:

> "Take some more tea," the March Hare said to Alice, very earnestly. "But, I've had nothing yet," Alice replied in an offended tone, "so I can't take more." "You mean you can't take less," said the Hatter. "It's very easy to take more than nothing." (Carroll, 1865)

3.8.2.2 Features of Cognitive Conflict

Cognitive conflict will ordinarily include a *but* in the middle—for example, "It is always nice to help people, but it is not nice to help your friends bully someone."

For cognitive conflict to exist, a person needs to agree with the points of view on either side of the *but*. For example, it would *not* be cognitive conflict to say, "Some people believe the world is flat, but of course the world is round," because that is refuting one point of view and believing in another.

The viewpoints on either side of the *but* should include the same subject. For example, it would not be cognitive conflict to say, "Fruit is good for you, but fried food is bad for you," because two different subjects—fruit and fried food—are compared. However, it could be written as, "Sugar is bad for you, but there is lots of sugar in fruit, and that is good for you," because sugar is now the focus on either side of the *but*.

Using *always* or *never* in the first assertion can be very useful because then you just need to find an exception in order to create cognitive conflict. For example, we should always tell the truth, but sometimes lying is the right thing to do (for example, telling young children that Santa brings gifts at Christmas); or you should never kill another person, but sometimes it is necessary to kill (for example, in times of war or for the purposes of voluntary euthanasia).

3.8.2.3 Best Types of Cognitive Conflict

When someone experiences cognitive conflict, they might respond badly to the confusion, or it might energize them to figure things out. As teachers, we are responsible for encouraging our students to do the latter; we need to help them respond proactively and positively to cognitive conflict. In doing so, we give them more opportunities to develop habits of good thinking, problem solving, and positive attitudes toward challenge.

There are many ways to create cognitive conflict in the minds of your students. Before I share some of these, they should all be underpinned by the following values.

- **Challenging, not point scoring:** The Learning Pit is designed to cause participants to think more deeply and more compellingly about their learning. It promotes a spirit of exploration to identify complexity and subtlety. It is not about scoring points, nor is it about putting someone else down to propel yourself further. Every interaction in Learning Pit (and indeed classroom) experiences ought to be underpinned by a sense of being in this together, the pursuit of awareness and understanding, and the synthesis of new ideas.

- **Humility and gentle humor:** These are difficult to convey in a book, but they are absolutely key aspects of Learning Pit experiences. Giving your students the impression that you are interrogating them in an effort to discredit or disprove their hypotheses is both arrogant and discouraging. Instead, you should take a lighthearted and self-effacing attitude. This means using phrases such as, "Sorry, I don't understand" or "I don't think I am very clear about this." It means laughing with, rather than at, your students; admitting you don't have all the answers; asking unpretentious questions; and using a tone of voice and body language that suggest you are in the pit with your students.

- **Playful trickery:** On some occasions, Learning Pit experiences feel a little like a form of language trickery or wordplay. This is by no means the intention and should be avoided where possible. However, in some ways, one person's playfulness is another person's trickery, so perhaps it can't be avoided altogether. It might be helpful, therefore, to think of the trickery of a children's magician rather than the trickery of a con artist!

3.8.2.4 Creation of Cognitive Conflict Through Questioning

In section 2.1.6 (page 46), I remarked that questioning is one of the best ways to engage your students. I also emphasized the importance of giving your students time to think (remember the three-second rule) and taking an authentic interest in their answers. Building on these important principles, figure 3.14 includes some questions that can help create cognitive conflict for your students.

Clarification

Are you saying that . . . ?

What does that mean?

Could you rephrase that?

Could you explain that a little more?

Could someone else say what they think this idea means?

Reasons

Why do you think that?

What evidence or proof do you have for saying . . . ?

Could you give us an example?

Could someone else give an example or counterexample?

Do your reasons support your conclusion?

Assumptions

What do we already know about this?

Are you assuming that . . . ?

What are we taking for granted?

Are you suggesting that . . . ?

How could we be sure of this?

Viewpoints

What would happen if . . . ?

Who or what would benefit from this?

Who or what would be disadvantaged by . . . ?

Are there alternative ways of looking at this?

When would it be better/worse/different?

Equivalence

Are there similarities between this and that?

What are the main differences between this idea and that one?

Is this the same idea as before but put in a different way?

Are these ideas of equal value?

How would you rank these ideas from most to least . . . ?

Which question led to the most (progress, thought, confusion, and so on)?

Figure 3.14: Question starters that can lead to cognitive conflict.

3.8.2.5 Creation of Cognitive Conflict With Wobblers

One of the best ways to create cognitive conflict is with *wobblers*. This is a term I first used in my earliest book, *Challenging Learning* (Nottingham, 2010). The term should evoke the sense of wobble we experience when learning to ride a bike—except that the shaky, unsteady feeling is likely to be in the minds, rather than the bodies, of your students.

Wobbler 1: If A = B

This involves asking what something is, taking whatever your students say, and then testing that response by turning it around and adding a conflicting example. For instance, if you are going to ask your students about being healthy, you could use a process that looks something like this:

If A = B, then does B = A?

A is the concept that you are considering—in this case, being healthy. *B* is a student's first response to your question.

So, let's say the student's first response is, "Being healthy is when you feel good about yourself." What you can then do is take their response and turn it around: "So, if I feel good about myself (B), does that mean that I am healthy (A)?"

Then you should add an example to increase the wobble—for example, "I might feel good about scoring points in a game, but does that make me healthy?"

Of course, this does not prove them wrong, but like on most occasions when I have used this technique, it does cause students to think more and to come back with an alternative response.

The last time I used the concept of being healthy, the dialogue progressed with a group of thirteen- to fourteen-year-olds in the way that follows. For reference, I have marked the concept each time with an *(A)* and the students' answers that I am testing with a *(B)*.

> *Teacher:* What does being healthy (A) mean?
>
> *Student 1:* It means feeling good about yourself (B).
>
> *Teacher:* So, if I feel good about myself (B), does that mean I am healthy (A)? For example, if I feel good about myself for scoring points in a game, does that make me healthy?
>
> *Student 2:* No, that's happiness—not healthiness. Being healthy (A) means being fit (B).
>
> *Teacher:* So, if I am fit (B), does that make me healthy (A)? For example, if I am fit enough to run up the stairs, does that make me healthy?
>
> *Student 2:* It depends on how many stairs there are and how quickly you run up them. Even my grandma can run up her stairs, but I wouldn't say she's fit.
>
> *Teacher:* Why not?
>
> *Student 3:* Because my grandma is old.

Teacher: Are you suggesting that old people can't be healthy?

Student 3: Well, no. For them, maybe they can be healthy just by running up one flight of stairs, but for us teenagers, we'd have to run up a lot more.

Teacher: How many more?

Student 4: It's not about how many stairs. It's about your heart rate, your blood pressure, your BMI, that kind of thing.

Student 5: Yeah, fitness is all sorts of things—like how far and fast you can run, or how much exercise you can do before you're out of breath.

Teacher: So, are you saying that the longer it takes you to get out of breath, the healthier you are?

Student 5: Yeah, kind of.

Teacher: So, someone who plays chess for five hours without getting out of breath (B) is healthier (A) than someone who gets out of breath after sprinting for thirty seconds?

Student 6: No, that's not right.

Teacher: Could you explain more, please?

Student 6: Well, obviously, chess isn't the same as sprinting. You need to be a lot fitter to sprint than you do to play chess.

Teacher: Are you suggesting that chess players are not healthy?

Student 3: No, I don't think she meant that. Did you? She meant that sprinting is tiring for the body, whereas chess isn't.

Teacher: So, do you think chess might not tire people out?

Student 7: Well, yes, it will—particularly five hours of it!

Student 4: Yeah, but that's a different kind of fitness—that's mental fitness.

Teacher: OK, so could we say there is being healthy in a physical sense but also being healthy in a mental sense too?

Student 4: Yeah, definitely—that's why people talk about mental health these days.

Teacher: So, do you think someone could be mentally healthy but not physically healthy—or the other way around?

Student 8: For sure.

Teacher: So, what does that mean for our thinking about being healthy?

Student 9: Well, you have to kind of look after both—your mind and your body—if you want to be healthy.

Teacher: So, if I look after my mind and my body (B), will that make me healthy (A)?

Student 10: Could be—it depends.

Teacher: On what?

Student 7: Ah, you're just trying to get us into the Learning Pit!

Teacher: I am indeed, because that will help everyone think a little more about our concept. So, I tell you what, let's pause there as a whole class and split into groups of three and four. In those groups, I'd like you to create a definition of healthy that you think no one else in the room will be able to challenge. Be careful to think it through before you report back, and anticipate the questions or challenges I, or other people, might have. The more watertight your definition, the better it will serve you later.

Wobbler 2: Not B

In effect, this is the opposite of the first wobbler. It involves asking what something is, taking whatever your students say, and then testing that response by turning it into a negative and adding a conflicting example. The process would look like the following:

If A = B, then if it's *not* B, does that mean it is not A?

A is the concept you are considering—for example, a river. *B* is a student's first response to your question.

So, let's imagine a student says, "A river is water flowing to the sea." I can then turn it around and add a negative by saying, "So, if there is no water (not B), does that mean it is *not* a river (not A)—for example, all the water has evaporated during a drought?"

Some examples of this process working in practice follow.

- If students say that music (A) is made of sounds including rhythm and melody that they enjoy (B), then I could say, "If I don't enjoy the sounds (not B) or can't hear the sounds (not B), does that mean it is not music (not A)?"
- If power (A) is the ability to influence people (B), then what about a president who is ignored by the people (not B)? Does that mean they have no power (not A)?
- If equality (A) means people have the same opportunities (B), does that mean that if we're not all given the same opportunity to answer a question during class (not B), we're not all equal (not A)?
- If numbers (A) are something we do mathematics with (B), but we're not doing mathematics (not B), does that mean they are no longer numbers (not A)? (For example, we're using the numbers on playing cards to win a game.)
- If social media (A) is an online platform that allows networking (B), but someone has no followers or contacts and is therefore prevented from networking (not B), does that mean they are not using social media (not A)?

Wobbler 3: General to Specific

Moving between generalizations and specific examples can make the first two wobblers work even more effectively. For example, if you were to ask what a friend (A) is and your students replied, "Someone who is nice" (B), then using wobbler 1 would look like this: "Does that mean someone who is nice (B) is your friend (A)?" And wobbler 2 would be like this: "Does that mean someone who is not nice (not B) is not your friend (not A)?"

If you then added a move from a generalization (G) to a specific example (S), the wobblers would look more like this: "Does that mean someone who is nice (B) to you today (S) would be your friend (A) forever (G)?" and "Does that mean someone who is not nice (not B) to you today (S) could never (G) be your friend (not A)?"

Here are two more examples, again with the main concept shown as *(A)*, the students' first answer as *(B)*, the generalization as *(G)*, and the specific example as *(S)*.

Example 1:

> *Teacher:* What is a friend (A)?
>
> *Student 1:* Someone who is nice (B).
>
> *Teacher:* Do friends always (G) have to be nice to each other? For example, what if your friend wasn't nice to you today (S); would that mean you were no longer (G) friends?

Example 2:

> *Teacher:* What are living things (A)?
>
> *Student 1:* Living things grow (B) and breathe and excrete.
>
> *Teacher:* What if a living thing did not grow for a few months (S)—would that mean it was no longer (G) living? For example, a plant does not grow throughout the winter months (S) but starts to grow again in springtime. Does that mean it was not living during winter?

Wobbler 4: Quantifiable

The final wobbler connects to asking for an amount or a circumstance. This is not a common wobbler, but when it is used, it can really help create cognitive conflict. In the following example, the quantifiable wobbler is marked with *(Q)*.

> *Student 1:* What is a friend (A)?
>
> *Student 2:* Someone you've known for a long time (B).
>
> *Student 1:* How long (Q)?
>
> *Student 2:* About two years.
>
> *Student 1:* So if I have known someone for two years (B), does that mean I am definitely friends with them (A)?

Student 2: No.

Student 1: And what about if I have not known someone for very long (not B)—let's say three weeks (Q). Does that mean I can't be friends with them (not A)?

Student 2: No. But the longer you know someone, the more chance you have of being friends with them.

Student 1: Really?

Teacher: You say that a friend (A) is someone you have known for a long time (B). When (Q) might that not be the case? And you say a friend (A) is someone who is nice to you (B). Can you think of an occasion when (Q) you've been friends with someone who wasn't nice (not B) to you? What did you do?

3.8.3 The Learning Pit Stage 3: *Construct*

You will know your students are in the pit because of the confusion they are experiencing. I do not mean the type of confusion someone feels when they have no idea what to do. I mean the confusion that comes with having so many options that it is difficult to know which one is best. That is why I use the term *cognitive conflict* for stage 2 of the pit, because it represents a conflict between *multiple ideas* in participants' minds. Some people prefer to use the term *cognitive dissonance*.

Once your students are experiencing this state of confusion, they will want to find a way out. On occasion, it is better to leave them in the pit (I cover the reasons why at the end of this section), but most of the time, you will want to help them climb out of the pit. This does *not* mean going back to the beginning or giving up; it means creating the conditions in which your students can construct a positive way *forward* so that they emerge *out the other side* with a more robust, well-thought-out answer. To do so will mean they have moved from an simple initial answer (stage 1) through a state of cognitive conflict (stage 2) to emerge with a much more robust, nuanced answer (stage 3).

3.8.3.1 The Way to Deal With Wrong Answers

Some teachers ask me what happens if students emerge from the pit with the wrong answer. I understand this worry, but there are so many ways to avoid it that I have never actually seen it happen!

First of all, any erroneous ideas or misconceptions will be uncovered long before your students begin constructing new ones. Your questioning—as they go *into* the pit—will reveal these. Any false information or ideas can then be gently corrected. This does not mean being confrontational or even evaluative. Instead, you can use responses such as, "Oh, that's interesting. Could you tell us more?" "Can you give us an example of how that works in practice?" "Can anyone think of any counterexamples?" and "Does anyone have an alternative point of view?" These types of questions should help your students discover errors themselves.

If this appeal to the floor doesn't work, then you could be a bit more direct with something along the lines of, "I've always understood it to work like this [insert correct idea] because [give reason]. So, for example . . ." And if that *still* doesn't work, then you might ask your students to take a moment to look up the correct information! Whichever of these approaches you take, make sure you give your students time to process and talk about the correct information *before* they begin constructing a way out of the pit.

It is interesting that Daniel Willingham (2021b), the professor of cognitive psychology that I mentioned in chapter 2 (page 19), says this about *discovery learning*:

> If students are left to explore ideas on their own, they may well explore mental paths that are not profitable. If memory is the residue of thought, then students will remember incorrect "discoveries" as much as they will remember the correct ones. . . . [So] discovery learning is probably most useful when the environment gives prompt feedback about whether the student is thinking about a problem in a useful way.

That is why your direction, your questioning, and your willingness to go through the Learning Pit with your students are crucial in making this approach successful.

3.8.3.2 Construction of Better Answers

When your students have been in the pit for a while, you will want to prompt them to move into the constructing phase. This involves using one or more problem-solving or higher-order-thinking strategies to make sense of their ideas.

Notice that I am being vague about the time frame by saying "when your students have been in the pit for a while." I say this purposefully because the actual length of time will be context dependent. For example, if you have only a few minutes available or you are working with very young students, then the "being in the pit" part might only last three to five minutes. But if you have curriculum freedom or middle or high school students, then your learners may well benefit from extended time in the pit. Thinking about how long you want your students to feel a sense of challenge will give you the answer to the question about length of time in the pit.

The typical way to begin the constructing phase is to encourage your students to list all the ideas they have come up with so far. Then, have them use this list to rank, filter, or connect their ideas in such a way that they can construct a well-thought-out, more precise answer than they had originally.

Let's imagine they have been thinking about what makes something fair. Perhaps they have come up with the following ideas through the process of their dialogue.

1. The people involved *think* it was fair.
2. No one was disadvantaged.
3. The rules were clear.
4. The rules were followed.
5. The judge, examiner, or referee was impartial.
6. Everyone (or everything) started from the same point.

7. The equipment used was the same for everyone.
8. In the case of a fair test, the instructions were followed exactly.
9. Justifications, including reasons, were given for the result.

3.8.3.3 Construction by Significance

Perhaps the best way to make sense of all the ideas your students have come up with so far is for them to decide on the relative significance of each one. They can do this using any of the ranking structures described in section 2.5.1 (page 67): diamond ranking, pyramid ranking, or line ranking.

Remind your students that the process of thinking is what is most important; they should not rush to an agreement. They should challenge each other, question each other, offer counterexamples, and so on. The purpose of any Learning Pit experience is to emerge with a more considered, robust, and nuanced answer. No points should be awarded for finishing first or making sure things are as effortless as possible for each other!

If your students use ranking to decide which of their ideas are the strongest ones, they can then combine the preferred ones into a more refined answer. For example, if they choose as their top ideas items 1, 2, and 5 from the selection in section 3.8.3.2 (page 138), they could construct a better definition along these lines: "Something is fair when an impartial observer judges it to be fair; when no one has been disadvantaged in any way; and when everyone taking part agrees it has been fair, even if they don't like the outcome."

3.8.3.4 Construction by Distinguishing Differences

It is often advantageous to describe something by comparing it with other connected things. For example, if your students wanted to explain a sport such as rugby to someone who has never seen it before, they could draw comparisons between rugby, soccer, football, and lacrosse.

In the case of the concept of fairness, you could use What's the Difference? (section 2.4.1, page 58) to prompt your students to compare their thoughts about the term *fair* with one of the following terms.

- Honest
- Correct
- Trustworthy
- Unbiased
- Equitable
- Just

For example, earlier, I suggested that a group of students decided that *fair* means the rules were clear and followed (ideas 3 and 4, page 138). If you were then to get them to think about the difference between fair and, for example, *unbiased*, they might come to realize that some rules are actually very biased, depending on who makes the rules! This, in turn, could lead them to refine their answer by saying it helps make something fair if the agreed-on rules that everyone follows are unbiased and trustworthy.

When you use the convention, "What's the difference between . . . ?" your students will typically compare their central concept with one other linked concept. An alternative is to use the Odd One Out strategy so that they compare their concept with two linked terms. (See section 2.4.2, page 60.) Using the format shown in figure 2.5 (page 63) can be helpful.

If your students are working in groups, each group could choose (or be given) two different concepts. If you then get them to give feedback to each other afterward, this could make their subsequent answers even more refined.

The strategies (1) What's the Difference? and (2) Odd One Out will help your students be more discerning about meanings. They will also offer them additional language to use in their subsequent answers. For example, they might develop their definition of *fair* to be more like this: "The term *fair* means different things in different contexts. It could relate to being trustworthy or honest, or it could be about everyone being given the same thing or opportunity. Another way of looking at it is in terms of justice or karma (for example, the result was fair)."

3.8.3.5 Construction by Refining Definitions

Another way for your students to climb out of the pit is for them to refine their definitions of the important concepts they have been thinking about. The following approaches can help with this.

- **Concept target:** Invite your students to place their ideas onto a concept target (see section 2.6.2, page 77), such as the one shown in figure 2.20 (page 78). For example, they might be inclined to place idea 1, "The people involved think it was fair," bang in the middle of the concept target because they think those who took part would be the best judges of whether something was fair. However, they might then be persuaded to place it in the outer ring—or maybe even outside the target altogether—if, for example, the people who took part were engaging in a "competition" in which they were all winners (such as a rigged election with only one serious candidate).

- **Concept line:** Take the same approach as with the concept target, but with a concept line (see section 2.6.1, page 76), your students should place their ideas on a line that runs from *is not that concept* on the left-hand side to *is that concept* on the right-hand side.

- **Venn diagram:** This diagram (see section 2.5.3, page 73) is a different way to help your students refine their definition. You (or they) will need to select a second concept to compare with their central concept. For example, your students might compare *fair* with *equal*. The last time I did this with a group of middle school students, they placed idea 2, "No one was disadvantaged," in the middle because they thought that was both fair and equal. They placed idea 3, "The rules were clear," in the fair category but not in the equal category because they thought the rules might have favored one group over another. And then they placed idea 1, "The people involved think it was fair," in the equal category but not the fair one because everyone might have been on the same side.

3.8.3.6 Construction by Being Open to Other Interpretations

The final category is about encouraging students to be aware of their own fallibility and to remain open-minded. Their answers will almost certainly have improved significantly throughout the course of the Learning Pit experience. However, this doesn't mean that the outcomes will be flawless—better, certainly, but not perfect. So, it is important to remind them that other people's views will differ from their own and that sometimes an answer that is perfect for one person is unacceptable or imprecise for another.

The three strategies I described in chapter 2 (page 19) that will help remind your students to remain open-minded are opinion lines (section 2.7.1, page 80), opinion corners (section 2.7.2, page 82), and thinking corners (section 2.7.3, page 83). Each of them has slightly different nuances, so I suggest you try them all over the course of a few weeks.

3.8.3.7 Notes to Accompany Stage 3

Stage 3 of the Learning Pit begins when your students start to clarify, connect, and sort the ideas they've been confused about. It is when the fog begins to lift and possible solutions present themselves. This sometimes takes place in an impromptu manner, whereas at other times, it requires the help of one of the strategies described in this section.

Almost always, the timing of students' ascent out of the pit varies considerably from student to student and context to context. This variability is not something to worry about—after all, it happens in every other lesson, whatever the subject—but it is something to be aware of.

Many people worry about this stage. Indeed, whenever I share the Learning Pit with teachers, there is always somebody who asks, "What happens if I get my students into the pit but I can't get them out again?"

My response to this question is as follows.

- Students resist going into the pit far more than they resist coming out of the pit, so in many ways, stage 3 is easier to lead than stage 2. When students are in the pit, they naturally look for ways to come out again by making sense of their conflicting thoughts and finding solutions to their conundrum. The main thing you will need to do is help your students identify and apply the best sense-making strategy at the right time; your students' desire for clarity will generate the momentum needed to climb out of the pit.

- The purpose of the Learning Pit is to think more, question more, and engage more. This means a quick exit from the state of cognitive conflict is not necessarily a good thing. Oftentimes, it is better to do what you can to keep your students in the pit longer. A technique that fits nicely with this idea is to pair a student who has come out of the pit with one who has yet to do so and then to give instructions along these lines: "The person who is out of the pit should try to help their partner who is still in the pit to come out. However, it is the responsibility of the person still in the pit to try to pull their partner back into the pit! Do not let them get away with easy answers! Question them, challenge them, and ask what-if and what-about questions. Make sure they haven't jumped out of the pit by sheer luck. We need to make sure everyone has developed a rock-solid understanding of the concept we're thinking about."

- Sometimes, it is advantageous to leave students in the pit so that they learn how to respond when answers are not readily available. Some students are already comfortable with this, but many are not because school tends to focus on accepted facts. Outside of school, however, young people might face many questions that do not yet have accepted answers. Examples include, What personal responsibility should someone take to ease climate change? Is a career worth having? Is it safe to post online? Should I use artificial intelligence to help with my studies? and Should the truth always be told even if it hurts others?

- Even in school, students will come across many topics that require them to be able to deal with uncertainty. Examples include, Is genetic modification a good thing? Who was to blame for the deaths of Romeo and Juliet? What makes a true hero? Should all laws be obeyed? Where does matter come from? Are exams easier or harder now than fifty years ago? and What makes us human?

3.8.3.8 The Eureka Experience

As your students climb out of the pit, they might experience the *eureka moment*, which is when a sense of clarity is reached spontaneously. It often includes the sudden realization that they now understand something that they didn't understand before. It doesn't occur every time, but when it does, it means two things: (1) your students have experienced enough cognitive conflict that the release from their sense of dissonance is visceral, and (2) they are likely to remember their learning much more vividly.

In section 2.0.5 (page 25), I mentioned that students engage much more when lessons follow the structure of a story. As I described in that section, stories set the scene, move to an incident that creates tension, add further crises to deepen tension, and then finish with a climax that makes everything clearer. Notice the similarities between this structure and the Learning Pit framework! With my model, you start with the key idea or concept; then you create cognitive conflict to provoke more spirited thinking. You give your students the opportunity to problem-solve using one or more of the dialogue structures I shared in chapter 2 (page 19), and this takes them out of the Learning Pit to a better sense of understanding. The more dramatic this resolution is, the more likely your students will experience a eureka moment.

Another connection is with the desirable difficulties (Bjork & Bjork, 2011) I mentioned earlier in this chapter. One of the categories is *generation* (see section 3.4.4, page 105), which is when students generate their own solutions rather than study a prefabricated answer. Bjork and Bjork's (2011) research shows this leads to much longer-lasting effects and greater chances of retrieval.

3.8.4 The Learning Pit Stage 4: *Consider*

The final stage of a Learning Pit experience is for your students to consider the learning journey they have been on and to look for ways to apply, adapt, and transfer their learning.

In his book *Unified Theories of Cognition*, researcher Allen Newell (1994) points out that there are two layers of problem solving: (1) applying a strategy to the problem at hand and (2) selecting and monitoring that strategy. Good problem solving, Newell (1994) observes, often depends as much on the selection and monitoring of a strategy as it does on its execution: "Competent or successful learners can explain which strategies they used to solve a problem and why, whilst less competent students monitor their own thinking sporadically and ineffectively and offer incomplete explanations" (p. 312).

Most of the meta-analyses use the term *metacognition* for the skill Newell is referring to. The overall effect size calculated from the twelve meta-analyses available is $d = 0.60$ (Hattie, 2023). So, the potential to accelerate student learning is considerable.

The good news is that metacognitive strategies can be learned and continually developed. They are not something that students either have or don't have. They can be acquired in a methodical way to begin with and then encouraged until eventually they become intellectual habits.

The questions in figure 3.15 will help your students develop their metacognitive habits. They are grouped according to the different stages of the Learning Pit. I am not advocating that you ask all of these! Instead, select two or three per section and then vary the questions from session to session. I would also encourage you to share with your students why you are asking these questions and what you expect them to gain from the experience.

Stage 1: Concept
1. Which concepts did you initially identify as interesting?
2. How did you choose your central concept?
3. Why did you choose that one rather than any of the other concepts?
4. Looking back, was that the best concept to go for?
5. What criteria did you use to decide which was the best concept?
6. What questions did you create around your chosen concept?
7. On reflection, would there have been any better questions to ask?
8. How did you choose the question you settled on?
9. What were some of your initial answers to your chosen question?
10. How accurate did these early answers turn out to be?
11. How confident were you with your early answers?
12. How did your thinking affect the first steps on your learning journey?

Stage 2: Conflict
1. What was it about the concept or the question that led to cognitive conflict?
2. Which two ideas formed the first cognitive conflict?
3. As you started to wobble, how did that make you feel?
4. How many examples of cognitive conflict did you create while you were in the pit? Can you list them?
5. Which two ideas conflicted the most and why?
6. Which ideas were easily dismissed and why?

Figure 3.15: Questions to encourage metacognition.   Continued →

7. Which skills of thinking did you use to analyze the conflict or confusion you felt in the pit?
8. Did you feel like giving up while in the pit? If so, how did you resolve to keep going?
9. Which questions did you (or somebody else) ask that helped you wobble even more?
10. On which occasions were you most aware of the importance of precise language?
11. Which of the wobblers did you use to create cognitive conflict?
12. Do you feel as if you examined all the options when you were in the pit?

Stage 3: Construct
1. When did you start to make sense of all the conflicting ideas you had in the pit?
2. Which thinking strategy did you use to help you connect and explain your ideas?
3. Which was the most useful revelation you discovered?
4. Which thinking skills were most helpful in constructing your answer?
5. How sure can you be that you did not accept easy answers?
6. At any point, did you think you'd found clarity only to find another problem? If so, please explain.
7. What misunderstandings, misconceptions, or assumptions did you uncover?
8. When you paired up with someone else who was already out of the pit, how did they help you?
9. Were you able to drag your pit partner back down into the pit? If so, how? And how did they respond?
10. What did you do to check the accuracy of your answer?
11. If you had had time, what could you have done to improve your answer even further?
12. Do you feel satisfied with the learning journey you have been on?
13. Did you have any ideas before you went into the pit that you later realized needed amending or abandoning altogether?

Stage 4: Consider
1. How did it feel to reach the eureka moment?
2. How do you know this was the eureka moment rather than merely a step on the way?
3. How did you self-regulate to help you on your learning journey?
4. In what ways do you understand the concept better now?
5. What would you do differently next time?
6. Which strategies did you use this time that you could use in other contexts?
7. Is there a different sequence you could use next time to be more effective?
8. How could you adapt your new learning to another situation?
9. What analogy, metaphor, or example could you create to explain your new learning?
10. What advice would you give others about going through the Learning Pit?
11. What questions do you still have?
12. What is the next concept that you would like to explore?
13. How might you use what you've found out this time in future sessions?

3.9 Challenge Summary

Learning is not linear. It doesn't go from one step to the second, to the third, and so on. It is far more complex than that and very contextual. However, for the purposes of this book, I have taken the liberty of imagining that the following three steps might be closely linked, even to the point of being consecutive.

1. Engage your students.
2. Encourage your students to step out of their comfort zones.
3. Use feedback to enhance the learning gains they make when they are out of their comfort zones.

This chapter has focused on the second of these steps: how to challenge your students so that they more willingly step out of their comfort zones. The research I've shared shows that this leads to enhanced learning outcomes—not necessarily in the moment, but certainly in regard to the longevity of memories and the ability of students to retrieve their learning when they need to. Indeed, researchers John F. Feldhusen and Mark D. Kroll (1991) found that students often begin with positive attitudes toward school but fail to maintain these attitudes because of the lack of appropriate challenge.

From the meta-analyses, it is clear that students engage more when the perceived challenge of a task and their own skills are high and in balance; instruction, activity, and explanation are relevant; and they have an opportunity to modify their assignment if the challenge-to-skill ratio gets off-kilter.

Researchers James L. Mandigo and Nicholas Holt (2006), for example, found that optimally challenging experiences were facilitated by (1) establishing opportunities to modify the challenge level of the activity and (2) possessing enough skill or ability to succeed eventually. When the balance was right, the experiences were associated with feelings of enjoyment and motivation to continue engaging in the activity. However, when students are given a choice of activities, they often choose easier options, not because choice is a bad thing but because they perceive—from previous rewards, grades, and praise—that many teachers prefer their students to experience straightforward success instead of problematic progress.

3.10 *Teach Brilliantly* Top Ten: *Challenge*

Challenge takes us out of our comfort zone. Vygotsky (1978) called this stepping into the zone of proximal development. I call it going through the Learning Pit.

1. **Challenge is a vital and necessary condition in the learning process.** Without it, there will be no growth, only practice.
2. However, challenge also causes performance and progress to slow down. Its benefits lie in **boosting long-term memory and the ability to retrieve learning** when needed.
3. **The Goldilocks principle applies** to challenge: it has to be just right. Too much challenge results in anxiety or disengagement; too little leads to boredom and lower

expectations. Wilson and colleagues (2019) calculate the optimum is **15 percent to 20 percent of any task should be beyond current abilities**.

4. Contrary to popular opinion, the brain is *not* designed for thinking (Willingham, 2021b). Whenever possible, it will rely on memory and rehearsed responses. **Challenge provokes an alternative response.**

5. Challenge **increases the need for higher-order-thinking skills** such as analysis, problem solving, creativity, evaluation, and metacognition.

6. **Challenge doesn't have to mean additional complexity or difficulty.** It can mean varying the conditions of learning with a different pedagogy or an alternative space, interleaving topics, or creating an opportunity for students to generate their own solutions.

7. Expectations, encouragement, psychological safety, and a sense of purpose contribute, but the **most significant factor influencing students' willingness to engage in challenge is their resolve**. They are the ones who will decide whether to try.

8. **Having a clear idea of the likely ups and downs of learning helps students prepare** and respond more effectively. The Learning Pit is very useful in this regard.

9. **The Learning Pit supports a culture of challenge**, showing students how to move from simple explanations to the construction of robust, nuanced solutions.

10. As well as being able to attend to the challenge itself, successful learners are able to determine which strategies to use when and why. This **metacognition is an important feature of navigating through the Learning Pit**.

CHAPTER 4

When *Feedback* Is Used Brilliantly, It Adds Significant *Value*

 *Improve every student's ability to receive feedback positively and use it wisely and productively.*

The impact of feedback on student learning is extraordinarily well researched. Hattie (2023), for example, includes more than 2,100 studies about feedback in *Visible Learning: The Sequel*. This compares with just 22 studies about school choice, 30 about screentime, and 181 about class size. You might think, therefore, that little more needs to be said about feedback. Yet thirty years into my work as a teacher and consultant, responses to the key points I share tend to be, "Why didn't we know this?" and "Why haven't we done this before?" and—perhaps more contentiously—"Why do leaders check that we've given feedback when the real impact comes from students' understanding and using our advice?" This is not to cast aspersions or apportion blame. It is to reflect, as the poet Maya Angelou is reported to have said, "You did what you knew how to do, and when you knew better, you did better" (Gaines, 1995).

THE BLUEPRINT

Purpose

The following lists the purposes of feedback within the learning process.

- Feedback should help students decide on the next steps in their learning journey.
- Feedback ought to be offered constructively and compassionately.
- Feedback's value rests in being received thoughtfully and used wisely.

> **What to Notice**
>
> The following lists what is important to notice about feedback.
>
> - **Notice its variability:** Feedback is a powerful influence on student learning, but its outcomes are more variable than most. One-third of studies show feedback has a negative effect.
> - **Notice its sequence:** Feedback should be guided by three questions: (1) What am I trying to achieve? (2) How much progress have I made so far? and (3) What should I do next to improve?
> - **Notice its congruity:** When feedback is clearly matched to agreed-on learning intentions and success criteria, students are more likely to trust, understand, and apply it. Matching also helps students generate more accurate self- and peer feedback.
> - **Notice its benefit:** Is your feedback leading to improved student learning? Look for evidence of impact. If there isn't any, then something needs to change.
>
> **Timing**
>
> Feedback that improves learning has to be timed in such a way that students have not only the opportunity to use it but also the expectation. Offer it too soon and you run the risk of providing your students with an unnecessary shortcut. Give it too late—most commonly after your students have finished their task—and you reduce the chances they will use your advice in any meaningful way.

4.0 What Is Feedback?

 *Give your students advice, help them understand it, and help them use it effectively. That's it; that's feedback. Everything else is a footnote.*

Are you still with me? If so, I'll happily offer you some footnotes. Brace yourself because there are quite a few of them.

Feedback redirects thinking, actions, or attention so that a learner more accurately aligns their activity with a desired result.

It does not *need* to be written down; feedback can be verbal. It can also be nonverbal, explained or implied, formal or informal. The laughter a student provokes when trying to amuse their friends is feedback that encourages the comedian to keep going. When you raise an eyebrow or make a strategic move toward a group of distracted students, you send feedback intended to modify their actions toward improved behavior. Conversely, the comments you write in students' books might *not* be received as feedback, no matter how much time and effort you put into them. But more on that later.

The good news is that feedback is one of the most significant ways to boost student learning. Put aside the factors you or I have little control over (for example, students' home lives and their parents' expectations, curriculum content, and class composition) and look purely at the elements we *can* influence, and feedback is among the very best ways to improve student learning. It also costs very little to implement and, as you'll see in this chapter, is based on extensive research evidence. So, if ever there was a place to start when on a mission to boost student learning, feedback is surely it!

However, feedback is almost impossible to isolate from other factors influencing student learning. The culture of the classroom, for example, can make or break the outcomes of feedback. If the culture is supportive of trial and error and of personal and academic growth, and it comes with a balance of challenge and success that leads to student (and teacher) self-efficacy, then feedback has the very best chance of success. Without any one of these factors, it is likely that positive gains that typically flow from feedback will be reduced.

4.1 Why Is Feedback So Complex?

Feedback is a powerful influence on student learning, but its outcomes are more variable than most. One-third of studies show a negative effect.

As well as being one of the most effective ways to improve student learning, feedback is also one of the most variable factors. At best, it can accelerate learning by as much as three times the normal rate (Lysakowski & Walberg, 1982). But researchers Avraham N. Kluger and Angelo DeNisi's (1996) analysis of three thousand studies found that in more than one-third of cases (38 percent), feedback leads to negative effects. The typical effect of students' effective use of feedback is an additional 50 percent gain compared to when they learn in the absence of feedback (Graham, Hebert, & Harris, 2015). However, Graham Nuthall (2007) found that 80 percent of the verbal feedback that students receive comes from other students, and most of it is wrong. So, although it has enormous potential, feedback also has many pitfalls.

Further, literally everyone in education already uses feedback. Have you ever heard of a teacher who doesn't? Yet so few of us get anywhere close to realizing the gains that research promises. So, it seems there's still a lot of work to do to maximize the gains of feedback.

When John Hattie (2009) published his first book on Visible Learning, he made more mentions of feedback than any other term apart from *teachers, schools, students,* and *reading*. He listed it as a single item (feedback) and quoted an effect size of $d = 0.79$ (Hattie & Timperley, 2007). In Hattie's (2023) book *Visible Learning: The Sequel*, he says feedback has an effect size of $d = 0.51$. (This indicates the overall effect of all factors relating to feedback.) Then he splits feedback into eight subcategories, all with differing effect sizes. I have listed them in descending order, from highest effect size to lowest.

1. Feedback (reinforcement and cues): 1.01
2. Feedback (timing): 0.89
3. Feedback (tasks and processes): 0.63
4. Feedback (technology): 0.55
5. Feedback (from students): 0.47
6. Feedback (from tests): 0.41

7. Feedback (comments versus grades): 0.19
8. Feedback (self): 0.14

Beyond those eight subcategories, Hattie also includes the following twelve variables closely related to feedback.

1. Classroom discussion: 0.82
2. Alternative assessment methods: 0.67
3. Success criteria: 0.64
4. Effects of testing: 0.59
5. Peer and self-grading: 0.54
6. Questioning: 0.49
7. Worked examples: 0.47
8. Clear goal intentions: 0.44
9. Peer assessment: 0.41
10. Formative evaluation: 0.40
11. Frequent testing: 0.39
12. Productive failure (errors): 0.39

I will describe each of these later in the chapter (see section 4.7, page 188). For now, I will refer to feedback as if it were one category. The two thousand studies and twenty-six meta-analyses included in Hattie's database make it possible to be much more discerning about the exact type and approach, but there is also benefit in starting with the aspects that are common to all.

4.2 Feedback's Guiding Questions

Feedback should be guided by three questions: (1) What am I trying to achieve? (2) How much progress have I made so far? and (3) What should I do next to improve?

To give feedback the best chance of being effective, it should always help students answer these three questions. These can be phrased in different ways, depending on preference and context. The next questions are followed by alternative ways to ask the initial questions.

1. What am I trying to achieve?
    a. Where am I going?
    b. What am I learning?
    c. What outcomes do I want?
    d. What is my target or goal?
    e. Why am I learning this?
2. How much progress have I made so far?
    a. How am I going?
    b. How much do I already know or understand?

      c. What steps have I taken so far?

      d. How close am I to achieving my goal?

      e. What is holding me back?

3. What should I do next to improve?

      a. What are my next learning steps?

      b. What should I do now?

      c. What will help me reach my goal?

      d. How can I overcome the obstacles?

A learner can effectively answer these questions when they know what they want to achieve (question 1) and have a clear idea of the progress they've made so far (question 2), and then are open to advice about what they could do next to improve (question 3).

In this video, James offers the key points about feedback.

4.3 Feedback's Essential Qualities

 *When giving feedback, make sure that it is good advice that is well used to improve learning or application.*

Feedback comes from a wide range of sources: a quizzical look, a nod, a smile, big green ticks and nasty red crosses, comments, grades, comparisons, and so on. Even silence is feedback. (In a sense, the absence of feedback is, indeed, feedback!) However, there will be times when you want to give your students premeditated, intentional feedback. This can be written down or spoken, formal or incidental. When you give this feedback, make sure that (1) it is advice, (2) it is well used, and (3) it improves learning and application. When leading workshops or giving keynotes, I often add, "Everything else is just white noise."

My purpose in adding this is to be provocative in the hope that people will remember it. I actually believe there are many other aspects of feedback—all of which are covered later in this chapter. Nonetheless, these three qualities are the ones most likely to influence how much students learn from the feedback they receive. Each of these dimensions is broken down as follows.

4.3.1 Feedback Should Be Advice

The type of feedback most likely to improve performance or learning is advice. An example is, "This is what I think you should do next. If you adapt this, build on that, repeat this, and clarify that, it should help you meet these criteria." Advice has the following characteristics.

- Advice will help your students answer the third guiding question of feedback: What should I do next to improve? When acted on, the advice becomes formative.
- Advice has the sense of being constructive, proactive, and encouraging. It is the opposite of nitpicky, critical, or overly judgmental.
- Advice supports the notions of growth, progress, and growth mindset. This is explained further in chapter 5 (page 215).

This sounds straightforward enough, but how often is our feedback *not* advice driven? In my experience, much of what is written in students' notebooks is anything but advice. There tend to be a lot of comments about what students have *done* rather than what they could do next. I also regularly see remarks about the quality of presentation, (presumed) application of effort, completeness of answers, or quantity of responses. These often come across very positively—so they are not bad, but they are *not* advice.

In addition to comments, I see grades or marks added in a lot of books. I cover this hot topic in more depth in sections 4.7 (Feedback [Comments Versus Grades]) and 4.9.7 (pages 188 and 210). For now, though, it's worth saying that grading does *not* help students, particularly if they are trying to answer the third of the three feedback questions: What should I do next to improve? Indeed, there is strong evidence that grades get in the way of learning—but more on that later.

Before I share some examples, let me say that written feedback isn't the only form of feedback; it's not even the best type in many situations. It is a very common practice, though it may be extremely time consuming. So, for those reasons, I think it is worth sharing some examples. If your feedback is nothing like the examples that follow, then bravo! You don't need to worry about tweaking anything. But if you do see some similarities, then I would gently suggest that there are more effective ways to offer feedback to your students!

First up, in figure 4.1, five-year-old Lucy is likely to be very happy with her teacher's feedback. She got everything right and was rewarded with a smiley face and a positive comment. However, what does Lucy do next? What response can she give to the third feedback question? (What should I do next to improve?) Doubtless, she'll feel proud for doing well, but this type of feedback is not going to help her do even better.

The feedback received by seven-year-old Gabe in figure 4.2 is like the response Lucy received. It is positive and encouraging. Gabe is likely to be very happy to receive it. However, I don't think he is going to do anything with this feedback apart from smile and think the equivalent of, "My work here is done!" Is this affirming? Yes! Is it productive? No! (Or, at least, it is very unlikely to be.)

In figure 4.3 (page 154), twelve-year-old Lela is happy with her teacher's feedback. She has even replied with a "thank you," as you can see! I wonder what the success criteria were. I'm guessing they were clearly stated somewhere because without them, the teacher's comment of "perfect attempt with good use of terminology" would have been less objective. My main concern, though, is that there are no recommendations for next steps, so what helps Lela know what to do better next time? Also concerning is the length of time it takes a teacher to review and respond to this quantity of homework from, say, thirty students in a class. What impact is that likely to have? It seems like a lot of input for little chance of improvement.

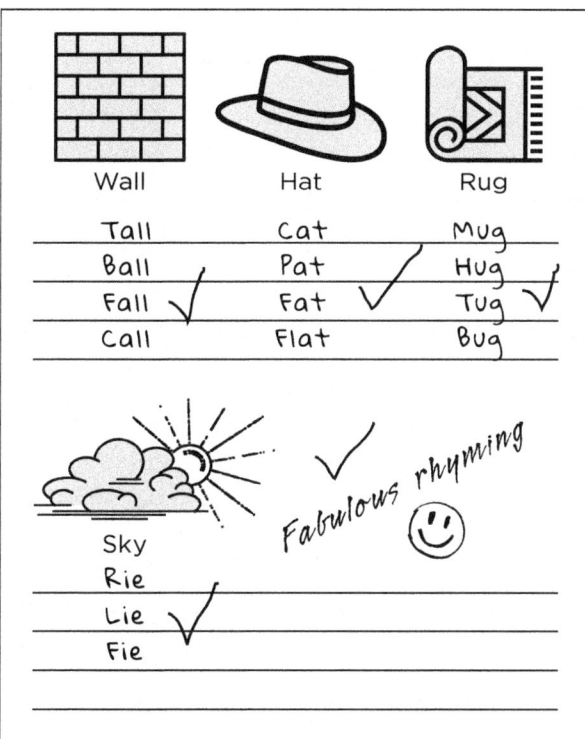

Five-year-old Lucy is likely to be very happy with her teacher's feedback. She got everything right and has been rewarded with a smiley face and a positive comment.

However, what does Lucy do next? What response can she give to the third feedback question (what should I do next to improve?). Doubtless, she'll feel proud for doing well but this type of feedback is not going to help her to do even better.

It won't prompt her to go further (for example, by going above and beyond the initial task).

Figure 4.1: Example of feedback to a five-year-old.

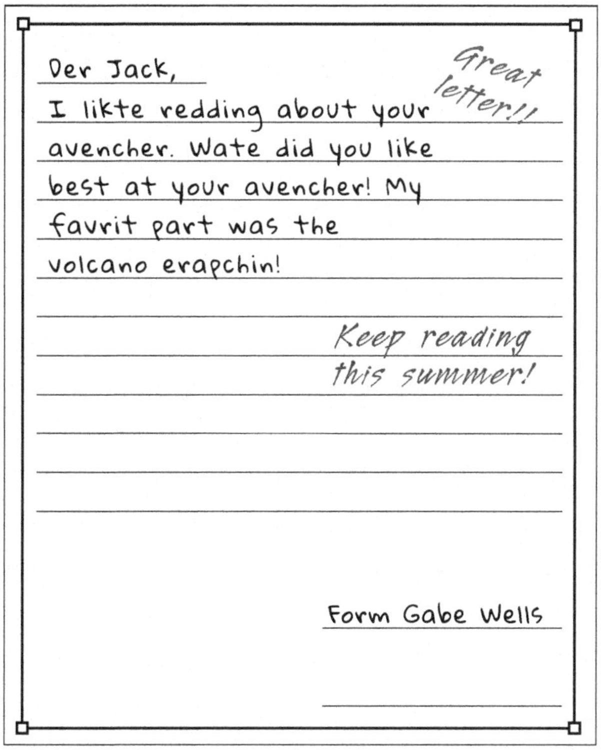

The feedback received by seven-year-old Gabe is like the response Lucy received in figure 4.1. The likelihood is that he will be very happy to receive it.

However, I don't think Gabe is going to do anything with this "feedback" apart from smile and think the equivalent of "my work here is done."

Is this affirming? Yes! Is it productive? No! (At least, it is very unlikely to be.)

Figure 4.2: Example of feedback to a seven-year-old.

Extension Task — *Wow! You show great understanding.*

Q. What happens when condensation takes place?
A. The water gets much cooler or gas turns into liquid.
Q. What does evaporation do to the water?
A. It turns the water into a gas or cloud.
Q. At what stage of the water cycle does precipitation happen?
A. The third stage.
Q. Why are plants and trees such a big part of the cycle?
A. Because without the plants or trees absorb the water from the surface flow.
Q. What does the cycle show?
A. How water moves around between the oceans, seas, rivers, and land.

Homework

Dear diary,
   You will never believe what happened to me today! So, early this morning I was chilling, you know, hanging out with the fish, and all of a sudden it got very warm and I mean VERY warm. Then I started to get so hot that I evaporated. I started floating. It felt very weird! Get yourself ready for this. I turned into a cloud or gas and I think some people call that <u>condensation</u>? But anyways, you'll never believe what happened next. I started to move over to a very weird and tall-looking rock. I started to feel very heavy until eventually I fell down, and landed on the rock or mountain. Someone said it was <u>precipitation</u>, whatever that means! I then started to run off the surface (<u>surface runoff</u>) of the rock. But then I went down into the ground, and someone flowing past me shouted, "<u>Infiltration</u>." I wasn't really paying attention cause I was going through <u>percolation</u>. Some of my friends did a <u>through-flow</u> and I felt so bad cause the plants and trees sucked them up. Then trees and plants did some <u>transpiration</u> to them. But I was so, so, so glad I was back with the fish.
   Your tired friend "The water droplet"

This is a perfect attempt with good use of terminology. Well done. — *thank you*

Twelve-year-old Lela is happy with her teacher's feedback. She's even replied with a thank you, as you can see!

I wonder what the success criteria were. I'm guessing they were clearly stated somewhere because without them, the teacher's comment of "perfect attempt with good use of terminology" would be less objective.

I have two main concerns. First, there are are no recommendations for next steps, so what helps Lela know what to do better next time? Second, the length of time it would have taken a teacher to review and respond to this quantity of homework from, say, 30 students in a class. What impact is that likely to have? It seems like a lot of input for little chance of improvement.

Figure 4.3: Example of feedback to a twelve-year-old.

I love how affirming and encouraging the comments in figure 4.4 are. If only we received similar responses after making presentations to *our* peers! Unfortunately, these comments are not feedback—at least not in the sense that to be so, they would need to answer the third question about what next. Imagine how effective this process could have been if peer responses had been invited after a practice run rather than after the final presentation and the comments had not just been positive but *also* included advice about ways to improve.

All four examples in this section show feedback that is more akin to praise than to advice. Some might say that these examples are unrepresentative of the norm and that I have deliberately chosen them to support my claim. If that were true, then I would be genuinely delighted that feedback isn't typically like this.

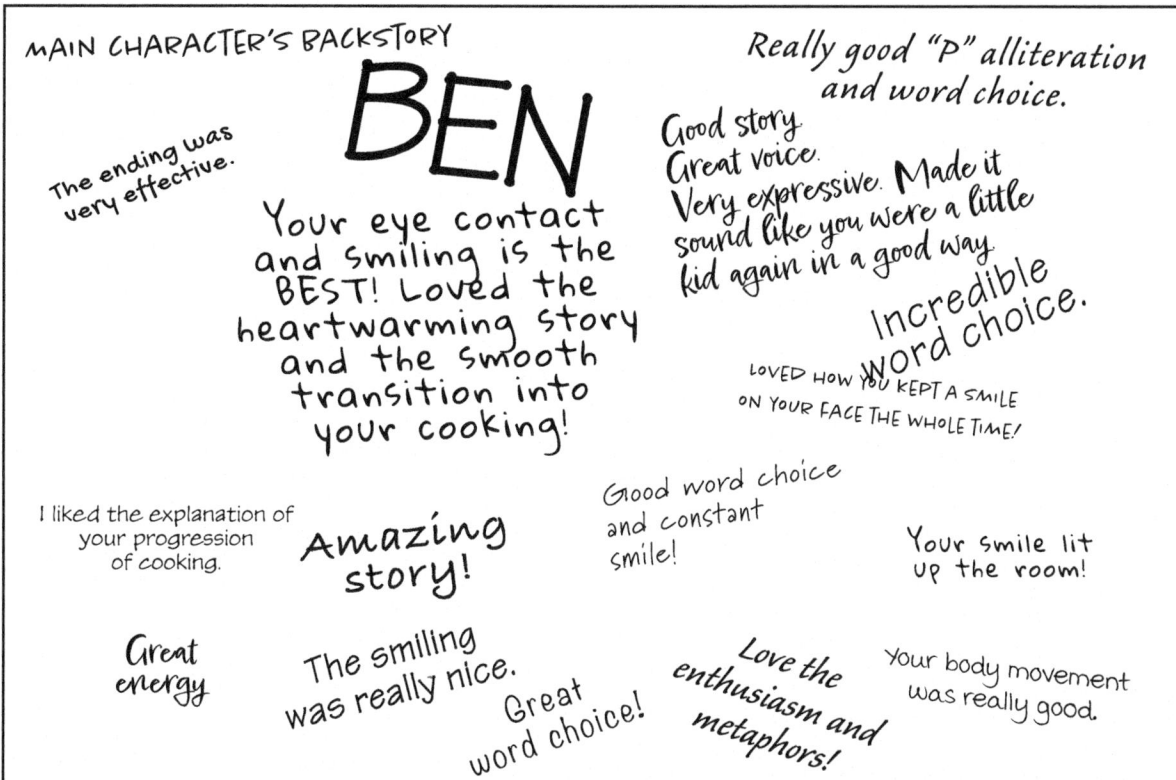

I love how affirming and encouraging these comments are. If only we received similar responses after making presentations to our peers!

Unfortunately though, these comments are just not feedback; at least, not in the sense that to be so, they would need to answer a third question about what next.

Imagine how effective this process could have been if peer responses had been invited after a practice-run rather than after the final presentation and the comments were just as positive but also included advice about ways to improve.

Figure 4.4: Example of feedback to a fifteen-year-old.

On the learning walks I go on around schools, the types of comments I see most frequently are as follows.

- Excellent.
- Gold star.
- Good effort.
- I enjoyed reading this.
- Interesting.
- Lovely handwriting.
- Nice ideas.
- This is really good.
- Well done.
- 10/10.

I've only included the favorable examples. I'll leave you to imagine the more neutral and negative versions, although thankfully, I don't see as many of those.

Since these comments are all positive, you might suppose that they won't do any harm. To a certain extent, that is true, but I explain the nuances—and dangers—of mixing praise with feedback in sections 4.4, 4.9, and 5.7.1 (pages 166, 198, and 253). For now, let's focus on the *function* of the comments. None of them could be construed as advice. They are intended to affirm and congratulate, not challenge or recommend. Because of this, they will *not* help with the feedback process. They won't offer answers to question three: What should I do next to improve? However, the following comments are advice. They help students have an idea about what to do next.

- Add a graphic to illustrate your point.
- Clarify this point.
- Correct this and explain the rule.
- Don't forget to reach a conclusion.
- Give a reason.
- Include definitions for the key terms.
- Show an example here.
- Show the calculation you used.
- Suggest alternatives.
- These are long sentences; can you split them into two or three more?

Here are four things to note about these examples.

1. They are all advice. They recommend what the student can do next to improve.
2. They work best—indeed, they might *only* work—when offered *before* a student has finished their assignment (see section 4.9.5, page 206).
3. Responding to these comments requires additional effort from the recipient. This means students should assume (1) an assignment is not finished until after they have applied the advice they've been given and (2) responding to that advice will take effort and time (which is probably why students tend to prefer praise to advice).
4. Although it is not clear from the information I have given you, all the advice should link to the agreed-on learning intention and success criteria. This is explained further in section 4.4 (page 166).

4.3.2 Feedback Should Be Well Used

The potency of feedback is realized only when it is used effectively. This sentence is enough to complete this section; everything else I write will be mere detail. I repeat: if your students do not use the feedback they receive, there is little point putting effort into creating your advice for them. No amount of guidance will have any efficacy if ignored or left to idle. "Feedback requires an additional condition—that it actually improves student learning—for it to be counted as good feedback" (Black & Wiliam, 1998a).

Figure 4.5 is an example of just such a situation. I was on a learning walk around one of the biggest international schools in the Middle East. I asked students what they were learning, how much progress they were making, and what they thought their next steps could be. (Sound familiar?) I asked some students to show me examples of the marking they had received. One boy showed me the following page about fossils.

After closely looking at the page, I asked him why he thought his teacher had written, "Trace fossils?"

He responded, "Perhaps she doesn't know what trace fossils are!"

"That's not very likely, is it?" I laughed.

	LO: To describe the process of fossilization	than the preserved remains of the body of the actual animal itself.
	FOSSILS	
	What's a fossil?	Mold fossils:
	Fossils are the preserved remains of plants or animals. For such remains to be considered fossils, scientists have decided they have to be over 10,000 years old. There are two main types of fossils: body fossils and trace fossils.	A fossil formed when an animal, plant, or other organism dies and is covered by sediment.
		Cast fossils:
	Body fossils:	Its flesh decays and bones deteriorate due to chemical reactions.
	Body fossils are the most common type of fossil found across the world. They are formed from the remains of dead animals and plants.	
	Trace fossils:	
	Trace fossils provide us with evidence of life in the past, such as the footprints, tracks, burrows, borings, and feces left behind by animals, rather	*Trace fossils?* *Well done! A good piece of research.*

Figure 4.5: Feedback that fails to elicit a response.

He agreed. "So, really, why do you think she wrote that?" I pressed.

"Maybe she wants me to write more about trace fossils," he said and shrugged.

"OK, so when will you do that?" I asked.

"I won't," he said with an air of *Why on earth would I?* "She's already marked my book, so she's not going to look at it again!"

How often does this happen? We spend hours writing brilliantly incisive, supportive, thought-provoking comments in our students' notebooks only for them to do nothing except smile, shrug, or sob!

To be clear, when we give our students feedback, we have to do so in such a way that they will use our advice to improve their learning or performance. So, timing and expectation are important too. I cover this in sections 4.3.3.1 and 4.7 (Feedback [Timing], pages 158 and 188).

Other core principles for ensuring feedback is well used include the following.

- Offering your feedback *before* your students complete their learning task
- Avoiding offering your feedback too early (Your students should have a chance to stretch themselves and try their very best before you give them ways to do even better.)
- Initiating feedback conversations with phrases such as, "Let's see how you're getting on *so far*," rather than "Hand in your completed work" or "Let me know when you're done" (These are important ways to indicate that feedback is part of your students' learning journey, not something that is only offered in retrospect.)
- Avoiding grading work at the same time as offering advice about how to improve (Grades or marks indicate that students have finished their work, whereas you want them to apply your fabulous advice first. This is covered in more depth in section 4.9.7, page 210.)

4.3.3 Feedback Should Improve Learning Outcomes

Feedback should bridge the gap between a student's current position and where you (and preferably, they) want them to be next. This gap can be bridged in two interrelated ways: (1) by accelerating their learning (this normally includes their finding out, understanding, or doing something they couldn't do before) and (2) by adjusting their application (or learning behaviors) toward their goal. Ways to achieve this include putting in more effort, better concentrating, adjusting their focus or sequence, examining their errors, and so on.

4.3.3.1 Improvement of Learning

Moving students from their current level of knowledge or ability to the next is perhaps the easiest way to describe learning. A useful illustration of this comes from the SOLO Taxonomy by Biggs and Collis (1982), an abridged version of which is shown in figure 2.2 (page 57).

The diagram tracks a learner's progress from knowing nothing (about a particular topic) to knowing something about it, to knowing lots about it, to being able to connect their new knowledge with other ideas within and outside the same domain, to applying and adapting their understanding in different contexts. To better understand how this might look in the classroom, consider the examples in figure 4.6.

As well as describing the different levels of knowledge, understanding, and application, the SOLO Taxonomy helps explain the difference between *surface learning* and *deep learning*. These two terms are sometimes bandied about without sufficient clarity as to their differences. Figure 2.2 (page 57) illustrates these terms and their relationship to each other.

Insects

0. I don't know what insects are.
1. I know the names of two or three insects.
2. I know the features of insects and can name ten or more examples.
3. I understand the similarities and differences between different types of insects, as well as the differences between insects, birds, fish, and mammals.
4. I am able to explain the defining features of insects and to design a superhero with insect qualities.

Metaphors

0. I don't know what metaphors are.
1. I can give an example of a metaphor.
2. I know the definition of a metaphor. I can also identify and give examples of metaphors.
3. I understand the similarities and differences between metaphors and other figurative language (and between their uses and effects).
4. I am able to explain the defining features of metaphors and can create my own metaphors.

Swimming

0. I don't know how to swim.
1. I know that I need to lie flat in the water, hips and shoulders in line and face down, and kick my legs.
2. I am trying to kick with my legs straight but not locked and my toes pointed, close to the surface.
3. I am able to perform the front crawl with increasing fluency and efficiency.
4. I understand why head position influences body position and why the kick should come from the hips, and I can adapt these to suit my body.

Figure 4.6: Examples of progress levels matched to the SOLO Taxonomy.

Learning is not about knowledge or understanding, nor is it about purely surface *or* deep learning. It should be about both. A novice must start at the surface, finding the most basic knowledge. As they discover more, this helps them deepen their knowledge. Eventually, they will want to move from knowledge to understanding and ultimately to application and adaptation. The problem is most curricula around the world overemphasize student knowledge to the disadvantage of deeper learning. Content is so overflowing that time to go deep is restricted. School days are filled with multiple short lessons that favor surface activities. The focus is more on *what* is taught than on *how* it is learned.

Imagine watching ten different box sets or reading ten different books—each one on a significantly different topic—in a week. Imagine that first thing, you are required to watch most of episode 5 of season 3 of one box set before moving straight to episode 1 of season 1 of an entirely different box set—but you don't quite finish it. Then you have to bounce to episode 15 of season 3 of yet another box set before taking a short break. After that, you have to crack on with the middle of chapter 16 of the third book you've started this week before trying to remember where you were in a totally different genre of book before lunch. Then you do this week in and week out . . . and get tested on everything at the end of term. Talk about pushing us toward skimming the surface rather than going deeply into characters, topics, themes, ideas, or points of view! This overemphasis on knowledge is a scourge of education.

That is not to say that knowledge is unimportant. Far from it. Without knowledge, one would be ill-informed and unable to gain any real depth of understanding. We need knowledge even in the age of artificial intelligence, perhaps more so than ever. We also need knowledge to think accurately, to make sense of information, and to make sense of our world.

However, knowledge is not the *only* thing we need. We also need to understand how to use that knowledge effectively. We need wisdom. We need skills. We need to develop good habits and attitudes. So, if knowledge is just one among many aspects of a broad and balanced curriculum, then why has it gained such a canonical position? Why has our education system been set up to privilege knowledge above all else?

I propose there are three main reasons. First, 'twas ever thus. Education for the many started with learning, typically by rote passages from holy books. For centuries, this is what schooling primarily consisted of. A good scholar was one who knew the scripture well enough to quote suitable text for every occasion.

Second, to test knowledge is far easier than to test skills, attitudes, understanding, and wisdom. Ask a knowledge-based question, and even a computer can check the validity of a student's answer. Ask students to create, imagine, enact, or perform, and the examiner's task becomes much more subjective.

Third, politicians like to promise to improve education. After all, this wins votes. But what does it mean, and what measures can be used? The answer, typically, is to raise standards; this, in turn, means improved test scores. Look for improved scores on knowledge-based tests and call that "raising standards." Rate schools and education systems according to how well their students do on tests. Pressure is applied to school leaders. Teachers, in turn, feel the pressure. And so, ruefully, an overemphasis is placed on teaching knowledge to the disadvantage of creativity, endeavor, and values. All of this occurs in spite of, rather than because of, educators' and parents' wish that young people be well rounded.

Enough of the soapbox, though; let's return to the SOLO Taxonomy. Using this model as the backdrop to students' learning can help move them from knowledge to understanding and from there to adaptation, application, and ultimately wisdom. It gives knowledge its rightful place as the foundation for learning. But it *also* prompts us to go deeper by moving to understanding and application.

This won't cure the education system of all its woes, but it will at least help you build a more holistic experience for your students despite the huge amount of content you have to teach.

4.3.3.2 Improvement of Application

To paraphrase some of the 20th century's best-loved philosophers, Fun Boy Three (1982) and Bananarama, it's not what you do, it's the *way* that you do it. It's not what you do, it's the *time* that you do it. It's not what you do, it's the *place* that you do it. That's what gets results (emphasis added). At the next staff-student event, I propose you and your colleagues dance onto the stage with this tune playing.

Believe it or not, my mentioning the '80s pop trios has a purpose, which is to move the emphasis from teaching students *what* to learn over to teaching them *how* to learn. This, of course, is not an either-or situation; we need to teach students both what and how to learn. This section focuses on how.

One way to frame teaching students how to learn is with the use of the ASK Model. The acronym *ASK* stands for *attitudes, skills,* and *knowledge*. I first proposed this model in my original book, *Challenging Learning* (Nottingham, 2010). I'm delighted to say the model has gained traction and is used in many schools around the world. It's not as popular as the Learning Pit, but then again, very few heuristics of learning introduced in the last thirty years are as widely used as the Learning Pit.

The ASK Model came from two provocations. The first was an invitation to develop a learning-to-learn program for a group of schools in North East England in the early 2000s. At that time, a review of approaches for developing pupils' thinking by the wonderful professor Carol McGuinness (1999) from Queen's University Belfast had just been published. This white paper provided a much-needed counterbalance to the National Curriculum for England and Wales, which was dominated by what pupils across these two countries should learn. McGuinness provided a timely reminder that teaching pupils how to learn is as important as teaching them what to learn, and her research showed that an emphasis on teaching thinking skills could help in this regard.

The second inspiration came from digging deeper into Bloom's (1956) taxonomy. In the late nineties and early 2000s, almost every teacher I knew was using Bloom's taxonomy of thinking skills. So, I wanted to include a list of these in the thinking-skills chapter of *Challenging Learning* (Nottingham, 2010). In book writing, there is a greater need to check sources and give full references than there is in everyday teaching. Indeed, this challenge is one of the main reasons why I go through the pain of book writing again and again! It lifts my practice and, therefore, my expertise. The same could be said of in-depth or postgraduate studies.

So, as I dug into educational psychologist Benjamin S. Bloom's thinking skills, I was surprised to find that he actually proposed a *Taxonomy of Educational Objectives* (Bloom, 1956). One small (but significant) part of this was thinking skills. He and his colleagues Max D. Engelhart, Edward J. Furst, Walker H. Hill, and David R. Krathwohl wrote about the need to develop students' abilities in three broad domains: (1) cognitive, (2) affective, and (3) psychomotor. These three together would, they proposed, go a long way toward developing well-rounded individuals capable of thoughtful, holistic lifelong learning. As I read about this, the irony was not lost on me. Bloom and his colleagues (1956) had proposed a wide-ranging classification of three broad domains that *together* would contribute toward the goals of holistic education. Yet, here we were in education using just one part of their proposal and referring to it as if it represented the whole.

Irony or not, the idea of developing students' *cognitive, affective,* and *psychomotor* skills appealed to me. I didn't think the language was particularly student friendly, which is why I used the terms *attitudes, skills,* and *knowledge*, as illustrated in figure 4.7 (page 162). After all,

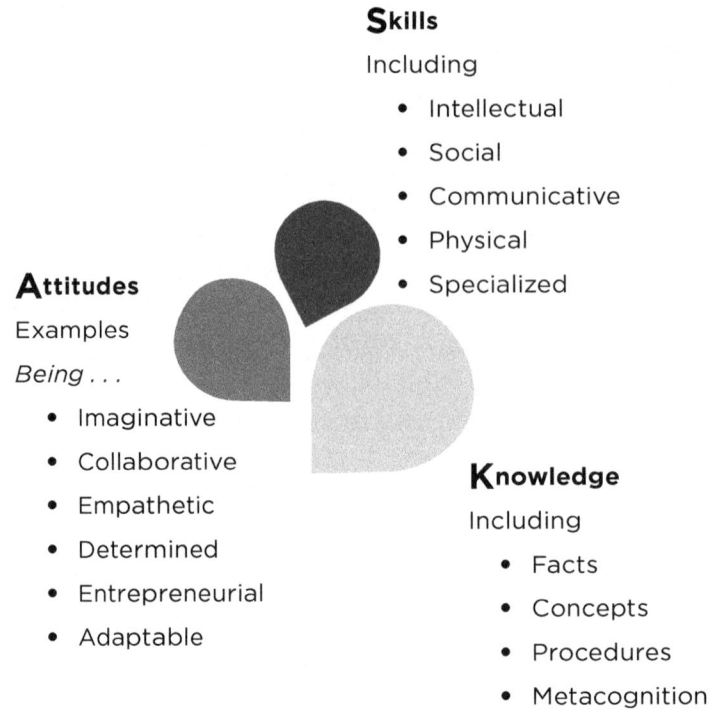

Figure 4.7: The ASK Model.

ideas that are easier to understand are easier to repeat. Ideas that are easier to repeat are the ones that transform teaching.

The purpose of the ASK Model is to remind us, as teachers, to design learning opportunities that will improve our students' attitudes and skills, as well as their knowledge. This has the bonus of providing a way to write learning intentions when the knowledge that students will engage with isn't clear from the beginning (for example, an inquiry-based lesson that begins with a story based on a wide range of themes that students might explore).

In my early days as a consultant, I often ran demonstration lessons in philosophy for children that typically began like this: I'd read a story and ask the students to draw out the themes, create questions together, pick the favorite question, and then inquire into that question, all the time searching for more depth of understanding. The staff observing these lessons would always appreciate the benefits of such an approach. However, their concern was how to write learning intentions when the theme that students would pick couldn't be predicted. My answer was always to refer to the ASK Model and pick an attitude (for example, to be able to strike a balance between being open-minded and being assertive) or a skill (for example, to understand the criteria needed when choosing the *best* question).

This approach can work in many lessons. When you want your students to engage in an open-ended experiment (such as in science), solve a task, or engage in a creative activity, the learning intention could be "to be able to collaborate effectively." You could then give them a collection of attitudes and skills, such as those in figure 4.8, to choose between. Note that the options in the middle column show attitudes. The other two columns show associated skills. All of these can be adapted to suit the context.

When I use this approach, I tend to split students into groups of three to five. I ask each group to select three criteria, one from each of the three columns shown. Their selections become their group's success criteria to help them toward the learning intention of collaborating effectively with each other. Every so often (typically, every ten to fifteen minutes), I pause all groups and ask them to answer the three feedback questions—in this case, the following.

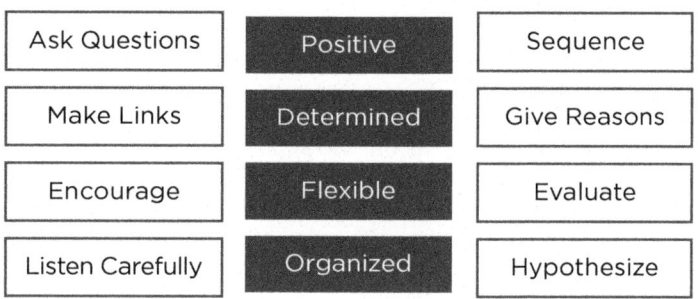

Figure 4.8: Group work attitudes and skills.

1. What did your group choose as your three success criteria?
2. How well are you doing so far in using these brilliantly?
3. What could you do next to do even better?

This is just one of many examples you could use to help your students develop skills and attitudes. In the next three sections, I describe the subcategories of attitudes, skills, and knowledge in more depth.

4.3.3.3 ASK Model: Attitudes

Attitudes are preferences or tendencies toward something and are usually reflected in behavior. They include mindset, outlook, and feelings. It is useful to categorize attitudes as having affective, behavioral, and cognitive components.

- **Affective components (feelings):** These involve a person's feelings or emotions about something. For example, if students feel positive about a curriculum area (perhaps because they enjoy the activities and like the teacher), their attitude toward that subject will be favorable.
- **Behavioral components (actions):** These involve the ways in which attitudes influence how we act or behave. So, when students have positive feelings and thoughts about learning, they are more likely to put in effort, listen carefully, and make sense of and connect ideas. Sadly, the reverse is also true.
- **Cognitive components (thoughts):** These involve the beliefs or knowledge a person holds about something. For example, if a student believes they are good at languages—typically because they have performed well previously—their attitude toward learning languages will be favorable. Again, as with the other examples given, the reverse is also true.

Attitudes are contextual and cultural, more so than skills and maybe even more so than knowledge. For example, hard work is strongly favored by some cultures but is relatively unimportant to others; the same goes for good humor in the face of difficulties. Because of this, I am hesitant to recommend specific attitudes.

However, teachers still ask me for suggestions. So, for what it's worth, here are some of the attitudes I nurture with my students. As you read them, think about your own students and what will help them be better learners, rather than looking at the attitudes as a list to check off. I have shown in parentheses the skill or behavior that students could use to demonstrate that particular attitude.

- Altruism (encourage others to take a turn)
- Attentiveness (focus your attention on the speaker)
- Connectivity (connect to what someone else has said)
- Constructiveness (build on other people's ideas)
- Courage (stand up for what you believe)
- Creativity (offer or explore alternatives)
- Curiosity (ask questions)
- Fallibility (admit your mistakes graciously)
- Openness (show a willingness to change your mind)
- Patience (avoid interrupting or rushing someone)
- Perceptiveness (clarify and make distinctions between ideas)
- Precision (ask for clarifications and definitions)
- Rationality (ask for reasons or criteria)
- Realism (find examples or counterexamples)
- Reasonableness (make decisions based on the quality of reasons)
- Resilience (overcome disappointments)
- Respect (recall other people's names, ideas, and contributions)
- Skepticism (question assumptions and conclusions)
- Tenacity (stick to the topic or task)
- Tolerance (listen carefully to ideas that differ from your own)

4.3.3.4 ASK Model: Skills

Skills are the abilities to carry out those processes necessary for gaining understanding or achieving excellent performance in any given field. Young people (and adults) develop their abilities through social interaction and from the social, cultural, and educational contexts of their lives.

- **Intellectual skills:** These include identifying, modeling, and altering relationships or concepts; understanding relevance; drawing conclusions; comparing and contrasting; asking relevant questions; and hypothesizing.

- **Social skills:** These include building rapport, respecting others' viewpoints, acting appropriately in particular contexts, self-regulating, working individually and as a team, and encouraging others.
- **Communicative skills:** These include being able to understand others and being understood, listening and responding appropriately to others, talking persuasively and respectfully, requesting things politely, paying full attention to a speaker, and reading body language.
- **Physical skills:** These include coordinating actions needed for such things as penmanship, manipulating objects to represent ideas, catching and throwing an object, dancing, participating in drama, riding a bicycle, making art, and playing sports.
- **Specialized skills:** These include the abilities we need for specific types of action, such as driving a car, using a map and compass, using a ruler or tape measure, using a paintbrush, using sporting equipment, weighing scales, and using a keyboard and touch pad or touch screen.

4.3.3.5 ASK Model: Knowledge

Having knowledge is being familiar with facts, truths, or principles. Knowledge is generally considered to be a step removed from understanding, which refers to when someone is able to relate, explain, and evaluate. Knowledge can be classified into four categories: (1) factual, (2) conceptual, (3) procedural, and (4) metacognitive (see figure 4.9).

Factual Knowledge
- Knowledge of terminology
- Knowledge of specific details and elements

Conceptual Knowledge
- Knowledge of classifications and categories
- Knowledge of principles and generalizations
- Knowledge of theories, models, and structures

Procedural Knowledge
- Knowledge of subject-specific skills and algorithms
- Knowledge of subject-specific techniques and methods
- Knowledge of criteria for determining when to use appropriate procedures

Metacognitive Knowledge
- Strategic knowledge
- Knowledge about cognitive tasks
- Contextual and conditional knowledge
- Self-knowledge

Figure 4.9: Four categories of knowledge.

4.4 Learning Intentions and Success Criteria

 *When feedback is clearly matched to agreed-on learning intentions and success criteria, students are more likely to trust, understand, and apply it. Matching also helps students generate more accurate self- and peer feedback.*

Learning intentions and success criteria have a mixed reputation. They are fabulously useful—and a necessary focus for good feedback—but they suffer from the evangelical approach many leaders take when first introduced to them. The erroneous ideas that every single lesson needs to have a learning intention displayed on the board, every learning standard has to be translated into *I can* statements, all curriculum documents have to be supported by multiple learning intentions, and success criteria are best served up with a rubric for every occasion make a lot of people tire of them before their value is realized. In this section, I aim to justify their use—in moderation and for the purposes of guiding feedback.

If you want feedback to be received well and used effectively, then it must be clearly linked to agreed-on learning intentions and success criteria. In fact, I would say to *stop giving feedback*; that is, unless you have a prior shared agreement with your students about what success looks like and the steps needed to get there. If you tell your students something positive without reference to agreed-on criteria, that is praise, not feedback. If you tell them something negative without reference to agreed-on criteria, that is criticism, not feedback.

Imagine your principal has asked me to walk around your school, make some observations, and then report back about the quality of teaching. In that report, I offer recommendations for each teacher. I give no explanations and no criteria, just recommendations based on my own beliefs about teaching and learning. How welcoming would you be to me coming into *your* classroom? I assume not very.

However, what if your principal said that the purpose (or learning intention) is for me to be able to offer ideas for improving student learning *and* that I am offering everybody a range of criteria to select from? Might you be a bit more open to me coming into your classroom?

The criteria I'm offering include the following.

- How well can students answer the three feedback questions: (1) What am I trying to achieve? (2) How much progress have I made so far? and (3) What should I do next to improve?
- How willing are students to ask questions during lessons?
- What do students do when they don't know what to do?
- Do students collaborate with each other effectively?
- What are some of the attitudes that students have toward the feedback they receive?
- How effective are students at giving each other feedback?
- What do students think is the purpose of feedback?
- When (under what conditions) do students feel they make the most progress?

- If students could change one thing that would improve the quality of their learning, what would that be and why?
- What do students think their teachers value most?

I invite you to select the criteria most relevant to you; I then focus my feedback entirely on these. I avoid judgmental or sycophantic responses. I am a fresh pair of eyes, offering information I gather on the criteria you have chosen.

I presume you would think this a whole lot fairer than the first proposal to focus on whatever I like without justification or explanation! That is the main purpose of learning intentions and success criteria: to be fair.

In the next five sections, I share a lot of details and possibilities. This makes the sections pretty chunky. That said, I expect you will skim over the examples from curriculum areas you don't teach and focus closely on those you do. In all cases, please note the following.

- Learning intentions and success criteria do *not* need to be part of every lesson. If there are occasions when feedback is not going to be part of your students' learning experiences, they may not be needed.

- Learning intentions and success criteria shouldn't be viewed as separate from the learning. They should be as integral to lessons as teacher instruction and student engagement.

- Ordinarily—though not always—you will create learning intentions in reference to your guidance documents, be they your national or state or provincial curricula, standards, or schemes of work. There will be occasions when you cocreate the learning intentions with your students, but most of the time, they will come from your short- and medium-term planning.

- Creating success criteria is likely to be more of a collaborative affair. Sometimes, you will formulate them at the same time as you create learning intentions. Other times, you will design some and ask your students to suggest others, or you will make the whole process a shared venture during the lesson.

In this video, James shows how the SOLO Taxonomy can help with the design of learning intentions.

4.4.1 Learning Intentions

A *learning intention* describes what students should know, understand, or be able to do by the end of the lesson or series of lessons. *Success criteria* are the key steps or components students need to be successful with the learning intention. They include the main things to do, include, or focus on.

In section 4.4 (page 166), I shared some ideas for using learning intentions and success criteria to individualize learning and to close the gap for at-risk students. In this section, I write in terms of helping *all* students move from knowing to understanding to being able to adapt and apply. I recommend that you match learning intentions to a clear sense of progress in learning. For this, I use the SOLO Taxonomy (see figure 2.2, page 57). In figure 4.6 (page 159), I gave three worked examples connected to the topics of insects, metaphors, and swimming. If I draw out the characteristics of those examples, they would look like the following.

For content-based learning:

0. I don't know
1. I can give an example
2. know the definition and can give examples
3. I understand the similarities and differences, uses, and effects
4. I can explain the defining features and can create alternatives

For skill-based learning:

0. I don't know how to
1. I know that I need to . . .
2. I am trying to . . .
3. I am able to perform with increasing fluency
4. I understand why . . . and can adapt . . .

Now, if I turn them from what a student can do at each level to how I recommend writing learning intentions, they would include these sorts of descriptors.

1. To know (some facts about, names of, examples of, ways to . . .)
2. To know (the features of, definitions of, reasons for, how to . . .)
3. To understand the similarities and differences between . . .
4. To be able to complete (various procedures) and create your own . . .

Shorthand versions could be:

1. Examples
2. Features
3. Connections
4. Applications and adaptations

I'm not suggesting that these are the *only* phrases or categories to use when writing learning intentions. However, I would say that you *do* need to have a schema that will ensure your students make good progress in their learning. I use the SOLO Taxonomy for this.

In the examples in figure 4.10, I give descriptions for all four stages of SOLO. This is so that you can match learning intentions to your students' individual levels. They won't all start at the same place; some students will already know a lot more than others. No matter where they start from, they should all make good progress. Having a clear sense of progression will make this much more likely.

These examples build on the examples from section 4.3.3.1 (page 158).

Content Area: **Insects**

Examples: To find out the names of three or more insects

Features: To know the features of insects

Connections: To understand the similarities and differences between different types of insects, as well as the differences between insects, birds, fish, and mammals

Applications and adaptations: To be able to explain the defining features of insects and to design a superhero with insect qualities

Content Area: **Metaphors**

Examples: To find examples of metaphors

Features: To know the definition of a metaphor and give examples

Connections: To understand the similarities and differences between metaphors and other figurative language (including their uses and effects)

Applications and adaptations: To be able to explain the defining features of metaphors and to create your own metaphors

Content Area: **Swimming**

Basics: To know the basics of the butterfly–simultaneous arms and dolphin kick

First goes: To try to move your arms from the hips simultaneously

Practice: To swim by alternating dolphin kicks and simultaneous arms

Perform: To swim multiple lengths, remember two-hand turns, breathe every other stroke, and kick from the hips

Additional Examples From Across the Curriculum

Content Area: **Art—Drawing Landscapes**

Basics: To know the difference between foreground and background

First goes: To know how to use the top and bottom of the page to represent foreground and background

Practice: To understand how changing the relative size of features in the foreground and background shows perspective

Perform: To be able to use perspective to create a landscape drawing that appears to be 3-D

Figure 4.10: Example descriptors for increasing depth of learning

Continued →

Content Area: **Design—Egg Drop**

Basics: To know why the key to a successful egg drop is slowing the speed of descent

First goes: To try drawing different plans to show ways to slow the speed of the egg drop

Practice: To build a prototype that tests which egg drops are likely to be successful

Perform: To build and develop your favored design, adjusting it to further increase the egg's protection

Content Area: **Geography—Water Cycle**

Examples: To know some of the features of the water cycle

Features: To know all major features of the water cycle by drawing and labeling them correctly

Connections: To understand the similarities and differences between evaporation and condensation in the context of the water cycle

Applications and adaptations: To be able to show how human activity and the water cycle affect each other and propose ways in which the negative influences can be minimized

Content Area: **History—Vikings**

Examples: To know who the Vikings were and when they invaded Britain

Features: To know key features of the Viking invasion and settlement

Connections: To understand the similarities and differences between the Vikings and Anglo-Saxons in terms of beliefs, customs, and ways of life

Applications and adaptations: To be able to explain the influence and impact the Vikings had on Britain then and now

Content Area: **Information and Communication Technology—Coding**

Examples: To know what coding is (in connection with computing)

Features: To define what coding is and give examples

Connections: To understand the basic variables and commands of coding and explain what each of them does

Applications and adaptations: To be able to use code to create a basic program and adjust as needed

Content Area: **Literacy—Letter Writing**

Examples: To know the basic format and structure of a letter

Features: To know the key features and tone of a formal letter

Connections: To understand the similarities and differences between formal and informal letters and the purpose of each

Applications and adaptations: To be able to compose a formal letter for a variety of purposes (complaint, information, thank you, request)

Content Area: **Modern Foreign Language—Conversation**

Examples: To know some words when accompanied by gestures or pictures

Features: To know some short phrases with common features, with supporting details

Connections: To understand simple questions and exchange simple answers using present tense in the first person

Applications and adaptations: To be able to ask and answer questions about a range of topics and opinions

Content Area: **Music—Rhythm**

Basics: To know what makes something a rhythm

First goes: To try copying rhythms after listening to someone else clapping

Practice: To understand how to create different rhythms using a range of instruments

Perform: To be able to adapt a rhythm by increasing tempo or altering the number of notes used

Content Area: **Numeracy—Patterns and Functions**

Examples: To know what patterns are in number sequences

Features: To know the features of different number sequences together with their patterns

Connections: To understand different patterns and predict the next set of numbers in a sequence

Applications and adaptations: To be able to find the nth term in a sequence using formulas (functions)

Content Area: **Physical Education—Throwing a Ball**

Basics: To know the basics of an overhand motion to throw a ball forward

First goes: To throw balls at a target using an overhand motion

Practice: To understand how the motion of the arm and the timing of the release impact the speed, direction, and accuracy of the throw

Perform: To be able to accurately hit a target from various angles and distances by adjusting the arm motion and the timing of the release

Content Area: **Science—Forces**

Examples: To name some examples of forces

Features: To explain the features of forces, giving real-life examples

Connections: To understand the laws that describe forces and how they interact with one another

Applications and adaptations: To be able to calculate the force on an object and show ways in which this can be adjusted

Content Area: **Social-Emotional Learning—Regulation**

Basics: To know the importance of being able to calm yourself when you are feeling frustrated

First goes: To try adjusting the energy and pattern of your breathing to increase your sense of calmness

Practice: To regulate your breathing in different ways at different times in the day to notice the effect this can have on your emotional state

Perform: To apply these regulation techniques in response to situations during the week and reflect on how these can be adjusted for even greater effect

4.4.1.1 Summary of Learning Intention Descriptors

Scanning the earlier examples, you will see certain phrases (and their variations) appear again and again. Using the phrases in figure 4.11 should help you design learning intentions.

Stage 1: Basic Knowledge and Skills
- Find out . . .
- Find the . . .
- Know a few . . .
- Know some of . . .
- Know that . . .
- Know the basics . . .
- Know the difference . . .
- Know the importance of . . .
- Know what . . .
- Know who . . .
- Know why . . .
- Name some . . .
- Notice . . .

Stage 2: Good Knowledge and Skills
- Copy a . . .
- Define what . . .
- Draw a plan . . .
- Explain the features of . . .
- Identify examples of . . .
- Illustrate . . .
- Know how to use . . .
- Know key features of . . .
- Know the definition . . .
- Know some of the features of . . .
- Label . . .
- Name . . .
- Show that you know . . .
- Try adjusting the . . .
- Try to . . .

Stage 3: Understand and Practice
- Mock up prototypes of . . .
- Play with . . . (regulate)
- Practice by . . .
- Understand different ways to . . .
- Understand how . . .
- Understand how to . . .
- Understand questions of . . .
- Understand the laws of . . .
- Understand the similarities and differences between . . .
- Understand the variables . . .

Stage 4: Apply, Perform, and Adjust
- Adjust . . .
- Alter . . .
- Apply . . .
- Be able to adapt . . .
- Be able to ask . . .
- Be able to compose . . .
- Be able to explain . . .
- Be able to find . . .
- Be able to show how . . .
- Be able to use . . .
- Build and develop . . .
- Create . . .
- Demonstrate . . .
- Design . . .
- Find the formula that . . .
- Propose ways in which . . .
- Teach . . .

Figure 4.11: Phrases to help design learning intentions.

4.4.2 Success Criteria

Success criteria are the key steps or components needed for students to fulfill the learning intention. Criteria should always flow from the learning intention and include the main things to do, include, or focus on. For example, if the learning intention is "to be able to identify and name equivalent fractions," then the success criteria could be the following.

- Use objects or drawings to show equivalent fractions.
- Explain to others how equivalent fractions have the same value.
- Show examples of equivalent fractions in number form.

Here are some other examples from across the curriculum.

Art

Learning Intention: To understand the differences in effect of a photograph and a drawing of the same image

Success Criteria:

- Identify similarities and differences between the drawing and the photograph.
- Predict which medium is best for different purposes.
- Explore the crossover between photographs and drawings.
- Propose which is the best way to record real life, and say why.

Geography

Learning Intention: To know how scale influences what is shown on a map

Success Criteria:

- Compare the similarities and differences of maps with different scales.
- Draw the same three features (for example, a house, a bridge, and a school) as they would appear on three different maps with different scales.
- Predict which features would appear on large-scale maps compared to those that would appear on small-scale maps.
- Assess the problems Google and other companies encounter when creating maps.

History

Learning Intention: To know about the effects of slavery on indigenous groups in Africa

Success Criteria:

- Use a range of maps to locate some of the different regional groupings across the African continent.
- Relate the main differences in features of regional groups (for example, North African and sub-Saharan) to the physical environment.
- Illustrate with reference to European shipping routes and trade winds which regional groups were most at risk from slave traders.

- Show sensitivity by using respectful language to describe the negative effects of slavery.
- Construct an overview of 15th century African society.

Literacy

Learning Intention: To be able to plan and produce a piece of recount writing (narrative)

Success Criteria:

- Identify the key features and structure of recount writing by examining other texts—for example, diaries, newspaper articles, and personal stories.
- Use a fortune line to chart the chronology and personal impact of events in the piece.
- Write in the first or third person.
- Make good use of the past tense.
- Accurately use time connectives in your writing.
- Focus on specific people or events rather than general topics.
- Engage the reader by using descriptive language.
- Discuss with your partner whether future events could ever be included in a piece of recount writing.

Mathematics (Geometry)

Learning Intention: To understand how to use sine, cosine, and tangent

Success Criteria:

- Locate the hypotenuse, adjacent side, and opposite side in a right-angled triangle.
- Explain what *SOHCAHTOA* stands for.
- Produce accurate formulas for trigonometric ratios.
- Justify why the sine, cosine, and tangent functions are important.

Music

Learning Intention: To be able to compose simple rhythms and melodies

Success Criteria:

- Identify the value of notes regarding their time value.
- Recognize what a minim and quaver represent in the music world.
- Identify the symbol for rest.
- Construct, write, and play a simple rhythm.
- In pairs, combine your compositions to form a new composition.

Religious Studies

Learning Intention: To know about some significant aspects of Hindus' belief in God

Success Criteria:

- Explain the beliefs that underlie the Hindu concept of God.
- Describe the Aum symbol and its significance for Hindus.
- Reflect on different ways of expressing beliefs about God.
- Use religious words accurately when explaining the meaning of worship.
- Identify the names of some of the Hindu gods and goddesses.
- Find links between the Hindu gods and the Viking and Roman gods.

Science

Learning Intention: To understand the properties of solids and liquids

Success Criteria:

- Correctly sort materials as liquid or solid using a Venn diagram (for example, wood, iron, shampoo, shaving foam, and so on).
- Describe similarities between solids and liquids (for example, solids and liquids can be measured).
- Describe differences between solids and liquids (for example, you can pour liquids but not solids).
- Classify items such as sponges, rice, and sand.
- Determine what something is called if it is neither a solid nor a liquid.

Social-Emotional Learning

Learning Intention: To understand what conflict is in its many forms

Success Criteria:

- Work together to discuss and question our interpretation of conflict in the pictures.
- Consider other situations of conflict we know about, including local, regional, national, and international situations.
- Define *conflict*.
- Justify and criticize the causes of conflict.
- Question your own response to conflict recently, and think about how you could make changes in the future.
- Explain how conflict begins and how it can affect different communities.
- Decide if conflict is always a bad thing or not.

4.4.3 Terms to Use When Designing Success Criteria

I mentioned Bloom's (1956) taxonomy in section 4.3.3.2 (page 160). The hierarchy of thinking skills that formed part of the broader set of educational objectives proposed by Bloom and his colleagues can be a very useful reference for when you are writing success criteria. This is particularly true if you are co-constructing criteria with your students (which I hope you are, at least some of the time).

It is strange that Bloom didn't include *reasoning* in his taxonomy, so I have added that category. Also, you will notice that some of the verbs I have suggested fit in multiple places. So, to avoid repetition, I have placed them where I think they fit best. The categories are listed from surface thinking to deep learning to match with the SOLO Taxonomy I shared in section 2.3 (page 56), as well as the hierarchy Bloom (1956) proposed.

Remembering

The following are terms to use when you want your students to show previously learned information.

Identify	Label	List	Match
Memorize	Name	Order	Outline
Recall	Recognize	Recollect	Remember
Repeat	Reproduce	Select	State

Understanding

The following are terms to use when you want your students to demonstrate an understanding of the facts.

Accept	Appreciate	Comprehend	Describe
Discuss	Distinguish	Explain	Give examples
Infer	Locate	Paraphrase	Rewrite
Review	Show	Show how	Translate

Applying

The following are terms to use when you want your students to apply their knowledge and understanding to other situations.

Apply	Change	Construct	Demonstrate
Dramatize	Employ	Extend	Illustrate
Interpret	Manipulate	Operate	Organize
Practice	Produce	Use	Write

Reasoning

The following are terms to use when you want your students to show that they are able to rationalize and interpret.

Choose	Connect	Decide	Deduce
Determine	Generalize	Give reasons	Hypothesize
Prove	Question	Rationalize	Show cause
Solve	Suppose	Test	Verify

Analyzing

The following are terms to use when you want your students to show they are able to analyze ideas and find evidence to support generalizations.

Analyze	Break down	Categorize	Classify
Compare	Contrast	Deconstruct	Draw
Examine	Experiment	Predict	Rank
Represent	Resolve	Sequence	Subdivide

Synthesizing

The following are terms to use when you want your students to pull together component ideas into a new whole.

Arrange	Assemble	Combine	Compose
Create	Design	Devise	Elaborate
Formulate	Generate	Modify	Prepare
Rearrange	Reconstruct	Relate	Reorganize

Evaluating

The following are terms to use when you want your students to show that they can make judgments or test them against agreed-on criteria.

Assess	Calculate	Conclude	Criticize
Critique	Defend	Discriminate	Estimate
Evaluate	Exemplify	Judge	Justify
Rate	Summarize	Support	Value

4.4.4 Co-Constructing (an Understanding of) Success Criteria

I have mentioned a few times that co-constructing success criteria with your students is a good way forward. Indeed, in many circumstances, it is the best way forward.

However, it's true to say there is a good deal of skepticism about this. Teachers ask, "How can students know what is relevant and what is not?" If students already know how to achieve something, then why do they need success criteria; and if they don't know how to be successful with something, then how can they come up with relevant criteria? They don't know what they don't know. A helpful way of approaching this is to think of it as co-constructing an *understanding* of criteria rather than of creating criteria from scratch.

Many students misunderstand or misapply success criteria. So, spending time co-constructing an understanding together—through guided exploration and application—can be time well spent. Other reasons for taking time to co-construct an understanding of success criteria include the following.

- You know what you mean, but that is not the same as having your students know what you mean!

- You can quickly gain a better sense of your students' starting points. Sometimes, confusion or misconceptions lurk where you didn't expect them to; other times, students show a greater awareness than you anticipated. Uncovering this early in the process can help with the task of setting appropriate challenge.

- Guided discussion about the success criteria can help build your students' language of learning, which in turn supports their abilities to self- and peer review.

Some of the best ways to engage your students in this process are as follows.

- **Here's one I made earlier:** Share an excellent example. Ask your students, in pairs, to identify the features they think are most effective.

- **The good, the bad, and the ugly:** Ask students to compare three examples of varying success. Draw out the similarities and differences—what worked and what didn't work. This can be particularly successful when using examples created by former students (anonymized, of course!).

- **Can you see what it is yet?:** Demonstrate a skill or create something in front of your students. Stop at key points to ask your students to share their observations: "What was I doing? What do you think I considered? What could I have done differently?" Use their answers to co-construct criteria for when they have their own goes at it.

- **Deliberate mistakes:** Do what you did in the previous cases, but with mistakes added for students to spot and call out.

- **Ready-Fire-Aim:** I will explain this phrase in more depth in section 5.8.1 (page 259). In the context of cocreating success criteria, it can work in this way.

  - *Ready*—Share the learning intention and an example of what success looks like.
  - *Fire*—Give your students time to experiment by making their first attempts at the task.
  - *Aim*—Reflect on what your students have managed so far, and draw out the features and actions they have found most productive. Turn these into success criteria so that all students can work toward them with later iterations.

4.4.5 Learning Intentions and Success Criteria: Some Final Thoughts

Learning intentions and success criteria will never be perfect. How could they be? Human endeavor is so broad. Students are so diverse. Our intentions are so varied. Even if the perfect ones did exist, matching our feedback against them would be complex. How do you judge a piece of writing if the learning intention is to be able to write a scary story? What makes something scary rather than cliché or predictable? Who decides if the adjectives add to the reader's enjoyment? Whether the verbs are interesting? If the characters come alive?

It's easier to be objective when giving feedback about closed or rules-based criteria—for example, when focusing on spelling, punctuation, or grammar. But even then, there is some degree of interpretation; for example, should I have started this sentence with *and* or can I start with *but*? Therefore, can it ever be satisfactory to judge a piece of writing purely on whether it follows the rules of language? I would be pretty disappointed if reviews of this book focused primarily on my punctuation!

Nonetheless, it still makes sense to be as fair and transparent as we can with the feedback we offer our students. Without doing so, we increase the chances that students who like the feedback they receive smile about it (but do nothing with it) and students who don't like the feedback they receive reject, ignore, or appeal against it for being too personal.

So, it will be imperfect. It will take effort. But the evidence is clear that feedback that closely references learning intentions and success criteria is more likely to be trusted and used and therefore more likely to be effective.

Make sure you create learning intentions that flow from your students' curriculum. Add a breadth of goals across the school year. Use the ASK Model to help you with this. Also, make sure there is a depth of learning. The SOLO Taxonomy can help with this.

Create a range of success criteria to go with each learning intention. Co-construct an understanding of them with your students. Use verbs from Bloom's (1956) taxonomy to guide you. Once you have made a good start with this process and you want to get into the nuances of learning intentions and success criteria, then check out the work of educator Shirley Clarke. Start with *Visible Learning: Feedback* by Hattie and Clarke (2019) and go from there. Also, check out the description of step 1 of the Seven Steps to Feedback (see section 4.9, page 198).

Remember: there is no perfect. Not when we have so many students to teach with so many needs. But that shouldn't stop us from trying—insofar as possible—to match feedback to clear agreements about learning intentions and success criteria.

4.5 Self- and Peer Feedback

Eighty percent of the verbal feedback students receive during the day comes from other students, and most of it is wrong (Nuthall, 2007). Therefore, one of the best ways to improve learning outcomes is to teach students how to give themselves and each other feedback.

In order to improve the outcomes of feedback, teaching students how to give themselves and each other feedback has to be a priority.

This 80 percent statistic comes from the work of Graham Nuthall, an educational researcher credited with doing one of the longest-ever series of studies on teaching and learning. His best-known work, *The Hidden Lives of Learners* (published posthumously; Nuthall, 2007), is widely regarded as a seminal text for understanding learning. His findings come from years of gathering evidence through recordings of student dialogues, pre- and post-testing, and extensive in-class observations. As you will recall, I also mentioned Nuthall's research in section 2.2.1 (page 50) in the context of the ways in which dialogue in classrooms is less productive than we would like it to be.

Reading Nuthall's work emphasizes how rarely students know how to assess their own learning. They need a lot of support to become proficient at it. They also need to be convinced of the purpose and benefits before they are likely to invest sincerity and energy in the process. In my experience, there are three principal steps to teaching students how to assess their own and others' work.

1. Stick as closely as possible to the learning intention and success criteria.

2. Encourage a dialogue between your students rather than asking one to mark or grade the other's efforts.

3. Time the conversations so that they coincide with students' readiness to move from surface to deep learning (from stage 2 to stage 3 of the SOLO Taxonomy). This will help them focus their conversations more on idea generation than on judgments of right, wrong, or bias.

In section 4.4.2 (page 173), I shared some examples of learning intentions and success criteria. Here are a couple of them again, together with samples of how peer assessments might flow from them.

Geography

Learning Intention: To know how scale influences what is shown on a map

Success Criteria:

- Compare the similarities and differences of maps with different scales.
- Draw the same three features (for example, a house, a bridge, and a school) as they would appear on three different maps with different scales.
- Predict which features would appear on large-scale maps compared to those that would appear on small-scale maps.
- Assess the problems Google and other companies encounter when creating maps.

And here is how a peer assessment might flow.

Student B (offering feedback): How much progress do you think you've made toward the learning intention?

Student A (responding to feedback): I've done pretty well so far, I think. I've looked at three maps, all with different scales: 1:25,000, 1:50,000, and 1:250,000.

Student B: What similarities and differences have you spotted?

Student A: The 1:25,000 shows a lot more detail than the 1:250,000. On the large-scale map, I can see houses, parking places, and footpaths. On the small-scale map, I can only really see major roads, whole

Student B: When I was looking at the maps I had, I saw lots of streams and contour lines on the large-scale map. These didn't show up on the small-scale map, although big rivers were shown.

Student A: Yeah, the large-scale map gives a lot more detail for someone walking around. The small-scale map would be better for someone driving a long distance.

Student B: Success criterion 2 says to draw three features for three different maps. Have you managed to do that yet?

Student A: Not yet. I was too busy comparing the differences between the maps. I was also confused by the yellow highlights on the 1:50,000 map.

Student B: I don't know what that is either. We'll have to ask. Anyway, what about the other two criteria? Did you have a go at either of those?

Student A: Well, the one about Google seems quite easy. They're not printing maps but making them for lots of different devices with different screen sizes. So, I guess they don't only have to create 1:25,000, 1:50,000, and 1:250,000 scale maps, but they also have to have everything in between, like 1:21,999. How do they decide what to include and what not to?

Student B: Good question! Also, they're adding live info that these printed maps won't include, such as traffic, roadwork, and so on. So, what's next for you? I'm thinking you should get on with criterion 2 next. What do you think?

Student A: Yeah, I suppose, though I do wonder why we're even looking at these printed maps when nobody uses them anymore. Why aren't we looking at Google Maps or Apple Maps?

As you read this interaction, you were probably wondering which students stick to the task like this. Good point! But I hope the lack of authenticity didn't get in the way of the interaction's purpose. I wanted to illustrate the characteristics of an optimal peer feedback conversation. Notice that it is much more of a guided dialogue than a passing of judgment from one peer to another. If you've read this chapter from the beginning, then this assertion won't come as a surprise, but to many teachers, it is a revelation. Peer feedback is not about having one peer tell another how well they've done, and it's certainly not about grading or passing some sort of judgment. Instead, it should be thought of as an interaction in which two minds are better than one and in which student B helps student A take stock of where they're at and what they could do next to stay on track toward achieving the learning intention.

Literacy

Learning Intention: To be able to plan and produce a piece of recount writing (narrative)

Success Criteria:

- Identify the key features and structure of recount writing by examining other texts—for example, diaries, newspaper articles, and personal stories.
- Use a fortune line to chart the chronology and personal impact of events in the piece.
- Write in the first or third person.
- Make good use of the past tense.
- Accurately use time connectives in your writing.
- Focus on specific people or events rather than general topics.
- Engage the reader by using descriptive language.
- Discuss with your partner whether future events could ever be included in a piece of recount writing.

Here is how a peer assessment might flow.

> ***Student B (offering feedback):*** How are you getting on?
>
> ***Student A (responding to feedback):*** Well, here's what I've done so far. What do you think?
>
> ***Student B (studying student A's first draft):*** First thing I notice is that you've gone for recounting your day. You've used, "I did this" and "I did that." So, you've gone for the first-person perspective. That meets criterion 3. You've also put everything in the past tense, so that sorts out criterion 4—although I'm not sure what it means by "make good use of the past tense"!
>
> ***Student A:*** Yeah, I don't know either, but anyway—yes, I went for the first person because I thought that was easiest for me. I don't think it's a very interesting recount, though.
>
> ***Student B:*** Which of the criteria do you think would help with that?
>
> ***Student A:*** Probably the seventh one: use descriptive language.
>
> ***Student B:*** I agree. Which sentences do you think you could add some more descriptive language to? How about this one? [Student B points to the third sentence.]
>
> ***Student A:*** Good idea. Maybe I'll add incredibly and completely in there?
>
> ***Student B:*** Or what about utterly or entirely? Tell you what, how about looking in a thesaurus?
>
> ***Student A:*** Yes, I could do that.

> ***Student B:*** One of the other criteria mentions using time connectives. I see you've used then, soon, and afterward. Which other ones might you use in the next section?
>
> ***Student A:*** I don't know. Maybe, next, first, second, third, and so on?
>
> ***Student B:*** My favorite ones are initially, meanwhile, and suddenly.
>
> ***Student A:*** Is suddenly a time connective?
>
> ***Student B:*** I think so. I guess it depends where you use it, and how.
>
> ***Student A:*** OK, thanks. I'll try those. I'll get a thesaurus as well!

Again, this all sounds very inauthentic, but I hope it nonetheless gives a sense of the spirit I'm aiming to recommend. It should be a guided dialogue, not a critique or judgment.

Mathematics (Geometry)

Learning Intention: To understand how to use sine, cosine, and tangent

Success Criteria:

- Locate the hypotenuse, adjacent side, and opposite side in a right-angled triangle.
- Explain what *SOHCAHTOA* stands for.
- Produce accurate formulas for trigonometric ratios.
- Justify why the sine, cosine, and tangent functions are important.

And here is how a peer assessment might flow.

> ***Student B (offering feedback):*** How do you feel you're doing?
>
> ***Student A (responding to feedback):*** Well, I know the hypotenuse is the long side, but I don't know which one is the opposite and which is the adjacent side.
>
> ***Student B:*** I think they change according to which angle you're trying to calculate, don't they?
>
> ***Student A:*** What do you mean?
>
> ***Student B:*** Well, if we're trying to work out which angle that is [student B points at the one to the bottom right], then the adjacent is that line because it's right next to it, and the opposite is that one across from it. The hypotenuse is always the longest side, so that doesn't change.
>
> ***Student A:*** Ah right, OK. That makes sense. So, if I'm trying to work out this angle [student A points to the other angle that isn't the right angle], then this line now becomes the adjacent and that one the opposite?
>
> ***Student B:*** Yes! Correct. So, that's the first criterion sorted. What about the second one? Do you know what SOHCAHTOA stands for?

Student A: Yes. Sine is equal to Opposite over Hypotenuse; Cosine is equal to Adjacent over Hypotenuse; and Tangent is equal to Opposite over Adjacent.

Student B: Great. So, how does that help you?

Student A: Well, if I want to calculate an angle in a right-angled triangle, then I can use SOHCAHTOA. For example, if I want to know the tan of this angle, then I would divide the length of the side opposite the angle by the length of the side adjacent to the angle.

Student B: Yes, that gives you the tan of that angle. Now how would you find the sin of the angle?

Student A: I would divide the length of the side opposite the angle by the length of the hypotenuse.

Student B: What if you know the sin of the angle is 0.5, and you know the hypotenuse is 3 centimeters, but you don't know the length of the opposite side?

Student A: I guess I could still use SOHCAHTOA to set up an equation. Because I know that sin is opposite over hypotenuse, I could set up this equation: $0.5 = x/3$. Then I would just multiply both sides by 3. The opposite side would be 1.5 centimeters.

Student B: Great, so I think you've definitely achieved criteria 1 and 2 and are well on your way to dealing with criterion 3. Do you have any thoughts about criterion 4?

Student A: Not really, no, other than sin, cos, and tan are needed to help work out angles in a right-angled triangle.

Student B: I couldn't really say any more either. Maybe we should ask someone else.

Before these examples, I mentioned there are three principal steps to teaching students how to assess their own and others' work. The first is sticking as closely as possible to the learning intention and success criteria. I hope these examples show that clearly.

The second is making sure any peer assessment comes in the form of a guided discussion rather than a critique or judgment. Again, the previous examples should illustrate this.

The third and final precept is making sure the conversation between peers takes place in the middle of the task, not at the end. If the reviews are left until your students have completed their tasks, it is going to be difficult to share anything other than summative comments ("This is how well I think you've done," "This is what I think was good or bad," "This is how well you attended to all the success criteria"). However, if the conversations take place one-third and two-thirds of the way through the task, they lend themselves much better to phrases such as, "This is how well I think you've done *so far*, and these are some of the ways I think you could continue."

Other phrases to encourage your students to use include the following.

- **So far:** As in, "How much progress have you made so far?" "What are the things you've done so far that you are happy with?" or "Which criteria have you attended to so far?"
- **Might or could:** As in, "What might your next steps be?" or "What could you do next?"
- **When:** As in, "When would it be good to . . . ?" or "I wonder if it would be good to add that when . . . ."

In other words, encourage your students to use provisional language during their conversations. They should think of themselves less as judges or referees and more as a second pair of eyes.

With elementary students, it may be necessary to directly support them rather than leave them to run their own peer assessments. For organizational reasons as much as pedagogical ones, I would ordinarily run these peer assessments as a whole-class or group activity.

As for self-assessments, the process is very similar. Encourage your students to stop midway through their learning task and consider how much progress they've made toward the learning intention, which success criteria they think they've attended to very well and which need more attention, and then what they think their next priority is. Getting into the habit of stopping, checking, revisiting, revising, and confirming is good practice not only for self-assessment procedures but also for exam practice, task success, and learning in general.

Finally, this section links very nicely with the earlier section on co-constructing success criteria. The same guidance applies. Model the right approaches with and for your students. Demonstrate what an assessment conversation should sound like. Emphasize the spirit of encouragement and inquiry. Draw attention to the provisional language and the questioning techniques that help maintain a focus on alternatives rather than rights and wrongs. Keep reiterating the three guiding questions: (1) What are you trying to achieve? (2) How much progress have you made so far? and (3) What could you do next? Figure 4.12 (page 186) offers some ideas for guidance to share with your students.

In this video, James gives a brief summary of the differences between formative and summative feedback.

> **Two Minds Are Better Than One**
>
> How to offer feedback to a classmate:
>
> 1. Pair up with someone who has made a good start on their learning task (not someone who has already finished).
> 2. Use the three feedback questions to guide your conversation.
>   a. a. What are you trying to achieve? (This should be answered by the learning intention and success criteria they are working toward.)
>   b. How much progress have you made so far?
>   c. What could you do next?
> 3. Remember: it is your job to be a curious friend, so ask interested questions.
> 4. Begin the conversation with, "Which criteria do you think you've satisfied?"
> 5. Listen to their responses, ask questions, give suggestions—but do not pass judgments.
> 6. Use these sorts of phrases.
>   - **So far**: For example, How much progress have you made so far? What are the things you've done so far that you are happy with? Which criteria have you attended to so far?
>   - **Might or could**: For example, What might your next steps be? What could you do next?
>   - **When**: For example, When would it be good to . . . ? I wonder if it would be good to add that when . . . .
> 7. After exploring how much progress your classmate has made, encourage them to think about what they could do next. Make sure these steps are in relation to the success criteria they are aiming to meet.

Figure 4.12: Guidance to share with your students.

4.6 *Formative* and *Summative*

 *When information is used to adjust teaching and learning, it becomes formative. When it is used to measure learning, it is summative.*

There is a lot of confusion about the terms *formative*, *summative*, *assessment*, *evaluation*, and *assessment for learning*. Oftentimes, they are used interchangeably. Sometimes, they attract reversed definitions. Additional complications arise when comparing the ways in which they are understood and used in the United States compared to the United Kingdom, Australia, and New Zealand. No wonder people are confused!

Originally, I was going to include these terms in the next section, listing all the different types of feedback, but they seemed too important to be just a few among many. They are often used prejudicially to argue which approach to assert and which to shun, so it seemed prudent to give them their own section.

Starting from the beginning, the terms *formative* and *summative* were first coined by professor Michael Scriven in 1967. He related them to timing and function. He described *formative evaluations* as considerations *during* a learning task that help a teacher *form* the next instructional steps. For example, teachers notice that some students are confused, some are making mistakes, and some are basing their actions on misconceptions—and they adjust subsequent explanations or activities to improve student learning. And Scriven (1967) described *summative evaluations* as the reflections at the *end* of a task that help *summarize* how much students have learned.

This all seems straightforward enough. When I'm teaching, I take notice of how well my students are understanding and engaging so that I can adjust interactions, activities, and explanations—in the moment—to maximize their learning. That is formative. However, after the lesson, when I'm staggering to the staffroom, reflecting on what just happened—for example, which students engaged and which didn't—that is summative.

Two years after Scriven coined these terms, Bloom (1969) made the case that assessments could help with these reflections. After all, tests can offer insights into student learning that classroom observations might miss. So, rather than teaching students first and then testing them afterward for the purposes of recording student achievement, Bloom (1969) recommended that teachers use assessments *during* a topic to check how well students are doing and make timely adjustments according to those findings.

Bloom's (1969) motive was to reduce the gap between underachieving students and their peers. He believed that the normal distribution of achievement was anything but natural. He argued that if instruction was more closely matched to student need—rather than determined by year group and curriculum—then every student would make excellent progress. Assessment, in the way in which he conceptualized it, would be instrumental in understanding each student's starting point.

Bloom's (1969) proposal makes sense. Interestingly, there are many connections between his theories and those of Alfred Binet (Binet & Simon, 1905), who I mention in section 5.3 (page 227) when describing the history of intelligence testing. Unfortunately, Bloom's (1969) theories led to unintended consequences. Rather than being considered *one way* to gather evidence to inform next steps—as Bloom had proposed—assessments became the primary way. Indeed, they were often viewed as the only reliable way. They still are, if the accusations that teacher assessments led to grade inflation during the COVID-19 pandemic are anything to go by.

So, decades after Bloom made his proposal, the terms *formative* and *summative* were inextricably linked to assessments. The direction of causation also switched. Instead of having information *from* assessments cause adjustments in teaching, all too often teaching was adjusted to cause improvements in assessment scores. To put it another way, testing for the purposes of (improving) teaching turned into teaching for the purposes of testing.

Then, in the mid-1980s, researcher Harry Black (Black & Wiliam, 1986) created the term *assessment for learning*. As his coauthor Dylan Wiliam notes, many teachers in the United States credit founder and retired president of the Assessment Training Institute Rick Stiggins (2005) with coining the term, but he cites Black as the original author.

Assessment *for* learning was introduced as a deliberate contrast to assessment *of* learning. There have been many definitions, but perhaps this is the clearest one: "Assessment for Learning is part of everyday practice by students, teachers and peers that seeks, reflects upon and responds to information from dialogue, demonstration and observation in ways that enhance ongoing learning" (Klenowski, 2009, p. 264).

Reading this, you could be forgiven for thinking that *assessment for learning* and *formative assessment* are the same thing. After all, isn't formative assessment an everyday practice that responds to a range of data that are then used to improve learning? Well, yes, except that their design is different. They might lead to the same outcomes, but they start from slightly different points.

Assessment for learning is designed to identify how well your students are learning and to adjust instruction accordingly, whereas formative assessment is when an assessment activity—normally designed for the purposes of certifying competence—is then used formatively to adjust subsequent teaching. Same outcomes, different design.

To some people, this distinction matters a lot. Personally, I'm a bit more sanguine about the differences. So long as we are using whatever reliable evidence we can gather to fine-tune our teaching so that it better meets students' needs, that is a good thing. The evidence we collect might come from assessments designed to certify competence (what we typically call *tests*). But it might just as well come from our assessments (professional judgments) of student engagement, curiosity, and thoughtfulness inferred from dialogue, observation, and interaction.

As for the difference between evaluation and assessment, it is a similarly blurred story. Some people think of assessments as tests or assignments completed under test conditions, whereas others see assessments much more broadly as any activities providing information that can be used as feedback to modify teaching and learning.

Some people think of evaluation as the *other* one. So, if they define assessment as *testing*, then they think of evaluation as gathering evidence from *other* sources. Or if they think of assessment as gathering evidence from a broad range of sources, then they think of evaluation as testing. So far, so murky!

In the research, I can't find a broad agreement about the definitions of *evaluation* and *assessment*. However, there is a very clear consensus about the following three definitions.

1. When assessment is used for the purposes of accountability or to certify competence, then it is *summative*.

2. When the information from an assessment is used to modify students' next steps or to adjust the teaching and learning that follow, then it becomes *formative*.

3. *Assessment for learning* is designed from the beginning to improve students' learning. It uses evidence from a range of sources to adjust instruction, typically during the lesson.

As Wiliam (2011) puts it, "There is now a strong body of theoretical and empirical work that suggests that integrating assessment with instruction may well have *unprecedented power to increase student engagement* and to improve learning outcomes" (p. 13, emphasis added).

4.7 A Wide Variety of Feedback Types

Feedback is varied. Its approaches vary. Its outcomes vary. They all tend to be positive, but some are more positive than others.

At the beginning of this chapter, I described how John Hattie used one term, *feedback*, in his original book, *Visible Learning* (Hattie, 2009). By the time he wrote his follow-up book, *Visible Learning: The Sequel* (Hattie, 2023), he had split feedback into eight subcategories and twelve other connected variables. I have already covered many of these, but some have yet to be touched on. So, here is the complete list, plus some others that other authors use when writing about feedback. As I did in section 4.1 (page 149), I have put them in order from highest effect size to lowest.

Feedback (reinforcement and cues; *d* = 1.01)

Positive reinforcement of the things that students are doing well, together with cues for their next steps, has a significant impact on student learning. However, there is a strong caveat to this. These gains are most likely to be at task level only rather than at process level or self-regulation level. The following paragraphs explain these terms further.

- **Task level:** This focuses on *what* students are trying to complete. Particularly suitable for someone working at the surface level, it generally focuses on what is right, what is wrong, and what steps could be taken next. Complexity of information offered should be kept relatively low. Feedback should be immediate, should be matched to success criteria, and may include scaffolding.

- **Process level:** This focuses on *how* students are working toward the desired outcome. It focuses on the approaches and strategies they are using, offering alternatives or refinements. It is particularly suitable for someone working beyond the surface level into the deeper areas of learning. Quantity and complexity of feedback can be greater than at the task level, and prompts and cues are often part of the advice offered.

- **Self-regulation level:** This helps students monitor their own progress and performance. It is suitable for students working at deep levels of learning. Prompts can include, How could you deepen your understanding? and Are you on track (and how do you know)? Feedback can be delayed since you are aiming to boost students' independent learning.

So, although positive reinforcement of the things that students are doing or getting right can lead to very positive outcomes (as evidenced by the effect size of 1.01), these gains tend to be at the surface level.

In some meta-analyses, a fourth category is mentioned: *self level*. This is another term for *praise*. Unlike the three other levels, self-level feedback is unrelated to what a student is doing and is more concerned with the person. Though appraisal feedback can be a source of comfort and support for students, it does little to enhance achievement or learning. This is explored further in the mindset chapter (see section 5.7.1, page 253).

Feedback (timing; *d* = 0.89)

The findings of the meta-analyses on this topic show that the timing of feedback should be matched to where students are in the instructional cycle.

When students are at the surface level of learning and focusing on the task, feedback should be immediate. When they have moved to a deeper level of learning by focusing on the strategies underlying the task, feedback can be slightly delayed. When they are thinking in a metacognitive way, considering how much progress they are making and if they could adjust anything, feedback is less sensitive to timing.

Classroom Discussion (*d* = 0.82)

Classroom discussion is one of the best ways to engage students and deepen their learning. It involves teachers and students building on each other's ideas, posing questions, and constructing interpretations together.

See chapter 2 (page 19) for an in-depth exploration of this topic.

Alternative Assessment Methods (*d* = 0.67)

This category relates primarily to the use of portfolios, which are typically created over a longer period of time. As such, they provide more opportunities for timely and relevant feedback that can be used formatively. The effect size of this category compares favorably with test-style assessments resulting in grades that are used summatively.

Success Criteria (*d* = 0.64)

Success criteria are the key steps or components needed for students to fulfill the agreed-on learning intention. They should include the main things to do, include, or focus on.

This category was covered in depth in section 4.4 (page 166).

Feedback (tasks and processes; *d* = 0.63)

This category focuses on feedback that helps students better understand the processes involved in completing tasks. It often includes analysis of good examples and how they were achieved. It can lead students to consider options for processing, strategies for detecting errors, better ways to find information, and different approaches to take.

Effects of Testing (*d* = 0.59)

Tests can offer insights into student learning that observations might miss. They are most effective when used formatively to identify adjustments that subsequent instruction might need. When used summatively, however—when they are given at the end of a unit of work and kept as a record of achievement—they offer little benefit. See sections 4.6 (page 186), 5.3 (page 227), and 5.5.2 (page 244) for further explorations of this topic.

Feedback (technology; *d* = 0.55)

Surprisingly, given how much money is invested in technology, only two meta-analyses on the topic are included in Hattie's database. They both relate to how effective computer-generated feedback can be in terms of improving learning outcomes.

There is evidence that students trust feedback from computers more than feedback from humans because of the inherent objectivity. Computers don't change their tone or message based on what mood they are in, how much they like students, or whether the recipient has special needs. Many students also report that they like being able to set the pace of feedback according to their own needs and preferences.

As technology is improving, more emphasis is being placed on elaborative as well as corrective feedback. This can make the feedback more beneficial, particularly at process and self-regulation levels.

Peer and Self-Grading (*d* = 0.54)

The meta-analyses on this topic give a number of varying conclusions. The most significant implication for our practice is that providing opportunities for students to actively engage in the grading process leads to many beneficial effects. These include a better understanding of success criteria, less suspicion about the way in which grade judgments are made, and a further opportunity to develop student metacognition.

All studies were run at the middle and high school levels, which is perhaps unsurprising. Interestingly, though, the effects were most powerful in the middle years. Encouragingly, these positive effects were noted in all curriculum areas. In all contexts, students who took part in self- and peer grading outperformed students not exposed to self-reflection on measures of academic achievement.

Beyond the grading exercises, the research also recommends providing metacognitive prompts to students. This often takes place in the last five minutes of a lesson, though of course it can take place at any point in the learning. As one meta-analysis concludes, "Providing metacognitive prompts to students . . . uses very little instructional time, and costs very little . . . [and is likely to lead to] a statistically significant, large effect size" (Youde, 2019, p. 54).

Questioning (*d* = 0.49)

Questioning is one of the most commonly used ways to engage students. Unfortunately, however, it all too often follows the Initiate-Respond-Evaluate (I-R-E) sequence. This sequence, together with the quick-fire pace, limits participation and, therefore, outcomes. Change this approach and learning is boosted significantly. See chapter 2 (page 19) for an in-depth exploration of this topic.

Feedback (from students; *d* = 0.47)

When feedback from students to their teachers is listened to and acted on, the impact of this feedback is significant.

However, not many teachers accept this feedback as credible. There are claims that student feedback is more akin to popularity ratings than teacher effectiveness. To an extent, this is borne out by the research. Researchers Herbert W. Marsh, Theresa Dicke, and Mathew Pfeiffer (2019) found that teacher expressiveness affected student ratings but had very little impact on student achievement, whereas lesson content made a difference to achievement but not to student ratings.

Strangely, teachers will often listen to feedback from adult observers who visit for short periods of time, but when it comes to feedback from students, they are skeptical even though students are the ones most familiar with a teacher's practice. There is very little evidence that collecting feedback from students leads to modifications to practice. If ever there was a topic worth digging into more, it would be this one!

Worked Examples (*d* = 0.47)

Worked examples show students the steps that could be taken toward a learning goal. In a sense, they are an instruction manual with explanations and possible solutions. A typical approach is to set a problem and then give a breakdown of the steps required to reach the solution.

Interestingly, particularly for those seeking ways to close the gap, the effects are much more pronounced for lower-achieving and at-risk students. This could have implications for your practice in that you might wish to provide worked solutions only (or initially) for those students struggling to access learning. This approach connects very much with the idea of preview that I write about in section 6.1 (page 272).

The research about worked examples is rooted in John Sweller's (1988) cognitive load theory. This theory states that we all have a limited working memory but an almost unlimited long-term memory. Our long-term memory holds schemas that help to make sense of the world. The more schemas we have, the less we have to hold in our working memory when accessing new information. For example, someone who plays a lot of computer games is likely to understand a brand-new game more quickly than someone who isn't a gamer. The schemas in their mind effectively make connections, make contrasts, and spot similar functions, whereas the non-gamer has to start from the beginning and rely much more heavily on their working memory. This leads to greater cognitive load for the non-gamer.

When the context is not gaming, but something regarded as fundamental to education—for example, numeracy or literacy—the stakes become *much* higher. Students who have lots of schemas to draw on encounter far less cognitive load when accessing new information than those who have fewer related schemas. This is why worked examples that help augment or create new schemas are so effective, particularly for at-risk students.

Incidentally, I make a link between cognitive load theory and growth mindset in section 6.4 (page 287).

Clear Goal Intentions (d = 0.44)

Learning goals describe what students should know, understand, or be able to do by the end of the lesson or series of lessons. When they are clearly understood by your students, learning becomes apparent and progress more likely. Without them, your students can still engage in tasks, but any attempt to extend or deepen their development is likely to be less precise. This category was covered in section 4.4 (page 166).

Feedback (from tests; d = 0.41)

Although the effect size shown is good, the range of effects depending on the type of feedback received after a test is enormously varied. Perhaps the biggest surprise for many teachers will be that feedback that merely indicates whether a response was right or wrong doesn't just have a limited impact; it actually leads to a slightly negative (–0.08) impact. For the feedback to have a positive effect, it needs to also include corrective information. If this is accompanied by explanation—or if students are guided enough that they come up with the correction themselves—then the effects improve to d = 0.31 (Kulik & Kulik, 1988).

The biggest gains are seen in pre- and post-test situations, with an effect size of 0.71 (Bangert-Drowns, Kulik, Kulik, & Morgan, 1991). I share ways in which these can work effectively in your classroom in section 5.5.2 (page 244).

Peer Assessment (*d* = 0.41)

Conventions such as "Three Before Me," in which students are encouraged to seek out three different people or resources before asking a teacher for help, are popular in many schools. However, students need to be taught how to engage in peer cooperation and peer assessment. Without this support, they may end up with incorrect or misleading advice or solutions, without realizing the errors. As I mentioned earlier in this chapter, Nuthall's (2007) research would suggest these erroneous responses are altogether far too common!

In section 4.5 (page 179), I shared some conventions that will help students learn how to effectively engage in peer assessment.

Formative Evaluation (*d* = 0.40)

I have written about this topic in section 4.6 (page 186). It is, however, worth adding that the effect size is lower than expected. Bear in mind that many researchers, not least Wiliam, recommend formative evaluation as one of the most effective practices teachers can use to improve student learning. So, an effect size of 0.40 seems low, certainly lower than the effect sizes of many other approaches to feedback.

However, as researcher Randy E. Bennett (2009) points out following a critical review of the field, there is no clear consensus about the meanings of the term *formative evaluation*. Therefore, the variability of effects from a magnitude of 0.25 to 0.70 is caused by differences in the way it is understood and, therefore, operationalized.

A 2011 meta-analysis included only thirteen studies because the authors, researchers Neal Kingston and Brooke Nash (2011), were highly critical of the quality of the research.

Frequently, a practice is described as *formative evaluation* when it is no such thing. It should only be called *formative* when the information gathered is used to adjust instruction. The data that inform the adjustments could come from tests, classroom interactions, reading of the room, gestures, questions, errors, or student accomplishments.

When it really is formative evaluation rather than a misnamed practice, it can indeed be one of the most effective ways to improve learning for all students.

Frequent Testing (*d* = 0.39)

If students always learned what they were taught, we would never need to test them; we could just keep records of the content covered. However, as we all know, students don't always learn. Indeed, sometimes we wonder whether they were even present in the lesson.

Hattie (2023) reports that tests including conceptual and problem-solving questions are better than only factual ones but that *the* most significant factor is making sure feedback is used in between tests. Giving tests by themselves doesn't make much difference, but administering tests, giving feedback, allowing students to learn from that advice, and then testing again increases the impact to $d = 0.62$.

Researchers Peter C. Brown, Henry L. Roediger III, and Mark A. McDaniel (2014) identify low-stakes testing as optimal for increasing retention of information. Low-stakes testing leads students to retain more than their peers who revise without being tested afterward.

If this topic interests you, I recommend checking out the meta-analysis by researcher Richard P. Phelps (2012) that I mention in section 5.5.2 (page 244).

Productive Failure (errors; *d* = 0.39)

Productive failure is an instructional design that implements a problem-solving phase before students receive advice and guidance from their teacher. It is particularly well tested within mathematics contexts. In section 5.8 (page 257), I write about it in a more general sense by discussing teaching students how to learn from corrected mistakes.

Feedback (comments versus grades; *d* = 0.19)

In her well-known study, psychology researcher Ruth Butler (1987) split 132 eleven-year-olds in Israel into three groups. The first group was given comments only, the second group was given grades only, and the third group was given what most students are given: grades and comments. She then looked at how much additional gain each group made as a result of the information they received.

As table 4.1 shows, the group that received only comments made an additional 30 percent gain in their learning. The group that received only grades made no additional gain. The worrying part is that the students who received grades and comments made no additional gain! The grades undid the positive effect of the comments.

Table 4.1: Comments Versus Grades

Group	Feedback Style	Pre-Post Gain	Student Attitudes
A	Comments only	30 percent gain	All students: Positive
B	Grades only	No gain	Top 25 percent: Positive Bottom 25 percent: Negative
C	Grades and comments	No gain	Top 25 percent: Positive Bottom 25 percent: Negative

Source: Adapted from Butler, 1987.

Feedback should tell your students what they have done well and what they should do next. Grades alone cannot tell them this. But when you put grades together with comments, too many students will look at their grade first and, if it is a good grade, think to themselves, "Why do I need to improve?" And if they get a bad grade, they will think, "Why should I try to improve? I'm no good at this anyway!" As researchers Paul Black, Christine Harrison, Clare Lee, Bethan Marshall, and Dylan Wiliam (2004) put it:

> Research experiments have established that, while student learning can be advanced by feedback through comments, the giving of numerical scores or grades has a negative effect, in that the students ignore comments when marks are also given. These results often surprise teachers, but those who have

abandoned the giving of marks discover their experience confirms the findings: students do engage more productively in improving their work. (p. 13)

You might be asking yourself why I'm drawing attention to this, bearing in mind that giving comments instead of grades has a *mere* 0.19 effect size. Good point! Except that it is a relatively easy win, so why not pursue it? If you can get an effect size of 0.19 just by keeping grades away from your feedback comments, you'd be foolish not to take it. That said, if you *are* obliged to grade students' work, then give your comments first, allow time for your students to apply your advice, and then grade at the end. I cover this in more detail in section 4.9 (page 198).

Feedback (self; *d* = 0.14)

This category relates to praise. Unlike other forms of feedback, this is unrelated to learning tasks. It is concerned with the person. In the mindset chapter, I explore the three main types of praise: (1) person, (2) process, and (3) product. The only one that leads to improvements in learning (the *d* = 0.14 effect size) is process praise. See section 5.7 (page 251) for more information.

Having described all the categories mentioned by Hattie in his Visible Learning Metax (n.d.) database, I think it is worth commenting on *feedforward*, as this is a particularly popular term in some parts of the world.

Some people use the term *feedforward* to ensure that necessary attention is given to looking forward, toward the next steps in the learning journey. In many ways, there is nothing wrong with this, and if you use the term, keep using it if you are particularly invested in it. However, there is a danger that using *feedforward* suggests *feedback* only involves looking backward, whereas for feedback to be effective, it necessarily *has to* include looking forward. The last of the three feedback questions makes this clear: (1) What am I trying to achieve? (2) How much progress have I made so far? and (3) What should I do next to improve?

So, if you use the term *feedforward*, I would make sure you place it under the umbrella term of *feedback*. For example, this might be a case of saying that you're engaging in the feedforward part of feedback, or summarizing the three guiding questions as (1) objective, (2) progress, and (3) feedforward.

4.8 Feedback and the Learning Pit

The best feedback helps students take their next steps in a learning journey. The Learning Pit provides a framework for this progress and the language to articulate it.

The main benefits of feedback come from helping students take steps forward in their learning journey. One way to frame this is by imagining their progress through the Learning Pit. This section describes the range of questions you could encourage your students to think about at each stage of their journey. Figure 4.13 (page 196) shows how these ideas fit with an illustration of the Learning Pit. A high-resolution pdf of this image is available to download from the Learning Pit website: www.learningpit.org/product/teach-brilliantly-downloads.

Stage 1: Preparing to Explore

Feedback questions should focus on how much your students understand the aim and purpose of the learning they are about to engage in. Consider questions such as the following.

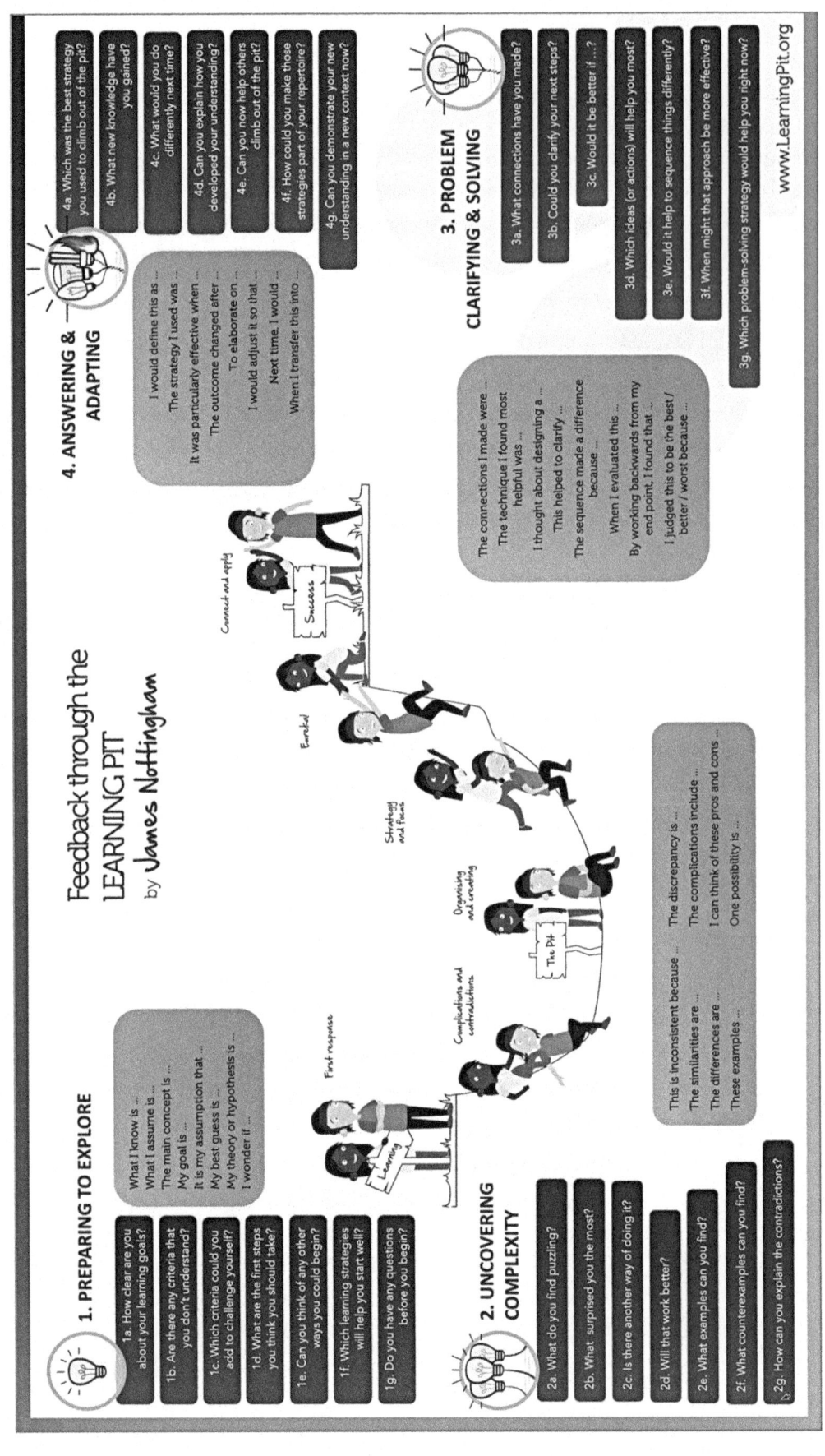

Source: © 2023 by James Nottingham.

Figure 4.13: Feedback questions through the Learning Pit.

- How clear are you about your learning goals?
- How much can you do or understand already?
- Are there any criteria that you don't understand?
- Which criteria could you add to challenge yourself?
- What are the first steps you think you should take?
- Can you think of any other ways you could begin?
- Which learning strategies will help you make a good start?
- Do you have any questions before you begin?

Terms your students might use when answering these questions include the following.

- What I *know* is . . .
- What I *don't know* is . . .
- What I *assume* is . . .
- I am *confused* by . . .
- The main *concept* is . . .
- My *goal* is . . .
- It is my *assumption* that . . .
- My best *guess* is . . .
- My *theory* or *hypothesis* is . . .
- I *wonder* if . . .

Stage 2: Uncovering Complexity

At this stage, your students are going into the pit. Therefore, feedback questions should focus on the examples and complications they are discovering, such as the following.

- What do you find puzzling?
- What surprised you the most?
- Is there another way of doing it?
- Will that work better?
- What examples can you find?
- What counterexamples can you find?
- How can you explain the contradictions?

Terms your students might use when answering these questions include the following.

- This is *inconsistent* because . . .
- The *similarities* are . . .
- The *differences* are . . .
- My *other idea* is . . .

- These *examples* . . .
- The *discrepancy* is . . .
- The *complications* include . . .
- I can think of these *pros and cons* . . .
- One *possibility* is . . .
- My *hypothesis* is . . .

Stage 3: Problem Clarifying and Solving

At this stage, your students should marshal their resources and select problem-solving strategies to help them climb out of the pit. To help them with these tasks, you could ask them some of the following feedback questions.

- What connections have you made?
- Could you clarify your next steps?
- Would it be better if . . . ?
- Which ideas (or actions) will help you most?
- Would it help to sequence things differently?
- When might that approach be more effective?
- Which problem-solving strategy would help you right now?

Terms your students might use when answering these questions include the following.

- The *connections* I made were . . .
- The *technique* I found most helpful was . . .
- I thought about *designing* a . . .
- This helped to *clarify* . . .
- The *sequence* made a difference because . . .
- When I *evaluated* this . . .
- By *working backward* from my end point, I found that . . .
- I *judged* this to be best, better, or worst because . . .

Stage 4: Answering and Adapting

At this stage, your students should be emerging from the pit with more robust solutions. They can then be given the chance to express their answers as well as to look for ways to adapt their learning to other contexts. The following metacognitive questions should deepen the feedback outcomes.

- Which was the best strategy you used to climb out of the pit?
- What new knowledge have you gained?
- What would you do differently next time?
- Can you explain how you developed your understanding?

- Can you now help others climb out of the pit?
- How could you make those strategies part of your repertoire?
- Can you demonstrate your new understanding in a new context now?

Terms your students might use when answering these questions include the following.

- I would *define* this as . . .
- The *strategy* I used was . . .
- It was particularly *effective when* . . .
- The *outcome* changed after . . .
- To *elaborate* on . . .
- I would *adjust* it so that . . .
- *Next time*, I would . . .
- When I *transfer* this into . . .

4.9 The Seven Steps to Feedback

 *The best feedback is guided by clear learning intentions and success criteria; is a mix of self-reflections, peer responses, and teacher advice; and is timed to create the opportunity and expectation that students will use it to improve their learning.*

Having gone through the main theory and practices of feedback, I think now is the time to pull everything together into a step-by-step guide. I call this the Seven Steps to Feedback. In reality, it is six steps plus a grading step at the end if you are required to grade. If you don't have to grade, lucky for you, and lucky for your students! Unfortunately, though, most of us have to. So, I've included the seventh step for you. The good news is that I include ways to stop it from being the negative distraction it so often is.

Whether you are interested in the first six or all seven steps, please note that each one relies on a set of values. These values include trust, engagement, and support. When these values are present, each step will lead to a more meaningful, lasting impact. Feedback without these is likely to be rejected, avoided, resented, or responded to under duress.

Of course, there may well be a bidirectional relationship between these values and high-quality feedback. So, if you develop trust, engagement, and support, then the outcomes of feedback are likely to be improved. And if you share high-quality feedback, then those same values are likely to develop along the way. So, choose a starting point and go for it!

The key is that feedback is not just influenced by the relationship between giver and receiver (although that is important). It is also affected by the prevailing culture of learning. So, pay close attention to this and ensure everyone knows their role in contributing to it.

Here are some messages to share with your students.

- No one has all the answers, but everyone can improve.
- Feedback is an important factor influencing our improvement.

- The best feedback shows us how much progress we've made and what we could do next.
- Feedback can be written or spoken, formal or informal.
- If we make mistakes, examining them can lead to even more learning.
- The power of feedback lies in the way in which we apply it thoughtfully.

And here are four messages to share with other adults in your classroom.

1. Students respond better to feedback when it is personalized, well timed, and constructive. *Constructive* does not mean the feedback is positive, as so many people assume. *Constructive* means it includes advice and ideas that will help students construct their next steps. Praise can distract from—and often, diminish—the impact of feedback. So, the safest bet is to keep praise out of the feedback process. That does not mean you should never praise! It just means you should keep it away from feedback. This is explored further in sections 4.4, 4.9, and 5.7.1 (pages 166, 198, and 253).
2. Feedback should help students make progress toward their learning goal. It should never be given—or perceived—as personal criticism.
3. Feedback is more effective when it is regular, cumulative, and developmental rather than random and unconnected.
4. We should all be seen to positively welcome and act on feedback. Walking the talk is crucial for the credibility of feedback.

The seven (six plus one) steps to good feedback are as follows.

1. **Agreement on learning goals:** Share learning intentions and associated success criteria. Co-construct an understanding of these when possible.
2. **First attempts:** Give your students an opportunity to take their first steps toward their learning goal.
3. **Self- or peer feedback:** Pause your students' learning journey. Refer to the success criteria, and ask them to identify how much progress they have made and what they could do next to move closer to their learning intention.
4. **Edits:** With their self-reflections (and peer reflections) in mind, your students should now take further steps toward their learning intention.
5. **Teacher feedback:** Once your students have gone as far as they can independently, offer them feedback that will help them reach or exceed their learning intention. Offer advice that can be understood and used effectively. Do *not* give them a grade at this stage (although you may wish to record a provisional grade for your own reference).
6. **Final edits:** Feedback has to be used effectively for it to be classified as good feedback. So, give your students time to apply your advice before they finish a learning episode.

7. **Grade (or no grade):** If you have to grade, do so at the end, *after* your students have used your feedback to improve their learning. Use the success criteria to justify the grade awarded. Ultimately, teach your students how to grade their own work.

The following sections take you through these seven steps in more detail.

In this video, James gives an overview of
The Seven Steps to Feedback.

4.9.1 Step 1: Agreement on Learning Goals

First things first, agree on learning goals with your students. If you don't have an agreement about these, don't offer feedback! You can challenge, prompt, or encourage, but do *not* give feedback. To do so would be to risk students' taking it personally.

At the beginning of this chapter, I mentioned the findings from Kluger and DeNisi (1996), who found that feedback led to negative outcomes in one-third of the studies they analyzed. By far the most common reason for these negative effects is students perceive the feedback to be related to them personally (to self) rather than to progress with a task. The best remedy for this, Kluger and DeNisi (1996) counter, is ensuring feedback is tied as closely as possible to learning intentions and success criteria.

Learning intentions should clearly state what your students will be *learning*, not what they will be *doing*. For example, "Complete tasks 1 and 2," is not a learning intention; it is a statement about activities. A good guide for writing learning intentions is to begin them with one of the following.

- To know . . .
- To understand . . .
- To be able to . . .

These help move students from surface learning (knowing) to deep learning (understanding) to transfer (applying).

In section 4.4.1 (page 167), I recommended using four levels of learning, each one matched with the SOLO Taxonomy (Biggs & Collis, 1982). This helps characterize learning as moving from (1) knowing a little to (2) knowing a lot to (3) understanding how these ideas relate to each other to (4) using and applying those ideas in different contexts.

Here are some example descriptors that you could use to build learning intentions that match with the SOLO Taxonomy levels.

4.9.1.1 Write Learning Intentions

Using the SOLO Taxonomy as your frame, you could use the following description starters for *discovering information* to indicate progress in learning.

- **To know:** To know some facts about, names of, examples of, ways to . . .
  - Building knowledge
- **To know:** To know the features of, definitions of, reasons for, how to . . .
  - Moving from knowledge to understanding
- **To understand:** To understand the similarities and differences between . . .
  - Applying and adapting
- **To be able to:** To be able to complete (various procedures) and create your own . . .

These are the descriptors I use when creating learning intentions. They have a lovely simplicity that leads to enhanced clarity. They are also matched to a clear sense of learning progress. So, from those points of view, they are a win-win.

There are other approaches, of course. The most common one I see is WALT, an acronym for *We Are Learning To*. As a sentence starter, it works well. It can also work with the deepening levels I shared earlier (for example, "WALT understand the similarities and differences between number and value").

Associated acronyms are WILF (*What I'm Looking For*) and WAGOLL (*What a Good One Looks Like*), but these are connected to success criteria rather than learning intentions. I have to say, though, I think it's time for WILF to retire! WILF is far too focused on teacher pleasing. Success criteria need to be objective (this is explained later on), whereas WILF implies a lot more subjectivity. WAGOLL works well, particularly when used as a prompt to co-construct success criteria. Again, this is covered in more depth later.

4.9.1.2 Connect and Decontextualize

Aim to connect learning intentions to the bigger picture or to students' lives. At the same time, make sure you decontextualize the learning. This is a balancing act.

For instance, go for this first example rather than the second so that you give a purpose to the learning intention.

- ✓ **To understand the role of evaporation and condensation in the water cycle**
- ✗ **To understand evaporation and condensation**

At the same time, try to decontextualize the learning intention so that it's more readily transferable to other contexts. For example:

- ✓ **To be able to use code to create basic program and adjust as needed**
- ✗ **To be able to use code using JavaScript on Bitsbox**

Here are some other examples of connecting learning intentions.

- ✓ **To know how to use the top and bottom of the page to represent foreground and background**

✗ **To know how to use the page effectively**

✓ **To know the importance of being able to calm yourself when you are feeling frustrated**

✗ **To know how to change your breathing**

And here are some other examples of decontextualizing learning intentions.

✓ **To know the key features and tone of a formal letter**

✗ **To know what to include in a letter of complaint**

✓ **To understand how to create different rhythms using a range of instruments**

✗ **To understand how to create rhythms on a drum**

As you will notice, the differences are subtle but, nonetheless, important. Students should know the reasons why they are learning what they are learning. Also, they should be learning something that can be applied in other contexts. This means starting with something transferable (for example, knowing the key features of a formal letter) rather than something specific (for example, writing a letter of complaint). They can then add a reason or justification (for example, understanding evaporation and condensation is important *because of* evaporation and condensation's central role in the water cycle, which itself is important to know about because of the water cycle's impact on all living organisms).

On learning walks around schools, I often ask students what they are learning and why. Most times, they can answer the first question, but rarely can they answer the second. They don't know their why. While writing this book, I visited eighth-grade students during a science lesson. They were testing the pH of cabbage. They were all engaged and on task. Every pair I spoke with knew what they were supposed to be doing, but not one of them could tell me why someone would want to know the pH of cabbage! In fact, many of them couldn't tell me what *pH* stands for, nor did they know how it relates to acidity.

So, when devising learning intentions, ask yourself, "What do I really want my students to learn from this lesson?" Then ask yourself, "And what will they need to do so that I can be sure they've learned it?" These will form the basis of the success criteria for the lesson or learning episode.

4.9.1.3 Write Multiple Learning Intentions

Ordinarily, each student will work toward a single learning intention in a lesson, although that is not to imply that thirty students will have thirty learning intentions between them! As I showed in section 4.4.1 (page 167), there are likely to be two or three different versions of the same learning intention in use at any one time, reflecting the varying depths of learning students in a mixed-ability class are working toward.

That said, in section 4.3.3.2 (page 160), I also wrote about the ASK Model. I created this framework to help move away from knowledge-dominated lessons to a more holistic focus on attitudes, skills, and knowledge. With this approach in mind, there will be times when it is preferable for students to be working toward more than one learning intention each. This would typically focus on two out of the three domains of attitudes, skills, and knowledge.

For example, students' focus might look something like this.

- **Knowledge focus:** To know key features of the Viking invasion and settlement

- **Skill focus:** To be able to write a diary or journal entry (to detail an Anglo-Saxon's first encounter with Vikings)

Or it might look like this.

- **Attitude focus:** To make good use of your curiosity
- **Skill focus:** To create a set of questions (about going back in time and asking questions of the Vikings)

Or, when you want the focus to be on attitudes and knowledge, it could look like this.

- **Attitude focus:** To use constructiveness and empathy to encourage everyone in your group (as you work together to investigate the Viking lifestyle)
- **Knowledge focus:** To understand similarities and differences (between the lifestyles of Vikings and Anglo-Saxons)

4.9.1.4 Share and Record Learning Intentions

Learning intentions do *not* need to be written on the board. They can be, and that is often helpful, but they do not need to be. Sometimes, just knowing the theme (for example, Viking lifestyles) is enough to signpost the lesson. Then your introduction—which should connect with previous lessons and prior knowledge—can lead into a full explanation and a more precisely worded learning intention.

Similarly, learning intentions do not need to be copied down in students' books. If you have a class of fluent writers, that task might not be a big deal, but most classes have a few students for whom it would be an unnecessary stumbling block. The practice at some schools is to print out learning intentions and paste them into students' books, but this can be a bit too static. What if you want to adjust the wording in light of student responses during your introduction? Maybe you realize they know more (or less) than you anticipated, so you wish to alter the level of challenge.

The critical factor for timing and sharing learning intentions is to do so in whatever ways will best support your students' learning. Sounds obvious, I know, but that's the golden rule. Ask yourself, "Will student engagement be hindered if I don't share the learning intentions straight away?" If not, then perhaps wait until you have introduced the topic, connected it to previous learning, and asked questions to engage students' interest. Then, as you're about to set students off with a task, share a clearly worded intention that will help guide their subsequent actions and ongoing feedback.

4.9.1.5 Choose Success Criteria

Success criteria are the key steps or components needed for students to fulfill the learning intention. Criteria should always flow from the learning intention and include the main things to do, include, or focus on. Sections 4.4.2 to 4.4.5 (pages 173 to 178) covered the key points about types of success criteria to use and ways to co-construct them with your students.

Some criteria are rules based (for example, *make sure spelling and punctuation are correct*), and others are more open and subjective (for example, *write persuasively, show your calculations, finish with a clear conclusion*, and so on).

Rules-based criteria have to be followed for students to be successful. If you notice a lot of students making the same mistakes or omissions, then this should prompt a whole-class or group review. If the errors are more individual, then quick annotations requiring the student to make a correction before completing the overall task can be easily administered.

For more open-ended criteria, the use of WAGOLL, mentioned earlier in section 4.9.1.1 (page 202), can be very productive. Typically, you would share a good example (or often two or three good examples) and ask students to draw out the success criteria. This gives you the chance to explain why the criteria are valuable and which characteristics will help determine whether a student has been successful.

In whichever way you create and share success criteria with your students, remember the mantra, "There should be no feedback without a clear agreement about intended outcomes and matched criteria."

4.9.2 Step 2: First Attempts

Once your students understand the learning goals (learning intentions) and what they should do to make progress (success criteria), they ought to be ready to begin. If their learning involves producing something (for example, an essay or a model), encourage them to say they are doing their *first draft* rather than their *work*. Similarly, if they are performing something (for example, a physical skill), get them to talk in terms of their *first attempt* rather than their *doing it*. The differences might seem subtle, but they can be significant.

First draft implies that there will be some editing to follow. It is the same with *first attempt*; there is the inference that adjustments will be made. If your students instead talk about *doing their work* or *doing it*, they might think that (1) if it doesn't work, they are a failure, or (2) once they've done it once, there is nothing more to be done. In both these cases, learning is likely to be constrained by a lack of revisions and edits.

4.9.3 Step 3: Self- or Peer Feedback

Self- and peer feedback is a vital step in helping your students grow their assessment capabilities. In section 4.1 (page 149), I shared Nuthall's (2007) finding that 80 percent of the verbal feedback students receive comes from other students, and most of it is wrong. So, if ever there was a way to improve learning outcomes, it would be by teaching students how to give themselves and each other feedback. This is what step 3 of these seven steps is all about—developing your students' assessment capabilities.

That said, if you are looking at the full list of seven steps and thinking that you'll never find time to fit in all seven, then perhaps step 3 is the one to omit, at least in the early days. However, know that if you leave this one out, you will forever be the hardest-working person in the classroom. Not only that, but your students will undo much of the good work you do for them by giving each other incorrect feedback. Talk about swimming upstream!

If you are going to include this step—and I hope you are, even if you don't do so immediately—make sure you encourage your students to follow these three steps.

1. **Look again at the learning intentions and success criteria:** These represent your learning goals. Remind yourself of these so that you can answer the first of the three feedback questions: What are you trying to achieve?

2. **Compare your first attempts against these goals:** Which criteria have you met, which have you exceeded, and which are you still working toward? If you are reviewing with a partner, remember to ask them to explain the reasons for their comments (for example, "Why do you say I have not quite met those criteria yet? What is missing or needs changing?").

3. **Based on your answers to the previous questions, think of the things you could do to move closer to your learning goals:** If this creates a long list of actions, prioritize them by choosing which ones you should do first, second, third, and so on.

Keep reminding your students to guide their reflections (or discussions in the case of peer feedback) with the three feedback questions.

1. What am I trying to achieve?
2. How much progress have I made so far?
3. What should I do next to improve?

It is important to resist the urge to offer your insights at this stage. Encourage and perhaps support the students who are giving the feedback, but do not offer your own feedback yet. Your students need the opportunity to develop their skills in giving feedback.

4.9.4 Step 4: Edits

Based on the feedback they have given themselves or each other, your students should now edit their work (or have another go if the context is a physical activity). This does *not* mean that they should redo the whole thing! Instead, they should make additions and corrections. They could do this with a different-colored pen if doing written work, by using track changes if doing something digital, or by attempting the skill again if engaging in physical learning.

As well as teaching your students how to give themselves and each other high-quality feedback, steps 1–4 will also help them develop good exam techniques, such as these four examples: (1) read the question carefully and make sure you know what is being asked of you, (2) write your first draft, (3) look back at the exam question and check whether you have answered all aspects of it by comparing your draft against the criteria, and, if needed, (4) edit your answer before moving on to the next question.

4.9.5 Step 5: Teacher Feedback

Only once your students have completed steps 1–4 is it time for some teacher-led (or other adult-led) feedback. Of course, you might have been giving feedback, guidance, and encouragement throughout the process, but step 5 is the time to give more formalized feedback.

When giving feedback, remember it should be advice that your students will understand and use effectively to improve their learning. Also, ensure the following.

- Your advice is focused on ways to move closer to the agreed-on learning intention.
- You reference the success criteria—for example, "I think you have succeeded with this criterion because [give reason or evidence]," "It looks as if you're well on the way to fulfilling this one because [give reason or evidence]," or "The criteria I think need more attention are these ones because [give reason or evidence]."
- You do *not* give a grade . . . *yet* (although you may wish to register a provisional grade for your own reference).

The advice you offer your students can include ideas about what could be changed, amended, left alone, added to, or scrapped altogether. It should always be focused on the task or the process, not on the students themselves. For example, provide the feedback, "Clarify your conclusion by shortening your sentences and making them punchier," rather than "There is some need for clarity here. I want you to try harder."

4.9.5.1 Are You a Coach or Referee?

At conferences, when I share these seven steps with teachers, there is always someone who suggests that giving feedback to your students before they have finished is cheating! This baffles me. How on earth can it be cheating to help students learn more? Isn't that teaching? Granted, *teaching* and *cheating* are anagrams of each other (presumably *not* by design), but still, the very purpose of teaching is to help students learn more than they might otherwise.

Of course, if we were to help our students during an exam, then that *would* be cheating. But during normal proceedings, our most important mission is to help students learn more—and one of the best ways to do that is to give our students feedback in such a way that they will use it effectively. The most motivated students might well use our feedback whenever we offer it, but the majority of students need feedback to be given *before* they have finished so that they have time to apply it effectively. Teacher feedback, therefore, should be offered at step 5, not step 7.

One way to imagine our role is to think of coaching rather than refereeing (unless your students are taking exams at the time!). The behaviors of a coach—in this case, a sports coach—have parallels to teaching as follows.

- Welcoming the team and engaging team members in an enjoyable warm-up (for nonsporty activities, this might be a brain teaser or stimulus for thinking)
- Giving them a clear sense of what the focus for the session is (This is identifying the learning intentions.)
- Asking them for suggestions about how they will achieve the learning goal or giving them a clear set of instructions (This is identifying the success criteria.)
- Inviting a more proficient performer (perhaps from another team) to demonstrate the skill (or sharing examples via video)
- Giving the players time to experiment and try out the skills (first draft)

- Circulating around the players and giving individualized attention, including feedback, encouragement, and additional challenges
- Splitting the players into groups and asking them to give each other feedback about how to improve the skills they are currently working on (self- or peer review)
- Giving more time to practice (edit)
- Offering expert guidance on how to improve (Those players who have met or exceeded the target would be given additional challenges or be asked to apply the skills in a game, those who are nearly there would be asked to keep working on the final bits of the skills, and those who are a long way off would be given some support so that they feel the session has not entirely been wasted and they have made some progress.)
- Expecting players to try out their new skills (This reiterates the context and purpose; most training sessions would finish with a game for this purpose.)

Compare those actions to the actions of an excellent referee, who would be doing the following.

- Reminding the players to play fairly
- Enforcing the rules of the game
- Acting as timekeeper
- Assigning punishments for serious offenses
- Keeping the game flowing as much as possible
- Providing the appropriate authorities with a match report
- Ensuring the safety of the players

Of course, teaching *is* different from the world of sports, but there are many parallels. And I hope by sharing these examples, I have drawn attention to how much more powerful feedback can be when you think of yourself as the coach rather than the referee.

4.9.5.2 Do Not Grade (Yet)

A point of utmost importance for step 5 is *do not grade your students' work*. Not yet, anyway. There are many reasons for this, the most important of which is that when students receive a grade, they assume their learning is complete. They see little point in adding or editing anything, because their grade will no longer be affected. A grade is like a rubber stamp, indicating that the assignment is over. So, any advice that you give following, or at the same time as, a grade is very likely to be ignored. At the least, it's not acted on.

It might be that you want to make a note—for your own purposes—of the provisional grade you would award, but in many circumstances, sharing that grade is likely to be disingenuous. If, for example, the provisional grade is a top one, many students will think it unnecessary to improve their work. The same could be said of any student receiving a grade that matches their aspirations. However, if the provisional grade is a disappointing one, many students will feel despondent and less inclined to try any further. Then those receiving the lowest of grades are likely to abandon all hope of ever having their learning be up to scratch.

The Kluger and DeNisi (1996) research that I mentioned earlier bears this out. Kluger and DeNisi examined 3,000 relevant studies published between 1905 and 1995. Of these, only 131 studies met their reliability criteria. Of the 131, there were 50 studies (38 percent) showing that feedback actually lowered average performance. And in every single case, grades were given at the same time as the feedback.

The authors identified eight possible responses students had when receiving a grade. Of these, six possibilities were negative. These are shown in bold in table 4.2.

Table 4.2: Negative Responses to Grades

Response Type	Grade Exceeds Student's Goal	Grade Is Short of Student's Goal
Changes behavior	**Exerts less effort**	Increases effort
Changes goal	Increases aspiration	**Reduces aspiration**
Abandons goal	**Decides goal is too easy**	**Decides goal is too hard**
Rejects feedback	**Ignores feedback**	**Ignores feedback**

Source: Adapted from Kluger & DeNisi, 1996.

When looking at table 4.2, one might wonder why on earth we give grades if their effects are often so negative. Robust arguments against grading have been made for a century or more (Black & Wiliam, 1998a; Brookhart et al., 2016; Crooks, 1933; De Zouche, 1945; Guskey, 2015; Kirschenbaum, Napier, & Simon, 1971, to name but a few), and yet the practice continues. On the flip side, many teachers report that grading motivates their students. "Will this be graded?" is often the first question asked, and the answer determines how much effort students apply subsequently.

I will explore grading in a bit more depth in step 7. For now, here are the two main points.

1. Do *not* give students a grade at the same time as you give them feedback. Be resolute with this. Say that you will grade their efforts *after* they have used your feedback to improve their learning, but not before.

2. If grading is part of your practice, make sure you match your advice against the grading criteria (for example, "If I were to grade this right now, I would award it a [*grade*] because of [give reasons and draw attention to evidence]. However, if you added this, changed that, and developed this section more, then I think you would lift the grade to [*improved grade*]").

4.9.6 Step 6: Final Edits

Using the feedback that you offered them at step 5, your students should complete their piece of work or performance. This might involve something as formal as a presentation piece, but more than likely, it will involve students' making corrections with a view to making their work the very best version it can be just now.

In chapter 5 (page 215), I explain the benefits of drawing attention to students' progress. Bearing that in mind, you might want to create a coding system for students' editing process. For example, you might ask them to write their first drafts in one style or color, make any edits at step 4 in a second style or color, and then make their final edits in a third style or color. Using markup in digital documents can achieve the same effect. If your students are engaging in something more performance based, then collecting photographs at steps 2, 4, and 6 achieves the same goal of drawing attention to progress.

4.9.7 Step 7: Grade (or No Grade)

If you are expected to grade students' work, then now is the time to do it. If you don't need to grade, then don't! You can happily ignore this step altogether.

There are so many problems with grading that I could start a whole new chapter and still not cover everything. Grading puts students' work into imprecise categories even though performance is continuous. If you have thirty students in your class, they are very likely going to be at thirty different points on a progress continuum. Grading systems don't allow for this variability. An A-to-E grading system provides five categories; the grade set of proficient, developing, and beginning that is common in the United States at the elementary level offers just three categories.

A-to-E grading becomes particularly problematic at the boundaries of the middle grades (one error can move a student from a C, which tends to be a pass, to a D, which often denotes a failing grade). Scaled scores are more precise and comparable because they are raw scores that are statistically adjusted and converted to account for differences in difficulty across questions (Tan & Michel, 2011). However, with the exception of reading ages and standardized testing, these are not commonly used because to calculate them is time intensive.

Many people argue that a grade is easier to understand than nuanced comments or scaled scores, and they're right. An A grade is easier to understand than a raw score of 39 out of 50 on a reading test converting to a scaled score of 108, or raw scores in the range of 53 to 57 out of 110 on a mathematics test converting to a scaled score of 99. Then again, it seems strange to argue that making the wrong thing easy to understand is a good thing!

Enough of the politics, though. We'll leave those for another time. If you really want to dig deeply into grading and assessment, I would recommend the work of Thomas Guskey (Guskey, 2011, 2015; Guskey & Brookhart, 2019). For the purposes of this chapter, let's look at four ways to make grading less problematic.

1. **Do not give grades at the same time as your feedback:** Keep them separate from each other. Refer to grades as *grades* and feedback as *feedback*, and never conflate the two. Grades are the rubber stamp. Feedback is the advice that will help your students improve.

2. **Be as precise as possible in linking grades with their criteria:** The more transparent the relationship between grades and success criteria, the better (for example, "This piece of work is awarded a [grade] because criteria x, y, and z were met; criteria a, b, and c were partially met; and criteria l, m, and n were missed").

3. **Teach your students how to grade their own work:** Help them become assessment capable.

4. **Use grades within a culture of progress, analysis, and correction:** I explain more in section 5.5.2 (page 244) when I show how effective pre- and post-testing can be.

4.9.7.1 Creating Time for the Seven Steps to Feedback

Seven steps seems like a lot, particularly if the typical convention in your school is the two-step approach of (1) students complete their assignment and (2) teachers assess it afterward. Having seven steps is indeed more time consuming than having two, but nowhere near as much as the ratio 7:2 would suggest.

Giving feedback to your students is the lengthiest process in both systems. Then again, it takes no more time to give feedback before your students finish their assignments than it does to give feedback afterward. The only real difference is that students are much more likely to use your advice when it's offered early than when it's offered afterward. Time doesn't increase, but impact does. How about that as a big win for the seven steps?

With regard to the time step 3 (self- and peer feedback) adds to the process, I would argue it is a necessary step. First, Nuthall's (2007) research (see section 4.1, page 149) shows us that students typically give each other misleading or incorrect feedback. So, something needs to be done to correct this. Second, when we teach students how to give themselves and each other feedback, they become less dependent on us. This is a good thing. While step 3 is the one to leave out if you really feel the need to shorten the process, know that if you do leave out this step, your students will continue to depend on you for advice.

That leaves us with the issue of giving feedback in one sitting and grades in another. In the usual system, teachers give grades and feedback at the same time, which is obviously quicker, but it is far less effective! The overwhelming weight of evidence shows that giving grades at the same time as advice will reduce the impact of feedback to nil (or worse). So, the choice is between using lots of time to give feedback and grades for little to no effect and using even more time but producing more significant gains.

One way to reclaim time is to reduce the number of feedback cycles. Instead of offering, for example, twelve in a term using the typical two-step system, you could reduce this to eight using the seven-step process. Insofar as anything can be guaranteed in education, eight rounds of the Seven Steps to Feedback *will* produce significantly more positive learning outcomes than twelve rounds of the normal two steps.

The other time-saver is giving verbal rather than written feedback. I mention this somewhat obvious solution because it is remarkable how many people worry that the Seven Steps to Feedback will take too long because they imagine steps 3, 5, and 7 all involve written feedback. They do not. Verbal feedback is just as effective, often more so, because your students can ask questions, and you can elaborate further. So, don't imagine that feedback must be written down. It can be, but it doesn't need to be.

4.9.7.2 Teaching Dogs to Whistle

Figure 4.14 (page 212) shows my dachshunds—five cuddly killers. Their favorite pastimes are snuggling on the shoulders of anyone sitting on our sofa and hunting bunny rabbits who foolishly hop into our garden.

Figure 4.14: I've taught my dogs to whistle.

All five are lovely, but not one of them is the brightest hound on the planet. Despite the figure caption, I certainly couldn't teach them how to whistle. Now, you might be wondering what on earth I'm talking about, and you have every right to, but there's a lovely story of two friends. The first friend says to the other, "I've taught my dog how to whistle."

The second friend says, "That's amazing! Let's hear him." The dog goes *woof*, and the friend says, "I thought you said you'd taught your dog to whistle."

"I did," the first one replies. "But I didn't say he'd *learned* how to."

The reason I've included this hilarious joke is that, too often, we focus on what we've *taught* our students rather than on what they've *learned*. In the context of feedback, this relates to looking for evidence of feedback having been given (taught) rather than evidence of feedback having been used (learned).

Teachers I meet tell me they are obliged to write feedback rather than speak it so that they can prove they've given it. If they ever give feedback verbally, then they are supposed to use the annotation *VF* in students' books. Thankfully, this isn't a practice everybody uses, but for those who do, it sounds a lot like compliance rather than a focus on student learning.

A much better system is to look for evidence that feedback has been understood and applied. So, by all means look through your students' books, but *not* for the messages given; look for the ways in which your students have used feedback to improve outcomes. This is another good reason for coding their edits (as recommended in the description of step 6), as this will support the evidence gathering.

So, there you have it. I'm finishing where I started. The power of feedback lies in its use. Think less about what your students receive and more about what they understand and do with it. Look for evidence of impact.

Always keep this as your guiding star: feedback becomes good feedback when it is used to improve learning.

4.10 *Teach Brilliantly* Top Ten: *Feedback*

 *Give your students good advice, help them understand it, and make sure they use it. That's the essence of feedback.*

1. Feedback is one of the **most effective ways to improve student learning**.
2. Feedback is also **one of the most variable factors**. It can accelerate learning by as much as three times the normal rate, but one-third of studies show negative outcomes.
3. Feedback **becomes good feedback when it is used** by students to improve their learning.
4. Feedback is not just marking and grading. **Feedback is any message, formal or informal, spoken, written, or inferred**, that redirects thinking, actions, or attention toward a desired result.
5. Feedback can be at **task level** (focusing on what students are trying to achieve), **process level** (focusing on how they are working toward their goals), and **self-regulation level** (monitoring their own progress). Avoid self-level feedback that praises or criticizes the person.
6. Feedback **should be guided by three questions**: (1) What am I trying to achieve? (2) How much progress have I made so far? and (3) What should I do next to improve?
7. **Connect feedback to agreed-on learning intentions and success criteria.** This enhances transparency, credibility, and usability.
8. Most of the verbal feedback students receive comes from each other, and most of it is wrong. So, **teach your students how to follow the three feedback questions and to stick to the agreed-on success criteria.**
9. **Give students feedback before they finish** their assignments to increase the likelihood that they will use it, and therefore benefit from it.
10. Grades tell students their work is done. So, **do not mix grades and feedback together**. Give feedback first, make sure your students apply it, and only then grade it (if you have to grade).

CHAPTER 5

When *Expectations* Are High, Everybody *Prospers*

 *Expectation matters. Students whose teachers have high expectations make progress at one to three times the normal rate; those whose teachers hold low expectations make progress at less than half the normal rate (Woolley et al., 2010).*

How we think about our students' abilities informs—and in many ways, directs—our actions toward them. It influences how much we challenge, expect, nurture, and encourage. It informs decisions about groupings and creates assumptions about the capabilities of each group. Little wonder, then, that teachers' expectations (of their students' abilities to learn) make such a radical difference to the ways in which students do or do not succeed.

THE BLUEPRINT

Purpose

The following lists the purposes of expectations within the learning process.

- It is far-fetched to expect all students to secure top grades, but holding high expectations for their growth is realistic as well as necessary.

- Believing in the potential of all students to improve requires a set of values and beliefs that are neatly captured by the theory of growth mindset.

- Growth mindset is rarely understood deeply or positioned effectively, but when it is, the effects on students' willingness to engage and persevere are pronounced.

- Being in a growth mindset also makes learners more receptive to feedback, better able to attend to challenges, and more likely to view mistakes and failure as learning opportunities.

- Notions of collective efficacy and self-efficacy are closely related to being in a growth mindset. They are both tied to the construct of agency (the ability to make things happen) and to proactivity when faced with opportunities or challenges.

What to Notice

The following lists what is important to notice about expectations.

- **Teachers' expectations significantly influence students' expectations:** We set the tone of the classroom. We design the levels of challenge and support within learning tasks. We choose how and when to give feedback, offer praise, and use questioning. We build rapport and create a safe learning space for our students. Together, we have the potential to transform expectations.

- **Teachers are not the only influence:** Factors that also affect a student's expectations include personality; social-emotional development, birth order, and gender; public recognition and approval; family traditions; proximity of resources; and historical forces, events, and trends (Feldman, 1991).

- **The emotional aspects of expectations are perhaps the strongest:** Maya Angelou writes, "I've learned that people will forget what you said, people will forget what you did, but people will never forget how you made them feel" (as quoted in Kelly, 2003, p. 263).

- **Expectations matter most for at-risk students:** Psychology researchers Victoria F. Sisk, Alexander P. Burgoyne, Jingze Sun, Jennifer L. Butler, and Brooke N. Macnamara (2018) suggest mindset has a bigger impact on academically high-risk and economically disadvantaged students than it does on other students.

Timing

Holding high expectations for all your students is always appropriate. How these transfer into actions, however, will differ according to circumstances. For example, it is usual to set different tasks for different students, expecting similar rates of success at whichever levels they are working at (the 80/20 principle described in section 3.5, page 106, is a useful guide here). At other times, however, you might give the same task to all students, expecting some to succeed with more of the task than others. High expectations in this second situation will be in terms of everyone progressing at similar rates rather than achieving at the same level of attainment.

5.0 Do You Hold Great Expectations for All Students?

All students have the same potential to learn. They won't all attain the same grades, but they can all make excellent progress from their starting point. Holding high expectations for this growth is imperative.

Do you hold great expectations for all your students? Surely your answer must be yes; otherwise, why choose teaching as a profession? There are many other jobs without such exacting standards, ones that don't require such tireless effort toward a greater good.

It's frustrating, then, that teaching is awash with terms, structures, and attitudes that bear false witness to such noble aspirations. There are students whom teachers think of as slow (calling them "bottom sets" in many schools). There are whispers about nonacademic kids and individuals who are never going to set the world alight, not to mention euphemisms and local slang that I would never print here.

We *know* that students differ from each other in their abilities. Some can ace a test that their peers can't yet understand. Some require frequent supervision, while others need minimal direction. Some have artistic flair; others appear not to. The same goes for mathematical thinking, athletic prowess, and scientific studiousness. Some seem to have it when many others don't. Or at least if they do, they're doing a good job of hiding their light under the proverbial bushel.

These differences in ability and attitude make it extraordinarily difficult to teach everyone in one homogeneous way. Indeed, why would we even want to? If I attended an adult learning center to study Mandarin, I wouldn't expect to be grouped with those already proficient in the language. It'd be the beginner's course for me. So, what's the problem with taking a similar approach in schools?

Well, seeing as you've asked, why don't you pull up a chair, and I'll begin! Here's what I'm going to cover.

- Why differences in students' current abilities are *incorrectly* assumed to be synonymous with potential
- The murky history of intelligence testing and why it has led to false notions about IQ
- Why common approaches to ability grouping are problematic and how we can improve them
- What all of this means for the ways in which you should interact with, group, challenge, and praise your students
- How to set up learning in such a way that everyone is able to make excellent progress, no matter where they are starting from

To begin with, I think it's important to be clear about language. Although many people use the terms *learning, achievement*, and *attainment* as if they were synonymous—and, therefore, use terms such as *learner, performance, high achiever*, and *A-grade student* interchangeably—it is helpful to be selective about which term to use and when. Across the more than 125 research papers and meta-analyses I have drawn from for this book, there are certainly differing, if not conflicting, definitions.

For example, when the topic of research is feedback, authors tend to describe (or assume) *learning* to be a process of acquiring information to move from surface knowledge to deep understanding. In studies about dialogic teaching, for example, the emphasis is more on the acquisition of knowledge, building of skills, and adaptation of dispositions.

The terms *achievement* and *attainment* are almost always used when learning has been assessed. Although they are sometimes used interchangeably, they are—theoretically at least—distinctive from each other. The research papers I've referenced use *achievement* to mean the assessed outcome of learning, whereas *attainment* is used when achievement is compared against a desired standard or benchmark.

As I say, clarity about these terms is helpful, particularly in the context of teacher and student expectations. So, throughout this chapter, terms are used in the following ways.

- *Learning* is the process of acquiring new capabilities. An added complication with *learning* is that it is both a verb and a noun. It is the process of acquiring new capabilities (verb) as well as the new capabilities themselves (noun).
- A *learner* is a person involved in the process of learning.
- *Achievement* is the assessed outcome of learning.
- An *achiever* is a person whose outcome of learning has been assessed.
- *Attainment* is the assessed outcome of learning when compared with an expected standard.
- An *attainer* is a person whose outcome of learning has been assessed and compared against the expected standard.

The purpose of sharing these definitions is to be clear from the outset that all students in a school have the same potential to learn. Some are starting further back than others (see section 5.1, page 220). Some will attain the required state, provincial, or national standards by the time they leave school, and some won't, but they all have significant potential to improve.

This is not to be apathetic about attainment; far from it. I believe we should do everything we can to help students make as much progress as they can so that they move ever closer toward the attainment levels we hope they reach—without exception. However, my experience and the experiences of my colleagues indicate a significant minority in our profession worry that this is all in vain. "In the real world," they say (always their first refrain), "students are going to be tested, and some just won't make the grade. It is futile to pretend otherwise." Having that mindset is a bit like starting a renovation job knowing you'll never be given enough time to finish the job.

So, let's be clear. Some students *are* unlikely to reach the state, provincial, or national standards within normal time frames. Their task is not *impossible*—they might, for example, reach these standards later than others, maybe after leaving school. But it is true to say that their attainment—on school-based assessments—is *likely to* be low. We should not pretend otherwise.

However, this does not contradict the evidence that all students' potential for growth remains high (Deslauriers, McCarty, Miller, Callaghan, & Kestin, 2019; Kalb, 2017; Maguire et al., 2000; Park et al., 2013). Indeed, a fundamental purpose of a professional learning community is to ensure all students learn at high levels (DuFour, DuFour, Eaker, Many, & Mattos, 2016).

Every student's learning can always be accelerated. Those students with lower-than-average achievement are starting further back, but they can still make—should still make—excellent progress. To assume otherwise is pessimistic, maybe even pernicious. Saying these students have little hope of learning would be akin to you and me turning up to an exercise class only to be told there's no point in joining in because we're never going to be as fit as some of the longtime members, or being advised to give up on ever driving because we've failed multiple driving tests, or choosing never to interview for another job again because of a few knockbacks.

I wrote a considerable amount of this book at the side of cricket fields across northern England and swimming pools across southern Scotland. This is the life of a sports parent, which many of us know well. All three of my kids are keen competitors, but they rarely seem to be on the winning team. Should they give up? They're not *yet* good enough to represent anything other than their local teams. They don't get chosen for regional or national events. They don't set records. They are never the first ones listed on the team sheets. So, what's the point in continuing? They've made good progress, but their attainment is a long way behind that of others in the county, if the one-sided match now taking place in front of me is anything to go by!

Well, indeed, what is the point—apart from the countless stories of world-class performers who were never considered the best among their peers at school! They stuck at it longer, desired it more, trained harder, and were encouraged and supported more optimistically beyond school. This idea applies to not just the athletes but the poets, actors, musicians, mathematicians, entrepreneurs, and job creators. Take a poll of one hundred people, and you will find dozens who didn't shine at school but are now wonderfully successful and happy today. Their attainment at school was low, but they continued learning, learning, learning—and now look where they are!

To summarize, almost every class has students whose achievement is lower than you would like, students whose achievement is higher than average, and lots of students whose achievement is in the middle. This spread of abilities can typically be represented with a bell-shaped curve of normal distribution. We must be very careful how we say it and to whom, but it *is* true to say that some students are low achievers, many are average achievers, and a few are high achievers. Let me emphasize this point. These terms are accurate *so long as* they are based on current performance on *recent* assessments. The greater the distance from the time when these assessments were taken, the less terms such as *low achiever* reflect reality, and the more they risk becoming self-fulfilling prophecies.

Imagine I go for a health checkup, and I'm told my blood pressure is raised. Immediately following the test, the medical professional would be accurate in saying I have high blood pressure. Would it still be accurate six months later? That would likely depend on what I've done in the intervening months. What if my medical visits followed the same intervals as most countries' national academic testing—every two to three years? Would I still be accurate in thinking of myself as a person with high blood pressure even if it has been more than two years since I was tested? Should I still be choosing what to do and what not to do based on that assessment?

How we think about our students' abilities informs—and in many ways, directs—our actions toward them. It influences how much we challenge, expect, nurture, and encourage. It informs decisions about groupings and assumptions about what each group of students is capable of, all of which make the biggest difference to how successful, happy, and satisfying students' experiences of education will be. We need to get it right. We *must* hold great expectations for every single student. Believe in their potential for learning, and view their current level of attainment as an indication of what they have achieved *so far*, not as a predictor of the future but as an idea of their current rung on the ladder we are helping them climb.

This then begs the question, Why are some students already much higher up the ladder of achievement than others? Well, dear reader, let's dive into that murky topic now.

5.1 Ability Is Not Genetic (Well, It Is Sort Of!)

The phrase *nature versus nurture* was first coined in the mid-1800s by the English polymath Francis Galton (1869). It offered expression to an already well-established debate about the extent to which talents, intelligence, and behavior come from inherited (genetic) or acquired (learned) sources. Galton (1869) also coined the term *eugenics* and wrote a book titled *Hereditary Genius*, so it is no surprise that he believed genetics to be the most significant influence on human capabilities.

Is this true, though? Do genetics really make the biggest difference to how talented or intelligent our students are?

We know for sure that everyone has a different set of genetics. Even an estimated 15 percent of identical twins have significant genetic variation from each other (Jonsson et al., 2021). So, it stands to reason that everyone will also possess different abilities, talents, and intelligence. Just as we differ in appearance, personality, and preference, so too do we vary in the attributes that influence success.

However, to take for granted that genetics are the main determining factor in how clever or talented someone is (or will be) is erroneous. Environment plays more of a role than first thought. We know with absolute certainty that intelligence and talents are malleable (Doidge, 2007; Merzenich, 2013; Merzenich, Tallal, Peterson, Miller, & Jenkins, 1999). Therefore, factors that can be adjusted—experiences and environment—are those most likely to influence outcomes, rather than inherited characteristics (Pietschnig & Voracek, 2015; Trahan, Stuebing, Fletcher, & Hiscock, 2014).

This assertion is relatively modern. For more than a century, opinions favored Galton's (1869) theories that genetics exert the greatest influence on a person's talents. With a few notable exceptions (I will come to Binet's story soon), researchers and opinion formers viewed success and failure through the lens of genetic causes. Sidestepping the most iniquitous and corrupt applications of this belief for a moment, this belief about genetics being the prime determiner of talent led to many school structures and educational attitudes that still persist today, including those I mentioned in this chapter's introduction.

A turning point occurred in the 1980s with the discovery that IQ scores had been steadily rising. Professor of politics James R. Flynn (1987) analyzed data from fourteen countries and found IQ increases ranged from five to twenty-five points in a single generation. These data were gathered by the military in each country. For example, in the postwar years, the Dutch military examined almost every eighteen-year-old male in the Netherlands. If boys passed a medical exam, they would then take a well-established IQ test, the Raven's Progressive Matrices test. Analyzing these results, together with those of thirteen other countries on six continents, led Flynn (1987) to conclude that "these data prove the existence of unknown environmental factors so potent that they account for 75 percent of the points gained" (p. 182). Flynn's research is so widely accepted that it is now often referred to simply as the "Flynn effect," referring to the observed rise in IQ scores over time (Trahan et al., 2014).

Some of these increases could be explained by better nutrition and understanding of healthy lifestyles. Also, they could be explained by an increase in the complexity of life, with people more often called on to think abstractly, which is something that IQ tests classically require people to do. Improvements in educational practices also contributed significantly. However, despite the difficulty in determining the exact contribution of each of these factors, whole populations were getting smarter not because of genetic changes but because of environmental improvements.

Nature will have played a role, of course, but nurture is the most significant determinant of success. It is as if genetics start the ball rolling, and then attitude, focus, dedication, and perseverance determine how far and fast the ball rolls.

A useful analogy is to think of identical twins separated at birth. Let's imagine that their genetics favor the acquisition of language. Because of this genetic predisposition, both twins show an early interest in words and sounds. Their new families encourage this interest, involving them in conversation as often as possible and giving every impression that reading is one of the best activities in the world. The twins become early talkers and passionate readers. When they start school, their love of and advanced skills in literacy are quickly recognized and built on by their teachers. More is encouraged and expected of them. Their sense that they are more talented than most steers them toward any literacy-based activity. By the time they move to middle school, their language skills are better than those of 95 percent of the general student population.

Now imagine that researchers tracked down each twin and tested their literacy acumen. It is likely that they would conclude the twins' advanced skills were largely genetic since that was the only constant shared by the pair. But some theories posit that these researchers would be wrong (Risch, 2002). It is more likely that the twins' genes gave them a disposition toward language but that their experiences and environment were what developed their aptitudes. Thus, the genetic effect is much more modest than has been claimed throughout most of history—including when our current education systems were first established.

In one sense, this debate is exactly that—a debate. We will likely never have conclusive proof about the relative balance between nature and nurture. We know that genetics and environment both play a role in determining intelligence and talent, but whether they contribute a 50/50 split, a 90/10 split, or indeed any other combination is unlikely to ever be known.

This lack of a definitive answer shouldn't make the topic any less important. Even if we find out sometime in the future that genetics make the biggest difference by far, this still will not change the fact that what you and I, as teachers, can affect is the learning environment. There is nothing we can do about our students' nature, but there are always things we can do to significantly influence our students' nurture. What you do, and how you think, will dramatically change the outcomes for your students.

What does this mean for educational practice today? I would suggest—nay, I would shout from the rooftops—that if a student isn't as adept or successful as their peers, in most cases, it is *not* because they lack potential; it is because they haven't *yet* had sufficient experiences to grow their talents in the same way. (I say *in most cases* because there are students with learning disabilities. They can still make excellent progress, but their growth is likely to be conceptualized differently than that of other students.) The *last* thing students need, therefore, is the faintest whiff that we, their intended champions, assume there is a glass ceiling to their talents. They mustn't think we believe them to be "bottom-set kids" or slow learners.

They have to know that we believe unwaveringly in their potential to grow and develop; that whatever they are capable of now is a step along the way; and that we will help them build the resilience, skills, and attitude they need to move further along the ability continuum.

This isn't just a philosophical stance, although it is also that. My assertion is *also* based on the latest evidence that shows time and again that intelligence is malleable and that talents are grown. Abilities are the outcomes of environment, experiences, *and* genetics. As teachers, we don't get to modify the last of these; the genetics of our students are already set. However, we do get to influence the first two; the classroom environment and our students' experiences *are* within our sphere of influence.

So, even if research later discovers that the evidence of today is wrong and that talents are 95 percent genetic, it still won't affect the validity of my assertion, for it matters little what the actual balance is between nature and nurture. What counts is that we act in accordance with the belief that transforming that which is malleable (environment and experience) *will* give our students the very best chance of making excellent progress. No longer can we accept the outdated belief that some students can, and some students can't, and that's just how it is.

It is true that every student is at a different place in their learning at any given moment. Some can complete assignments with aplomb, whereas others don't know where to begin. Their genetics will have played a role in this reality. But by far the biggest influence on current ability is that some students have already made a lot more progress to this point than others have. Their *potential* (for growth), however, is more or less the same as each other's—that is, unless students' self-concepts, teachers' beliefs, society's attitudes, and the educational systems push back against this opportunity.

All of this makes a significant difference to expectations. If we think that our students are either clever or not, talented or not—and that we're only really helping them make the most of what they've been given—then expectations are likely to be lower than they might otherwise be. If we instead assume that talents and intelligence are there to be grown—not just tinkered with but created—then we tend to hold much higher expectations.

The more malleable something is, the more it is worth dedicating ourselves to the cause; and the more we dedicate ourselves to that, the higher our expectations will rise. Exactly the same can be said of students and their expectations for their own growth.

5.2 We're All on a Continuum

Believing in the power of nurture creates the attitude that those who struggle need remedies, not labels, and those who excel do so because of their successful application.

Imagining that every student is on a continuum along which they can move makes a difference to the way we teach and the expectations we hold. If we view every strength as evidence they have learned and every weakness as an indication they have yet to learn, then our responses will differ from those that come from thinking strengths and weaknesses are primarily determined by genetics.

No one was born knowing calculus or being able to move a ball with pinpoint accuracy; people have developed their abilities. So rather than congratulating them for winning the genetic lottery, instead show admiration for a well-executed process.

I am a sports fan, and I often hear phrases such as these about the top players.

- He is one of the most gifted players of his generation.
- She has a natural talent.
- They were born to do this.

There's no denying they are much, much better than almost everyone on the planet at what they do. However, select a book or film about any prodigious talent, and sure as night follows day, you will discover a story of growth. In fact, I challenge you to find even one example of someone arriving fully formed because of hereditary traits! I am willing to bet a lot of money that every single prodigious talent has trained for years before becoming an "overnight" success. Even child prodigies—or maybe even especially those wunderkinds—have devoted their lives to excelling. Genetics almost certainly will have given them an advantage, but their determination and dedication are what have taken them so much further along the continuum than most.

So, let me share with you three improvised graphs. The first one, figure 5.1, shows the scores achieved on a test by six fictitious students. You choose the context, whether it is reading, mathematics, or any other subject. The scale is 0 to 700, but feel free to adjust it if that helps. When we have scores such as these, what do they tell us?

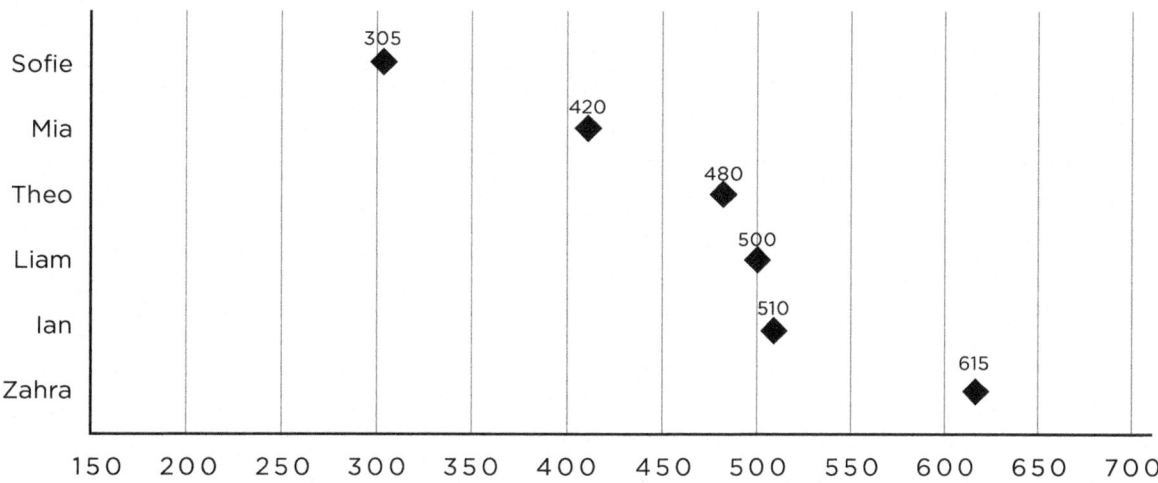

Figure 5.1: Scores achieved by six fictitious students.

Figure 5.2 (page 224) shows two scores for each student. The diamond-shaped points give the same data as shown in figure 5.1. The dots to the left are the scores the students each achieved on an equivalent test twelve months ago. The lines connecting the two points show the magnitude of improvement (effect size) from last year to this.

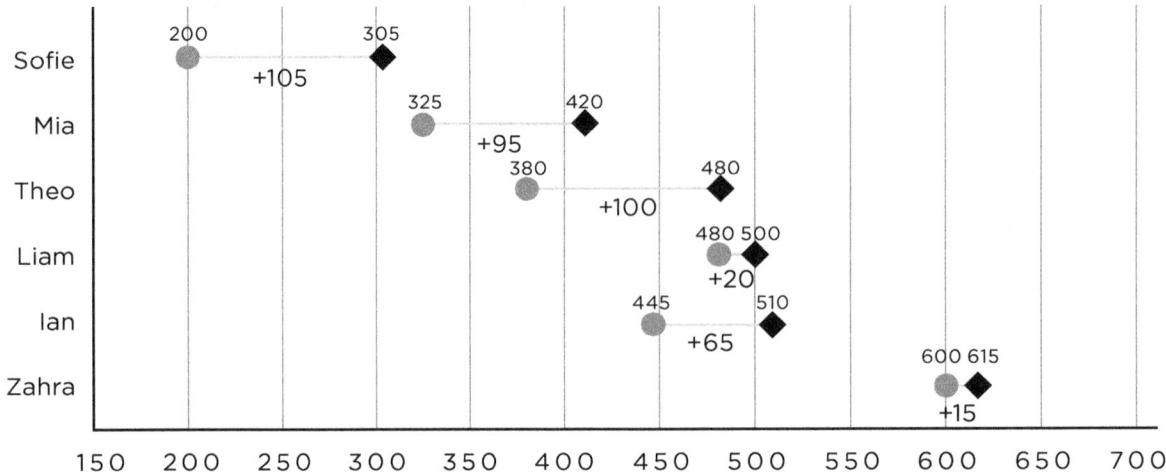

Figure 5.2: Progress made between assessments 1 and 2.

Note that in figure 5.2, only part of the 0–1,000 scale is shown so that differences in the students' scores are easier to read. As you can see, the progress for each student is as follows.

- Sofie has improved from 200 to 305 (+105).
- Mia has improved from 325 to 420 (+40).
- Theo has improved from 380 to 480 (+100).
- Liam has improved from 480 to 500 (+20).
- Ian has improved from 440 to 510 (+65).
- Zahra has improved from 600 to 615 (+15).

Figure 5.2 tells us a lot more about the six students than figure 5.1. Figure 5.1 doesn't tell us anything beyond the scores achieved on one assessment, which can lead to labels such as the ones I mentioned in my introduction. For example, Zahra—the outlier with a score of 615— might be described as bright, clever, advanced, gifted, or even a natural. Sofie, with her score of 305, might be thought of as slow, not so bright, or not very academic, or lead some to wonder if she's ever going to achieve much in this subject. As for the students in the middle, how might they be described? Average? Middle band? Doing OK?

However, figure 5.2 gives us pause for thought. Are terms such as *fast learner* for Zahra and *slow learner* for Sofie even accurate? Putting aside the ethics of using these labels, can it really be right to say Sofie is a slow learner when she has a progress score of +105 or to think of Zahra as a fast learner with a modest +15 progress score?

Now, moving away from intelligence labels for a moment, how about contrasting the ways these two graphs might influence your teaching? With only the data to generate figure 5.1, what might you conclude? Do you know whether to adjust the levels of challenge for any of these students? Design different learning activities? Teach higher? Teach lower? Or might you think most students are doing well and this is as expected? Alternatively, how many more questions could you generate from the data in figure 5.2? Here are a few thoughts to consider.

- What is going on with Liam and Zahra? Their progress from last year to this is +20 and +15, respectively. These rates of progress are much lower than expected. Have they plateaued? Do they need more challenge? Are opportunities to further their learning readily available to them? Are they suffering social or emotional difficulties that are getting in the way of their learning? Putting aside the ethics of calling anyone *slow* or *fast*, *worst* or *best*, is it even accurate to think of these students as two of the best learners given that their rate of learning is slower than most?

- Looking across the whole group, why are some making much better progress than others? What explains these differences? What can be done to accelerate those whose progress is slower? How can those who are making very good progress be supported to continue on the same trajectory?

Notice how these questions shift the focus from each student's perceived cleverness to how much progress each is making. Later in the chapter (see section 5.5, page 240), I share some strategies for amplifying progress to give it even more attention and credence. For now, though, notice (1) how impactful it is to think of students as being on a continuum of learning rather than possessing a set of abilities that sort them into smart, average, and not-smart categories and (2) how using data to recognize students' progress along this continuum can be stunningly useful feedback to us, as teachers, about what to do next to maximize our students' opportunities for learning.

Before I round off this section, let me show you one more improvised graph. Figure 5.3 shows three scores for each student. The first two are taken from figure 5.2. The additional square-shaped point for each student shows the score they go on to achieve three months from now.

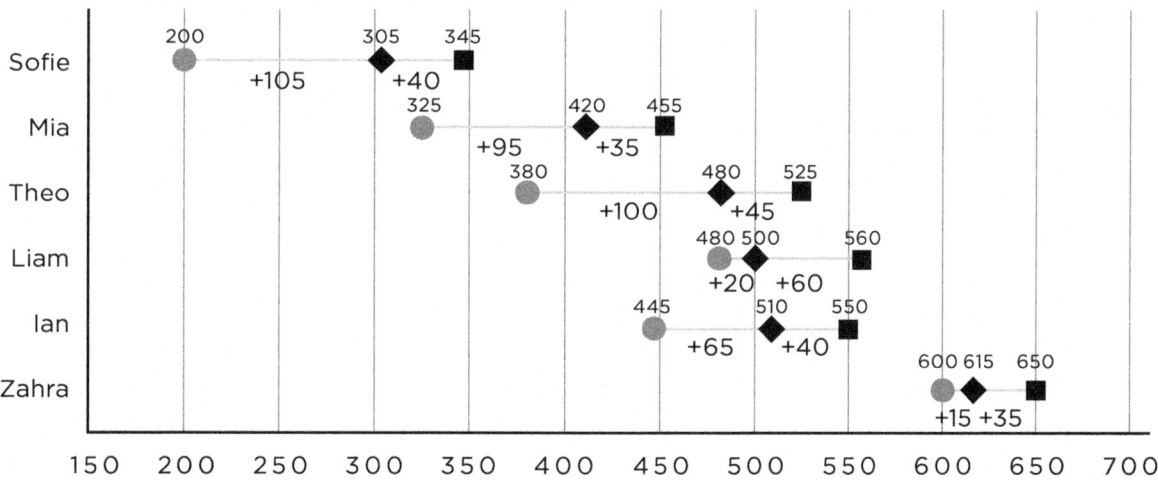

Figure 5.3: Progress made between assessments 1, 2, and 3.

The changes in scores from test 2 to test 3 are as follows.

- Sofie has improved from 305 to 345 (+40).
- Mia has improved from 420 to 455 (+35).
- Theo has improved from 480 to 525 (+40).
- Liam has improved from 500 to 560 (+60).
- Ian has improved from 510 to 550 (+40).
- Zahra has improved from 615 to 650 (+35).

What does this additional information tell us? The biggest difference is that the assessing interval has changed. Time is not a variable shown on the graph, but as described earlier, I have imagined that assessments 1 and 2 are twelve months apart, whereas assessments 2 and 3 are just three months apart. I have done this because I want to emphasize how fruitful it can be to use evidence formatively. Instead of waiting until the end of a course or school year to find out how much progress our students have made, running assessments at more frequent intervals allows us to more accurately adjust our teaching in light of the evidence they present. This is not to say we should teach to the test; I am certainly not an advocate for that! It is to say that assessments (which are not necessarily tests and certainly do not have to be under exam conditions) can offer us, at the very least, the following insights.

- How much progress is each student making at the moment?
- Having adjusted my teaching in response to assessment 2, does assessment 3 show me that these refinements are working as hoped?
- Figure 5.3 (page 225) shows that Liam has made particularly good progress in the last three months. What can Liam tell me about this? Does he have a sense of some of the reasons why and what he can do to keep going with the excellent rate of learning?
- How does Zahra feel now that she has significantly increased her progress between assessments 2 and 3, compared with assessments 1 and 2? Does it seem to her that she is now being more appropriately challenged? Has she experienced some breakthrough moments that led to this change? If so, what attitudes or strategies led to these, and what can she do to take similar approaches again?

5.2.1 Student Data and a Learning Continuum

I know this section doesn't do enough to prove that we are all on an ability continuum. However, I hope it has at least raised some questions for you about the relationship between achievement, progress, and learning.

For me, if I see assessment scores for a group of students, I want to know, So what? How did they perform three months ago? Six months ago? This time last year? In the first term at this school? What is their trajectory? Are they all making good progress? Do some need more of something—for example, challenge, support, encouragement, or guidance? Have there been significant events in their lives that may have impacted their performance? I want to think about their learning.

After all, we are in the business of accelerating student learning. If we're not helping students make more progress than they might otherwise do, then what is our function—being social workers? Childcare officers? Supervisors? Of course, we *also* seem to be expected to assume those roles, but our primary function as teachers is to boost students' learning. Others might sort and classify them, but we should guide them, challenge them, and encourage them to go beyond whatever they are capable of right now. If their achievement tells us what they have learned so far, and their attainment gives an indication of how well they're doing compared to recognized benchmarks, it is their learning that we can boost tomorrow. The more we do that, the greater their future achievements will be, and the closer they will come to meeting and exceeding state, provincial, or national standards.

Your students are on a continuum, and it is your responsibility to be a significant influencer in moving them further along that scale. It's better to think *less* in terms of who is clever and who isn't (which are the conclusions prompted by the data in figure 5.1, page 223) and more in terms of how much progress your students are making and what can be done to help them even more (which are what the data in figure 5.3 lead toward).

None of this is new, though. Indeed, the differing conclusions drawn from the testing of students have a very checkered past, as I will now show.

5.3 The World of Intelligence Testing Is Murky

The first practical IQ test was created by the French psychologist Alfred Binet (Binet & Simon, 1905). Contrary to the dominant practice of the day, it sought not to label students but to identify which of them needed alternative pedagogies so that everyone could learn. Only once Binet's test was translated into English did it become riddled with unethical practices.

The debate about the balance between nature and nurture, between genetics and experiences, isn't just a scientific or philosophical one. It is also highly political, with a very murky past. The present isn't as bright as it ought to be, either.

I mentioned Francis Galton (1869) earlier. As well as coining the term *eugenics*, he was one of its strongest advocates, recommending economic and medical measures to prevent people deemed "unfit" (Galton's term) from reproducing. Later, the eugenicists' ideal that a population should improve its genetic stock became one of the most cited claims by defendants at the Nuremberg trials (Pressel, 2003).

Before returning to Galton, I would like to go a bit further back to a man who should be judged much more favorably by history, Alfred Binet. This French psychologist invented the first practical IQ test with his colleague Théodore Simon in 1904 (Binet & Simon, 1905). They did so to meet the French Ministry of Education's desire to identify those students most in need of alternative education. Though this might seem unremarkable at first glance, bear in mind the prevailing wisdom at the time was to place "slow" students into an asylum, rather than to adjust pedagogy to the needs of the student. So, Binet's (Binet & Simon, 1905) work was pretty radical for its time. Carol S. Dweck, the Stanford University professor of psychology whose research I cover in section 5.4 (page 230), credits Binet as one of the earliest advocates of growth mindset (C. Dweck, personal communication, September 2, 2019).

The Binet-Simon test involved a series of tests for six- to fourteen-year-olds. Some of the simplest tasks assessed whether a child could follow a beam of light or talk back to the examiner. Slightly harder tasks required children to point to various named body parts, repeat simple sentences, and define words like *house*, *fork*, or *mama*. More challenging tasks included asking children to repeat back seven random digits and to find three rhymes for particular French words, such as *obéissance*.

The examples used for the reasoning elements would probably be regarded as inappropriate for today's young people because they included asking what is wrong with the following statements:

- An unfortunate bicycle rider smashed his head and died instantly; he was taken to the hospital and it is feared he may not recover.
- A railroad accident took place yesterday. It was not a serious one; only 48 people died.
- Yesterday the body of an unfortunate young woman, cut into eight pieces, was found on the fortifications. It is believed she killed herself.
- My neighbor has been receiving strange visitors. He has received in turn a doctor, a lawyer, and then a priest. What is taking place? (Binet & Simon, 1905, p. 252)

More important than the content of these tests were Binet's (Binet & Simon, 1905) beliefs about testing. He was forthright about the limitations of any testing scale. His warnings included the following.

- Intellectual development progresses at variable rates and is influenced by the environment. Therefore, any comparisons should be done only between children with comparable backgrounds.
- Tests can only show what a person has learned up to that point; they cannot be used to predict a person's future success or aptitude. Intelligence is malleable, and therefore, any test will show only a point in time, not a fixed quantity.
- Tests are imperfect, but they can be better than the subjectivity of adult opinion. For example, Binet wrote:

  > Teachers in standard schools might denigrate troublesome students' competence to have them removed from the classroom; conversely, teachers in special schools might exaggerate their students' achievements to boost their own success as instructors. Parents might overstate the accomplishments of their children to avoid the embarrassment of special school placements or understate them if they wished to escape responsibility for the child. (as cited in Siegler, 1992, p. 182)

- Tests should not be done in isolation and then over-relied on for months, even years to come. If testing is to be used, then it should be done frequently, partly because all tests are fallible but mainly because intellectual development progresses at variable rates.

Does this last point sound familiar? If it doesn't, see the notes accompanying figure 5.3 (page 225).

In summary, Binet and Simon (1916) assert, "A child scoring poorly in one test might, only a few months later, score very highly in another. This unpredictability would, in part, be explained by the different rates of maturation and educational experiences in between times" (p. 257).

Binet's proposed approach was philosophically sound and very much in keeping with the latest findings in research, discovered more than a century after his death. So why does testing suffer from such a bad reputation, and why does it create so many problems in modern education? The answer lies in its travel from France to the United States.

5.3.1 From French to English (and From Malleable to Fixed)

Unfortunately, Binet's work was published in French. That's not a problem in itself, but when it was translated into English, the values on which it was based changed dramatically. The principal translator was American psychologist H. H. Goddard, a champion of the eugenics movement. He promoted the Binet-Simon IQ test for reasons entirely antithetical to Binet's theories.

Goddard put forward the original work as if it could be used to measure "genetically determined" intelligence. His translation referred to a "general intelligence" despite Binet's strong assertion that no test could establish such a generalizable construct. Worse still, Goddard concluded that measuring IQ could be used to "separate 'superior' people from the 'inferior.' Specifically, he found utility in mental testing as a way to support his belief in the 'superiority of the white race'" (as cited in Siegler, 1992, p. 179).

For Stanford University psychologist Lewis Terman, Goddard's translation of Binet's intelligence test provided an ideal way to establish a "scientific" justification for White superiority (Leslie, 2000). He further adapted the test so that it would be culturally and linguistically accessible for White Anglo-Saxon Protestant children and less so for all other groups. Running huge trials across the United States, he identified 1,528 people aged three to twenty-eight whom he dubbed brilliant. Of these, two were Black, six were Japanese American, one was Native American, and 1,519 were White. All were urban and middle class.

Terman's adaptation of Binet's test later became the Stanford-Binet intelligence test. Now in its fifth edition, it is still used as an IQ test in 2023. "Few American children have passed through the school system in the last 80 years without taking the Stanford-Binet or one of its competitors" (Leslie, 2000).

Advocates considered intelligence to be the most valuable human quality. With the Stanford-Binet test, they now had a mechanism for identifying who was most qualified to lead and who should follow. Many influential individuals, including Terman, Galton, economist John Maynard Keynes, and British prime minister Winston Churchill, promoted ways to increase a nation's overall intelligence, including discouraging individuals with low IQ scores from having children and granting important positions based on high IQ scores alone. As Terman and his colleagues at Stanford noted (using biased and hurtful language) in their handbook, *The Measurement of Intelligence*:

> High-grade or borderline deficiency . . . is very, very common amongst Spanish-Indian and Mexican families of the Southwest and also among negroes. Their dullness seems to be racial, or at least inherent in the family stocks from which they come . . . Children of this group should be segregated into separate classes . . . They cannot master abstractions, but they can often be made into efficient workers . . . from a eugenic point of view they constitute a grave problem because of their unusually prolific breeding.
> (Terman, 1916, pp. 91–92)

When Binet heard about Terman's corruption of his life's work, he argued that "foreign ideas being grafted on his instrument . . . were done so with brutal pessimism and deplorable verdicts" (as cited in White, 2000, p. 33). Binet (1975) writes:

> A few modern philosophers seem to lend their moral support to these deplorable verdicts when they assert that an individual's intelligence is a fixed quantity, a quantity which cannot be increased. We must protest and react against this brutal pessimism. . . . With practice, training, and, above all, method, we manage to increase our attention, our memory, our judgment and literally to become more intelligent than we were before. (pp. 105–106)

Terman's goal was to classify people on a scale so that they could be assigned a suitable job or, in the case of children, be put on an appropriate job track. He believed IQ is inherited, stable, and generalizable. He also believed IQ is the strongest predictor of a person's ultimate success in life. Binet's goal was to identify children who needed additional support. He believed IQ is significantly influenced by the environment and builds at variable rates according to experience and maturity. He rejected the idea of a general form of intelligence, stating instead that intelligence is remarkably diverse in terms of origin, function, and applicability.

There have been many other critical figures in the development of IQ testing and the wider debate about the nature of intelligence. These include Françoys Gagné (study of giftedness), Cyril Burt (study of twins), Jean-Jacques Rousseau (theory of the "noble savage"), Reuven Feuerstein (mediated learning and human potential), and Francis Galton (founding of eugenics). However, I have chosen to focus on Terman and Binet in this chapter partly because they have had particularly significant influences on current attitudes about intelligence and partly because their attitudes paint a clear picture of the topic for the next section: fixed and growth mindsets.

In this video, James gives a short summary of the pros and cons of growth mindset.

5.4 Is Growth Mindset Worth the Hype?

Mindset plays a significant role in determining expectations. It's much better to be in a growth mindset than a fixed one. However, overclaims abound and effect sizes are lower than expected, so a deeper understanding is needed of why growth mindset matters and when.

Growth mindset refers to a belief that intelligence and abilities can be grown through experience, effort, strategy, and support from others. The term is most closely associated with professor Carol Dweck (2017). By contrast, being in a *fixed mindset* is a belief that intelligence and abilities are mostly innate, changing very little over time.

The impact of being in one or the other of these mindsets is significant, as the decades of precise research by Dweck (2017) and her team prove. Having co-presented with Dweck on many occasions, I aim to separate fact from fiction, reality from hype.

Table 5.1 gives an overview of the differences between fixed and growth mindsets, using a different example for each segment. Most people experience both mindsets, often at the same time. For example, someone might believe they can grow their talents in a sport through focus, effort, and determination (growth mindset thinking) and at the same time assume there is next to nothing they can do to become more artistic, mathematical, or multilingual (fixed mindset thinking). As Dweck often teases, "claiming you are always in a growth mindset is a very fixed mindset thing to say!" (C. Dweck, personal communication, August 16, 2017).

Table 5.1: Comparisons of Fixed and Growth Mindsets

Fixed Mindset: Abilities are fixed.	Growth Mindset: Abilities are grown.
The belief that abilities and intelligence are fixed by nature and are relatively innate	The belief that abilities and intelligence are grown through nurture and are relatively malleable
"I have always been good at this." "I don't have the mind for that."	"I have developed a talent for this." "I have never tried learning that."
Saying Usain Bolt, Marie Curie, Leonardo da Vinci, Albert Einstein, Whitney Houston, Steve Jobs, Hedy Lamarr, and Wolfgang Mozart were successful because of the gifts they were born with	Saying the people mentioned in the left-hand column turned their natural advantages into world-beating excellence through extraordinary drive, ambition, effort, opportunity, culture, and resilience
Fixed Mindset: Know your limitations.	**Growth Mindset: Test your limitations.**
The belief that our limitations tell us how far we can go before we can expect to fail	The belief that our limitations are there to be tested, stretched, and overcome
"I know and accept my limitations."	"I want to test my limitations to the maximum to see if I can go past them."
Quickly concluding others can't do something because they are female, are disabled, are poor, have ADHD, are from the wrong side of the tracks, have a bad attitude, and so on	Thinking of athletes at the Paralympics and people like Dame Evelyn Glennie, Stephen Hawking, Rosa Parks, and Oprah Winfrey
Fixed Mindset: *Prove* your ability.	**Growth Mindset: Improve your ability.**
Abilities and intelligence are relatively fixed. Therefore, it is important to prove one's talents.	Abilities and intelligence are relatively malleable. Therefore, it is important to grow and improve.
"I have always been really good at that." "I can't do this, but that's OK because I'm better at other things."	"I would love to have a go at improving that." "I have never had much success with this, so I'm trying to improve it now."
Choosing activities that are likely to end in success	Choosing activities that are likely to take you out of your comfort zone

Continued →

Fixed Mindset: I *can't* do that.	Growth Mindset: I *can't* do that yet.
Earlier failures or anticipated failures indicate that you can't do it.	Earlier failures or lack of familiarity indicate you can't do it yet.
"I know I can't do that." "I've tried it before and proved I'm hopeless at it."	"I know I can't do it yet, but I'm willing to have a go." "I'm hopeful I can do it better next time."
Saying, "I can't do it," as an excuse for not joining in	Saying, "I can't do it yet," to reflect the possibilities of future success, and to signal a willingness to try
Fixed Mindset: *Avoid* challenges.	**Growth Mindset: *Seek* challenges.**
Challenges are uncomfortable, so they should be avoided unless absolutely necessary.	Challenges are stimulating, so it is good to seek them out whenever appropriate.
"Why would I want to try that and make a fool of myself?" "That looks far too difficult."	"I would love to have a go at that to see how I get on with it." "That looks really exciting."
Using excuses and diversionary tactics to avoid challenges	Looking for opportunities to have a go at different challenges
Fixed Mindset: Struggling indicates *inadequacy*.	**Growth Mindset: Struggling indicates *learning*.**
Talented people can do things with ease. So, if you are struggling, then that means you are inadequate.	Talented people have been through many struggles to get where they are today. So, if you are struggling, then maybe you are on your way, too.
"I hate struggling. It shows I can't do it, and that's embarrassing. I get frustrated when I struggle and feel like giving up."	"Struggling means I am trying to learn. When I'm struggling, I reassure myself that the outcome is going to be worth it."
Trying not to show anyone that you are struggling; asking to be rescued or giving up too quickly	Persevering through the struggle; even growing to find joy in the knowledge that struggling leads to growth and personal development
Fixed Mindset: *Hide* mistakes.	**Growth Mindset: *Examine* mistakes.**
Mistakes are embarrassing because they indicate a lack of talent, understanding, or attention.	Mistakes can lead to a better understanding of what might be needed for increased success.
"I hate making mistakes; they show that I'm not concentrating or, even worse, that I can't do it."	"Mistakes are not great, but I can turn them into something positive if I learn from them."
Hiding mistakes from other people; pretending (sometimes even to yourself) that they never happened; blaming circumstances	Examining what went wrong, lessons learned, and possible solutions; deciding cause and effect rather than blame and punishment
Fixed Mindset: Feedback is *criticism*.	**Growth Mindset: Feedback is *information*.**
Feedback is a euphemism for *criticism*. It leaves the receiver feeling inadequate and crestfallen.	Feedback is not personal; it is information that could be used to improve future performance.
"Please be gentle when giving me feedback." "So basically, what you're telling me is that I'm not good enough?"	"Feedback helps me to understand how well I am doing and what I could do next to improve."

Thinking feedback is directed toward the person and their inadequacy; preferring feedback to be praise based rather than critique based	Thinking feedback is directed toward process and improvement of future performance; wanting clarity and purpose rather than flattery or false praise
Fixed Mindset: Mottoes	**Growth Mindset: Mottoes**
"Fortune favors the strong."	"Fortune favors the brave."
"If you're really good at something, you shouldn't need to try."	"No matter how good you are at something, you can always improve."
"If you have to try, you must be stupid; effort is for losers."	"If you have to try, you must be learning something; effort is how people succeed."
"Don't try too hard; that way, you have an excuse if things go wrong."	"Always try hard; that way, you have a greater chance of succeeding and making progress."
"No pain, no pain."	"No pain, no gain."

5.4.1 Is Mindset Important?

The positive effects of growth mindset are well established (Yeager et al., 2019). It is not, as some commentators claim, pseudoscientific, new-age thinking. As Dylan Wiliam (2020) posted:

> I think we have to distinguish between small, well-established effects (e.g., growth mindset) and those for which there is no reliable evidence (Brain Gym, learning styles). Given that growth mindset interventions typically take less than an hour, not using them seems odd to me.

Patricia A. Smiley and colleagues (2016) provide useful clarity on the impact of growth versus fixed mindsets:

> Students who endorse an incremental theory of intelligence are more likely to make plans to improve their performance after a setback, due in part to their holding learning goals in academic situations and to their focus on the positive role that effort can play in achievement. In comparison, students who hold ability goals are more likely to withdraw from challenges, due in part to their focus on lack of ability as the reason for failure and their tendency to experience deactivating loss of interest/excitement after a setback. (p. 890)

In general terms, mindset is important. However, as with most aspects of education, it works better for some students than others and better in some situations than others. Some key points include the following.

- There is some hype about growth mindset, as well as too much overclaiming of its benefits. However, the research supporting growth mindset is robust and reliable (Burnette, O'Boyle, VanEpps, Pollack, & Finkel, 2013; Sisk et al., 2018; Yeager et al., 2019).
- Across the four meta-analyses investigating the impact of growth mindset (see section 5.4.2, page 235), the range of effect sizes is $d = 0.08$ to 0.28. These are lower than the average effect across all interventions of $d = 0.40$ (see section 1.5, page 10).

The range is nonetheless positive, and given that most were achieved following an online intervention of just fifty minutes, the effects are considerable.

- Analysis of the research by Sisk and colleagues (2018) suggests mindset has a bigger impact on academically high-risk and economically disadvantaged students than it does on other students.
- Growth mindset may have a detrimental effect on students who are confident in, or rely on, their "natural" talents (Yeager & Dweck, 2020).

In all cases, mindset does not matter very much when you are in your comfort zone. When engaged in easy tasks, you have no need to question your abilities or find alternative solutions. A similar thing could be said of grit, determination, and self-efficacy (all of which are linked with growth mindset): they are all unnecessary when tasks are straightforward.

Mindset becomes relevant when faced with situations that give rise to questions such as, Is it worth persevering in the hope of finding a better solution, or should I admit defeat before I embarrass myself? Will I be able to outdo myself, or have I reached my limit? Is it better to involve others or to cover up my failings? Why can't I do this? Why do others succeed seemingly with ease when I find it so difficult?

In these situations, someone in a growth mindset tends to choose the positive, proactive option. They do so because they believe talents are malleable, and with that comes the recognition that effort, strategy, and perseverance will make breakthroughs more likely. Those in a fixed mindset, however, believe that everyone has limitations; therefore, setbacks and failure are likely to indicate they have reached, or are close to, their natural limits.

Other situations in which mindset is important include the following.

- **Feedback:** Being in a growth mindset helps learners be more receptive to feedback. They seek out ways to improve because they believe progress is possible. They know that if they take good advice and apply it properly, outcomes will be better. This compares to someone in a fixed mindset who is primarily interested in how well they did and how this compares with other people's achievements.

  You can link these findings with the differences between formative and summative assessments. Those in a fixed mindset tend to use feedback summatively (by wanting to know how well they did), whereas those in a growth mindset use feedback formatively (by seeking to understand what they could do next to improve).

- **Challenge:** Being in a growth mindset engenders a positive attitude toward challenge. When someone believes improvements are possible given the right adjustments, they are much more willing to engage in short-term discomfort to secure longer-term benefits. But those in a fixed mindset tend to worry about the negative outcomes or long-term effects of mistakes or failure.

  That is not to say that mindset is the only factor influencing attitudes to challenge. Other aspects include how often someone has succeeded with similar tasks, how much they trust the intentions of the person setting the challenges, and whether they value the intended outcomes. In other words, are they likely to succeed, do they trust the situation, and is the pain worth the gain? If the answer to these questions is no, then mindset is unlikely to be important, whereas if the answer is yes (or a borderline yes), then being in a growth mindset could very well make the difference between taking on challenges and avoiding these challenges.

- **Failure:** When I was gathering together the research available to write *Challenging Mindset* (Nottingham & Larsson, 2018), the analysis I was most fascinated by was the conclusion that a teacher's attitude toward failure is more influential than their mindset is. As I will show in section 5.8 (page 257), a teacher's mindset is important. However, anyone else's mindset is difficult to detect without an interview or focused observations; their attitude toward mistakes and failure is visible and therefore much more likely to be of influence.

  Thus, teachers who respond to failure with despondency are likely to put their students into a fixed mindset, whereas those who respond as if failure is a learning opportunity that always has options for improved iterations are more likely to encourage students into a growth mindset.

To summarize, being in a growth mindset is particularly important when your students are:

- Out of their comfort zone
- Nervous about their chances of success
- Faced with setbacks or failure
- Setting goals or choosing tasks
- Responding to feedback
- Comparing themselves with others
- Imagining what they are capable of

As a footnote to this section, growth mindset is not the be-all and end-all. Developing interests and talents is complex and multifaceted. In *Nature's Gambit: Child Prodigies and the Development of Human Potential*, researcher David Henry Feldman (1991) concludes that talent is the result of a lucky coincidence of factors. This includes a willingness to put in the hours necessary to improve, the proximity of the resources needed, healthy social-emotional development, birth order and gender, public recognition and approval, family traditions, historical forces, events, and trends.

5.4.2 When Is Mindset Most Effective?

In this section, I share some of the findings and nuances of the research. These are drawn from four meta-analyses covering 283 studies about the effect size of growth mindset.

- Overall effect of mindset on student achievement: 0.15
- "Implicit Theories of Intelligence and Academic Achievement: A Meta-Analytic Review" (Costa & Faria, 2018), 46 studies: 0.14 effect size
- "To What Extent and Under Which Circumstances Are Growth Mind-Sets Important to Academic Achievement?" (Sisk et al., 2018)

- Growth mindsets, 123 studies: 0.20 effect size
- Growth mindsets interventions, 29 studies: 0.08 effect size

• "Mind-Sets Matter: A Meta-Analytic Review of Implicit Theories and Self-Regulation" (Burnette et al., 2013), 85 studies: 0.19 effect size

These meta-analyses show the effects of growth mindset on student achievement are positive. However, given the significance of the attitudes and behaviors associated with growth mindset (setting aspirational targets, being more willing to accept and use feedback, persevering in the face of setbacks, and so on), it is surprising that the effects are smaller than the average effect of 0.40 (see section 1.5, page 10).

There are many reasons why these effects, though positive, are below average, including the following five reasons.

1. A significant proportion of the interventions included in the meta-analyses took less than an hour to administer. For example, researcher David S. Yeager and colleagues (2016) ran a web-based intervention involving two twenty-five-minute sessions with 7,335 students in the United States that significantly lowered the dropout rate among socially and economically disadvantaged students. Three years later, Yeager ran the same intervention with a nationally representative sample of 12,490 ninth graders attending 65 schools. The results were particularly effective with lower-achieving students, raising their GPAs by an average of 0.10 grade points (on a 4.0 scale) in core classes. This represents a substantial increase when compared with other equivalent educational interventions (Yeager et al., 2019).

   Beyond the United States, researcher Mari Rege and colleagues (2021) ran Yeager's intervention with 6,541 high school students in Norway, prompting significantly more students to enroll in higher mathematics classes the following year.

   So, although many homegrown mindset projects are designed to run throughout a school year, most of the data included in the meta-analyses are based on just two twenty-five-minute sessions with students. Being able to achieve effect sizes between 0.08 and 0.20 (20 percent to 50 percent improvement) with such a low-cost, time-effective approach is remarkable.

2. The strength of the relationship between growth mindset and achievement is dependent on the many factors shaping the culture of learning. For example, it is difficult to maintain a growth mindset if asking thought-provoking questions or seeking more challenging work is met by the scorn of peers; the same could be said of giving too much attention to test taking such that other educational aims are displaced.

   This interpretation is supported by the largest study to examine growth mindset and achievement, administered as part of the Programme for International Student Assessment (PISA), the testing program by the Organisation for Economic Co-operation and Development (2019). Questions designed to identify a link between mindset and performance on the rest of the test were asked of 500,000 fifteen-year-old students in seventy-nine countries. Those in a growth mindset scored on average thirty-two points higher on the reading portion of the test than those in a fixed mindset. The examiners also concluded that being in a growth mindset was positively associated with setting higher learning goals, being motivated to master tasks, and perceiving value in attending school. There was also a strong correlation between growth mindset increasing and fear of failure decreasing.

However, when the data were broken down by country, these effects were large in some and nonexistent in others. The conclusion was that the role of context is very significant. It is false to say that growth mindset works everywhere, every time. There are many factors that lead to successful outcomes, and mindset is just one.

3. The growth mindset theory is correct, but the implementation takes more care and attention than is often given. For example, many educators and researchers have created their own interventions rather than replicating the successful methods used by others.

   Reading through the meta-analyses makes it clear that the interventions with the highest effect sizes have all been administered by trained instructors taking an iterative approach. They have begun with an already-proven strategy and then used participant interviews to identify what was engaging, clear, and meaningful. Their collected data have then been used to further refine later iterations. No wonder these researchers have had more success than the busy teacher for whom growth mindset is just one of the many strategies they're using to engage and extend their students' learning!

   Connected to this is Dweck's concern that too many people have oversimplified growth mindset such that it has become mainly about praising students' efforts. She has noted that students are too often praised even if their efforts have been misdirected or fruitless (Dweck, 2016). This is despite her assertions that growth mindset theory actually demands that feedback be gathered about what went wrong, and that new strategies be developed after the feedback is considered to overcome failure or mistakes.

4. When staff promote growth mindset but do so superficially or are themselves in a fixed mindset, they are likely to convey mixed messages. Of course, we all start as novices with more enthusiasm than understanding, so mistakes are inevitable. So, the examples shown in table 5.2 (page 237) are illustrations, not accusations!

5. Higher-achieving students often don't gain as much from growth mindset as their lower-achieving or at-risk peers. This whole chapter could be given over to exploring why this might be, and still there would be gaps. So, for now I will offer just a few reasons. It's worth bearing in mind that all four meta-analyses quoted show the biggest gains for at-risk and lower-achieving students. So, even if you don't agree with the why, you can be confident of the what.

Table 5.2: When Growth Mindset Is Poorly Implemented

Growth Mindset *Intention*	Growth Mindset *Misapplied*	Conflicting Fixed Mindset *Action*
Using process praise (for example, extolling strategy and determination) to emphasize that everyone can improve and grow	Using phrases such as, "Good effort" or "Well done," even when efforts were misdirected or ineffective (such that praise is thought of as unrelated to achievement)	Celebrating the achievements of someone who succeeds with ease more than those of someone is trying hard but not quite reaching their goal (such that praise feels like a consolation prize)
Examining mistakes to better understand their causes, solutions, and ways to avoid repeating them	Giving the impression that the errors themselves are causes for celebration	Showing annoyance, frustration, or disappointment when making or discovering mistakes
Developing students' agency and self-efficacy by teaching them how to be proactive when faced with setbacks and failure	Telling students not to worry when faced with setbacks and failure without also teaching them a range of next steps	Implying that failure is the end of the road and should be avoided at all costs, or that some people are (for example) creative and some are not

Understanding Old Ideas Versus New Theory

Lower-achieving students and those with risk factors for graduation often conclude that their lack of success is due to inherited traits or personality defects—for example, "I'm not academic, because my parents aren't," or "I'm just impulsive by nature." So, when they learn about growth mindset, they start to believe (and act in the belief) that improved efforts, determination, and strategy will improve outcomes. But many—maybe even most—successful students already know (often because they have been told so) that doing extra studying or asking for advice generally leads to better performance on an assignment or test. For them, growth mindset merely adds a language or a justification for what they already do.

Maintaining an A Is Less Noticeable Than Moving From D to C Grades

For students who are already securing top grades, improvements will be harder to spot than for those starting from a lower grade with plenty of room for improvement. It is but one of the many drawbacks of using national, provincial, or state grading systems as the main (or sometimes only) measure of student learning. If a student achieves an A grade every time, then the only obvious marker of their learning is to maintain that A. But when students who are normally awarded Ds and Es (or Fs) begin to apply themselves more effectively (because of their newly acquired understanding of growth mindset), their gains are likely to be much more noticeable—particularly if this grade improvement carries with it a move from fail to pass.

So far, so obvious! Of course those for whom growth mindset confirms they're on the right path will make fewer gains than those who choose a better path altogether! But now for the lesser-known fact (whisper it quietly): some students in a fixed mindset achieve more than those in a growth mindset.

Figuring Out If It's the Chicken or the Egg

Until now, I have written in terms of "evidence indicates that you will probably do better if you are in a growth mindset," but what happens when students who do very well explain their successes in fixed mindset terms? When an interviewee says they do well at something because they're naturally good at it or they've always found it easy, researchers have to take them at their word. They don't have the resources to uncover the interviewee's early experiences, home life, resources, or opportunities, whereas if, for example, renowned runner Usain Bolt said he is the fastest man on the planet because he is Jamaican, we'd assume he was being flippant because we're aware that his extraordinary dedication, training, and physique have also contributed to his successes. Being Jamaican might be a factor—athletics is the number-one sport in his country—but we know it's just one of many factors.

Interestingly, there are incidents of outstanding performers not wanting researchers to dig too deeply for fear that they might unearth a mix of factors so mundane that the "magic" will be lost! When the reasons for success are so complex and the naming of every factor so difficult, it is sometimes better to accept the success for what it is and enjoy the ride!

5.4.3 Is Growth Mindset Worth Investing In?

Although the positive effects might be smaller than expected, growth mindset tends to be good value for money. It doesn't require hours of extra effort in the way that engaging parents does, it doesn't require a significant change to marking and assessment practices as feedback does if you are going to make the outcomes worth the efforts, and it doesn't bring with it the enormous financial burden that reducing class sizes or investing in technology does.

Growth mindset means talking about talent creation in particular ways: being careful to praise actions rather than individuals; responding to mistakes, setbacks, and failures in such a way that will teach students not to fear them, but to harness them for deeper understanding; and drawing attention to students' progress as well as their achievements.

Investing in growth mindset, therefore, should not mean more. Your teaching load should not increase. You shouldn't be required to add yet another thing to the curriculum. The only additional efforts are likely to be during your professional learning time. After that, growth mindset should be a way of interacting with your students, no more, no less.

Growth mindset also makes a significant difference to expectations—yours and your students'. Being in a growth mindset includes believing that abilities and intelligence are malleable; limitations are there to be tested, stretched, and overcome; and no matter how good you are at something, you can always improve. All these beliefs contribute to raising expectations.

So, how do you make growth mindset a reality for all your students? The following section has some ideas to get you started.

5.4.4 How Do You Make Growth Mindset a Reality for Your Students?

Mindset interventions hinge on their ability to persuade participants to shift their mindsets from fixed to growth. One of the meta-analyses quoted in this chapter (Sisk et al., 2018) shows that only 54 percent of mindset interventions achieve this shift. So, don't be tempted to pick just one of the recommendations in the following five sections. Instead, plan to integrate them all into your teaching over time. Together, they will give you the best chance of convincing your students to adopt growth mindset beliefs. The following are five recommendations for creating growth mindset beliefs.

1. Explain the neuroscience (see discussion after this list).
2. Privilege progress (see section 5.5, page 240).
3. Be careful with rewards (see section 5.7, page 251).
4. Learn from mistakes (see section 5.8, page 257).
5. Build efficacy (see section 5.9, page 263).

The interventions that have been consistently successful have all involved teaching students about the malleability of intelligence and, more broadly, growth mindset theory. So, even if this isn't your starting point, make sure it is at least a point along the journey.

One of the more fascinating experiments I came across in the meta-analyses involved college students writing to at-risk middle school students. They were asked to share what research is revealing about human intelligence. The college students who took part reported greater enjoyment of and engagement in the academic process and obtained higher grade point averages than their counterparts in two control groups (Aronson, Fried, & Good, 2002).

The best starting point for teaching students about growth mindset is using the free materials created by Standford University on the Mindset Kit website (visit https://mindsetkit.org/topics/teaching-growth-mindset and www.healthline.com/health/growth-mindset-neuroplasticity).

5.5 Improve Everyone's Learning by Amplifying Progress

The miracle, or the power, that elevates the few is to be found in their industry, application, and perseverance under the prompting of a brave, determined spirit.

—Mark Twain

Holding high expectations involves not only *believing* that you can make significant progress, but also having enough proof that you *know* you can. This section shows how to make this more likely.

Take a look at the fabulous drawing in figure 5.4. It was created by a five-year-old named Silja in one of the preschools I've worked with in Denmark. If one of your students created something as impressive, particularly considering their age, would you display it for all to see? I ask this because the practice in so many schools is to do exactly that.

In many regards, it would be lovely to display such a fabulous creation. However, there is a drawback. Doing so risks drawing too much attention to achievement and not enough to progress.

Let's say you displayed six students' artwork—including Silja's. How would that be very different from showing off the test results of the six students included in the data in figure 5.1 (page 223)?

Granted, butterflies are more aesthetically pleasing than a data graph. But they would share the same principle: behold the achievement of our students!

I realize this doesn't automatically happen, but why even risk having onlookers jump to conclusions about who is the better or best artist? Were that to happen, it wouldn't be much different from having someone look at a list of test scores and make assumptions about who is cleverest and who is not.

Figure 5.4: Butterfly by five-year-old Silja.

Don't worry, though! I'm not about to suggest we stop displaying or sharing students' artwork! After all, it *can be* really positive, particularly in boosting a sense of belonging in the learning space. A much better practice is to display finished work *together with* earlier iterations. Continue to share your students' fabulous creations, but *also* draw attention to the progress they have made along the way. For example, don't display figure 5.4, but do show figure 5.5 instead.

Figure 5.5: Silja's progress in drawing a butterfly.

At the risk of coming across as anti-art (which I definitely am not), I think the displays in art rooms are often misdirected. All too often, they *only* show stunning pieces of artwork. This can be inspiring for some but intimidating for others. Too many of us (adults as well as young people) look at the fabulous creations and think, "That is amazing, but I could never do that." It's a bit like going to an IT suite and seeing only coding diagrams on the wall. It's inspiring for those who have made huge progress already, but it's inaccessible to most.

This is *not* to suggest that schools should never host an art exhibition. Of course, they should! Excellence should be celebrated. We *should* hold chess competitions, spelling bees, sporting events, and science and technology fairs. But inside school—*during normal proceedings*—the emphasis should be on progress. Special events such as performances, exhibitions, and competitions can celebrate achievement. Classrooms should be for everyone, not just the best of the best.

School classrooms—including art rooms, sports facilities, drama studios, computer rooms, science labs, and the like—should warmly welcome every single student. They should never be intimidating places for students who already feel as if they're far behind others. Every single space should say, "You are welcome here! Come in, and let's *all* learn together."

I spent the first thirty-three years of my life thinking I wasn't creative. There were always artistic students at school, but I was never one of them. Those students received extra attention and favor from the art teachers (or so it seemed to me), getting better and better as a result. Soon, those of us who were left out were left behind.

So, what happened when I was thirty-four? In 2004, I attended a lateral thinking course by professor Edward de Bono, the creator of the Six Thinking Hats (de Bono, 1999). By the end of that course, de Bono had convinced everyone—me included—that we could all be creative. Indeed, we *are* all creative. Use the right strategies and adopt important principles, and you, too, can be creative. It was a revelation. Part of me wanted to go back to school and show my teachers what I was capable of. Then I remembered my 1980s hairstyle and thought better of it.

At the ripe old age of thirteen, we accepted our fate that we were *never* going to be creative (or sporty, mathematical, linguistic, dramatic, inventive, or scientific). We decided that school was a place to find our niche and stay there (or hide there, maybe?). We did not venture into other areas of the curriculum, even if they seemed fascinating. After all, only ridicule awaits those who start much further back than others—or at least that's what we scholars thought.

Fortunately, my schooling was in the 1970s and 1980s, and we've come a long way since then! And yet, I have heard these themes repeated again and again during student voice activities in more recent years. In fact, it's very rare that students *don't* have the impression that some subjects are the sole preserve of some rather than all.

5.5.1 Examples of Progress

Achievement is important; so is progress. Both should be valued in educational contexts. The motto, "Proving is good; improving is better," captures the essence of this assertion.

Drawing attention to progress won't change everything, but it's a great start. In fact, I would argue it is an absolutely necessary action to take if (1) you believe your job is to help your students improve, and (2) you want to make growth mindset the attitude your students take toward their learning and their lives.

Of course, this is not just about displaying progress in art. It's not even about displaying any type of work. It's about what we draw attention to. Wider society already celebrates top grades, outstanding performances, and the best of the best. We have prize-giving ceremonies, awards, merits, and enhanced reputations for those who achieve more than others. This is not about getting rid of those systems and structures, dubious though some of them might be. This is about *also* drawing attention to students' progress, also amplifying their growth, and also emphasizing that school has as much to do with growing, improving, and developing as it does with recognizing achievements.

In 2006, I set up a company to share some really effective teaching practices that my colleagues and I had been developing. By 2014, I employed thirty staff in seven countries. Our motto during that time was very much in keeping with the recommendations I make in this section: "Proving is good; improving is better."

Notice that this says, "Proving is good." It doesn't say, "Achievement isn't worth celebrating." Of course, achievement is important. We want all our students to achieve well. As leaders, we hold similarly high hopes for our colleagues and ourselves. However, achievement is not everything. Progress is also important. Indeed, the more progress you make, the higher your achievement is going to be! One leads to the other. There is not the sort of false dichotomy that some people claim in which we can't value progress because we have to value achievement instead. They say, "In the real world, it is achievement that matters. That is what gets graded. That is what universities and businesses want." (Why do they always start with "in the real world," as if education *isn't* the real world?)

In most cases, universities and businesses want brilliant learners, and they also want good qualifications. But (and here *is* a false dichotomy) if they had to choose between someone with a PhD who thinks they know it all and someone with average qualifications but a thirst for learning, many—probably most—recruiters would go for the learner option first.

So, what does amplifying progress look like in practice? Here are some ideas. It is by no means an exhaustive list.

- **Beginning, middle, end:** Early in a topic, ask your students to write down everything they already know about the topic, together with any questions they might have. At the midway and end points of the topic, invite them to add extra detail. If they use a different-colored pen for each of these stages, it will be easier to draw attention to the progress they are making in their studies.
- **Markup:** Engage the markup feature when your students use Microsoft Word (or the equivalent). This will create the same effect as the first idea.
- **Revisiting earlier iterations:** Periodically, return to something that your students have created previously. Then invite them to use their newly improved skills and understanding to edit their original creations to make them even better than they were before. Examples include essays, paintings, models, scientific write-ups, and so on. This should show the students how much progress they have made in the intervening period.

- **Annotating books:** Invite your students to browse through their books, annotating the progress they think they have made with either sticky notes or comments in the margins. You could also ask them to identify their favorite examples.
- **Reviewing video evidence:** Record your students performing a skill in sports, drama, group work, and so on. Share the recordings with them and ask them to identify what they would like to improve next. Record their subsequent attempts and highlight the improvements.
- **Attitudes, skills, and knowledge (ASK):** Similarly, record some of the activities that students are engaged in. Look for signs of increasing confidence, curiosity, reasoning, interpersonal skills, and so on. The ASK Model, as described in section 4.3.3.2 (page 160), can be a source of inspiration for this.
- **Beating their personal bests:** During physical education lessons, record your students' performances over a few months. For example, see how fast they can run one hundred meters, how far they can jump, how accurately they can throw a ball, and so on. This allows you to focus on the progress they are making as well as their performances in competitions.
- **Thinking journals:** Create thinking journals in which your students record their reflections following different learning activities. They can add further ideas over time or extend their original ideas that they recorded earlier in their journal. These journals will show your students, their parents, and you how their ideas are gaining in complexity over time.
- **Learning conferences:** Host learning conferences in which students show their parents the progress they have been making recently. This gives your students the opportunity to show examples of what they have been learning and improving. If these conferences are used in conjunction with some of the other ideas here, each student should have ample examples to showcase.

5.5.2 Tests That Show Progress

Researcher Richard Phelps (2012) found that testing can have a significantly positive impact on student learning. This is particularly true when teachers use results to adapt later instruction and students use corrections from initial tests for further study.

I have already written about tests on a number of occasions (see sections 3.4.4 and 4.6, pages 105 and 186). To say that the use of tests is contentious would be an understatement. Advocates claim that testing causes students to put more effort into their studies; prepare more effectively for national, provincial, or state exams; and gain a better sense of whether they're on track to achieve the grades they want or need. Opponents argue that frequent testing—and teaching that is directed specifically toward answering test questions—leads students to become good test takers rather than develop the broader set of skills and knowledge intended by a school curriculum.

The most notable analysis about the effects of testing was completed by researcher Richard P. Phelps (2012). He summarized 669 studies conducted between 1910 and 2010. He included only studies that found effects on student achievement or teacher instruction, rejecting more than two thousand that were incomplete or had no comparative control group. Among the 177 quantitative studies, he found an effect size of 0.55. From the surveys, polls, and qualitative studies (for example, asking students if tests helped prepare them more effectively for their exams), he calculated an effect size of 0.50 (Phelps, 2012). So, it would seem from these data that tests boost student achievement considerably.

Opponents would still argue that the types of gains are too narrow; they show students are more successful test takers rather than, for example, more engaged, collaborative, and thoughtful citizens. Nonetheless, the magnitude of the gains is considerable, even if those gains are not as holistic as they (or I) would wish.

With that all said, here is why I'm wading into this. The more interesting data, at least in terms of growth mindset, were when students received the opportunity to take a pretest and a post-test. In these instances, the effect size almost doubled to 0.96. And when the tests were used to improve instruction, the effect size similarly increased to 0.90 (Phelps, 2012). The conclusion from this is that we should *not* administer tests as one-offs. Rather, we should always give a pretest followed by a post-test. This is by far the most effective way to test students.

Give your students a pretest (call it a *practice* or *tryout* if that helps) followed by targeted instruction (remediation) and additional study time *with the marked pretest in front of them.* Then give them the post-test (or actual test). It doesn't need to involve twice as much grading work for you. For example, you could (1) run the pretest; (2) share the right answers or mark scheme; (3) ask your students to mark their own (or each other's) answers; (4) give targeted instruction or additional study time; and then (5) administer the actual test in the way you would normally.

In most cases, the pre- and post-tests ought to be similar but not the same. This will help sidestep any complaints that testing is becoming more heavily reliant on just memorization. For example, if you are testing your students on their knowledge about trigonometry, then ask them to calculate angles of triangles on the first test and then angles of different triangles on the second. If it's a language test, then give them situations to describe or vocabulary to explain on the first test and then similar or connected examples on the second test.

Sometimes, it makes sense to have identical pre- and post-tests. For example, here in the United Kingdom, it is commonplace to give primary school students spelling tests. Typically, a new list of words is given each week, students have a few days to memorize the answers, and then they are tested. The usual suspects score 100 percent every time, while others score poorly most times. There are many problems with this approach, including the following.

- For some students, there is no challenge. They have no need to practice before the test because they already know the answers. This might sound reasonable enough, but the flip side is that it may also risk having students think teachers are more interested in passed tests than in the further development of talents.

- The students who get 100 percent every time, particularly those who do so with ease, may start to believe they are good spellers, which is fine until their egos begin to rely on this assertion. Ultimately, they may get to the point where they dare not get things wrong for fear of losing their clever status. This thinking can lead them to take evasive action, including sticking to what they know to be correct, taking fewer risks, and choosing to remain in their comfort zones.

- Then there are the students who never do very well. They might believe they are just not good at spelling. That sense of incompetence can lead students (and maybe even their onlookers) to the fixed mindset conclusion that they are naturally untalented.

So, is there anything positive to say about spelling tests? Well, there could be if we take a growth mindset approach with the following steps.

1. Before handing out the new set of words for the week, give your students a pretest.
2. Share the correct answers so that they can mark their own or each other's pretests.
3. Remind anyone who scores lower than, say, 70 percent to concentrate particularly on the words they got wrong (together with any spelling rules that might apply) as they prepare for the actual test. Give an additional set of words with more complex spellings to learn to anyone who achieves a higher score. This emphasizes the importance of challenge as well as gives them more opportunities to show progress.
4. Once the students have had the chance to prepare, give them the post-test.
5. Gather only the progress scores (the difference between each student's pretest score and their post-test score).

This isn't perfect. (Show me the test or task that is, and we'll all use that!) However, not only is it better than the traditional way to run spelling tests, but it is also much more in keeping with growth mindset. It helps emphasize how interested you are in your students' growth and development. It also reduces the likelihood that students will suppose some people are naturally good at spelling and others aren't.

The same can be said for the likelihood that they will compare final scores with each other. My experience is that they still want to know how well their friends did, but they tend to focus more on each other's progress scores. It's still not perfect, but I'd rather a student with lower scores compare their own progress from 1 to 9 with their friend's move from 6 to 13 (their progress scores being 8 and 7, respectively) than draw fixed mindset conclusions as to why their friend scored 13 when they themselves only got 9 correct.

Whenever I suggest this idea to staff, there are always a few teachers who fold their arms as if to say, "This will never work." They predict that their students will get wise to the format and deliberately score poorly on the pretest so as to avoid harder options. I understand this concern because my own students did the same thing in the early days. However, when this approach (to progress testing) goes hand in hand with extolling the virtues of seeking challenges, beating personal bests, and testing the limits of their knowledge—and then smashing those barriers— this sort of work-shy behavior lessens over time.

5.5.3 Identification of the Type of Progress You Want

 *Do not ask what teachers do. Instead, ask students what their teachers value.*

I can't imagine any teacher or school leader disagreeing with the idea that their students should make progress. But a significant question remains: Progress in what? As the adage goes, before putting effort into climbing the ladder, make sure it's leaning against the right wall.

Another way to think about this is with the statement that starts this section. It can be a very powerful one. The leaders' equivalent is, "Don't show me your mission statement. Show me your budget, and I'll tell you what you really care about." Ouch.

Returning to the teaching emphasis once more, what type of progress would you like your students to make? Having a clear idea about this will help you know what to put effort into and what to draw attention to. For example, if you want your students to develop reasonableness, then one focus ought to be teaching them how to reason (since reasoning is at the heart of being reasonable). How can you emphasize reasoning within different curriculum areas? Within class or group dialogue? How can you use your questioning to direct your students more toward giving reasons and justifications?

Guy Claxton's work in this field is brilliant. Indeed, Claxton himself is brilliant; I definitely recommend reading any of his books. His recommendations for *Building Learning Power* (Claxton, 2002) would be particularly relevant in helping identify the dispositions you would like your students to make progress with. The ASK Model is also a good inspiration, though I say so myself. I have written about this in some depth in chapter 4, section 4.3.3.2 (page 160).

Once you have chosen which attitudes, skills, and knowledge you would most like your students to make progress in, the following questions could help you take the next steps.

- What would visitors looking at the displays in, and the setup of, your classroom infer that you value: achievement or progress or both?
- What would students' parents and caregivers infer that you value based on your communication with them: achievement or progress or both?
- If you decide to make any changes to your teaching or approaches to student learning so that they are even more progress oriented, how might you communicate those decisions to your colleagues and students?

5.6 Group Students for Maximum Growth

Earlier, I wrote that testing is contentious. However, it's like taming a cute puppy compared to the bear poking that accompanies any mention of tracking, streaming, and ability grouping! Some people are so attached to the approach that they can't imagine how students can be taught adequately without some sort of ability grouping. Others point to the damage it does to those in the lowest groups, arguing that the negative effect on their self-concept as learners—and the lowering of their expectations—is a price too high to pay. I'm *not* saying ability grouping is like smacking, but the debate *about it* reminds me of the polemic years ago surrounding corporal punishment as a way to discipline children.

As a teacher reading this, you probably think you have little to no influence on systemwide tracking or streaming. You're assigned classes and you teach whoever turns up. For that reason, I won't linger on the wider topic. Instead, I will focus on what we *can* normally influence—the within-class grouping. For the sake of background, though, here is a very brief summary.

Tracking or *streaming* is the system of creating different classes for different ability groups. Typically, there are top, middle, and bottom groups. According to the Organisation for Economic Co-operation and Development (OECD, 2012), almost half of all students across the OECD countries are grouped this way, with 75 percent of students being streamed for at least one subject, normally mathematics or literacy.

Researchers Saiying Steenbergen-Hu, Matthew C. Makel, and Paula Olszewski-Kubilius (2016) synthesized thirteen meta-analyses. They concluded that "tracking has minimal effects on learning outcomes; no one profits" (Steenbergen-Hu et al., 2016). The effect sizes ranged from 0.06 for the top groups to 0.04 for the middle groups to 0.03 for the lower-ability groups. The researchers did point out that three meta-analyses showed students taking part in accelerated learning classes made significant gains ($d = 0.70$), but that these gains were quickly lost when they rejoined their peers, the conclusion therefore being to accelerate learning for everyone, not just the chosen few.

There is an even bigger equity issue when it comes to tracking. Researchers Jeannie Oakes and Martin Lipton (1990) analyzed 1,200 elementary and high schools in the United States and found that minority and low-income students are seven times more likely to be placed in a low-ability class. In England, 5,481 of the children who were tracked as part of the Millennium Cohort Study (a longitudinal study following the lives of almost twenty thousand children in the United Kingdom in the year 2000) were sampled and analyzed. From the data, researcher Tammy Campbell (2013) reported the following outcomes noted even by the age of seven.

- 78.8 percent of students were ability grouped in class for most or all teaching.
- 92.6 percent of students who were in the highest stream or track for literacy were in the highest groups for all subjects.
- 88.6 percent of students who were in the lowest stream for literacy were in the lowest groups for all subjects.
- 70.7 percent of students born in September (the oldest in each year group in England) were placed in top streams, with 19.5 percent placed in the middle streams.
- 26.2 percent of students born in the following August (the youngest in each year group) were placed in bottom streams, with 44.3 percent placed in the middle streams.

The astonishing degree to which age positioning within a year group influences educational opportunities is not just an England-based phenomenon. There exists a vast amount of international research on the month-of-birth effect. It *uniformly* indicates that a student's age within their year group has a statistically and educationally significant relationship with a variety of outcomes and experiences. They include academic achievement (for example, Crawford, Dearden, & Greaves, 2011); likelihood of being diagnosed with special educational needs (for example, Sykes, Bell, & Rodeiro, 2009); participation in further and higher education (for example, Bedard & Dhuey, 2006); and propensity to be bullied (for example, Crawford et al., 2011).

There are only two principal arguments for tracking. The first is that we've always done it this way ("and it never did me any harm," as the script usually goes). The second, and much more persuasive, is that it reduces within-class variance, making classes easier to teach. The latter, however, is not supported by the research. If we assume *easier to teach* means improved learning outcomes, then there just isn't any evidence of this.

If, however, *easier* means *less need for behavior management strategies*, then that might be true—in top groups at least. After all, students with behavior or attention difficulties are overwhelmingly placed into bottom groups, leaving top groups freer from "those kinds of students." No wonder senior teachers view the teaching of top groups as their sole preserve! Before I risk alienating too many people, let me finish this overview with the following question: "Why, in the light of all the research evidence that tracking is harmful to students in the lower tracks and that high achievers can function well in heterogeneous groups, is the practice so widespread and entrenched in our schools?" (Oakes & Lipton, 1990, p. 187).

Yet, grouping is a necessary process.

5.6.1 Grouping Is Necessary

Despite everything I have written so far in this section, groupings *are* necessary. We simply can't teach all our students as if they belonged to one homogeneous group. Even streamed classes have a broad mix of abilities within them, although they're assumed not to be mixed ability. Every class of students needs different approaches, varying degrees of attention, and starting points that are matched on a case-by-case basis.

For example, in section 3.5 (page 106), I mentioned that the optimum level of challenge is for students to be able to succeed independently with about 80 percent of a task. The other 20 percent of a learning task should be beyond them, at least without the guidance or suggestions of others. This 80/20 split begins and ends at different points for every student. Add in their varying literacy rates, self-esteem, self-efficacy, familiarity with the classroom context, relationships with peers, and any neurodivergence or special needs, and little wonder that a class of students needs dividing up into smaller groups. Practically speaking, we can't create enough groups to closely match to every single student, but we can have a sorting system that will at least reduce the margin of error. So, doesn't that bring us back to ability grouping?

Not exactly! Among the more damaging aspects of ability grouping are the following.

- **Ability grouping is too often a static affair:** Once a student is placed in a group, they tend to stay in that group, as if what they do won't change how clever or otherwise they are.

- **Stasis within ability groups leads to the formation of labels:** Think of labels like *bottom groups*, *highfliers*, and *middle groups*, or their thinly veiled code names such as *starfish*, *rainbow fish*, and *fish out of water*. (OK, I made the last one up.)

- **Labels lead to expectations that can be crippling:** For example, being part of a bottom group creates all sorts of negative expectations. A group of sixteen-year-olds I worked with told me they were VCAL students. When I asked what that meant, they told me, "The clever kids do VCE, but dumb kids like us do VCAL." (Students in the Australian state of Victoria who study for the Victorian Certificate of Education [VCE] are considered to be more academically prepared for university compared to those studying for its vocational equivalent, the Victorian Certificate of Applied Learning [VCAL], now referred to as the Vocational Major [VM].) "It basically means we use our hands, not our heads." Astonishing! Eleven years at school had taught them they were "dumb."

- **Even top groups don't thrive as much as many parents, or even teachers, assume:** Significant evidence shows (Lo & Porath, 2017; Oakes, 2005; Puzio & Colby, 2010) students in top groups ask fewer questions (for fear of revealing they don't know enough answers to remain in the group), have higher levels of anxiety (impostor syndrome), and are mistaken about their success relative to that of others (when they compare themselves to other groups, they assume the other groups are more advanced than they really are, or when they compare themselves to the other students in the top group, they think of themselves as nowhere near as talented as they really are).
- **Teachers' expectations are unduly affected by ability grouping:** For example, many of us assume that if students in a bottom group don't understand something, it's because they're bottom-set kids, whereas if students in a top group don't understand, adjustments to our teaching will soon put that right. There are indications we also don't differentiate as much as we should for students in top groups or bottom groups, assuming them all to be of a similar level.

So, what's the alternative? I will keep the answer to this question focused on what we, as teachers in a classroom, can do. If you are a teacher working with whichever class of students you are given, my recommendations are as follows.

- **Create flexible groupings:** The more students move within and between groupings, the more likely these groups will be associated with dynamic learning rather than with fixed notions of intelligence. Remember that fluid groupings encourage growth mindsets; static groupings encourage fixed mindsets.
- **Create groups based on *current* levels and needs:** Rather than using the results of a national test taken months or even years ago, find out where your students are now, and group them accordingly. I expand on this idea after the list.
- **Make the criteria for grouping clear:** Talk about groupings in such a way that your students know the criteria for selection are based on the next step you would like them to take in their learning, *not* on who is who. Once they have successfully taken that next step, they will be moving into the next group ready for the next challenge. Your students need to know that what they do and how they apply themselves today *will* make a difference to their learning. Too many students in fixed ability groups don't know this.

5.6.1.1 Using the SOLO Taxonomy

An excellent way to create groups is by matching them to SOLO Taxonomy levels. I shared an abridged version of this model in figure 2.2 (page 57). Because most students so easily understand it, it brings an air of transparency to the criteria that need to be met in order to make progress from one group to the next (another characteristic that is typically *not* met by static ability groups).

In section 4.4.1 (page 167), I shared lots of examples of learning intentions matched to SOLO Taxonomy levels. You can use any of those—or any others you create—to set up groupings.

In the case of the following worked example, I use the descriptions I created to help students understand the water cycle.

1. **Examples:** To know some of the features of the water cycle
2. **Features:** To know all major features of the water cycle by drawing and labeling them correctly
3. **Connections:** To understand the similarities and differences between evaporation and condensation in the context of the water cycle
4. **Applications and adaptations:** To be able to show how human activity and the water cycle affect each other and propose ways in which the negative influences can be minimized

For this example, I would create four groupings, each one matched to one of the levels described. So, I would have some students working in group 1, who would be finding out about some of the features of the water cycle—perhaps by viewing an explanatory video on their devices, looking through some of the topic books, or receiving some instruction from me. Those working in group 2 would already know the basics, so they would now be drawing and labeling the features. A few students may already have studied the water cycle (perhaps because I've used a preview strategy, as described in section 6.1, page 272). So, these students would be in a third group identifying the similarities and differences between evaporation and condensation in the context of the water cycle.

At the beginning of the topic, it is unlikely that any students will be working at level 4. Over time, though, most will make their way to this fourth level, and groupings connected with levels 1 and 2 will no longer be needed.

Depending on the context of the classroom, I might even set up the groupings I've described in different areas of the room so that students physically—as well as intellectually—move from one level to the next. This isn't a necessary feature, however, just one that works nicely in some situations.

Have a look at all the examples I included in section 4.4.1 (page 167) to see how this strategy can work with the students you teach. As I mentioned, depending on the context, you might start with levels 1, 2, and 3 at the beginning of the topic and then progress to just two levels at the end (levels 3 and 4). Or you might start with levels 2, 3, and 4 because of the preview work you've done with those students who might ordinarily be further behind (see section 6.1 on page 272 for a description of preview techniques).

5.7 Know How to Praise and What to Reward

One of the most frequently used ways to raise expectations—and encourage actions toward those higher goals—is through praise. It is a very powerful motivator. At least that is what many people say. Yet, the research on how praise affects students' motivation (and achievement) is somewhat contradictory.

On the one hand, many mid- to late-20th century studies find that praise can effectively reduce behavioral problems and encourage students to learn (Harris, Wolf, & Baer, 1967; Madsen, Becker, & Thomas, 1968; O'Leary & O'Leary, 1977); on the other hand, more recent studies find it to be largely ineffective (Beaman & Wheldall, 2000; Bhanji & Delgado, 2014; Gunderson et al., 2018). Some have even found it to be dysfunctional (Birch, Marlin, & Rotter, 1984; Brummelman, Nelemans, Thomaes, & Orobio de Castro, 2017; Meyer, 1992; Mueller & Dweck, 1998). Add into this the complication that it is difficult to separate the effects of praise from other factors, such as teacher attention, special privileges, student personality, and so on, and the way forward is unclear.

One possible explanation for such contradictory findings is that the *type* of praise matters more than *if* praise has been given. The biggest difference can be noticed between praise that is directed at the person (for example, *good boy* or *clever girl*) and praise that focuses on an aspect of the person's performance (for example, *good effort* or *clever idea*).

Researchers Jennifer Henderlong Corpus and Mark R. Lepper (2007) conducted two studies to identify the motivational consequences of person versus performance praise. The first study focused on differences in the ways preschool girls and boys responded to feedback. In the second study, five-year-old preschool students in a nursery school in California were given four interesting puzzles, two designed to lead to success and two to failure. The students were then asked to indicate how much they enjoyed the puzzles based on a scale of five schematic faces ranging from a frowning face to a smiling face. Next, perceived competence was measured by students' responses to the question, Are you good at these kinds of puzzles or not so good at these kinds of puzzles? Finally, attributions for failure were measured by students' responses to the question, Did you have trouble on the second puzzles because you didn't try hard enough or because you aren't good enough at these kinds of puzzles?

As the students worked on the two success puzzles, they were praised three times—once after completing the first puzzle, once during the second puzzle, and once after completing the second puzzle. Students in the *neutral* feedback condition were given a positive-sounding *OK* at each of these points, whereas the other students were praised as follows (Corpus & Lepper, 2007).

- Praise statements for students in the *person* condition included:
    - You're really good at this!
    - You must be good at puzzles!
    - You are a great puzzle solver!
- Praise statements for students in the *product* condition included:
    - Good job on that one!
    - You're getting a lot of pieces!
    - You finished one again!
- Praise statements for students in the *process* condition included:
    - You must be working hard!
    - You're really thinking!
    - You're finding really good ways to do this!

This being a research study, the students were of course randomly assigned to one of the four conditions: (1) *person*, (2) *product*, (3) *process*, (4) or *neutral*.

The next stage of the study involved the two failure puzzles that were impossible to solve successfully because the pieces had been switched (Corpus & Lepper, 2007). The students were given seventy-five seconds for the first one before being told, "Time is up. Let's move on to the next one." No other comments were made. Then after another seventy-five seconds attempting the second puzzle, the students were told, "Time is up. You didn't finish the puzzles." The students were asked the same questions as before: How much did you enjoy the puzzles, and are you good at these puzzles or not? They were also asked which of these three reasons best explained why they had done badly on the last two puzzles: (1) "I didn't try hard enough," (2) "I'm not smart enough," or (3) "I ran out of time."

After this, the children were asked to sit at an activity table and to play with anything they wanted to. Seventy percent of the children given product praise and 60 percent of the children given process praise chose to persevere with the puzzles. Whereas only 35 percent of the children offered person praise, and 15 percent who were not praised at all, continued with the puzzles.

The more significant results, however, were noticed days and weeks later (average time lapse of ten days) when the children were observed engaging with the puzzles during regular classroom activities. The amount of time they spent on the puzzles varied considerably so the researchers converted it (using logistic regression) into a scale shown from 0 to 3.

The time score for children receiving product and process praise was 3.0 compared to 1.75 for those receiving person praise and only 0.5 for those receiving no praise. This was with pre-school children. When Corpus and Lepper (2007) ran similar experiments with upper-elementary children, the differences were even more pronounced, with potentially harmful effects noted as a result of person praise, particularly on the motivation of girls. As the paper summarizes, "The research suggests that praise linking children's performances to their personal traits should be used only with caution because of the vulnerability it may create when children are subsequently faced with challenging experiences" (Corpus & Lepper, 2007, p. 506).

Incidentally, if you are worried about the effects of the failure part of the experiment, then you will be relieved to know the students were told afterward that no one could have solved the puzzles because the pieces had all been mixed up. The mistake was later corrected, and the students were given time to complete the puzzles successfully.

5.7.1 So, Is Praise a Good Thing or Not?

Praise is a positive judgment. Though the positive part feels nice, problems may often result from the judgment.

Notions of praise, when to give it, how much to give, and whom to give it to are wrapped up in culture, historical era, and personality. So, the answer to whether to praise is complex to say the least. Of all the studies on praise, I share the Corpus and Lepper (2007) findings partly because the results are statistically significant, which is a good start, but mainly because the recommendations are not about either *do* or *don't*; instead, they are about *type* of praise.

That compares favorably with some of the more simplistic texts in the field, some of which say *never* praise, whereas others say praise *lots*. That seems to me a false dichotomy. Students are complex creatures (staff even more so), so to say, "This always works, and therefore, the opposite can never work," masks the splendid diversity of education.

Figure 5.6 gives some examples of three categories of praise. Person praise is the riskiest, product praise is somewhat neutral (with a caveat about the effects of extrinsic motivators—see section 5.7.2), and process praise is generally the best.

Person Praise	Product Praise	Process Praise
Praises the person	Praises the end result	Praises the actions
Nouns such as *artist*, *linguist*, *mathematician*, and *player*	Nouns such as *result*, *answer*, *model*, and *outcome*	Verbs such as *thinking*, *trying*, *working*, and *developing*
Examples		
"You're a brilliant swimmer."	"Brilliant result! Well done."	"That's brilliant swimming."
"You are a fantastic mathematician."	"Fantastic! Your answers are all correct."	"Fantastic! You've answered them all correctly."
"Wow, you are so clever!"	"That's a very clever answer."	"That was a really clever way to solve the problem."
"What a brilliant artist you are."	"What a brilliant piece of artwork you've created."	"What a brilliant way to add perspective to your art."
"You are the best player on the team."	"You were the best player in that match."	"You played brilliantly in that match."

Figure 5.6: Examples of three types of praise.

On the face of it, all these types of praise seem positive, and in the moment, they typically do feel good. However, as researchers Melissa L. Kamins and Carol S. Dweck (1999) and researchers Eva M. Pomerantz and Sara G. Kempner (2013) show, using person praise may lead students to assume they are worthy only when they have succeeded and not worthy when they have failed. For example, when adults tell students they are clever, brilliant, bright, or talented when things go well, it feels nice. However, when things go badly and there's no praise, *some* students assume the opposite is true. Some now think of themselves as stupid, slow, or incapable.

To many people, this might seem to be an overly sensitive exaggeration of the possible downsides of person praise. Think about it for a moment. How many people do you know who succeeded many times early in their lives and have since found setbacks extraordinarily difficult to deal with? How many high school students who were previously told they are clever or bright have hit a crisis of confidence when things have gone wrong for them? They have gone from being showered with praise to noticing the absence of it and then starting to wonder if they are now the very opposite of clever or talented.

So, if you're going to praise—and generally speaking, I hope you do—then by far the best type to use is process praise. Focus on students' thoughts, words, and deeds, *not* on their personality, identity, or nature. It's not just because of the risk that students might think the opposite when praise is removed, but as explained on page 253, product and process praise are more effective at engaging students than person praise. Also, make sure you praise what your students have control over (for example, praise ideas, actions, use of language, or determination). This connects to self-efficacy (see section 5.9, page 263). Further, ensure you do the following.

- **Be specific:** Praise that is too general can result in inadvertent consequences. For example, "Well done, that was great!" seems to be a good thing to say, but if your students don't know what was great, it might be misinterpreted. Are you praising the attention they were giving the task? That would be process praise. Praising the fact that they were getting it right would be product praise. Praising them for being the best at it would be person praise. Each of these interpretations will lead to quite different conclusions about what you think is important.

- **Be genuine:** Ensure praise is given when it is deserved. Don't praise effort if your students haven't needed to put effort into finishing the task; and don't say an outcome is excellent unless it quite clearly is. If your students feel patronized or undeserving of praise, they are likely to question your motives or to think you have lower expectations for them than they hoped you would.

Finally, remember that praise is a little like currency in that the more of it that exists, the less valuable it becomes. Don't be so difficult to impress that you never give praise; but similarly, don't be so easily impressed that you give the impression you are impressed by *anything* students do! As Dweck (2017) states in the updated edition of her best-selling book, *Mindset*:

> Some teachers and coaches are using effort praise as a consolation prize when kids are not learning. If a student has tried hard and made little or no progress, we can of course appreciate their effort, but we should never be content with effort that is not yielding further benefits. We need to figure out why that effort is not effective and guide kids toward other strategies and resources that can help them resume learning. (p. 213)

For a more extensive exploration of this topic, I invite you to read chapter 9 of *Challenging Mindset* (Nottingham & Larsson, 2018).

5.7.2 Be Careful About What You Reward

In section 3.6 (page 109), I shared the evidence that when we give students a choice of tasks or assignments, they learn less rather than more (Carolan et al., 2014). The main reason they do this is because students assume they will receive more reward if they complete tasks with ease than they will if they struggle. This is obviously a problem! After all, we *want* students to struggle—not forever but enough that they will learn more and remember their lessons longer. So evidently, we need to be wary about what we reward.

What I didn't mention when I originally shared Thomas F. Carolan and colleagues' (2014) research is that this only applies to school-age children. It turns out that when we give preschoolers choice, they learn more, not less! Young students, typically in the preK–2 bracket, go for whatever looks exciting. They don't do a cost-benefit analysis, unlike secondary-level students, who often make decisions based on what's going to give them the greatest reward for the least effort. Students in the early years select whatever interests them most. As B. F. Skinner (1948), considered the father of behaviorism, wrote in his novel, *Walden Two*, "No one asks how to motivate a baby. A baby naturally explores everything it can get at, unless restraining forces have already been at work. And this tendency doesn't die out, it's *wiped* out" (p. 114).

Researchers Edward L. Deci, Richard Koestner, and Richard M. Ryan (1999) ran a meta-analysis of 128 studies examining the effects of rewards on intrinsic motivation. They found that all rewards—actual and expected—undermined students' motivation. These included rewards for engaging, for completing tasks, and for performing successfully (d = -0.40, -0.36, and -0.28, respectively). Negative results were also found in terms of students' self-reported interest.

There is some good news, though. Providing feedback that gave students the sense they were making good progress *during* a task led to positive outcomes (d = 0.33), and when rewards were offered for engaging with, and completing, the most *un*interesting tasks, the gains were a respectable d = 0.18 (Deci et al., 1999). So, offering rewards for engaging with, or completing, most learning tasks is ill-advised. Dangling the carrot when there is absolutely no inherent pleasure or other perceived gain connected with a task *might* lead to a positive effect.

Offering encouraging feedback during a task is the best form of reward, but even that has its dangers. Be careful that your affirmation doesn't become the reason why students engage. For example, if your students have already chosen to throw themselves into a task—and they have done so because of an intrinsic motivation (for example, curiosity, a desire to see if they can complete it, or camaraderie with peers)—then you have to make sure your offer of a reward enhances rather than replaces that motivation.

As researcher Ann Boggiano and her colleagues (1989) discovered, "Children who adopted an extrinsic rather than an intrinsic orientation toward schoolwork were more likely to do poorly on overall achievement, as indexed by national test scores, even when controlling for achievement scores from the previous year" (p. 24). The best rewards in schools, therefore, should be the joy of learning, the intrinsic pleasure derived from discovering and developing, and the satisfaction of making progress.

Of course, this is much easier said than done, particularly for the resolutely disengaged students—or for those hooked on extrinsic sweeteners. Merits, stars on a behavior chart, or the promise of grade credits *can* help when interest levels begin at rock bottom. But they should not be necessary as standard features of everyday classroom life—unless your students' lessons are utterly uninspiring every day! Keep the cavalry in reserve. Don't send them out as your first line of defense.

In this video, James gives an insight into turning mistakes into learning opportunities.

5.8 Turn Mistakes and Failure Into Learning Opportunities

 *The best teacher we ever had was Miss Takes. She showed us the error of our ways. Examining what she showed us made us the learners we are today.*

Too often, mistakes and failure lower students' expectations of success. Therefore, teaching your students how to respond positively and proactively to these stumbling blocks is an important step in helping raise expectations and their associated efforts.

In section 5.5.2 (page 244), I shared the fascinating research from Phelps (2012), who, after analyzing 669 studies stretching back over a century, concluded that the best way for a student to prepare for a test or performance is to revisit their corrected mistakes. Rereading textbooks, creating flash cards, or going over perfected techniques again and again will help. But even more effective is to take practice tests or do trial runs, identify mistakes, correct them, and then study from those. This practice comes with an effect size of $d = 0.96$.

To emphasize the magnitude of this effect, only three factors I mention anywhere in this book have higher effect sizes (collective efficacy at $d = 1.36$, the jigsaw method $d = 1.20$, and feedback [reinforcement and cues] at $d = 1.01$. These are covered in sections 5.9, 6.5, and 4.1, pages 263, 292, and 149). This is an astonishing effect, but bizarrely, up to this point, it has not been widely recommended. For the first seventy years of the 1910–2010 period that Phelps (2012) examined, conventional wisdom declared that mistakes should be avoided. And that is still good advice when they risk safety or are made in high-stakes environments such as exam rooms.

However, in a learning environment—and this is important, so I will emphasize it again—in a *learning environment*—when our purpose is to improve, making mistakes and correcting them can be much more powerful than making no mistakes. Making a mistake as you cross the road is not recommended. Saying the wrong thing to the wrong person at the wrong time is to be avoided. Making a silly mistake because you're not concentrating can make the difference between one grade and the next on an assessment. So, mistakes in and of themselves are not to be recommended. Making mistakes in a learning environment, however, *and correcting them* is what leads to the positive outcomes.

It is the spotting of the mistakes and the thinking that goes into, and comes out of, correcting them that improves learning. Researchers Barbie J. Huelser and Janet Metcalfe (2012) find a similar impact from their meta-analysis: "Producing an error, so long as it is followed by corrective feedback, has been shown to result in better retention of the correct answers than does simply studying the correct answers from the outset" (p. 514).

These same authors also find that students make more use of metacognitive strategies after making errors. Bearing in mind metacognitive thinking—such as reflecting on the why, when, and how of a particular strategy—is closely linked with improved learning outcomes, it is clear that the examination and correction of mistakes is particularly beneficial. Unfortunately, many students are quickly discouraged when they make mistakes, and some teachers are too quick to rescue their students the moment they make mistakes or ask for help.

So, communicating growth mindset attitudes toward mistakes, and acting in ways that are consistent with those beliefs, is a very good way to increase your students' understanding, investment, and efficacy as learners. Here are three principle starting points.

Principle 1: Mistakes Are *Not* Marvelous

More than once, I've heard the phrase *marvelous mistakes* used in classrooms. Although I recognize this as shorthand for a more complex message, I worry that many students will miss the intended nuance and instead conclude that mistakes are good things in and of themselves. Most of the time, that's not true; we do not *want* to make mistakes! A significant portion of instruction and feedback is designed to boost accuracy. We implore our students to concentrate, read carefully, and think before they act. So, it seems contrary or confusing to some to then talk about mistakes as if they were marvelous!

A better way to talk about mistakes is to say *learning from* mistakes is marvelous! It's a shame that this loses the lovely alliteration of *marvelous mistakes* but, nevertheless, the message is more precise.

Principle 2: Mistakes Are *Not* Embarrassing

I often ask audiences which of two situations more commonly occurs in classrooms when a student recognizes they have made a mistake and asks their teacher for help. Option 1 involves the teacher helping the student correct the mistake, whereas in option 2, the teacher invites the whole class to examine and correct the mistake so that everyone can learn from the experience. Most people tell me that option 1 is by far the more common practice in schools, and I would agree. However, option 2 is more in keeping with a growth mindset.

A common refrain is, "But getting others to look at the mistake risks embarrassing the student who made it." Others say the student culture isn't supportive enough to make this a positive experience. I understand these misgivings, and I'm certainly not suggesting we go for option 2 irrespective of who might be flustered or mortified by it. However, I *am* suggesting we put into place many of the strategies I recommend in this chapter, reiterating again and again how much learning comes from examining mistakes, how *everybody* makes mistakes (which means *nobody* should be embarrassed to make them), and how no one should be made fun of or belittled for sharing their fallibility. Instead, they should be commended and thanked for sharing their learning opportunity with others.

I realize this sounds very idealistic. But if teaching isn't idealistic, then I don't know what is! Better to be idealistic and fall short than be pessimistic and never try.

Principle 3: Students and Their Teachers Are *Not* Infallible

I know it goes without saying, but I'll say it anyway: if we want our students to respond positively to making mistakes, we have to model growth mindset attitudes. Someone in a fixed mindset would:

- Think mistakes are embarrassing, assuming they indicate a lack of talent, understanding, or attention
- Hide mistakes from other people, pretending (sometimes even to themselves) that they never happened
- Blame others, circumstances, or factors outside of their control

Someone in a growth mindset would:

- Think of mistakes as opportunities to better understand a situation by identifying what doesn't work (as well as what does)
- Examine mistakes, often alongside others
- Identify the steps they can take to be more successful next time around

5.8.1 Ready-Fire-Aim

A really nice way to weave the learning that can come from mistakes into lessons is with the Ready-Fire-Aim approach. This phrase influences my thinking so much that I even considered using it as the title for this book—that is, until I discovered there are at least eight books using the same title!

I first used the term in my original book, *Challenging Learning* (Nottingham, 2010), having drawn inspiration from the way in which Guy Kawasaki, one of the people responsible for the success of the Mac computer, described how he writes books: "First, I make the slides (Ready). Then I give the presentation many times (Fire). Then I write the book (Aim). If your speeches work, then your book will too. The opposite is not true" (Kawasaki, as quoted in Nottingham, 2016, p. xvi).

As I read this, it was as if Kawasaki were speaking on my behalf. His approach was my approach. I like to examine meta-analyses so that I can design presentations (Ready), try them out with staff in many different contexts (Fire), and then gather questions and skepticism so that I can write better guides (Aim) for transferring research into practice.

I would also use Ready-Fire-Aim if I were ever responsible for redesigning initial teacher education. I'd recommend splitting the postgraduate training in half. The first half would be to help trainees prepare for teaching, just as now (Ready). Then, with half their training completed, I'd suggest trainees get some real-life experience under their belts by teaching for a year or two (Fire), rather than doing the few short teaching practices most do now. After that, they could return to their teacher education center to complete their course of study (Aim) with a much better sense of who they are as teachers and what questions they have, and a more prepared and open mind for considering the purpose and philosophy of education. But I digress! So, let's return to the matter at hand, which is how to use Ready-Fire-Aim to help students make better use of the mistakes they make.

- **Ready:** Give your students the shortest introduction possible, thereby saving time for the Aim phase later. Make sure you include phrases along the lines of, "I'm giving you just enough to make a start with this. As you try these tasks out, I want you to be experimental and open-minded. Don't worry about making mistakes. In fact, I'm taking this approach in the hope that you will be out of your comfort zones and therefore more likely to make mistakes that we can learn from."

- **Fire:** Give your students time to make their first attempts at the tasks you've set. Expect them to be out of their comfort zone. If they're not, then increase the challenge by adding or removing a variable. Remind them to persevere even if they feel unsuccessful. If anyone asks for help, be circumspect with your support; only help them if it doesn't rescue them altogether. Remember, you want them to make mistakes so that these can be the focus for reflection and correction afterward.

- **Aim:** During the Fire phase, collect examples of the mistakes your students are making so that you can share them during this Aim phase. If you are only just starting to develop growth mindset attitudes with your students, you will probably need to anonymize the examples before sharing them. Whichever approach you use—anonymizing or asking for volunteers—I recommend that you share the examples via a document camera or screenshare so that the whole class can see them and suggest answers to the following questions.
    - Who can spot a mistake?
    - Could you describe the mistake?
    - Can someone else say what might have led to the mistake?
    - What options are there for more accurate ways to solve or complete this?
    - What is the general principle we can use in future to avoid making the same mistake again?

Throughout this convention, keep reiterating the three principles mentioned in the previous section (mistakes are marvelous when we learn from them; mistakes are not embarrassing; and none of us is infallible).

5.8.2 Responding to Failure

What happens when mistakes become failures? The latter make the former feel like a pale comparison. Even the term *failure* causes a shudder for some people. I once presented to a group of PhD students and university lecturers at the Melbourne Graduate School of Education, and their first question was, "Can you give us a more positive term than *failure*? It feels so final!"

Then again, one of the quirkiest events I've ever spoken at was a FUN (F*Up Nights) event in Leeuwarden, northern Netherlands. Five of us were invited to each make a short presentation about our biggest failures, describing the circumstances and the learning that came from them. It was inspiring and fascinating in equal measure. What I didn't know before I attended was that FUN is a global movement with events in more than three hundred cities in eighty countries. So, it seems lots of people believe it is fun to celebrate their failures! Is failure good or bad, then? I guess it depends on who you ask and what their approach is.

This isn't just a philosophical question. It is also an important educational one because of the evidence that adults' attitudes toward failure dramatically influence young people's mindsets. Indeed, when I was digging as deeply as I could into Dweck's research ahead of writing *Challenging Mindset* (Nottingham & Larsson, 2018), I was interested to note that responses to failure are, in many ways, *more* likely to influence those around us than even whether we are in a fixed or growth mindset!

For example, researchers Kyla Haimovitz and Carol Dweck (2016) ran a series of studies that showed that parents who believed failure is debilitating had children who were significantly more likely to be in a fixed mindset than parents who believed failure is enhancing. Before I give an insight into the detail of that research, I should define the difference between a *performance orientation* and a *learning orientation*, since these terms are both used throughout.

A performance goal or performance orientation focuses on demonstrating competence relative to others, generally in an attempt to look clever or to avoid looking stupid. A learning goal or learning orientation, on the other hand, focuses on learning and improvement relative to self (beating your personal best would be a classic learning orientation). Researchers Jeni L. Burnette, Ernest H. O'Boyle, Eric M. VanEpps, Jeffrey M. Pollack, and Eli J. Finkel (2013) find the difference in effect size of these two were $d = 0.32$ for learning orientation and $d = -0.02$ for performance orientation.

So, to return to Haimovitz and Dweck's (2016) research, they found the following across the four studies involving approximately 470 parents and 300 children.

- All people have a mindset that shapes behavior and aspirations. Parents' beliefs are most likely to shape children's beliefs if they lead to practices that children notice.
- A parent's attitude toward failure is more visible to a child than their mindset is and, therefore, more likely to influence their child's attitude.
- Parents who believed failure is debilitating had children who were significantly more likely to be in a fixed mindset.
- The more that parents believed failure is debilitating, the more likely they were to worry about their child's ability and the less likely they were to react with support for their child's learning and improvement.
- Older parents were more likely to believe that failure is enhancing and less likely to endorse performance-oriented responses.
- Children were much more accurate when identifying their parent's attitude toward failure than they were when identifying their parent's mindset.

To find out whether parents believed failure is debilitating or enhancing, those involved in the studies were asked how much they agreed with the following statements:

- The effects of failure are positive and should be utilized.
- Experiencing failure facilitates learning and growth.
- Experiencing failure enhances my performance and productivity.
- Experiencing failure inhibits my learning and growth.
- Experiencing failure debilitates my performance and productivity.
- The effects of failure are negative and should be avoided. (Haimovitz & Dweck, 2016, p. 861)

Those who most agreed with the first three statements were deemed to believe failure is enhancing, whereas those who showed more agreement with the last three were thought to believe failure is debilitating.

These answers were added to the results of a scenario in which parents imagined their child had returned home from school with a failing test grade. The participants were asked how likely they were to have each of several reactions. These included performance-oriented responses such as the following:

- I might worry (at least for a moment) that my child isn't good at this subject.
- I'd try to comfort my child to tell him it's OK if he isn't the most talented in all subjects.
- I'd probably find myself dwelling on his performance. (Haimovitz & Dweck, 2016, p. 863)

And they included learning-oriented responses such as the following:

- I'd encourage my child to tell me what she learned from doing poorly on the test.
- I'd discuss with my child whether it would be useful to ask the teacher for help.
- I'd let my child know that this is a great opportunity to learn this material well. (Haimovitz & Dweck, 2016, p. 863)

At this point, it would be interesting to consider your own responses to the scenario. Interestingly, the statements that the children were given so that they could indicate their level of agreement or disagreement included the following:

- My parents would be pleased if I could show that school is easy for me.
- My parents ask me how my work in school compares with the work of other students in my class.
- My parents want me to understand homework problems, not just memorize how to do them.
- My parents think how hard I work in school is more important than the grades I get. (Haimovitz & Dweck, 2016, p. 863)

How much would your own students or your own children agree with these statements? And what can you do about it if their responses indicate fixed mindset thinking?

Researchers Andrew J. Elliot and Todd M. Thrash (2004) reported that fear of failure, which can elicit avoidance behavior, is often passed from parent to child. Parents of children in a growth mindset encourage their children to persist, offer support, and teach their children new strategies when faced with failure. In contrast, parents of children in a fixed mindset offer less help and encourage their children to quit when a task seems too hard.

A similar impact has been noted inside schools as well as within students' homes. For sure, teachers who respond to failure with despondency are likely to put their students into a fixed mindset, whereas those who respond to failure as a learning opportunity with many options for improved iterations are more likely to encourage students into a growth mindset.

What does this mean for classroom practice? Here are some suggestions for you to choose from (what you pick will depend on your students' ages and the subjects you are teaching them).

- Make FAIL an acronym for *First Attempt in Learning*.
- Think of failure as if a child learning to ride a bike had just fallen off. What would you do? I'm guessing you wouldn't suggest they give up! Instead, you would check

they weren't hurt, and then you'd encourage them back onto the bike. You might give additional temporary support to get them started again (not the same as taking over or doing it for them), but one way or another, you'd get them to have another go—with adaptations. I recommend that you take this same approach to any type of learning failure, whether it is in an academic, creative, social, or performance-based field.

- Use the power of eavesdropping! When your students (or your own children) overhear a conversation that they are not part of, they tend to listen much more carefully, particularly if it is about them! So, use this psychology to good effect. Talk about the ways in which they can use failure for good effect, how you always see failure as instructive, what steps or strategies could be taken next, and so on.

The messages about failure that are likely to put others into a fixed mindset include, "That was a stupid thing to do," "Why did I ever think that could work?" and "I won't be trying that again!" The messages that are more likely to lead to growth mindset thinking include, "I wonder why that didn't work," "What can I do next time so I don't repeat the same mistakes?" and "What will I definitely not do again, and what will I?"

To return to the request of the PhD students in Melbourne for a different word for *failure*, if we do not first change the messages and mindsets associated with failure, then any word we choose will eventually have the same stigma.

5.9 Boost Self-Efficacy and Collective Efficacy

 *Efficacy is the term most closely connected with mindset. With a strong sense of efficacy, people know there is always something they can do to improve outcomes and figure things out.*

Along with growth mindset, the most effective way to raise your students' expectations of success is by boosting their self-efficacy; this is the notion that a person has about their ability to create new outcomes. Useful synonyms include *potency* and *influence*.

Stanford University psychologist Albert Bandura (1997) proposed the term *self-efficacy* as an alternative to the more widely used term of *self-esteem*. Whereas the latter relates to how a person esteems or likes themselves, self-efficacy relates more to a person's belief in being able to effect (not just affect) new outcomes. It refers to "beliefs in one's capabilities to organize and execute the courses of action required to produce given attainments" (Bandura, 1997, p. 3).

In her meta-analysis on teacher efficacy Rachel Jean Eells (2011) summarizes the various work of Albert Bandura, stating, "Efficacy involves more than positive thinking or optimism. It is tied to the construct of agency (the ability to make things happen) and to action" (p. 5).

Students who rate themselves very highly and yet are defeatist when faced with challenges could be said to have high self-esteem but low self-efficacy. Indeed, it is these students who tend to be quickest to shrug their shoulders and say something along the lines of, "I don't care that I can't do it; I'm happy as I am." In some circumstances, that might sound reasonable, but what happens when it is actually coming from a fear of failure rather than a genuine disinterest?

What if the shoulder shrug is a defense mechanism rather than a show of contentment? This is where self-efficacy comes in. If we help our students develop their self-efficacy, then they will be more likely to make decisions from a position of aptitude rather than aversion. Knowing they are in a position to effect or create a new outcome if they wish to is preferable to avoiding new experiences because of a sense of foreboding or fear.

Table 5.3 summarizes the differences between low self-efficacy and high self-efficacy. As you read through it, make a note of the similarities between fixed mindset and growth mindset.

Table 5.3: Comparing Low and High Self-Efficacy

People With *Low Self-Efficacy* Tend to Be:	People With *High Self-Efficacy* Tend to Be:
Rigid in their thinking	**Flexible** in their thinking
Fearful of new and unfamiliar situations	**Keen** to experience new situations
Wary of change	**Open** to change
Cautious of other people	**Cooperative** with others
Keen to **prove** themselves	Keen to **express** themselves
Reassured by the **familiar**	Excited by **challenge**
Evasive in what they say	**Honest** in what they say
More likely to **give up**	More likely to **persist**
Easily **frustrated**	Tolerant
Less equipped to cope	Quicker to **bounce back**

As you will have noticed, the similar traits of those with low self-efficacy and those in a fixed mindset include that both are wary of change, both prefer to prove rather than improve themselves, and both are likely to be frustrated by challenges. Conversely, the similarities in behavior between those with high self-efficacy and those in a growth mindset include having good coping strategies, being open to new situations as well as to change, and choosing growth and expression over playing it safe or showing off to others.

Note also that while boys often have a greater sense of self-efficacy than girls, this is not always the case and might not be particularly prevalent in some countries. Take a look at this quotation from Carol Dweck (2007):

> Confusion is a common occurrence in math and science, where, unlike most verbal areas, new material often involves completely new skills, concepts, or conceptual systems. So we created a new task for students to learn, and for half of the students we placed some confusing material near the beginning.
>
> What we found was that bright girls didn't cope at all well with this confusion. In fact, the higher the girl's IQ, the worse she did. Many high IQ girls were unable to learn the material after experiencing confusion. This didn't happen to boys. For them, the higher their IQ, the better they learned. The confusion only energized them.

> Since our high IQ girls had done wonderfully well when they didn't bump up against difficulty, what we're looking at here isn't a difference in ability, but a difference in how students cope with experiences that may call their ability into question—whether they feel challenged by them or demoralized by them. (pp. 47–48)

Part of the difference might come from the amount of criticism that boys receive compared to girls. Not that criticism is in itself beneficial for self-efficacy, but consider the implications of the following examples.

- "John, if only you could sit still for a minute and listen, you'd do much better."
- "Paul, if you put as much effort into your work as you do into messing about, you could really achieve."
- "Ringo, as for you, young man, you need to focus more! I'm fed up with repeating myself for your sake."

All the messages state that by concentrating more, trying harder, listening better, and so on, the outcomes will improve. Those are strong self-efficacy messages. It is a pity they come in the form of criticism but, nonetheless, they are influence-driven messages. They are also much more powerful than the person-focused messages that girls so often receive: *good girl, clever girl*, and so on.

Not that it is always *boys this* or always *girls that*, but if boys receive more of the type of criticism shown and girls receive more of the type of praise shown, then it might go some way to explaining the situation Dweck found, as shown in the earlier quotation.

Returning to the general concept of self-efficacy and its impact on motivation and expectation, Bandura (1997) finds that efficacy influences a student's level of effort, persistence, and choice of activities (Carpenter, 2007; Çikrıkci, 2017; Huang, 2016). Those with a high sense of efficacy for accomplishing an educational task will participate more readily, work harder, and persist longer when they encounter difficulties than those who doubt their capabilities.

Self-efficacy is also correlated with various outcomes including self-regulatory behavior such as awareness of learning approach used and time taken, motivation constructs, and academic performance (Zimmerman, Bandura, & Martinez-Pons, 1992).

The importance of a person's efficacy, therefore, cannot be underestimated. It influences the courses of action your students choose to pursue, their expectations, their motivation, and how much effort they will expend in given situations. So, to raise their expectations, a big step in the right direction will be to boost their sense of self-efficacy.

5.9.1 How to Boost Student Self-Efficacy

Here are three of the most effective ways to boost your students' sense of self-efficacy.

1. **Guide your students through the Learning Pit:** Overcoming challenges is the surest way to build self-efficacy (Çiftçi & Yildiz, 2019). Doing so and then reflecting on the personal and intellectual resources used gives students the sense that it is possible for them to figure things out and, therefore, it is likely that they will be able to do so again. This is the basis for self-efficacy. One way to frame this

process is with the Learning Pit, described in detail in sections 3.7 and 3.8 (pages 113 and 124).

2. **Ensure your students make the most of any relevant feedback they receive:** Feedback is at its most effective when students respond appropriately to the three guiding questions: (1) What am I trying to achieve? (2) How much progress have I made so far? and (3) What should I do next to improve? The more your students apply their feedback productively, the more they will notice how much more progress they are making. This will enhance their sense of efficacy because they will see how their efforts and strategies make such a big difference to outcomes.

3. **Use process praise, not intelligence praise:** Praise can influence self-efficacy for better or for worse, depending on the type used. Person praise (for example, "You are a clever child") is likely to decrease self-efficacy, whereas process praise (for example, "That was a clever thing to do") is likely to increase self-efficacy because it focuses on actions, which are something that your students are able to control. Praising concentration, effort, strategy, focus, collaboration, and perseverance (for example) adds building blocks to your students' sense of self-efficacy.

5.9.2 Collective Efficacy

Collective efficacy is strongly associated with student achievement. That in itself is enough to provoke interest. The moment the effect went straight to number one as the most powerful influence included in Hattie's Visible Learning Metax (n.d.) database, it became intriguing. What is it, how is it created, and could our school have the capacity to make it a reality?

Since this is a book for teachers and the term *collective efficacy* applies to an approach for teams, I will give just a short summary of the influence. There are three meta-analyses about collective teacher efficacy available (Çoğaltay & Karadağ, 2017; Eells, 2011; Norris, 2018). Together, they analyze eighty-five studies, giving a combined effect size of $d = 1.36$. This is the equivalent of students' progressing at three times their normal rate. That is extraordinary!

Collective efficacy represents the beliefs a group of staff hold about their combined ability to create positive learning for *all* their students. Teams with the strongest sense of self-efficacy feel highly optimistic about their students' success. This comes from knowing they have the abilities and resources to ensure every single learner thrives. These beliefs are underpinned by meaningful evidence of progress. It is therefore about not *only* believing in their potential as a team (although that is crucial) but *also* having enough evidence to show that this is a reality: "Our students don't just grow, they flourish with—and because of—us." The ideas recommended in section 5.5 (page 240) make a very good start toward this.

This sense of collective efficacy engenders positive thinking. Limitations are seen as challenges rather than roadblocks. What can be influenced and adapted is, and what can't be changed is mitigated. As Bandura (2011) puts it, "the power of uncontrollable circumstances is weighed against that which can be controlled" (p. 38).

There are many scales that are designed to measure collective efficacy. The types of statements that are used for measurement include the following, all of which I have adapted to suit the context of a school team.

- We all share a sense of purpose in helping every single student make excellent progress.
- Everyone on our team believes that all students are capable of learning, even if they face additional social, emotional, or intellectual difficulties.
- We are able to identify how much progress our students are making, and are quick to respond effectively when someone needs more (or less).
- Not one of our students is left behind.
- Everyone on our team is able to adapt when our students' needs change.
- Most of the people on our team can see who needs help and when.
- In critical situations, our team can be relied on to do the right thing.
- People in our building will work together to overcome obstacles.

5.10 *Teach Brilliantly* Top Ten: *Expectations*

Holding high expectations for all students boosts learning outcomes for everyone. This is not just a philosophical position but a practical and ethical one, too.

1. Every single student has the potential to grow and improve. Some won't achieve top grades, but **everyone is capable of making significant progress** from wherever they are starting from.

2. Believing in everyone's ability to grow means we should **adjust instruction for those who are struggling** and frame success as the outcome of determination, effort, strategy, and purpose.

3. For all students to make excellent progress, every member of **staff must hold the highest of expectations**. No exceptions.

4. **Students whose teachers have high expectations make progress at one to three times the normal rate.** Those whose teachers hold low expectations make progress at less than half the normal rate.

5. Holding high expectations includes believing intelligence and talents are incremental. Better known as being in a growth mindset (Dweck, 2006), this outlook accepts that **experiences and environment influence abilities more than hereditary factors do**.

6. Emphasizing that everyone is capable of growing their talents requires assessments that **draw attention to progress**, and feedback that, when applied, improves learning outcomes.

7. Praise can be a powerful motivator but only when directed discerningly. Of the main categories, **process praise is by far the most effective**. This focuses on actions and uses verbs such as *thinking, trying, working,* and *developing*.

8. Students should be grouped according to current learning needs rather than historical levels of achievement. **Create flexible groupings that reorganize** as individuals move from surface knowledge to deep learning.

9. **Mistakes and failure** (in learning contexts) **should be welcomed as opportunities for closer inspection** and deeper understanding. The Ready-Fire-Aim structure can help normalize their role as potent provocations for learning.

10. Boosting **students' sense of efficacy contributes significantly to raising their expectations** of success. One of the best ways to achieve this is by guiding them through the Learning Pit. This experience of overcoming challenges and improving outcomes substantiates their feelings of agency.

CHAPTER 6

When There Is *Equity*, There Is *Fairness*

 *Equity provides individuals with what they need and removes barriers so they can enjoy the same opportunities as their peers.*

This is *not* a book about equity. Many outstanding titles already exist about—and I am by no means an expert in—this essential field. Equity, though, must never be ignored.

So, for this final chapter, I offer you another view of the strategies I have recommended throughout this book. This time, I will cover them through the lens of equity. The practices I have shared, the values I have promoted, and the research I have annotated should all make significant contributions toward addressing inequality and promoting equity for and with your students.

Equity will be realized when demographics don't predict outcomes—when the barriers of systems, attitudes, and prejudicial behaviors no longer exist.

6.0 Equity, Equality, and Fairness

The first time I became aware of equity, or rather the brutal effects of inequity, was in 1989. Two years prior to this, my father had evicted me. So, to put myself through school, I worked on a local pig farm and in a chemical factory before a friend offered me a way out. He told me about a group heading to South Africa to engage in voluntary work in some of the country's squatter camps. No sooner had he given me the scantest of details than I boarded a ferry to Amsterdam and from there a flight to Cape Town, where we were met by our hosts. We followed them to the train station and boarded a third-class carriage. Back then, in apartheid South Africa, only White folk were permitted to buy first- or second-class tickets, and since we were a multiracial group, we traveled third class.

When we finally reached our destination—Crossroads, a huge squatter camp on the outskirts of Cape Town, home to more than one hundred thousand people—we caused quite a stir. Some of our team was White—me included—and ordinarily, the only White folk to enter shantytowns were security forces with ruthless orders to carry out. So, to say people were understandably wary of us, at least at first, would be an understatement. Was this what it was like, we wondered, to be regarded with suspicion because of skin color? We guessed so, except that our experience was a moment in time, which is hardly comparable to a lifetime of prejudice.

The conditions the people there endured beggared belief. Entire families—sometimes multiple families—sharing tiny makeshift structures of cardboard, wood, or scrap metal. No running water or sewer systems. All the living conditions were exacerbated by forced racial segregation.

During the months we spent there, we volunteered at a women's cooperative and in a men's hostel. We also helped out at one of the makeshift schools. Five hundred students and three teachers. Classes were forty to fifty students ranging from late teens to babies in arms, with every age in between. We had no experience. No teacher training. No idea, except that of being impostors. We were extra pairs of hands, and for that, we were welcomed warmly, more than I had ever been before—or indeed have ever been since.

These memories are as vivid today as they were in 1989. It was these experiences that proved to be the turning point for this school dropout with a deep despair of his own education. I became a man on a mission to do everything in my power to add value to education. As South African president Nelson Mandela—whose release after twenty-seven years in prison we witnessed live—once said, "Education is the most powerful weapon which you can use to change the world" (Lib Quotes, n.d.).

Notice, though, my phrasing in the sentence before Mandela's quote: "I became a man on a mission to do *everything in my power to add value* to education." Talk about privilege. I have power, and I know I can add value. As a White man from an affluent Western country, I face almost no obstacles in doing so. I am able bodied. English is my mother tongue. I belong to a white-collar profession. All of this makes life easier for me.

My mother died when I was young, and my father was an excessively strict military man. These circumstances, together with other negative experiences in and out of school, meant I was considered a vulnerable student. Yet, I could walk out the door without suffering racism, sexism, ableism, or other forms of prejudice. I was judged by my thoughts, words, and deeds, not my demographics.

This is as it should be, except it isn't for so many. Not just for the people of Crossroads, although they are particularly stark examples. People everywhere, very likely including students in your school, are prejudged because of their demographics. Some of the students you are responsible for are blamed, ignored, denied the benefit of the doubt, assumed less of, and treated as if they are less capable. Equity means removing all these barriers to learning.

Student outcomes are connected far too closely to identity and not enough to actions (Datnow & Park, 2018; Education Endowment Foundation, 2017). The field on which students play is not level. Race, culture, gender, socioeconomic status, comparative age, and special education needs can all be used to predict who is most likely to succeed and who is not; who is likely to be sanctioned for discipline infractions and who is not; who will graduate, be involved in criminal justice, win awards, receive grants, or be chosen to represent their school. It shouldn't, but a student's identity matters.

In 1996, I wrote my undergraduate dissertation: *Children's Attitudes Towards Africa and Africans: A Study of the Implications for Primary School Geography* (Nottingham, 1996). Flicking through it today, I don't suppose very much has changed. I don't mean in terms of quality or methodology—both need serious upgrades! I mean in terms of the pupils' responses to my questions. For one activity, I shared an outline of Africa and an outline of the United Kingdom and asked four sixth-grade classes (126 students) to write descriptions for each. Two students correctly identified one was a continent and the other a country. Otherwise, descriptions were worryingly prejudiced. Terms such as *poor, dirty, desert, unemployed, homeless people, hungry, bad education, sunny, musical, thin, sporty,* and *Black* were the ones most frequently attached to the outline of Africa. *Clever, fat, rich, White, expensive, cities, fast cars, nice food, money,* and *boring* were used in connection with the United Kingdom.

I then shared a range of photographs of children from the United Kingdom and from African countries. I asked the children to choose three they thought would make good friends and one they thought would not. The expressions in the photos played a part, but skin color correlated much more closely with the children's choices. My approach was hardly watertight, but even if I improved it dramatically before sharing it with my current students, I would be willing to bet their assumptions wouldn't be so different.

This cannot be allowed to continue. If we want the best for *all* our students—and frankly, all educators worthy of the title do—then we must do what we can whenever we can to change this untenable situation. Improving equality is a good start, but boosting equity would be better still.

These are two terms that often get misunderstood. *Equality* is about providing the same for everyone. *Equity*, on the other hand, is about recognizing that everyone starts from a different place, faces different obstacles, and, therefore, needs different adjustments. Get this right, and outcomes become equal. It might not feel like it at the time; giving a boost to some students and not others feels unfair. However, those you choose to boost will be the ones most in need of boosting due to all the unfair disadvantages they face in their lives. They're probably not suffering as many barriers as the people of Crossroads, but their obstacles are pervasive and pernicious nonetheless.

Offering all school graduates an unpaid internship is not equitable. Some students can afford to volunteer; many others cannot. Therefore, the goal of equitable practice is to redress the balance, close the gap, or level the playing field—whichever phrase you want to use—so that *everyone* thrives. And that means giving a leg up over the obstacles or, better still, removing the obstacles altogether.

The strategies I recommend in this book can help you with that cause. Until now, I have described them as methods to use with all students. However, this chapter will show you how to use them more equitably by using them with only the students most in need. That doesn't mean you should never use them with a whole class or year group. Of course, you can, and I hope you do. However, to be serious about equity means to be partisan with your approach.

Throughout the text, I refer to students *at risk* of not graduating from K–12 education. In many cases, you will see the shorthand *at-risk students*, which is rapidly and justifiably falling out of favor, but nonetheless, it is the term most frequently used in the research I mention in this chapter. Other expressions used include *vulnerable students, minority students, disadvantaged students,* and *students at promise*. Many of these also have problematic aspects to them, but all are used to cover students who face obstacles because of one or more of the following: racism, sexism, classism, religious discrimination, linguistic discrimination, sexual discrimination, gender identity discrimination, nationalism, or special education needs.

In this video, James describes the ways preview strategies can be used to boost equity.

6.1 Preview Strategies

Preview strategies can do more to close the gap for disadvantaged students than any other pedagogical strategy.

Preview strategies are among the best ways to close the gap between the performance of disadvantaged students and the performance of the rest of their peers (often referred to as the *attainment gap*). Flipped learning is the most familiar form, but it is not the only approach to preview. I describe both terms—*flipped learning* and *preview*—later in this chapter. First, though, a story to illustrate the potential of previewing.

At school, I hated French lessons. I've got nothing against the language. In fact, I tend to choose foreign-language films when I can, and I have a particular fondness for *cinéma français*. In high school, my fear and loathing of French came from two sources. Most profoundly, two months into starting high school at the age of eleven, I was sent away from the side of my mother's hospital bed to complete my French homework. It was the last time I saw my mother alive. It was also the last time I ever completed any homework (perchance that was a reason why I was placed in detention so many times).

The second source—and one that is much more common—was that French lessons were so unfair! They appealed to students who already had a smattering of French, but not to the rest of us. Those privileged students who had been to France with their families or had studied French during primary school were able to access the activities. The rest of us sat on the periphery of the conversations between the teacher and the "keen kids," wondering what on earth they were *parlez*-ing about.

Preview techniques could have helped. These involve giving students the opportunity to prepare themselves in advance of a lesson. For our high school French lessons, the teacher could have told us about the topic for next week and offered some phrases and vocabulary to learn ahead of time. Those students with competent levels of French had already taken part in a luxury version of preview (their holidays in France), so this teacher-initiated preview would have been a catch-up session for the rest of us.

Back in the 1980s, we didn't have the luxury of the internet. We had to rely on finding one of the few textbooks available or being given a poorly photocopied resource sheet. These days, students can find all sorts online, not just lists of phrases and vocabulary but translators to turn whatever phrase they want into workable French (or Spanish or Japanese or whatever suits their context). There are even thousands of videos to choose from that offer guides to pronunciation as well as phraseology.

Of course, students with risk factors are the ones most likely *not* to have reliable access to the internet, so you will need to find a workaround for that issue. In the schools I've taught at, I've created a preview room where students can go to access resources and additional support. A well-resourced school library, if you have one, is ideal for this purpose, but even just a mobile device and a place to study can be enough to make a start. The following sections offer additional details on previewing effectively.

6.1.1 Five Ways to Preview

For my high school French lessons, I would have gained so much by turning up to class with some ready-made, rehearsed phrases to try out. I could have then joined in with the classroom activities and received the sort of encouragement and feedback that the more privileged students had benefited from for so long. As it was, I disengaged because I didn't have two French words to rub together.

Learning vocabulary ahead of a lesson isn't the only way to preview, though. What follows are five other approaches to try out. Which ones you choose will depend on the subject you're teaching and the age of your at-risk students.

1. **Use flipped learning:** This is the best-known approach to preview. It normally involves having students watch explanatory videos and complete formative assessment quizzes before any classes are held about the topics covered in the videos. Class time is then used to clarify students' understanding and to engage in problem-solving activities. Among the first to use the term *flipped learning*, educators Jonathan Bergmann and Aaron Sams (2012) define it as a method where that which is "traditionally done in class is now done at home, and that which is traditionally done as homework is now completed in class" (p. 13).

   Flipped learning tends to be used with older students and with a whole class. For the purposes of equity, I recommend that you use the approach primarily with your students with risk factors. If you have the time and inclination to create your own videos, then this can often be the best way forward. However, two sites that come highly recommended are Khan Academy (https://khanacademy.org) in the United States and the BBC's Bitesize (https://bbc.co.uk/bitesize), which is only available within the United Kingdom.

2. **Dig for information:** Tell your students which new topics are about to be covered, and give them the opportunity to dig for information. You might want to frame it with something like *5-4-3-2-1*. This stands for:

   a. Find five pieces of information

   b. Find four images linked to the topic (could be diagrams, cartoons, photographs, and so on)

   c. Create three questions that they're keen to answer

    d. Unearth two facts that surprise them
    e. Create one statement that captures the essence of the topic
3. **Try a new skill:** Preview doesn't need to be about information. It can be—and often is—about trying out a new skill before everyone else has a go or revisiting and refreshing a previously learned skill. This might be throwing, catching, displaying ball control, using a compass, drawing cartoons, creating charts and diagrams, or any skill that is likely to be useful in subsequent lessons.

   As I describe in more detail in section 6.1.2 (page 275), this is *not* about expecting students to turn up to class having already covered, discovered, or perfected everything they are going to need. Instead, it is about having them familiarize themselves enough with the content so that when they join in with everyone else, they will be starting further along the progress continuum than they otherwise might. In other words, the gap will have closed a little (or hopefully a lot) before the lesson begins.

4. **Follow a how-to guide:** The potential for learning is greatest with this approach because (a) reading and understanding instructions is one of the few really generalizable skills needed in almost every context; (b) students can move at their own pace and skip or repeat as needed; and (c) instructions can readily be differentiated to meet the needs of a diverse group of students. However, this last characteristic also brings with it the need to get the Goldilocks principle (see section 3.5, page 106) of challenge just right. Any how-to guide must be accessible enough for your at-risk students to make sense of but also involve challenge to extend their learning in preparation for the following lessons.

5. **Watch a film:** Preview doesn't *have* to feel like learning! It could be that you recommend a film for your students to watch. For example, watching a film version of a play they are about to study, watching a documentary that will give them a head start with a history topic, and watching the biography of the inventor of a scientific principle they are about to study are popular approaches.

Those five descriptions show the ways I most commonly preview with my students. They are by no means an exhaustive list. Other approaches include the following.

- Finding conflicting opinions in different sources of information (for example, differences of opinion on the way we should respond to climate change)
- Identifying connections between a new topic about to be studied and content previously learned
- Recording real-life examples (for example, a video of evaporation in action ahead of a topic about the water cycle)
- Collecting resources that will help in class (for example, photographs, brochures, materials to be used in a collage, and objects that can be used for impromptu music lessons)
- Reading the next chapter or two in the textbook, play, or class novel
- Finding out key points from older or former students
- Creating a sketch, plan, prototype, or proposal

6.1.2 What Evidence Supports Preview

According to Hattie (2023), there are forty-eight meta-analyses covering almost 2,500 studies about preview. Their combined effect size is $d = 0.56$. However, the range across all these studies is 0.19 to 1.19. That is an astonishing variance, reminiscent of the scales associated with feedback that I described in section 4.1 (page 149).

Bear in mind that I recommend preview strategies for the purposes of equity, whereas the research studies primarily report on approaches with all students in a school or class. Nonetheless, the findings are as follows.

- The major advantage of preview is extended exposure to content. Repeating the same information in subsequent lessons is a good thing, despite the sometimes bad reputation with students that repetition suffers from!

- When preview includes—or results in—quizzes, results *must* be used formatively; otherwise, the impact will be lower than if quizzes are not used at all. So, if you are going to give tests as part of preview, make sure you use the results to adjust subsequent instruction!

- Higher gains are noted when subsequent lessons involve direct instruction, labs, and demonstrations. Surprisingly, lessons that include active learning immediately following the use of preview seem to lower the impact of preview.

- Alignment is needed between preview content and lesson activities. This may seem an obvious point, but it is worth mentioning anyway. Previewing content or skills that are not then used in subsequent lessons does not improve learning outcomes.

6.1.3 Why Previewing Does Not Spoil the Surprise

I was amused the first time someone asked me, "But won't previewing spoil the surprise?" Thereafter, I have been perplexed. If surprise is the main part of our pedagogy, we might want to expand our skill set! Previewing does *not* give away closely guarded curriculum secrets, nor does it steal lessons' thunder! Rather, previewing gives students the opportunity to prepare their minds (or bodies in the case of skills) so that they are better able to focus and engage in lessons. When used solely with students who have risk factors, it also goes a long way toward closing the gap between them and other, more privileged students.

"If I've already introduced the topic to students, what do I teach them?" some will ask. Here are three answers to that particular worry.

1. The research shows repetition is good (Barber, Rajaram, & Marsh, 2008; Ebbinghaus, 1964; Zhan, Guo, Chen, & Yang, 2018)! That's me repeating the information I shared in the previous section.

2. There is always more to learn and always more refinements to develop. Increased exposure helps with this.

3. You already have a mix of abilities in each class. What preview does is move everyone who takes part one step further in their learning.

To expand on that last point, in section 4.4.1 (page 167), I shared some examples of progress connected to the SOLO Taxonomy. Here are three of those examples again, which you will find in figure 4.10 (page 169).

- **Example 1: Coding**
    - *Examples*—To know what coding is (in connection with computing)
    - *Features*—To define what coding is and give examples.
    - *Connections*—To understand the basic variables and commands of coding and explain what each of them does
    - *Applications and adaptations*—To be able to use code to create basic program and adjust as needed
- **Example 2: Letter Writing**
    - *Examples*—To know the basic format and structure of a letter
    - *Features*—To know the key features and tone of a formal letter
    - *Connections*—To understand the similarities and differences between formal and informal letters and the purpose of each
    - *Applications and adaptations*—To be able to compose a formal letter for a variety of purposes (complaint, information, thank you, request)
- **Example 3: Rhythm**
    - *Basics*—To know what makes something a rhythm
    - *First goes*—To try copying rhythms after listening to someone else clapping
    - *Practice*—To understand how to create different rhythms using a range of instruments
    - *Perform*—To be able to adapt a rhythm by increasing tempo or altering the number of notes used

For the first example, coding, I would give my students the opportunity to play with the Hour of Code website (https://hourofcode.com) or have a go with any of the coding games we have available in our school. Even half an hour of exploring either of these would help them know what coding is (the unistructural stage of SOLO) or even begin defining what coding is and giving examples (the multistructural stage of SOLO). As you can see from the preceding descriptions, there would still be more than enough for them to explore later in the lesson!

For the second example, letter writing, I would ask my at-risk students to collect as many examples of letters as they can find. These might include letters of complaint, love letters, letters of historical importance, and so on. If I could create the opportunity, I would then have them work together to identify common features of those letters. Doing so would help them consolidate stage 1 of the SOLO Taxonomy or move on to stage 2—either of which would be a brilliant starting point for the subsequent lesson.

For the third example, rhythm, I could get my students to sample some of the rhythms they like best and learn a rhythmic pattern so that they have one to teach others in the lesson. As you can see from the preceding descriptions, this would move the students to at least stage 1 of SOLO, probably to stage 2, or maybe even to stage 3.

It is important to note that I would *not* give an independent preview task to students if I thought there was a good chance that this would lead to some misconceptions. I never ask students to find a method for long division. Just imagine the work I would have to put in to undo the wacky ways they would find for that! I also don't ask them to set up a science experiment using hydrochloric acid. I'd be struck off the teaching register!

When choosing preview activities, use the "do no harm" principle as guidance. The purpose is to help your students, particularly your vulnerable ones, move one or two steps forward in their learning so they are not starting from scratch at the beginning of the lesson. Preview is not about replacing teachers. It is about giving our students and us more to work with.

6.1.4 Preview Notes

In no particular order, here are some additional notes to go with the idea of preview.

- If any of your students access extra support from additional needs assistants, then encourage that some of this time be spent previewing. My first school-based job was as a teaching assistant in a school for deaf children. I can't tell you how much time was wasted helping students complete time-filler tasks. If only I'd known about preview back then, I could have helped the students I supported so much more effectively. I would have asked the teachers what they were going to be teaching over the coming days, what was most relevant, and what I could usefully cover ahead of time. My students would have been so much more willing to engage in subsequent lessons if they had had the chance to prepare something beforehand, even if this was—or maybe particularly if this was—practicing the sign language vocabulary they needed to ask questions or give fuller, more descriptive answers.

- The same theory applies for students who are English learners (ELs). Use preview to familiarize your EL students with the key terms that will be used in subsequent lessons. This usually involves giving them the opportunity to translate the terms into their own languages, practicing using the terms in context, checking on pronunciation, and so on.

- If you set homework, turn some of it into preview tasks. However, do so with care because the effects are varied, and often misreported. When researchers Harris Cooper, Jorgianne Civey Robinson, and Erika A. Patall (2006) found that homework had almost zero effect on achievement, some schools ditched after-school assignments altogether. Unfortunately, further meta-analyses have not supported this conclusion. Although the effect of homework in elementary schools is indeed low ($d = 0.15$), in middle schools it is better ($d = 0.30$), and in high schools it is significant ($d = 0.48$; Ozyildirim, 2022; Trautwein, 2007). Digging deeper, the best outcomes come from homework that is short (it depends on age group, but generally less than thirty minutes) and does not require parental supervision. This explains why high school homework has a higher effect than elementary school homework, because teenagers don't ask for—or even want—help, whereas the parents of elementary-age children often end up doing their work for them! Most importantly, for homework to be effective, it should be valued at school, whether marked, built on, or in some way responded to in a timely manner. This last characteristic is a cornerstone of preview tasks, so that is one advantage already. Then, as long as you ensure the other two guidelines are followed (the tasks are relatively brief and don't require adult supervision), then preview homework should add value to your students' learning.

- The most significant effect of preview homework is to re-engage hard-to-reach parents! This recommendation might appear to contradict the earlier point about adult supervision, but I have experienced many occasions when this has worked. My favorite example comes from a school in Devon, England, where I engaged in a three-year project. During my first visit, one of the dads complained, "Now that we're not allowed to hit kids, you tell me how we're supposed to discipline them." A year later, the same dad started the parents' meeting with, "Whatever this school is doing for these kids needs to happen in every school in the country. My kids love this place, and so do I, especially the homework!" When I asked for details, he and the other parents in the focus group sang the praises of the new preview homework that they were allowed to get involved with. Many said that they hated school when they were students. Now, they could enjoy learning, and their children loved it.

- Another assignment involved parents and their children in making houses as preparation for the history topic of the Great Fire of London. The fourth-grade teachers asked students to find out what they could about this topic before the lessons began and to bring in cardboard boxes that could be used to represent the houses that caught fire in 1666. A week later, the students came in with such beautifully decorated houses that the school staff didn't have the heart to burn them on the school field as originally planned. Instead, they made a display out of them and burned some plain boxes instead. Whether the students enjoyed making the houses as much as their parents did is still debated in the town.

- Granted, this is but one story among many, and it hardly proves anything. But knowing the school community as I came to it and how significant this moment was for parents to engage more fully in their children's education, I think it is noteworthy enough. And while the research says that homework has the best effect when parent support is not required, note that in stories like this (and there are many like it), support wasn't *required*—it was *chosen*. That makes a big difference.

- I've mentioned resourcing a few times already, but it is always one of the biggest concerns for teachers when I mention previewing. The simplest form of preview is to print off some additional information for students to take home and read sometime before the lesson covering that topic begins. That is the starting point. However, if you have the possibility to take it further, then so much the better. Enhanced preview means ensuring your students have access to appropriate resources. If you use the approach to support students with risk factors, the obstacles to this will be greater but not normally insurmountable. For example, which devices and online connections will your students be able to use? Will they choose the websites they visit, or will you give them direction (and age-related restrictions)? Could they arrive before school starts or leave later so that you can give them the resources and the study space to engage properly? If this is out of the question, are there times during the school day that could be used for this purpose without feeling like punishments?

- Preview doesn't have to be reserved only for your vulnerable students; you could use it with all your students. During my full-time teaching years, I used the approach so much that I rearranged the ways in which I taught units. For example, instead of teaching a unit in, say, four lessons stretching over two weeks, I would take the last half lesson of each unit to preview the next topic. I would also turn one of the two homework tasks into a preview opportunity. When I taught primary school classes, I would take some time on Friday afternoon to preview key points for the following week. I'd also ask students to think about, find, or watch something connected with one of the main topics they were about to study.

6.1.5 Preview Detentions

I must have spent a minimum of twelve hours *every week* throughout my entire high school career (eleven to sixteen years old) in detention, mostly because I hadn't done my homework (see my French lessons story in section 6.1, page 272) or because I had been caught playing the class clown yet again. However, if those detentions had been turned into preview opportunities, I feel sure I would have committed fewer misdemeanors!

Like so many students who struggle, I used the power of distraction to avoid scrutiny of my work. If a teacher ever wandered close to where I sat, I would throw a pen, drop my book, or shout out or do anything else to draw their attention away from the blank page in my exercise book. "What are you doing? Get out!" they would admonish me. And off I'd skip, happy to have escaped the lesson without anyone noticing I didn't understand what I was supposed to be doing. My belief was it's much better to be thought of as naughty than to be thought of as stupid! In fact, every single time a teacher talked to me about my behavior was a small victory in my mind. In my teenage mind, I had won (by distracting their attention away from my lack of understanding) and they had lost (by falling for the oldest trick in the book yet again).

Imagine that detentions had consisted of previewing a forthcoming topic. Instead of completing irrelevant tasks, I could have spent time preparing to engage in future lessons. If I had been able to rock up to the next lesson in French or history or physics—or whichever subject I'd earned my detention in—with an idea of what was going to be studied and, more importantly, what I could do to join in rather than opt out again, then maybe, just maybe, I wouldn't have wasted so many hours on detention.

Old-school teachers hate this idea. They want detentions to be all about the punishment. They think it is wrong to give an advantage to anyone who, by rights, should be placed in the stocks and pelted with rotten tomatoes! To be clear, though, preview does *not* run contrary to punishment. When a student is placed in detention, they have their liberty removed; *that* is their punishment. If they require more punishment than that, extend the length of detention or give them another one. Don't also get them to complete meaningless tasks!

If you think this is pointless, and you would rather have helped me avoid going to the detention hall again and again, then preview can help. Of course, some students who are placed in detention know perfectly well how to access lessons, but many like me do not. So, for those students, previewing can be a big step toward reducing recidivism and, therefore, boosting equity.

6.2 Growth Mindset for Low-Socioeconomic-Status Students

 *Growth mindset interventions reduce educational disparities. Conveying the belief that all students have the capacity to learn and improve has a particular positive effect with disadvantaged and at-risk students.*

In a moment, I will share reasons why growth mindset practices make an even bigger difference to disadvantaged students than to others. Before that, though, I want to share some worrying research. Researchers Shwetlena Sabarwal, Malek Abu-Jawdeh, and Radhika Kapoor (2022) analyzed survey data from twenty thousand teachers in nine developing countries. What Sabarwal and colleagues (2022) found should worry us all.

- Forty-three percent of the teachers surveyed believe "there is little they can do to help [disadvantaged students] learn" (p. 73).
- More teachers believe that students deserve more attention if they are performing well than if they are lagging behind.

These findings are pronounced, and I hope unrepresentative of the school you teach in. If these beliefs are present in your building, then your disadvantaged students likely face even more obstacles than they might otherwise.

Before we dwell too much on this disheartening message, let's move swiftly to some good news instead. Beliefs can be changed, and growth mindset approaches can go a long way toward improving the education and life chances of your at-risk students. In section 5.4.2 (page 235), I wrote a summary of the four meta-analyses that have been published about mindset. The impact of these is significant for all students. For vulnerable students, the outcomes are even more positive. Across the four meta-analyses (Burnette et al., 2013; Costa & Faria, 2018; Sisk et al., 2018), the following has been found to result from growth mindset.

- Lower-achieving students who believe they are naturally unacademic learn how malleable talents and intelligence really are.
- Economically disadvantaged students whose families tell them their only hope is to win the lottery begin to understand that a myriad of factors lead to success and that they can significantly influence many of them.
- Students with risk factors become aware of negative stereotypes about themselves (the stereotype threat from Aronson et al., 2002) and begin to understand the erroneous nature of stereotyping and how malleable intelligence is.

These findings ought to be enough to put growth mindset on your priority list. However, there is more. A study published in 2023 shows even more astonishing gains for low-socio-economic-status (SES) students (Hecht et al., 2023). The researchers assigned 155 teachers (5,393 students) to receive an intervention and 164 teachers (6,167 students) to receive a control module. All the educators involved in the study worked at high schools in a southern U.S. state. The study focused on encouraging teaching practices that would lead to a growth mindset in students and emphasized the importance of the following actions (Hecht et al., 2023):

- Conveying a belief in all students' capacity to learn and improve in the course
- Putting less emphasis on students' current levels of performance and more emphasis on improvement over time
- Taking every opportunity to make clear to students that what the teacher really cares about is that students put in the effort to push the limits of their learning
- Providing assurance that if students put in that effort, they (the teacher) would provide the necessary support to ensure that that effort paid off (p. 2)

The intervention urged teachers to make these ideas a regular and central part of their classroom communication so that even skeptical students would eventually be persuaded that these beliefs were sincere and central to the teachers' philosophy of instruction.

Here is where the study gets really exciting: the impact was hugely significant and even more so for at-risk students. The intervention improved learning outcomes as follows (Hecht et al., 2023).

- Effect on pass rates:
  - Overall effect—6.31 percentage points, equivalent to an effect size of *standardized mean difference* (*SMD*) = 0.13
  - Effect in majority low-SES classes—10.65 percentage points, equivalent to an effect size of $SMD = 0.22$
- Effect on course grades:
  - Overall effect—0.14 grade points (effect size of $SMD = 0.10$)
  - Effect in majority low-SES classes—0.36 grade points (effect size of $SMD = 0.25$)
- Effect on rates of earning college credit:
  - Overall effect—4.19 percentage points (effect size of $SMD = 0.09$)
  - Effect in majority low-SES classes—7.35 percentage points (effect size of $SMD = 0.15$)

Note that the effect sizes are quoted differently than previous effect sizes in this book. As Cameron A. Hecht, Christopher J. Bryan, and David S. Yaeger (2023) state, they have used standardized mean differences (SMDs), which are conceptually equivalent to Cohen's d (the convention I have used before now) but calculated from raw data. For the purposes of comparison, a fifth of an SMD (that is, $SMD = 0.20$) is considered a large effect in real-world educational settings. This is roughly equivalent to Cohen's effect size of $d = 0.40$. An effect of $SMD = 0.20$ corresponds roughly to the following.

- The amount of improvement shown on students' standardized test scores after a year of classroom learning in high school (Hill, Bloom, Black, & Lipsey, 2008)
- The effect of having a high-quality teacher (versus an average teacher) for one school year (Hanushek, 2011)
- The most optimistic estimates of the effects of costly interventions that are difficult to scale, such as individualized tutoring (Kraft, 2020)

Bear in mind that the only extra work that teachers in the study took part in was a forty-five-minute interactive online intervention training module. After that, they were urged to make the growth mindset ideas shown in points 1–4 (page 281) regular and central parts of their classroom communication. That was it. And yet look at the astonishing results. The effect on pass rates was *SMD* = 0.13 overall and *SMD* = 0.22 for students in majority low-SES classes. That is the equivalent of two years' schooling in one year! Course grades improved even more, and college credit increased significantly also.

The only caveat I would offer is that this is a study and not a meta-analysis. However, since one of the authors is David Yeager, who has published many peer-reviewed studies connected with growth mindset, I would suggest the study is more reliable than most single studies (Yeager & Dweck, 2020; Yeager et al., 2019). The findings are also in keeping with the four meta-analyses published so far. Therefore, with that caveat aside, I would like to finish by shouting from the rooftops: If you are serious about equity, then you *must* make sure growth mindset features in your plans for intervention!

6.3 Further Strategies to Boost Equity

Large socioeconomic inequalities have long persisted in the education system. One way to change this is to motivate teachers to adopt equity-based beliefs. Unfortunately, scalable methods to make this a reality have proven elusive. As teachers, we already face overwhelming demands on our time and attention. We also assume we already have the right values and beliefs!

So, there is an understandable skepticism about professional development advice that comes from experts who conduct their research under lab conditions rather than in real-life classrooms. That is why using practical teaching strategies that are aligned with relevant core values is often the best way to improve learning outcomes. This can be for all students or for a target group—which, in the case of this chapter, is your disadvantaged and low-SES students.

I have already shared the two most effective strategies: (1) preview and (2) growth mindset. Here are some other approaches. They have all previously been mentioned in the book, but this time, I take an equity approach to them.

6.3.1 Extending Thinking Time

Increasing thinking time for students is an important equity practice. All students benefit from an increase to three or more seconds of wait time; low-SES students benefit most of all.

In section 2.1.3 (page 38), I shared Mary Budd Rowe's (1986) research about increasing wait time during questioning sequences. Her recommendation was to increase the wait time in these two situations.

1. After you have asked a question and before a student answers
2. After a student answers and before you respond (or someone else does)

Increasing these wait times to at least 2.7 seconds creates significant results for all students. The following are even more pronounced for disadvantaged students.

- The length of student responses increases between 300 percent and 700 percent, even more in the case of at-risk students:

    Under the usual 1-second average wait times, responses tend to consist of short phrases and rarely involve explanations of any complexity. Wait time two is particularly powerful for increasing probability of elaboration. (Rowe, 1986, p. 44)

- The variety of students participating voluntarily in discussions increases, and the number of unsolicited but appropriate contributions increases:

    Typically, six or seven students capture more than half of the recitation time. Under the 3-second regimen, the number of students usually rated as poor performers who become active participants increases. Interestingly, this change in verbal activity gradually influences teacher expectations . . . (Verbal competence appears to be a salient factor in teacher judgments concerning a student's capabilities.) (Rowe, 1986, p. 44)

- Expectations improve for the performance of certain students:

    Previously "invisible" people become visible. Expectations change gradually, often signaled by remarks such as "He never contributed like that before. Maybe he has a special 'thing' for this topic." This effect was particularly pronounced where minority students were concerned. They did more task relevant talking and took a more active part in discussions. (Rowe, 1986, p. 45)

The rest of Rowe's research, together with subsequent studies by researchers Ken Tobin (1987), Robert Stahl (1994), and Dan Rothstein and Luz Santana (2011), showed that gains made were even more significant for at-risk and minority students. For example, researcher Wayne A. Winterton (1977) found that minority students who were previously described by teachers as nonverbal contributed spontaneously twice as often during the longer wait time classes as their counterparts did in other, more typical science classes. Thus, improving the length (and quality) of thinking time during lessons is of benefit to students generally but is of utmost importance for practices of equity.

6.3.2 Reducing Polarization and Increasing Dialogue

In section 2.2.1 (page 50), I shared Gad Yair's (2000) research about engaging students in dialogue. Before we view this research through an equity lens, I want to share another aspect of Yair's research, that of polarization.

Yair (2000) shows that teachers put more effort into *instructing* their high-achieving students, whereas they direct more *affective* efforts toward their lower-achieving students. There is evidence that parents mirror this approach. Low-SES families tend to evaluate students according to behavioral and disciplinary comments made by teachers (Alexander, Entwisle, & Bedinger, 1994). This contrasts with parents of high-SES backgrounds, who mainly focus on cognitive and achievement criteria.

Yair (2000) calls this a *polarization approach*, which is instructing one group and nurturing the other. In the case of teachers, this does not seem to be a planned interaction. It is likely, as Yair (2000) suggests, a rational tactic that allows the double tasks of teaching and controlling. Unfortunately, the outcomes of high-polarization classes are the achievement of low-SES students drops and the social gap in student achievement widens. Therefore, polarization is a bad thing.

On the other hand, dialogue is a good thing. Let's look back through Yair's (2000) research, this time with an equity lens. Yair noted the following evidence when he asked students in grades 6, 8, 10, and 12 what was on their mind at eight randomly chosen moments during their school day.

- The students were engaged in their lessons only 54 percent of the time. There was very little variation relative to student ability or curriculum subject.
- Students in earlier grades engaged more than students in higher grades.
- External preoccupations distracted all students 36 percent of the time and students with risk factors 42 percent of the time.
- Teachers talked for 70 percent to 80 percent of class time. They talked more in classes with a majority of students from low-SES backgrounds.

The few bits of good news were that students' engagement improved significantly when they (Yair, 2000):

- Studied in laboratory classrooms or took part in group activities (73 percent engagement for all students, 84 percent for low-SES students)
- Were involved in group presentations (67 percent engagement for all, 76 percent for low-SES students)
- Participated in discussions that were at the heart of their learning (63 percent engagement for all, 72 percent for low-SES students)

So, the lessons from these findings are clear: do not polarize your students, and engage everyone in as much high-quality dialogue as you can. The first of these means giving more (not less) cognitive and achievement instruction to your students with risk factors, and the second means teaching them how to engage in exploratory talk. If you wanted to take this second recommendation a step further, you could engage your students in dialogue about equity itself.

To facilitate that exact outcome, I created examples for some in-service training for the trainers working with Show Racism the Red Card (https://theredcard.org), the United Kingdom's leading antiracism educational charity. This fabulous organization brings together youth workers and ex-professional footballers to deliver educational workshops in schools, workplaces, and sports arenas. I am delighted to work with them from time to time. Figure 6.1 shows the first Odd One Out example I used with the Show Racism the Red Card team.

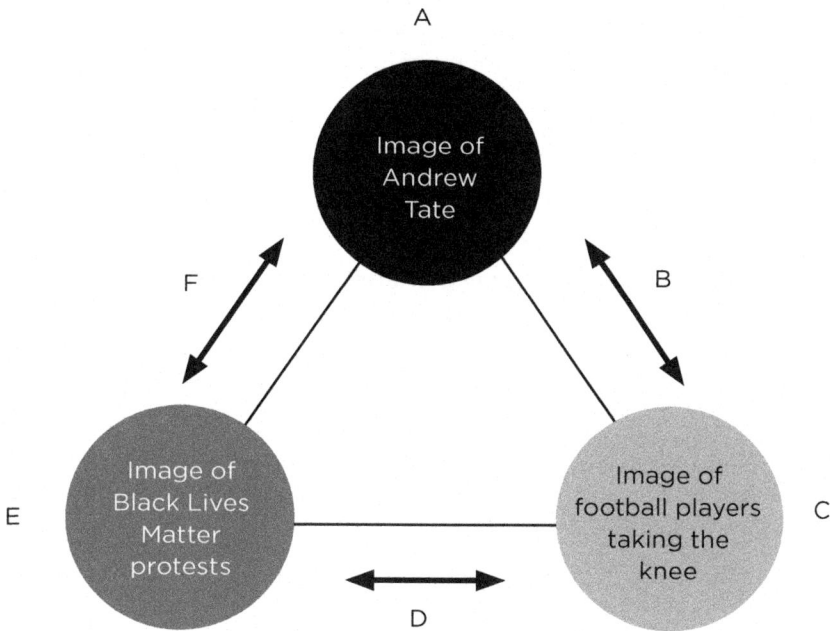

Figure 6.1: Odd One Out example for an antiracism workshop.

For that workshop, I used images where you see circles here, but for copyright reasons, I have given the descriptions instead. I think the examples are relatively well known internationally, but just in case, here is a brief summary of each one.

- **Andrew Tate:** Tate is a British-American kickboxer who has attracted controversy for his misogynist views. In June 2023, he was charged with human trafficking and forming an organized crime group to sexually abuse women (Williamson & Wright, 2023). His social media posts are widely viewed and talked about, and at the time of the workshop, they were a main topic of conversation among teenagers in the United Kingdom. This led to some debate about whether schools ought to ban conversations about him or tackle the issues head-on (Das, 2022).

- **Black Lives Matter protests:** Following the death of George Floyd in May 2020, antiracism protests and riots transpired across the United States, as well as in Europe. Assuming that the workshop participants would unanimously be in favor of the protests, I wanted to use an image that would provoke a bit more cognitive conflict. So, I chose the scene of protesters spraying graffiti on a statue of Winston Churchill alleging that Churchill was racist (Adam & Booth, 2020).

- **Football players taking the knee:** Players in England's Premier League have been making this gesture of antiracism before select games since June 2020. The image I chose was of Marcus Rashford, who has won as many plaudits for his off-field charity work as for his excellent performances for England and Manchester United. He was one of the standout performers at the UEFA Euro 2020 championship, and yet after he missed a penalty in the final, fans who had previously been cheering him on unleashed a torrent of racist abuse on social media (Premier League, 2023).

The two main purposes for using an Odd One Out strategy are (1) to notice connections and distinctions between the images or ideas selected and (2) to use cognitive conflict and respectful dialogue to build familiarity with exploratory talk. The examples I chose served just those purposes for the Show Racism the Red Card team. I subsequently used the examples with high school students in England and Scotland.

For younger students in primary and middle schools, I use different images. The ones I tend to select from are the following, which are widely available online.

- An ex-professional footballer wearing a T-shirt with the Show Racism the Red Card logo
- Players taking the knee (This is widely recognized and reported on in the United Kingdom and suitable for students from second grade onward.)
- The three England players who each missed a penalty in the Euro 2020 final (This was a widely reported event in England that most primary school students know the story of, even those who aren't football fans.)
- Colin Kaepernick taking the knee to protest Black oppression in the United States
- A multiracial group of students hanging out together
- Protesters holding Black Lives Matter banners
- The rainbow flag (LGBTQ pride) flying outside a school
- The word *racism* being rubbed off a classroom board
- A child of color being left out of a game by a group of White children
- Olympic 100-meter sprinters, 100-meter swimmers, and cross-country skiers
- A comparison of sports pundits from the 1980s (all White) and current TV pundits
- Refugees on an overcrowded boat
- Jeff Bezos on his $500 million yacht
- A Black child and a White child hugging

Odd One Out isn't the only strategy that can be used, of course. Indeed, any of the strategies described in sections 2.4 to 2.7 (pages 58 to 80) are suitable. Examples of the sorts of concepts that can be used with these strategies include the following.

Bias	Discrimination	Intersectionality	Supremacism
Bullying	Dog whistling	Prejudice	Whataboutery
Color	Ethnicity	Racism	Xenophobia
Culture	Institutional racism	Stereotyping	

6.3.3 Supporting Students Who Are English Learners

The strategies I have mentioned in this book all lend themselves to supporting your EL students. The particularly effective ones are those I have mentioned in this chapter, starting with preview.

The research is clear that there is a positive and significant link between English learners' use of multiple strategies and learning outcomes (Baker & Boonkit, 2004; Green & Oxford, 1995; Zhang, Gu, & Hu, 2008). By introducing and using many different strategies for making meaning, you will provide your non-native speakers of English with a set of tools that they can choose from. Strategies like Odd One Out allow English learners to use their home language to support their thinking. They can say or write terms and then work with others to translate them into English.

Some teachers worry EL students will feel excluded from activities such as going through the Learning Pit. Many cognitive demands are already placed on students as they move from holding a few ideas to understanding lots of ideas to using those ideas in different ways. So, to do all of this in another language can be overwhelming. My response to these concerns is this.

- The Learning Pit is a collaborative exercise (at least it should be). Therefore, your EL students should not find themselves in the pit by themselves. Using exploratory talk (see section 2.1.1, page 31) with the students they are collaborating with, together with language prompt cards and lots of thinking time (see section 6.3.1, page 282), should provide the right scaffolds to allow all students to take part, including your EL students.

- Using preview strategies (see section 6.1, page 272) to familiarize your EL students with the terms and key concepts ahead of Learning Pit activities will help significantly.

- Having a bilingual image of the Learning Pit, such as the one shown in figure 3.8 (page 119), will also help.

If you work with younger bilingual students, then using prompt cards with terms or phrases in both languages should already be standard practice. Making sure this is the case when you ask groups to engage in any of the strategies described in sections 2.4 to 2.7 (page 58 to 80) will be a good use of this approach.

6.4 Cognitive Load Theory

The only social media platform I visit more than once in a blue moon is X (formerly Twitter). Shouty elements aside, through following the right accounts, I find it a useful way of reading up-to-date news and ideas that mainstream media sources often avoid for fear of upsetting their paymasters. Of the educational accounts I follow, the one I find most engaging is that of professor Dylan Wiliam (@DylanWiliam), who posted on January 26, 2017, "I've come to the conclusion Sweller's Cognitive Load Theory is the single most important thing for teachers to know."

When Wiliam said cognitive load theory is that important, I decided I needed to know more. I realize it is *ad hominem* to think something is worthwhile because of who said it rather than what it is they said. However, bearing in mind Wiliam's deep understanding of education (as evidenced by the fact I've referenced his work in all twelve books I have written so far, including this one; see the introduction, page xi) and my use of his guidance on many occasions in the classroom, I think it important to lean into what makes this concept so vital.

Cognitive load theory, as first researched by Australian educational psychologist John Sweller (1988), describes learning as something that best happens when conditions are aligned with human cognitive architecture. Although this architecture is not known precisely, experimental research leads to the conclusion that working memory is limited in its capacity, whereas long-term memory is almost limitless. I will share the importance of this distinction in more detail soon. For now, know that if you are already familiar with a topic and have committed a clear understanding to your long-term memory, then you will be able to attend to new information you come across in this field using both your long- and short-term memory. This means you will handle that information very efficiently. However, if a topic is brand new to you and you don't have any reliable schemas to draw on, then your short-term (or working) memory will do all the work. This creates several issues that I'll return to.

I mentioned *reliable schemas*, which are cognitive frameworks (or concepts) that help organize and interpret information. They come in many forms and describe patterns of thinking and behavior that are used to interpret the world. For example, *social schemas* include what it means to be respectful and what is expected when a group of people are asked to settle a bill (which, of course, may differ from one context or culture to another). *Event schemas* include how you greet another person and what is appropriate to wear (again, both are context specific though they have generalizable dos and don'ts). *Self-schemas* include how smart you think you are, how you regard your personality, and what you view as your purpose in life.

Jean Piaget, often regarded as one of the two founding fathers of educational psychology, along with Lev Vygotsky (who I mentioned in section 3.0.1, page 93), wrote that a schema is both the category of knowledge and the process of acquiring that knowledge (Huitt & Hummel, 2003). He believed that people are constantly adapting to the environment as they take in new information and learn new things. For example, a young child may first develop a schema for a cow. She knows that a cow is large and has hair, four legs, and a tail. Then, when the child encounters a horse for the first time, she might initially call it a cow. After all, this fits in with her schema for the characteristics of a cow; it is a large animal that has hair, four legs, and a tail. Once she is told that this is a different animal called a horse, she will modify her existing schema for a cow and create a new schema for a horse.

Imagine, though, this same child comes across a different type of animal that has similarities to both a cow and a horse. (You're trying to think of one now, aren't you?) Does this animal— let's say, a zebra—fit into her schema of a cow? Or should it fit with her schema of a horse? Or does a zebra require its own schema? Then, what about a pony? Or a bull? A donkey? A buffalo, a yak, a bison, or a beefalo? (Yes, I had to look up beefalo too.)

What on earth has all of this got to do with education or, more particularly, to do with equity? First, the more general question, which is, What role do schemas play in the learning process? Consider the following.

- **Schemas influence what we pay attention to:** If new information associates easily with one of our current schemas, we will pay attention to it more than if it doesn't. For example, if I see a complex algebraic equation on the board, I will pay less attention to it than a mathematician would. Right now, I don't have any schemas that will help me make sense of it. I know what algebra looks like, so I can recognize it as such, but that is pretty much my limit. However, if there are any spelling mistakes or geographical errors on the board, my pedantic mind will home in on them straight away.

- **Schemas help simplify the world:** When we come across new information, we can classify and categorize it by comparing it to existing schemas. A novice teacher, for example, might look at chapter 4 (page 147) and be awed by the volume of detail it contains, whereas an expert teacher will cut through all the detail because it's familiar to them, and they will quickly identify what is of most relevance to them. In other words, without a schema, everything is new. With a schema, you can move directly to nuance.

- **Schemas help us think quickly:** If you or I visit someone else's classroom—even if it's in a very different context—we are likely to be able to make quick decisions about what students need and how to proceed effectively. Adults not in teaching are likely to use a lot more energy trying to understand the intentions and needs of thirty diverse students. As experienced teachers, we make it look so easy! Every profession is the same. The experts make it look effortless, and in some ways, that is because much of the processing of information has already been done. That's why the best of the emergency services handle crises so calmly.

- **Schemas determine how we interpret information (warning!):** It shouldn't come as a surprise when people on opposite sides of the political divide interpret the same information in completely different ways, but it is still perplexing. You might ask yourself, "How did they come to *that* conclusion from *that* information?" At that very same time, others are likely thinking the same about your assumptions!

- **Schemas create prejudice:** The role schemas play in creating prejudicial practice is one of the reasons I included cognitive load theory in this chapter. For example, to a racist, the actions of a Black man are symptomatic of "all Black men," whereas the actions of a White man are his own business. Therefore, if a student who is a person of color commits a misdemeanor, it's expected behavior. If a privileged student makes the same mistake, it's because they are having a bad day or it's otherwise "out of character."

Where does all of this leave us with cognitive load theory? First, the schemas your students hold will influence their long-term memory, which will make a significant difference in how they interact with, and respond to, learning. If a topic is familiar to them—if it connects with one of their schemas—then they should be able to make good progress with assimilation of new information. However, if they have no schema to help make sense of the topic, then they are likely to struggle. The cognitive load will be too much. According to researchers Susan E. Gathercole and colleagues (2008), classic indications of this include:

- Incomplete recall of new information
- Failure to follow instructions
- Forgetting where they got to (place-keeping errors)
- Abandoning the task (and potentially causing a nuisance to distract others' attention away from this)

From an instructional perspective, information contained in materials and explanations will first be processed by students' working memory. If this fits with one or more of their schemas, then their long-term memory will be able to do much of this processing. This is likely to lead to a good pace of progress.

Your students with risk factors are likely to encounter significant problems in this regard. The fewer schemas they have, the more they will have to rely on their working memory to process the information (and remember, working memory is far more limited than long-term memory). There are many categories of vulnerability, of course, and not all of them result in less expansive long-term memory. It is a common trait, though.

Betty Hart and Todd R. Risley's (1995) landmark study is influential in this regard. They wanted to know why, despite best efforts to promote equity in preschool programs, children from low-income homes remain well behind their more economically advantaged peers years later in school. Each month, they recorded an hour of conversations in the homes of forty-two families, categorized as professional, working-class, or welfare families. Two and a half years of coding and analyzing every utterance in 1,318 transcripts led to the discovery that the average vocabulary of three-year-olds varied as follows (Hart & Risley, 1995).

- 1,116 words for children with professional parents
- 749 words for children with working-class parents
- 525 words for children with welfare-dependent parents

There is some evidence that this effect is partly due to differences in parents' knowledge about child development (Bornstein, Cote, Haynes, Hahn, & Park, 2010). Parents who know more about how children learn talk to their children in more complex ways and more often invite ideas from their children. More often than not, it is the high-SES parents who have this knowledge. Furthermore, when the home is crowded, parents are more likely to talk to children briefly and in directives. Also, children in low-SES families are read to less often and watch more television than their high-SES counterparts. Finally, more-educated parents are more concerned about spending time with their children, which significantly contributes to their language development (Bornstein et al., 2010).

Does this extraordinary difference in the number of words young people learn make a big difference to their schemas and to the cognitive load that they encounter? Probably. We don't understand that enough yet. For example, it might be not the number of words but how they are used that makes the biggest difference. Are the words primarily used in short, sharp instructions or in the to-and-fro of conversation? In the latter case, schemas are likely to be more developed despite lower levels of vocabulary. Could gestures that accompany words make a difference in the development of schemas? Again, probably.

The point is, whatever the reason for the differences in vocabulary and schemas between low- and high-SES students, there is no denying that some students we work with have a more acutely developed understanding of the world (because of their schemas) than other students do. Therefore, some students process new information quickly because their schemas make sense of it almost subconsciously, whereas other students in the same class don't have the relevant schemas, and so require a lot more effort from their working memory to process it in the same way. No wonder EL students, neurodiverse students, and other students with special needs are so tired by the end of the day. Either that or they opt out so as to conserve energy.

6.4.1 Preventing Cognitive Overload

When the demands placed on working memory are too high, your students might give up in frustration. Or they might fail to comprehend. Either way, their learning will be limited. When this cognitive overload happens, it does *not* mean that those experiencing it are less intelligent than others. It means their working memory has to put in more effort than others' working memories do.

That said, there must be *some* cognitive load, or else there will be nothing much to think about; students will simply be able to do rather than think. Getting the balance right is exactly as tricky as I have mentioned many times in this book—for example, when describing desirable difficulties in section 3.4 (page 101), when showing why we ought to guide our students through the Learning Pit (section 3.7, page 113), and when identifying the Goldilocks principle of challenge (section 3.5, page 106).

Here are some ways to avoid cognitive overload. Think of them primarily as ways to support your students with risk factors. Of course, they can be appropriate for all students, particularly placed side by side with the cognitive conflict strategies I've mentioned previously.

- **More signal, less noise:** The *signal* is the core message or concept you want your students to think about. The *noise* is any extraneous information that detracts from the intended focus. By removing unnecessary complexity and distraction, you will remove some of the cognitive overload. I often think about this when listening to someone presenting their research findings. They put so much text on the screen together with graphs that require time to process and *then* read their notes without pausing for breath. Talk about cognitive overload (or death by PowerPoint). As the saying goes, if you're repeating all the words on your slides, one of you is redundant!

- **Stop and think (turn and talk):** Earlier, I shared Yair's (2000) research (see section 2.2.1, page 50) showing that teachers talk for 70–80 percent of a lesson. Wow, that's a lot of talking—a seemingly unbelievable statistic—yet this research comes from thousands of hours of observations, so he's got a better chance of being right than what my gut instinct tells me! But even if we speak for only 50 percent of a lesson, that is still a lot of information for our students to process, considering every lesson of every day. It's even more to process if the information is new or doesn't clearly connect with students' schemas. So, make sure you stop to give students time to think. Also, teach them how to turn and talk effectively with each other (see sections 2.4 to 2.7, pages 58 to 80, for ideas). The following structures can help with this.

  - Name or describe or define the main idea or concept you've just heard.
  - Create a definition of this concept.
  - Complete these sentences: *This would be useful when . . .* ; *The most important part of this is . . .* ; *What would happen if . . . ?*; and *One application of this could be to . . .*
  - Create a beginner's question.
  - Predict what will happen next.
  - Make a connection to another topic or curriculum area.

- **Worked examples:** I wrote about this in section 4.7 (Worked Examples, page 188). Worked examples show students the steps they can take toward a learning goal—for example, "Here is how to draw a graph to represent . . ." or "Here is what a good opening paragraph or definition or description looks like." Connected to the previous strategy of turn and talk, you could give each pair a worked example and then ask them to create another one using different words, ideas, or elaborations (with the caveat that this strengthens the signal rather than adds more noise).

  As I mentioned in section 4.7, the general effect of worked examples is $d = 0.47$, but the effects are much more pronounced for lower-achieving and at-risk students. So, make sure you have worked examples ready to go! Equity in your classroom depends (in part) on having worked examples.

- **Clearly presented instructions:** This seems so obvious that it is almost patronizing to mention. Give clear instructions. Avoid lots of subclauses. Match them to a clear learning intention. Print a summary of the instructions on the board, or have them ready as a handout. I'm not talking about dumbing down the instructions, going interminably slow, or repeating yourself over and over. I'm talking about ensuring your students with risk factors use less energy on procedural thinking and, therefore, have more energy to direct toward the key concept or bank of knowledge you would like them to learn about.

- **Concise writing:** Concise writing is a straightforward way to reduce cognitive load. Long-winded explanations, obtuse instructions, and irrelevant content make unnecessary demands on your students' working memories. A study by researchers Richard E. Mayer, William Bove, Alexandra Bryman, Rebecca Mars, and Lene Tapangco (1996) had participants read passages of different lengths about a weather process. Students who were given the 500-word description learned the least. Those who read very short summaries learned the most (as evidenced by improved retention and transfer rates). "Conciseness is cool," says the author writing yet another 145,000-word book!

6.5 Equity Summary

Equity should not—must not—be ignored. Our responsibility is to help every student grow and flourish. We don't get to pick and choose; we have to help everyone. We are not there to teach some of our students some of the time or to help only our favorites or the ones who are a pleasure to teach.

Creating equity means removing the barriers that some students face. To do this, we should use some—or maybe even all—of the following strategies.

- **Give previews:** Give your disadvantaged students an opportunity to prepare themselves more effectively for forthcoming lessons. Offer them insights into vocabulary, concepts, main ideas, features, or simply an advanced copy of the notes that you will use in the coming days. This extended exposure to content gives your vulnerable students a chance to make progress toward most other students' starting points.

- **Convey growth mindset messages:** All four meta-analyses about mindset show the impact of being in a growth mindset is even more powerful for low-SES students than for others. That in itself ought to be enough for every single educator to adopt (or double down on) these strategies. However, a study by Hecht and colleagues (2023) shows even more impressive gains, particularly for disadvantaged students. That study's intervention shows improvements of 10.65 percentage points on pass rates for low-SES students (compared to 6.31 for all students), 0.36 grade points on course grades (compared to 0.14 for all students), and 7.35 percentage points on college credits (compared to 4.19 for all students). Bearing in mind these gains came *not* from an intensive intervention but from classroom teachers *merely* emphasizing the teaching practices shown in this section, these results are astonishing.

  So, if you're not already championing these approaches, make absolutely sure that you do so from now on, and try to persuade everyone else to do the same. Even if you think they're hocus-pocus, try these approaches anyway! Your most in-need students have so much to gain from them that they're as close as you can get to the pedagogical non-negotiables in the following list:
  - Conveying a belief in all students' capacity to learn and improve in the course
  - Putting less emphasis on students' current levels of performance and more emphasis on improvement over time
  - Taking every opportunity to make clear to students that what the teacher really cares about is that students put in the effort to push the limits of their learning
  - Providing assurance that if students put in that effort, the teacher would provide the necessary support to ensure that that effort paid off (Hecht et al., 2023, p. 2)

- **Extend thinking time:** When you are using questioning to engage your students and deepen their thinking, make sure you give them plenty of time to think. The two wait times to extend are (1) after you have asked a question and before a student answers, and (2) after a student answers and before you respond (or someone else does). The more important of these (and often the harder to get into the habit of) is wait time two. Both should last at least three seconds (gains start to occur after 2.7 seconds). The gains are impressive for all students; for at-risk students, they are even more powerful.

- **Reduce polarization:** Many of us in education put more effort into instructing our highest-achieving students; when it comes to lower-achieving students, our effort goes into affective platitudes such as, "You're doing really well," "Keep concentrating," "That's great," and "I'm so impressed." Yair (2000) calls this *polarization.*

  Thinking the cognitive domain is more important for the clever students and the affective domain is more important for the others leads to a widening of the gap, not a narrowing. If we find this is how we think, then we are part of this problem! Therefore, the onus is on us to become part of the solution instead. Holding equally high expectations (of progress) for all students includes making the topics of interaction the same across the board. Don't talk to some students about their behavior and others about their learning. Instead, interact with *all* students within both cognitive *and* affective domains.

- **Teach students how to engage in dialogue:** Engagement improves significantly when students receive the opportunity to engage in dialogue. However, most group work is unproductive because students haven't been taught how to interact with each other effectively. The remedy is exploratory talk (see section 2.1.1, page 31). This is by far the most productive form of dialogue. When you teach your students to use this type of talk, they learn how to question, challenge, and encourage in a reasoning and reasonable way. The potential gains for students are significant; for students with risk factors and low-SES students, they are especially consequential.

- **Reduce cognitive overload:** Cognitive load theory states that we have two types of memory: (1) a short-term working memory and (2) a long-term memory. When we concentrate on something, both are used. *How much* each one is required depends on the quality and quantity of the schemas that form the basis of our long-term memory. These schemas—or mental models—help us make sense of information efficiently. For example, if I have a schema about mapping—I know what maps represent, what sorts of details go onto them, what their purpose is, what they don't include, and so on—then a glance at a map should be enough for me to make sense of it. I don't need to study the details, wonder what the symbols mean, or try to understand the scale. I've already done this so many times that this sense making takes place subconsciously. On the other hand, if I *don't* have a concept of what a map is, then I will need to put significant mental effort into interpreting it first before I can learn anything new. To do this, I will call on my working memory more than my long-term memory. When this happens, I risk cognitive overload.

  Students with fewer schemas (concepts) require strategies for lowering demands on short-term memory. This does not mean dumbing something down or lowering expectations. It means providing scaffolds, which are ways to reduce the strain without reducing the challenge, a bit like distributing a heavy weight across your shoulders rather than bearing the same weight with your hands. Your at-risk and low-SES students will be most in need of these load-reducing strategies.

- **Use the jigsaw method:** I haven't written about the jigsaw method yet, at least not in this book. So, including it in this chapter summary perhaps feels strange. However, there are two very strong justifications for including it. First, it was originally designed to reduce racial cliques in forcibly integrated schools. So, for sure, it belongs in a chapter about equity. Second, Hattie (2023) reports that "of all the teaching methods that have been studied using meta-analysis, [the jigsaw method] has the highest effect size" (p. 387).

  A degree of skepticism should be maintained in regard to the latter of these two claims. The single published meta-analysis (Batdı, 2014) covers thirty-seven studies that were all carried out in one country. Therefore, the robustness score is just 1 out of 5. Nonetheless, the effect size is extraordinary ($d = 1.20$). So, even if only half that effect can be achieved elsewhere, it is still *very* much worth considering. The jigsaw method was designed by social psychologist Elliot Aronson (1978). What follows is an abridged version of the information found on the Jigsaw Classroom website (https://jigsaw.org).

6.5.1 Using Jigsaw in Eight Easy Steps

Use the following steps to engage students in a jigsaw activity.

1. Divide your students into groups of five. These are the home groups.
2. Divide the activity into five segments. For example, if you want history students to learn about Anne Frank, you might divide a short biography of her into stand-alone segments on (1) her early life; (2) the period before going into hiding; (3) life in her hiding place; (4) her arrest, deportation, and death; and (5) her legacy.
3. Give each home group one of the segments to read. Give them time to question each other, discuss difficult words, and make notes.
4. Ask the students in each home group to number themselves 1 to 5.
5. Person 1 from each home group then moves to sit with all the other number 1s at a table, person 2 sits with all other number 2s at another table, and so on. These new groups are the away groups.
6. All members of the away group take turns presenting their segments to the other students in this new group. By sharing the information that they are expert in, the whole group develops a full picture of the topic.
7. Once all the information has been shared in the away group, the students can return to their home group and share what they have learned about the other segments. This step is important for securing the learning. However, it is often left out. Taking the time for students to share with their home group gives them the opportunity to uncover valuable connections they made during the mixed-groups time. These connections could also be shared with the whole class.
8. Each of the students now knows about one aspect of the topic in depth and the whole topic in breadth. A quiz can be given to help the students realize how much they have learned about the whole topic from their dialogue with each other.

Researcher Veli Batdi's (2014) meta-analysis shows that jigsaw is an effective intervention for increasing interdependence between students and fostering prosocial behaviors that increase trust and social connection. More recent research has focused on jigsaw's strong effects on academic learning and has largely overshadowed the original purpose of improving social interactions and inclusion.

It's strange, given the magnitude of effects—socially as well as academically—that jigsaw is not already used in every school around the world! Maybe your quest to improve equity for your students can be the basis for changing this.

6.5.2 Using Jigsaw as Part of Your Professional Learning

Jigsaw isn't just for students. It also works brilliantly as a routine for investigating pedagogical topics as a collaborative team. For example, there are six chapters in this book. Chapters 1 and 6 are the most succinct and could be grouped together. So, you could divide this book into five jigsaw pieces and follow the steps described in the preceding section.

Alternatively, bearing in mind there is so much content throughout the book, you might want to jigsaw the chapters as you use the book for a yearlong or multiyear study. Two options are shown here, but I also challenge you to be creative and find a jigsaw routine that works for your team.

- **Option A:** Start the year with chapter 1 (page 1) and then follow that up with chapter 2 (page 19) a couple of weeks later, after your team has had time to think about teaching and learning and how they are connected. Approximately every six weeks thereafter, take on a new chapter (in the order that makes the most sense for your team's journey). Teachers can use the six weeks between chapters for Ready-Fire-Aim (see section 5.8.1, page 259).

  Divide chapter 1 as follows.

  - Sections 1.1 and 1.8
  - Sections 1.2, 1.3, and 1.8
  - Sections 1.4 and 1.8
  - Sections 1.5 and 1.8
  - Sections 1.6, 1.7, 1.8, 1.9, and 1.10 (Note that 1.8 is the glossary of terms, so it is a good idea for all staff to make themselves familiar with these terms.)

  Divide chapters 2–5 as follows.

  - Sections X.1 and X.2
  - Sections X.3 and X.4
  - Sections X.5 and X.6
  - Sections X.7 and X.8
  - Sections X.9 and X.10

  Divide chapter 6 as follows.

  - Sections 6.0 and 6.2
  - Section 6.1
  - Section 6.3
  - Section 6.4
  - Section 6.5

- **Option B:** Start the year with a jigsaw of chapter 1 as in option A, but then allow teachers to select one of chapters 2–5 that addresses a teaching focus that matches their needs. Each chapter team will engage in a lesson study to become experts over the course of the term. At the end of the term, jigsaw the four chapters and allow teachers to choose a new focus for the next term (by selecting a different chapter and a new team). You could do this for several terms before bringing the whole staff together to jigsaw chapter 6 as in option A.

Finally, if you visit the Teach Brilliantly website (http://teach-brilliantly.org), you will find lots of suggestions for Professional Pauses that will help you and your colleagues with reflections and next steps.

EPILOGUE

Post-Credit Encores

I've always enjoyed post-credits scenes in films. I think I'm right in saying the first one I ever saw was in *The Muppet Movie* (Frawley, 1979). My favorites were the bloopers. I deeply appreciate getting a glimpse into the efforts of making a film, the enjoyment of mistakes, and the willing removal of facade. In my opinion, everyone wears a mask, but only some are willing to remove theirs in self-deprecating, humanizing ways. Sadly, this section does not contain bloopers. A selection of the edits I've needed to make to this book—even the slightly amusing ones—would be anything but engaging. Soporific, maybe, but certainly not humorous.

Instead, I wanted to end the book with a few comments that I hope will add something extra. Coming where they do in the book makes them feel a little like an add-on at the end, which is what made me think of the post-credits encores.

At the beginning of the book, I wrote about the magic that takes place "inside the black box" (see the introduction, page xi). The term comes from a book that was very influential in my early days of teaching, *Inside the Black Box* by Black and Wiliam (1998b). The authors' point is that governments and administrators bequeath inputs such as curricula, exam content and schedules, resources, buildings, and the like and then expect excellent outcomes to follow. What they overlook—or, at least, don't give enough esteem to—is the pivotal, make-or-break influence of teachers.

When educators get it right, the outcomes are indeed excellent; but when they don't, then no matter how impressive the inputs are, the outputs just will not be that great. Of course, what it means to *get it right* is different in different contexts. We know that pedagogy, culture, expertise, and timing all play a role. Defining the exact blend of these, though, is close to impossible. Despite the many easy (overly simplistic) answers that journalists and barroom commentators offer, classrooms are just too complex to be straightforward. What takes place inside them is hard to understand, at least for those looking on from afar. This is why Black and Wiliam (1998b) chose the term *black box*.

Perhaps confusingly, the concept of a black box is used in two mildly conflicting ways. The first is how Black and Wiliam (1998b) use it: observing behavior only in terms of inputs and outputs by willingly overlooking the process that takes place between the two. The other way it is used refers to the flight data recorder that all aircraft need to have. Ignoring the fact that these devices tend to be yellow, these aircraft black boxes collect detailed information for later analysis. So, one type of black box overlooks anything that takes place between input and output, whereas the other records almost everything that happens in between the two!

The contrary uses of the term *black box* lend themselves well to the context of this book. On the one hand, the interaction between teachers and their students *is* what drives education. Leaders, facilities, resources, prior learning, and the community the school serves all play their role, but by far, the biggest influence on learning is what teachers and students do together.

So, rightfully, this book focuses on just that: our interactions with our students. How can we enhance their learning further still? Not through extra work or shiny new programs. Not by heaping more onto the curriculum or our workloads. But by thinking about what takes place inside the black box and deciding what we can tweak, modify, and time differently so that everyone gains. We gain, our students gain, their communities gain.

Then there is the other type of black box, the one that collects data for further analysis. I have also offered you that angle by sharing ways to determine what to prioritize and what to drop. In chapter 1 (page 1), I began with an examination of effect sizes and decision making, not because these are particularly exciting topics but because time and resources are finite. So, all decisions we make should be justifiable, not least because they each come with an equivalent decision *not* to do something else. We can't fit everything in, much as some people expect us to. So, we need to be as discerning as possible about what we choose. Our students, colleagues, and communities rely on us to do this wisely. Our colleagues do; our communities do.

Everything I've included in this book is driven by evidence. I realize that is a cliché these days. It's also rather tautologous. After all, if evidence includes gut instinct—for example, noticing a student's frown or sensing that someone doesn't understand—then isn't all teaching driven by evidence? How can it not be? The same could be said of brain-based learning. After all, what other type of learning is there other than brain-based?

I am being genuine when I say this book is driven by evidence. I have not gone looking for evidence to back up my pet theories. Instead, I have looked at the evidence first and then shown how this ought to influence our practice. Evidence first, followed by practice. Review that practice to see if it worked as expected. Compare it with the evidence. Redesign if needed and try it again. Or to put it more succinctly, use Ready-Fire-Aim (section 5.8.1, page 259).

- *Ready* is exploring the evidence and planning an approach that flows from it.
- *Fire* is trying out that idea or strategy.
- *Aim* is reviewing how successful the approach was (ordinarily in terms of boosting students' learning in some way) and planning the next steps.

So, there you go. There's my purpose for writing this book. I hope very much that you find this book useful and that it becomes a source of inspiration as well as information and helps you make whatever goes on inside the black box of *your* classroom even more effective. I'd like to finish with a story.

Many years ago, on a visit to a local castle (there are many on the border between England and Scotland), I spotted a fabulous photo opportunity. From one of the windows, I could get a clear view across the ramparts, over the beach, and out to sea to the site of the Vikings' first landing in Britain. My youngest daughter was just a baby at the time, so rather than try to compose the shot while carrying her, I popped her on the floor and asked my son to watch over her. As I prepared to take the photograph, a bright yellow air-sea rescue helicopter was flying toward the castle. In the next few seconds, it was going to be within my photo frame. I could barely contain my excitement. Thoughts of photography awards burst into my imagination. Just as I was about to press the shutter, I glanced down to check my kids were OK.

I never did capture the moment a Sea King helicopter from RAF Boulmer positioned itself perfectly between Bamburgh Castle and Holy Island. Instead, I took the photograph in figure E.1. I very nearly missed the most beautiful moment because I was planning the perfect one.

Figure E.1: It's the moments that count.

And this is where I would like to finish, by remembering that planning is important. Alignment is crucial. If we can synchronize our practice with the most credible research, then everyone is a winner. And yet, none of it matters in comparison to the humanity of teaching. It is the moments that bring meaning—the moments that sustain and lift us all.

References and Resources

Abuhamdeh, S., & Csikszentmihalyi, M. (2012). The importance of challenge for the enjoyment of intrinsically motivated, goal-directed activities. *Personality and Social Psychology Bulletin, 38*(3), 317–330.

Adam, K., & Booth, W. (2020, June 8). Britons cheer toppling of slave trader statue but are divided over tagging of Winston Churchill as racist. *The Washington Post.* Accessed at www.washingtonpost.com/world/europe/churchill-statue-racism-british-black-lives-matter-protests/2020/06/08/33f68146-a991-11ea-9063-e69bd6520940_story.html on September 1, 2023.

Alexander, K. L., Entwisle, D. R., & Bedinger, S. D. (1994). When expectations work: Race and socioeconomic differences in school performance. *Social Psychology Quarterly, 57*(4), 283–299.

Alexander, R. J. (2001). *Culture and pedagogy: International comparisons in primary education.* Oxford, England: Blackwell.

Alexander, R. J. (2017). *Towards dialogic teaching: Rethinking classroom talk* (5th ed.). York, England: Dialogos.

Alexander, R. J. (2018). Developing dialogic teaching: Genesis, process, trial. *Research Papers in Education, 33*(5), 561–598. https://doi.org/10.1080/02671522.2018.1481140

Anderson, J. (2022, April 5). Learning the right way to struggle. *The New York Times.* Accessed at www.nytimes.com/2022/04/05/science/education-learning-challenge.html on August 28, 2023.

Anderson, L. W., & Krathwohl, D. R. (Eds.). (2001). *A taxonomy for learning, teaching, and assessing: A revision of Bloom's taxonomy of educational objectives* (Complete ed.). New York: Longman.

Applebee, A. N., Langer, J. A., Nystrand, M., & Gamoran, A. (2003). Discussion-based approaches to developing understanding: Classroom instruction and student performance in middle and high school English. *American Educational Research Journal, 40*(3), 685–730.

Archambault, I., Janosz, M., Fallu, J.-S., & Pagani, L. S. (2009). Student engagement and its relationship with early high school dropout. *Journal of Adolescence, 32*(3), 651–670.

Aronson, E. (1978). *The jigsaw classroom.* Beverly Hills, CA: SAGE.

Aronson, J. (2002). Stereotype threat: Contending and coping with unnerving expectations. In J. Aronson (Ed.), *Improving academic achievement: Impact of psychological factors on education* (pp. 281–301). New York: Academic Press.

Aronson, J., Fried, C. B., & Good, C. (2002). Reducing the effects of stereotype threat on African American college students by shaping theories of intelligence. *Journal of Experimental Social Psychology, 38*(2), 113–125.

Baker, W., & Boonkit, K. (2004). Learning strategies in reading and writing: EAP contexts. *RELC Journal, 35*(3), 299–328. https://doi.org/10.1177/0033688205052143

Bandura, A. (1977). Self-efficacy: Toward a unifying theory of behavioral change. *Psychological Review, 84*(2), 191–215.

Bandura, A. (1997). *Self-efficacy: The exercise of control.* New York: Freeman.

Bandura, A. (2011). The social and policy impact of social cognitive theory. In M. M. Mark, S. I. Donaldson, & B. Campbell (Eds.), *Social psychology and evaluation* (pp. 31–71). New York: Guilford Press.

Bandura, A., Freeman, W. H., & Lightsey, R. (1999). Self-efficacy: The exercise of control. *Journal of Cognitive Psychotherapy, 13*(2), 158–166. https://doi.org/10.1891/0889-8391.13.2.158

Bangert-Drowns, R. L., Kulik, C.-L. C., Kulik, J. A., & Morgan, M. (1991). The instructional effect of feedback in test-like events. *Review of Educational Research, 61*(2), 213–238.

Barber, S. J., Rajaram, S., & Marsh, E. J. (2008). Fact learning: How information accuracy, delay, and repeated testing change retention and retrieval experience. *Memory, 16*(8), 934–946.

Barker, G. P., & Graham, S. (1987). Developmental study of praise and blame as attributional cues. *Journal of Educational Psychology, 79*(1), 62–66.

Batdı, V. (2014). A meta-analysis study comparing problem-based learning with traditional instruction. *Elektronik Sosyal Bilimler Dergisi, 13*(51), 346–364.

Beaman, R., & Wheldall, K. (2000). Teachers' use of approval and disapproval in the classroom. *Educational Psychology, 20*(4), 431–446.

Becker, B. E., & Luthar, S. S. (2002). Social-emotional factors affecting achievement outcomes among disadvantaged students: Closing the achievement gap. *Educational Psychologist, 37*(4), 197–214.

Bedard, K., & Dhuey, E. (2006). The persistence of early childhood maturity: International evidence of long-run age effects. *Quarterly Journal of Economics, 121*(4), 1437–1472.

Bennett, R. E. (2009). *A critical look at the meaning and basis of formative assessment* (Report No. RM-09-06). Princeton, NJ: Educational Testing Service.

Bergmann, J., & Sams, A. (2012). *Flip your classroom: Reach every student in every class every day.* Eugene, OR: International Society for Technology in Education.

Berry, A. (2022). *Reimagining student engagement: From disrupting to driving.* Thousand Oaks, CA: Corwin Press.

Bhanji, J. P., & Delgado, M. R. (2014). The social brain and reward: Social information processing in the human striatum. *Wiley Interdisciplinary Reviews: Cognitive Science, 5*(1), 61–73.

Biggs, J. B., & Collis, K. F. (1982). *Evaluating the quality of learning: The SOLO Taxonomy (structure of the observed learning outcome)*. New York: Academic Press.

Binet, A., & Simon, T. (1905). Application of the new methods to the diagnosis of the intellectual level among normal and subnormal children in institutions and in the primary schools. *L'Année Psychologique, 12*, 245–336.

Binet, A., & Simon, T. (1916). *The development of intelligence in children (the Binet-Simon scale)* (E. S. Kite, Trans.). Baltimore: Williams & Wilkins.

Birch, L. L., Marlin, D. W., & Rotter, J. (1984). Eating as the "means" activity in a contingency: Effects on young children's food preference. *Child Development, 55*(2), 431–439.

Bjork, R. A. (1994). Memory and metamemory considerations in the training of human beings. In J. Metcalfe & A. P. Shimamura (Eds.), *Metacognition: Knowing about knowing* (pp. 185–205). Cambridge, MA: MIT Press.

Bjork, E. L., & Bjork, R. A. (2011). Making things hard on yourself, but in a good way: Creating desirable difficulties to enhance learning. In M. A. Gernsbacher, R. W. Pew, L. M. Hough, & J. R. Pomerantz (Eds.), *Psychology and the real world: Essays illustrating fundamental contributions to society* (pp. 57–68). New York: Worth.

Black, H., & Wiliam, D. (1986). Assessment for learning. In D. Nuttall (Ed.), *Assessing educational achievement* (pp. 7–18). London: Falmer Press.

Black, P., Harrison, C., Lee, C., Marshall, B., & Wiliam, D. (2004). Working inside the black box: Assessment for learning in the classroom. *Phi Delta Kappan, 86*(1), 8–21. https://doi.org/10.1177/003172170408600105

Black, P., & Wiliam, D. (1998a). Assessment and classroom learning. *Assessment in Education: Principles, Policy & Practice, 5*(1), 7–74.

Black, P., & Wiliam, D. (1998b). *Inside the black box: Raising standards through classroom assessment*. London: GL Assessment.

Black, P., & Wiliam, D. (2002). *Inside the black box* (Updated ed.). London: GL Assessment.

Blackburn, B. (2018). Productive struggle is a learner's sweet spot. *Educational Leadership, 14*(11). Accessed at www.ascd.org/ascd-express/vol14/num11/productive-struggle-is-a-learners-sweet-spot.aspx on September 7, 2023.

Blatchford, P., & Kutnick, P. (2003). Developing group work in everyday classrooms: An introduction to the special issue. *International Journal of Educational Research, 39*(1), 1–7.

Blatchford, P., Kutnick, P., Baines, E., & Galton, M. (2003). Toward a social pedagogy of classroom group work. *International Journal of Educational Research, 39*(1–2), 153–172.

Bloom, B. S. (Ed.). (1956). *Taxonomy of educational objectives: The classification of educational goals; Handbook I: Cognitive domain*. New York: McKay.

Bloom, B. S. (1969). Some theoretical issues relating to educational evaluation. In R. W. Tyler (Ed.), *Educational evaluation: New roles, new means* (Vol. 68[2], pp. 26–50). Chicago: University of Chicago Press.

Boakye, J. (2022). *I heard what you said: A Black teacher, a White system.* London: Picador.

Boaler, J. (2022). *Limitless mind: Learn, lead, and live without barriers.* Glasgow, Scotland. Harper Collins.

Boggiano, A. K., Main, D. S., Flink, C., Barrett, M., Silvern, L., & Katz, P. A. (1989). A model of achievement in children: The role of controlling strategies in helplessness and affect. In R. Schwarzer, H. M. van der Ploeg, & C. D. Spielberger (Eds.), *Advances in test anxiety research* (Vol. 6, pp. 13–26). Amsterdam: Swets & Zeitlinger.

Booth, D., & Hachiya, M. (Eds.). (2004). *The arts go to school: Classroom-based activities that focus on music, painting, drama, movement, media, and more.* Markham, Ontario, Canada: Pembroke Publishers Limited.

Bornstein, M. H., Cote, L. R., Haynes, O. M., Hahn, C.-S., & Park, Y. (2010). Parenting knowledge: Experiential and sociodemographic factors in European American mothers of young children. *Developmental Psychology, 46*(6), 1677–1693. https://doi.org/10.1037/a0020677

Brookhart, S. M., Guskey, T. R., Bowers, A. J., McMillan, J. H., Smith, J. K., Smith, L. F., et al. (2016). A century of grading research: Meaning and value in the most common educational measure. *Review of Educational Research, 86*(4), 803–848.

Brown, P. C., Roediger, H. L., III, & McDaniel, M. A. (2014). *Make it stick: The science of successful learning.* Cambridge, MA: Harvard University Press.

Brummelman, E., Nelemans, S. A., Thomaes, S., & Orobio de Castro, B. (2017). When parents' praise inflates, children's self-esteem deflates. *Child Development, 88*(6), 1799–1809.

Bruner, J. S. (1957). On perceptual readiness. *Psychological Review, 64*(2), 123–152.

Burnette, J. L., O'Boyle, E. H., VanEpps, E. M., Pollack, J. M., & Finkel, E. J. (2013). Mind-sets matter: A meta-analytic review of implicit theories and self-regulation. *Psychological Bulletin, 139*(3), 655–701. https://doi.org/10.1037/a0029531

Butler, A. C. (2010). Repeated testing produces superior transfer of learning relative to repeated studying. *Journal of Experimental Psychology: Learning, Memory, and Cognition, 36*(5), 1118–1133.

Butler, R. (1987). Task-involving and ego-involving properties of evaluation: Effects of different feedback conditions on motivational perceptions, interest, and performance. *Journal of Educational Psychology, 79*(4), 474–482.

Cameron, W. B. (1963). *Informal sociology: A casual introduction to sociological thinking.* New York: Random House.

Campbell, T. (2013). *In-school ability grouping and the month of birth effect: Preliminary evidence from the Millennium Cohort Study.* London: Centre for Longitudinal Studies.

Carolan, T. F., Hutchins, S. D., Wickens, C. D., & Cumming, J. M. (2014). Costs and benefits of more learner freedom: Meta-analyses of exploratory and learner control training methods. *Human Factors, 56*(5), 999–1014. https://doi.org/10.1177/0018720813517710

Carpenter, S. L. (2007). *A comparison of the relationships of students' self-efficacy, goal orientation, and achievement across grade levels: A meta-analysis* [Master's thesis, Simon Fraser University]. Summit Research Repository. https://summit.sfu.ca/item/2661

Carroll, L. (1865). *Alice's adventures in Wonderland.* London: Macmillan.

Cazden, C. B. (2001). *Classroom discourse: The language of teaching and learning* (2nd ed.). Portsmouth, NH: Heinemann.

Chin, C. (2006). Classroom interaction in science: Teacher questioning and feedback to students' responses. *International Journal of Science Education, 28*(11), 1315–1346.

Çiftçi, S. K., & Yildiz, P. (2019). The effect of self-confidence on mathematics achievement: The metaanalysis of Trends in International Mathematics and Science Study (TIMSS). *International Journal of Instruction, 12*(2), 683–694.

Çikrıkci, Ö. (2017). The effect of self-efficacy on student achievement. In E. Karadağ (Ed.), *The factors effecting student achievement: Meta-analysis of empirical studies* (pp. 95–116). Cham, Switzerland: Springer International.

Claxton, G. (2002a). *Building learning power: Helping young people become better learners.* Bristol, England: TLO Limited.

Claxton, G. (2002b). Education for the learning age: A sociocultural approach to learning to learn. In G. Wells & G. Claxton (Eds.), *Learning for life in the 21st century: Sociocultural perspectives on the future of education* (pp. 21–33). Oxford, England: Blackwell.

Claxton, G. (2017) *The learning power approach: Teaching learners to teach themselves.* Carmarthen, Wales: Crown House Publishing

Clinton, J., & Dawson, G. (2018). Enfranchising the profession through evaluation: A story from Australia. *Teachers and Teaching, 24*(3), 312–327. https://doi.org/10.1080/13540602.2017.1421162

Coe, R., Aloisi, C., Higgins, S. & Major, L.E. (2014). *What makes great teaching? Review of the underpinning research.* London, England: Sutton Trust.

Coe, R. (2018a, September 5). *Serious critiques of meta-analysis and effect size: researchED 2018.* Accessed at www.cem.org/blog/serious-critiques-of-meta-analysis-and-effect-size-researched-2018 on July 13, 2023.

Coe, R. (2018b, September 6). *What should we do about meta-analysis and effect size?* [Blog post]. Accessed at www.cem.org/blog/what-should-we-do-about-meta-analysis-and-effect-size on July 13, 2023.

Çoğaltay, N., & Karadağ, E. (2017). The effect of collective teacher efficacy on student achievement. In E. Karadağ (Ed.), *The factors effecting student achievement: Meta-analysis of empirical studies* (pp. 215–226). Cham, Switzerland: Springer International.

Colman, A. M. (2015). *A dictionary of psychology* (4th ed.). Oxford, England: Oxford University Press.

Connolly, M. [@martinC_CT]. (2023, April 20). *Michelangelo's Moses includes one very small muscle in the forearm—it contracts only when lifting the pinky, otherwise it's invisible. He's lifting his pinky finger, so it shows tiny muscle is contracted. What a detail.* [Post]. X. Accessed at https://twitter.com/martinC_CT/status/1649163344262119428 on August 28, 2023.

Conoley, J. C., & Kramer, J. J. (Eds.). (1989). *The tenth mental measurements yearbook*. Lincoln, NE: University of Nebraska Press.

Cooper, H., Robinson, J. C., & Patall, E. A. (2006). Does homework improve academic achievement? A synthesis of research, 1987–2003. *Review of Educational Research, 76*(1), 1–62. https://doi.org/10.3102/00346543076001001

Corpus, J. H., & Lepper, M. R. (2007). The effects of person versus performance praise on children's motivation: Gender and age as moderating factors. *Educational Psychology, 27*(4), 487–508.

Costa, A., & Faria, L. (2018). Implicit theories of intelligence and academic achievement: A meta-analytic review. *Frontiers in Psychology, 9*, Article 829. https://doi.org/10.3389/fpsyg.2018.00829

Crawford, C., Dearden, L., & Greaves, E. (2011). *Does when you are born matter? The impact of month of birth on children's cognitive and non-cognitive skills in England*. London: Institute for Fiscal Studies.

Crooks, A. D. (1933). Marks and marking systems: A digest. *Journal of Educational Research, 27*(4), 259–272.

Csikszentmihalyi, M. (1990). *Flow: The psychology of optimal experience*. New York: Harper & Row.

Csikszentmihalyi, M. (1997). *Creativity: Flow and the psychology of discovery and invention*. New York: HarperCollins.

Das, S. (2022, August 6). Inside the violent, misogynistic world of TikTok's new star, Andrew Tate. *The Guardian*. Accessed at www.theguardian.com/technology/2022/aug/06/andrew-tate-violent-misogynistic-world-of-tiktok-new-star on August 31, 2023.

Datnow, A., & Park, V. (2018). Opening or closing doors for students? Equity and data use in schools. *Journal of Educational Change, 19*(2), 131–152. https://doi.org/10.1007/s10833-018-9323-6

de Bono, E. (1999). *Six thinking hats* (Revised ed.). New York: Back Bay Books.

DeCharms, R. (1968). *Personal causation: The internal affective determinants of behavior.* New York: Academic Press.

Deci, E. L., Connell, J. P., & Ryan, R. M. (1989). Self-determination in a work organization. *Journal of Applied Psychology, 74*(4), 580–590. https://doi.org/10.1037/0021-9010.74.4.580

Deci, E. L., Koestner, R., & Ryan, R. M. (1999). A meta-analytic review of experiments examining the effects of extrinsic rewards on intrinsic motivation. *Psychological Bulletin, 125*(6), 627–668.

Degoumois, V., Petitjean, C., & Doehler, S. P. (2017). Expressing personal opinions in classroom interactions: The role of humor and displays of uncertainty. In S. P. Doehler, A. Bangerter, G. de Weck, L. Filliettaz, E. González-Martínez, et al. (Eds.), *Interactional competences in institutional settings: From school to the workplace* (pp. 29–57). Cham, Switzerland: Palgrave Macmillan.

Deslauriers, L., McCarty, L. S., Miller, K., Callaghan, K., & Kestin, G. (2019). Measuring actual learning versus feeling of learning in response to being actively engaged in the classroom. *Proceedings of the National Academy of Sciences, 116*(39), 19251–19257.

Dewey, J. (1916). *Democracy and education: An introduction to the philosophy of education.* Toronto: Collier-Macmillan.

De Zouche, D. (1945). "The wound is mortal": Marks, honors, unsound activities. *The Clearing House: A Journal of Educational Strategies, Issues and Ideas, 19*(6), 339–344.

Doidge, N. (2007). *The brain that changes itself: Stories of personal triumph from the frontiers of brain science.* New York: Viking.

DuFour, R., DuFour, R., Eaker, R., Many, T. W., & Mattos, M. (2016). *Learning by doing: A handbook for Professional Learning Communities at Work* (3rd ed.). Bloomington, IN: Solution Tree Press.

Dunlosky, J., Rawson, K. A., Marsh, E. J., Nathan, M. J., & Willingham, D. T. (2013). Improving students' learning with effective learning techniques: Promising directions from cognitive and educational psychology. *Psychological Science in the Public Interest, 14*(1), 4–58.

Dweck, C. S. (2000). *Self-theories: Their role in motivation, personality, and development.* Philadelphia: Psychology Press.

Dweck, C. S. (2006). *Mindset: The new psychology of success.* New York: Random House.

Dweck, C. S. (2007). Is math a gift? Beliefs that put females at risk. In S. J. Ceci & W. M. Williams (Eds.), *Why aren't more women in science?: Top researchers debate the evidence* (pp. 47–55). Washington, DC: American Psychological Association.

Dweck, C. S. (2015). Carol Dweck revisits the "growth mindset." *Education Week, 35*(5), 20–24.

Dweck, C. S. (2016). Review of *Challenging Learning: Theory, Effective Practice and Lesson Ideas to Create Optimal Learning in the Classroom* (2nd ed.), by J. Nottingham. Accessed at www.learningpit.org/resources/books/#learning on September 7, 2023.

Dweck, C. S. (2017). *Mindset: The new psychology of success* (Updated ed.). New York: Random House.

Ebbinghaus, H. (1964). *Memory: A contribution to experimental psychology* (H. A. Ruger & C. E. Bussenius, Trans.). New York: Dover. (Original work published 1885)

Education Endowment Foundation. (n.d.a). *Oral language interventions*. Accessed at https://educationendowmentfoundation.org.uk/education-evidence/teaching-learning-toolkit/oral-language-interventions on August 23, 2023.

Education Endowment Foundation. (n.d.b). *Teaching and learning toolkit: An accessible summary of education evidence*. Accessed at https://educationendowmentfoundation.org.uk/education-evidence/teaching-learning-toolkit on April 6, 2023.

Education Endowment Foundation. (2017). *The attainment gap: 2017*. Accessed at www.educationandemployers.org/research/the-attainment-gap-2017 on September 7, 2023.

Eells, R. J. (2011). *Meta-analysis of the relationship between collective teacher efficacy and student achievement* [Doctoral dissertation, Loyola University Chicago]. Loyal eCommons. http://ecommons.luc.edu/luc_diss/133

Eisenberg, N. (Ed.). (2006). *Handbook of child psychology: Social, emotional, and personality development* (Vol. 3, 6th ed.). Hoboken, NJ: John Wiley & Sons.

Elliot, A. J., & Thrash, T. M. (2004). The intergenerational transmission of fear of failure. *Personality and Social Psychology Bulletin, 30*(8), 957–971.

Fasano, J. [@Joseph_Fasano_]. (2023, April 20). *What's your favorite detail of any work of art? I think the right hand of Michelangelo's David is one of the greatest things ever made* [Post]. X. Accessed at https://twitter.com/Joseph_Fasano_/status/1649143104086179840 on August 28, 2023.

Feldhusen, J. F., & Kroll, M. D. (1991). Boredom or challenge for the academically talented in school. *Gifted Education International, 7*(2), 80–81.

Feldman, D. H. (1991). *Nature's gambit: Child prodigies and the development of human potential*. New York: Teachers College Press.

Feuerstein, R., Feuerstein, R. S., Falik, L., & Rand, Y. (2006). *Creating and enhancing cognitive modifiability: The Feuerstein Instrumental Enrichment Program*. Jerusalem: ICELP.

Fleckenstein, J., Zimmermann, F., Köller, O., & Möller, J. (2015). What works in school? Expert and novice teachers' beliefs about school effectiveness. *Frontline Learning Research, 3*(2), 27–46.

Fleming, V. (Director). (1939). *Gone with the wind* [Film]. Selznick International Pictures.

Flowerday, T., & Schraw, G. (2003). Effect of choice on cognitive and affective engagement. *Journal of Educational Research, 96*(4), 207–215.

Flynn, J. R. (1987). Massive IQ gains in 14 nations: What IQ tests really measure. *Psychological Bulletin, 101*(2), 171–191.

Frawley, J. (Director). (1979). *The Muppet movie* [Film]. ITC Entertainment.

Freire, P. (2000). *Pedagogy of the oppressed* (M. B. Ramos, Trans.; 30th anniversary ed.). New York: Continuum. (Original work published 1970)

Fun Boy Three. (1982). *Fun Boy Three* [Album]. London: Chrysalis Records.

Gaines, P. (1995, January 13). How Oprah's confession tumbled out. *The Washington Post*. Accessed at www.proquest.com/historical-newspapers/how-oprahs-confession-tumbled-out/docview/903277472/se-2 on September 1, 2023.

Galton, F. (1869). *Hereditary genius: An inquiry into its laws and consequences*. London: Macmillan.

Galton, M., Hargreaves, L., Comber, C., & Wall, D. (1999). *Inside the primary classroom: 20 years on*. London: Routledge.

Gathercole, S. E., Alloway, T. P., Kirkwood, H. J., Elliott, J. G., Holmes, J., & Hilton, K. A. (2008). Attentional and executive function behaviours in children with poor working memory. *Learning and Individual Differences, 18*(2), 214–223.

Gerull, F. C., & Rapee, R. M. (2002). Mother knows best: Effects of maternal modelling on the acquisition of fear and avoidance behaviour in toddlers. *Behaviour Research and Therapy, 40*(3), 279–287.

Gibbons, P. (2002). *Scaffolding language, scaffolding learning: Teaching second language learners in the mainstream classroom*. Portsmouth, NH: Heinemann.

Gibbons, P. (2014). *Scaffolding language, scaffolding learning: Teaching English language learners in the mainstream classroom* (2nd ed.). Portsmouth, NH: Heinemann.

Good, T. L., & Brophy, J. E. (1997). *Looking in classrooms* (7th ed.). New York: Longman.

Goswami, U., & Bryant, P. (2007). *Children's cognitive development and learning* (Primary Review Research Survey 2/1a). Cambridge, England: University of Cambridge Faculty of Education.

Graham, S., Hebert, M., & Harris, K. R. (2015). Formative assessment and writing: A meta-analysis. *The Elementary School Journal, 115*(4), 523–547.

Green, J. M., & Oxford, R. (1995). A closer look at learning strategies, L2 proficiency, and gender. *TESOL Quarterly, 29*(2), 261–297. https://doi.org/10.2307/3587625

Green, M. (2016, July 3). Develop mental agility with a plunge into the Learning Pit. *Financial Times*. Accessed at www.ft.com/content/72ce62fc-3ea7-11e6-8716-a4a71e8140b0 on September 1, 2023.

Gunderson, E. A., Sorhagen, N. S., Gripshover, S. J., Dweck, C. S., Goldin-Meadow, S., & Levine, S. C. (2018). Parent praise to toddlers predicts fourth grade academic achievement via children's incremental mindsets. *Developmental Psychology, 54*(3), 397–409.

Guo, G., & Stearns, E. (2002). The social influences on the realization of genetic potential for intellectual development. *Social Forces, 80*(3), 881–910.

Guskey, T. R. (2011). Five obstacles to grading reform. *Educational Leadership, 69*(3), 16–21.

Guskey, T. R. (2015). *On your mark: Challenging the conventions of grading and reporting.* Bloomington, IN: Solution Tree Press.

Guskey, T. R., & Brookhart, S. M. (Eds.). (2019). *What we know about grading: What works, what doesn't, and what's next.* Alexandria, VA: ASCD.

Gustafsson, M. (2018, November 13). Challenging learning kommer till de svenska skolorna i Vanda—Lärare: "Jag är mycket ivrig, det nya tänkesättet aktiverar eleverna." *Svenska Yle.* Accessed at https://svenska.yle.fi/a/7-1344313 on September 1, 2023.

Haimovitz, K., & Dweck, C. S. (2016). Parents' views of failure predict children's fixed and growth intelligence mind-sets. *Psychological Science, 27*(6), 859–869. https://doi.org/10.1177/0956797616639727

Hanushek, E. A. (2011). Valuing teachers: How much is a good teacher worth? *Education Next, 11*(3), 40–45.

Hardman, F., Smith, F., & Wall, K. (2003). "Interactive whole class teaching" in the National Literacy Strategy. *Cambridge Journal of Education, 33*(2), 197–215.

Harris, F. R., Wolf, M. M., & Baer, D. M. (1967). Effects of adult social reinforcement on child behavior. In S. W. Bijou & D. M. Baer (Eds.), *Child development: Readings in experimental analysis* (pp. 146–158). New York: Appleton-Century-Crofts.

Hart, B., & Risley, T. R. (1995). *Meaningful differences in the everyday experience of young American children.* Baltimore: Brookes.

Hattie, J. A. C. (2003, October). *Teachers make a difference: What is the research evidence?* [Paper presentation]. Australian Council for Educational Research conference, Melbourne, Australia.

Hattie, J. A. C. (2009). *Visible learning: A synthesis of over 800 meta-analyses relating to achievement.* New York: Routledge.

Hattie, J. A. C. (2017). Foreword. In J. A. Nottingham, *The learning challenge: How to guide your students through the Learning Pit to achieve deeper understanding* (pp. xvii–xix). Thousand Oaks, CA: Corwin.

Hattie, J. A. C. (2023). *Visible learning: The sequel—A synthesis of over 2,100 meta-analyses relating to achievement.* New York: Routledge.

Hattie, J. A. C., & Clarke, S. (2018). *Visible learning: Feedback.* New York: Routledge.

Hattie, J. A. C., & Timperley, H. (2007). The power of feedback. *Review of Educational Research, 77*(1), 81–112.

Hawking, S. W. (1988). *A brief history of time: From the big bang to black holes.* New York: Bantam Books.

Hecht, C. A., Bryan, C. J., & Yeager, D. S. (2023). A values-aligned intervention fosters growth mindset–supportive teaching and reduces inequality in educational outcomes. *Proceedings of the National Academy of Sciences of the United States of America, 120*(25), e2210704120.

Hetland, L. (2000). Listening to music enhances spatial-temporal reasoning: Evidence for the "Mozart effect." *Journal of Aesthetic Education, 34*(3/4), 105–148. https://doi.org/10.2307/3333640

Hill, C. J., Bloom, H. S., Black, A. R., & Lipsey, M. W. (2008). Empirical benchmarks for interpreting effect sizes in research. *Child Development Perspectives, 2*(3), 172–177.

Hodges, T. (2018, October 25). *School engagement is more than just talk*. Gallup. Accessed at www.gallup.com/education/244022/school-engagement-talk.aspx on August 28, 2023.

Howe, C., & Abedin, M. (2013). Classroom dialogue: A systematic review across four decades of research. *Cambridge Journal of Education, 43*(3), 325–356. https://doi.org/10.1080/0305764X.2013.786024

Howe, C., McWilliam, D., & Cross, G. (2005). Chance favours only the prepared mind: Incubation and the delayed effects of peer collaboration. *British Journal of Psychology, 96*(1), 67–93.

Huang, C. (2016). Achievement goals and self-efficacy: A meta-analysis. *Educational Research Review, 19*(4), 119–137.

Hubbard, E. (1927). *The notebook of Elbert Hubbard: Mottoes, epigrams, short essays, orphic sayings and preachments, coined from a life of love, laughter and work*. New York: W. H. Wise.

Huelser, B. J., & Metcalfe, J. (2012). Making related errors facilitates learning, but learners do not know it. *Memory and Cognition, 40*(4), 514–527. https://doi.org/10.3758/s13421-011-0167-z

Huitt, W., & Hummel, J. (2003). Piaget's theory of cognitive development. *Educational Psychology Interactive, 3*(2), 1–5.

Jeong-Hwa, L., & Byung-Gee, B. (2019). A meta-analysis of feedback effects on academic achievement. *The Journal of Child Education, 28*(2), 39–66. https://doi.org/10.17643/kjce.2019.28.2.03

Jonsson, H., Magnusdottir, E., Eggertsson, H. P., Stefansson, O. A., Arnadottir, G. A., Eiriksson, O., et al. (2021). Differences between germline genomes of monozygotic twins. *Nature Genetics, 53*(1), 27–34. https://doi.org/10.1038/s41588-020-00755-1

Kalb, C. (2017). What makes a genius? *National Geographic, 231*(5), 30–55.

Kamins, M. L., & Dweck, C. S. (1999). Person versus process praise and criticism: Implications for contingent self-worth and coping. *Developmental Psychology, 35*(3), 835–847.

Kämpfe, J., Sedlmeier, P., & Renkewitz, F. (2011). The impact of background music on adult listeners: A meta-analysis. *Psychology of Music, 39*(4), 424–448.

Kapur, M., & Bielaczyc, K. (2012). Designing for productive failure. *Journal of the Learning Sciences, 21*(1), 45–83. https://doi.org/10.1080/10508406.2011.591717

Keller, A. S., Davidesco, I., & Tanner, K. D. (2020). Attention matters: How orchestrating attention may relate to classroom learning. *CBE Life Sciences Education, 19*(3), fe5.

Kelly, B. (2003). *Worth repeating: More than 5,000 classic and contemporary quotes.* Grand Rapids, MI: Kregel.

Kerr, R., & Booth, B. (1978). Specific and varied practice of motor skill. *Perceptual and Motor Skills, 46*(2), 395–401. https://doi.org/10.1177/003151257804600201

Kidd, C., Piantadosi, S. T., & Aslin, R. N. (2012). The Goldilocks effect: Human infants allocate attention to visual sequences that are neither too simple nor too complex. *PLoS One, 7*(5), e36399.

Kingston, N., & Nash, B. (2011). Formative assessment: A meta-analysis and a call for research. *Educational Measurement: Issues and Practice, 30*(4), 28–37.

Kirschenbaum, H., Napier, R., & Simon, S. B. (1971). *Wad-ja-get? The grading game in American education.* New York: Hart.

Klenowski, V. (2009). Assessment for learning revisited: An Asia-Pacific perspective. *Assessment in Education: Principles, Policy & Practice, 16*(3), 263–268.

Klinzing, H. G., & Klinzing-Eurich, G. (1988). Questions, responses, and reactions. In J. T. Dillon (Ed.), *Questioning and discussion: A multidisciplinary study* (pp. 212–239). Norwood, NJ: Ablex.

Kluger, A. N., & DeNisi, A. (1996). The effects of feedback interventions on performance: A historical review, a meta-analysis, and a preliminary feedback intervention theory. *Psychological Bulletin, 119*(2), 254–284.

Kornell, N., & Bjork, R. A. (2008). Learning concepts and categories: Is spacing the "enemy of induction"? *Psychological Science, 19*(6), 585–592.

Kraft, M. A. (2020). Interpreting effect sizes of education interventions. *Educational Researcher, 49*(4), 241–253.

Kulik, J. A., & Kulik, C.-L. C. (1988). Timing of feedback and verbal learning. *Review of Educational Research, 58*(1), 79–97.

Kyriacou, C., & Issitt, J. (2008). *What characterises effective teacher-initiated teacher-pupil dialogue to promote conceptual understanding in mathematics lessons in England in Key Stages 2 and 3: A systematic review* (Report No. 1604R). London: EPPI-Centre.

Landers, R. N., & Reddock, C. M. (2017). A meta-analytic investigation of objective learner control in web-based instruction. *Journal of Business and Psychology, 32*(4), 455–478. https://doi.org/10.1007/s10869-016-9452-y

The Learning Pit. (n.d.). *John Hattie interviews.* Accessed at www.learningpit.org/John-Hattie on July 13, 2023.

Leslie, M. (2000, July/August). The vexing legacy of Lewis Terman. *Stanford Magazine.* Accessed at https://stanfordmag.org/contents/the-vexing-legacy-of-lewis-terman on July 26, 2023.

Levin, T., & Long, R. (1981). *Effective instruction.* Alexandria, VA: ASCD.

Lewin, K. (1952). Group decision and social change. In G. E. Swanson, T. M. Newcomb, & E. L. Hartley (Eds.), *Readings in social psychology* (pp. 459–473). New York: Holt.

Li, Y., & Bates, T. (2018). *Do parents' and teachers' failure mindsets influence children's intelligence mindset?* Accessed at www.research.ed.ac.uk/en/publications/do-parents-and-teachers-failure-mindsets-influence-childrens-inte on July 27, 2023.

Lib Quotes. (n.d.). *Nelson Mandela quotes.* Accessed at https://libquotes.com/nelson-mandela/quote/lbl8m7d on September 1, 2023.

Lipman, M. (1987). Critical thinking: What can it be? *Analytic Teaching, 8*(1), 5–12.

Lo, C. O., & Porath, M. (2017). Paradigm shifts in gifted education: An examination vis-à-vis its historical situatedness and pedagogical sensibilities. *Gifted Child Quarterly, 61*(4), 343–360.

Lyle, S. (2008). Dialogic teaching: Discussing theoretical contexts and reviewing evidence from classroom practice. *Language and Education, 22*(3), 222–240. https://doi.org/10.1080/09500780802152499

Lysakowski, R. S., & Walberg, H. J. (1981). Classroom reinforcement and learning: A quantitative synthesis. *Journal of Educational Research, 75*(2), 69–77. https://doi.org/10.1080/00220671.1981.10885359

Lysakowski, R. S., & Walberg, H. J. (1982). Instructional effects of cues, participation, and corrective feedback: A quantitative synthesis. *American Educational Research Journal, 19*(4), 559–578.

Madsen, C. H., Jr., Becker, W. C., & Thomas, D. R. (1968). Rules, praise, and ignoring: Elements of elementary classroom control. *Journal of Applied Behavior Analysis, 1*(2), 139–150.

Maguire, E. A., Gadian, D. G., Johnsrude, I. S., Good, C. D., Ashburner, J., Frackowiak, R. S. J., et al. (2000). Navigation-related structural change in the hippocampi of taxi drivers. *Proceedings of the National Academy of Sciences, 97*(8), 4398–4403.

Mandigo, J. L., & Holt, N. L. (2006). Elementary students' accounts of optimal challenge in physical education. *Physical Educator, 63*(4), 170–183.

Marsh, H. W., Dicke, T., & Pfeiffer, M. (2019). A tale of two quests: The (almost) non-overlapping research literatures on students' evaluations of secondary-school and university teachers. *Contemporary Educational Psychology, 58*, 1–18. https://doi.org/10.1016/j.cedpsych.2019.01.011

Marsh, R. J., Cumming, T. M., Randolph, J. J., & Michaels, S. (2021). Updated meta-analysis of the research on response cards. *Journal of Behavioral Education*, 1–24. https://doi.org/10.1007/s10864-021-09463-0

Maslow, A. H. (1968). *Toward a psychology of being* (2nd ed.). New York: Van Nostrand Reinhold.

Mason, L. (2007). Introduction: Bridging the cognitive and sociocultural approaches in research on conceptual change—Is it feasible? *Educational Psychologist, 42*(1), 1–7.

Mayer, R. E., Bove, W., Bryman, A., Mars, R., & Tapangco, L. (1996). When less is more: Meaningful learning from visual and verbal summaries of science textbook lessons. *Journal of Educational Psychology, 88*(1), 64–73.

McGuinness, C. (1999). *From thinking skills to thinking classrooms: A review and evaluation of approaches for developing pupils' thinking* (Research Report No. 115). London: Department for Education and Employment.

Meaney, M. J. (2004). The nature of nurture: Maternal effects and chromatin remodeling. In J. T. Cacioppo & G. G. Berntson (Eds.), *Essays in social neuroscience* (pp. 1–14). Cambridge, MA: MIT Press.

Mehan, H. (1979). *Learning lessons: Social organization in the classroom.* Cambridge, MA: Harvard University Press.

Mercer, N. (1995). *The guided construction of knowledge: Talk amongst teachers and learners.* Clevedon, England: Multilingual Matters.

Mercer, N. (2000). *Words and minds: How we use language to think together.* New York: Routledge.

Mercer, N., & Hodgkinson, S. (Eds.). (2008). *Exploring talk in schools: Inspired by the work of Douglas Barnes.* London: SAGE.

Mercer, N., & Howe, C. (2012). Explaining the dialogic processes of teaching and learning: The value and potential of sociocultural theory. *Learning, Culture and Social Interaction, 1*(1), 12–21. https://doi.org/10.1016/J.LCSI.2012.03.001

Mercer, N., & Littleton, K. (2007). *Dialogue and the development of children's thinking: A sociocultural approach.* London: Routledge.

Mercer, N., & Wegerif, R. (2002). Is "exploratory talk" productive talk? In K. Littleton & P. Light (Eds.), *Learning with computers* (pp. 93–115). New York: Routledge.

Merzenich, M. (2013). *Soft-wired: How the new science of brain plasticity can change your life* (2nd ed.). San Francisco: Parnassus.

Merzenich, M., Tallal, P., Peterson, B., Miller, S., & Jenkins, W. M. (1999). Some neurological principles relevant to the origins of—and the cortical plasticity-based remediation of—developmental language impairments. In J. Grafman & Y. Christen (Eds.), *Neuronal plasticity: Building a bridge from the laboratory to the clinic* (pp. 169–187). Berlin, Germany: Springer-Verlag.

Meyer, W.-U. (1992). Paradoxical effects of praise and criticism on perceived ability. *European Review of Social Psychology, 3*(1), 259–283.

Miskin, R. (2006). *Read Write Inc. phonics handbook 1.* Oxford, England: Oxford University Press.

Montessori, M. (1967). *The absorbent mind* (C. A. Claremont, Trans.). New York: Holt.

Moon, C. E., Render, G. F., & Pendley, D. W. (1985). *Relaxation and educational outcomes: A meta-analysis* [Conference paper presentation]. Annual meeting of the American Educational Research Association, Chicago. Accessed at https://files.eric.ed.gov/fulltext/ED263501.pdf on July 26, 2023.

Mueller, C. M., & Dweck, C. S. (1998). Praise for intelligence can undermine children's motivation and performance. *Journal of Personality and Social Psychology, 75*(1), 33–52.

Murphy, P. K., Wilkinson, I. A. G., Soter, A. O., Hennessey, M. N., & Alexander, J. F. (2009). Examining the effects of classroom discussion on students' comprehension of text: A meta-analysis. *Journal of Educational Psychology, 101*(3), 740–764.

Nakamura, J., & Csikszentmihalyi, M. (2002). The concept of flow. In C. R. Snyder & S. J. Lopez (Eds.), *Handbook of positive psychology* (pp. 89–105). Oxford, England: Oxford University Press.

Newell, A. (1994). *Unified theories of cognition.* Cambridge, MA: Harvard University Press.

Newton, P., Driver, R., & Osborne, J. (1999). The place of argumentation in the pedagogy of school science. *International Journal of Science Education, 21*(5), 553–576.

Norris, B. D. (2018). *The relationship between collective teacher efficacy and school-level reading and mathematics achievement: A meta-regression using robust variance estimation* (Publication No. 10817564) [Doctoral dissertation, State University of New York at Buffalo]. ProQuest Dissertations & Theses Global. Accessed at www.proquest.com/dissertations-theses/relationship-between-collective-teacher-efficacy/docview/2124052293/se-2 on August 31, 2023.

Nottingham, J. A. (1996). *Children's attitudes towards Africa and Africans: A study of the implications for primary school geography* [Unpublished dissertation]. Lancaster University.

Nottingham, J. A. (2007). Exploring the Learning Pit. *Teaching Thinking and Creativity, 8:2*(23), 64–68.

Nottingham, J. A. (2010). *Challenging learning.* Berwick-upon-Tweed, England: JN.

Nottingham, J. A. (2016). *Challenging learning: Theory, effective practice and lesson ideas to create optimal learning in the classroom* (2nd ed.). New York: Routledge.

Nottingham, J. A. (2017). *The learning challenge: How to guide your students through the Learning Pit to achieve deeper understanding.* Thousand Oaks, CA: Corwin.

Nottingham, J. A. (2020). *The learning pit.* Berwick-upon-Tweed, England: JN

Nottingham, J. A., & Larsson, B. (2018). *Challenging mindset: Why a growth mindset makes a difference in learning—and what to do when it doesn't.* Thousand Oaks, CA: Corwin Press.

Nottingham, J., & Nottingham, J. A. (2018). *Learning challenge lessons, elementary: 20 lessons to guide young learners through the Learning Pit.* Thousand Oaks, CA: Corwin.

Nottingham, J., Nottingham, J. A., & Bollom, M. (2019) *Learning challenge lessons, secondary English language arts: 20 lessons to guide students through the Learning Pit.* Thousand Oaks, CA: Corwin.

Nuthall, G. (2002). The cultural myths and the realities of teaching and learning. *New Zealand Annual Review of Education, 11,* 5–30.

Nuthall, G. (2007). *The hidden lives of learners.* Wellington, New Zealand: NZCER Press.

Nystrand, M. (1997). *Opening dialogue: Understanding the dynamics of language and learning in the English classroom.* New York: Teachers College Press.

Oakes, J. (2005). *Keeping track: How schools structure inequality* (2nd ed.). New Haven, CT: Yale University Press.

Oakes, J., & Lipton, M. (1990). Tracking and ability grouping: A structural barrier to access and achievement. In J. I. Goodlad & P. Keating (Eds.), *Access to knowledge: An agenda for our nation's schools* (pp. 187–204). New York: College Entrance Examination Board.

O'Leary, K. D., & O'Leary, S. G. (1977). *Classroom management: The successful use of behavior modification* (2nd ed.). New York: Pergamon Press.

Organisation for Economic Co-operation and Development. (2012). *Equity and quality in education: Supporting disadvantaged students and schools*. Paris: Author.

Organisation for Economic Co-operation and Development. (2019). *PISA 2018 results (volume III): What school life means for students' lives*. Paris: PISA.

Orwell, G. (1945). *Animal farm*. London: Secker & Warburg.

Overskeid, G., & Svartdal, F. (1996). Effect of reward on subjective autonomy and interest when initial interest is low. *Psychological Record, 46*(2), 319–331.

Ozyildirim, G. (2022). Time spent on homework and academic achievement: A meta-analysis study related to results of TIMSS. *Psicología Educativa: Revista de los Psicólogos de la Educación, 28*(1), 13–21.

Park, D. C., Lodi-Smith, J., Drew, L., Haber, S., Hebrank, A., Bischof, G. N., et al. (2013). The impact of sustained engagement on cognitive function in older adults: The Synapse Project. *Psychological Science, 25*(1), 103–112.

Parker, L. E., & Lepper, M. R. (1992). Effects of fantasy contexts on children's learning and motivation: Making learning more fun. *Journal of Personality and Social Psychology, 62*(4), 625–633.

Patall, E. A., Cooper, H., & Robinson, J. C. (2008). The effects of choice on intrinsic motivation and related outcomes: A meta-analysis of research findings. *Psychological Bulletin, 134*(2), 270–300.

Phelps, R. P. (2012). The effect of testing on student achievement, 1910–2010. *International Journal of Testing, 12*(1), 21–43.

Pietschnig, J., & Voracek, M. (2015). One century of global IQ gains: A formal meta-analysis of the Flynn effect (1909–2013). *Perspectives on Psychological Science, 10*(3), 282–306.

Pittman, L. D., & Richmond, A. (2007). Academic and psychological functioning in late adolescence: The importance of school belonging. *Journal of Experimental Education, 75*(4), 270–290.

Pomerantz, E. M., & Kempner, S. G. (2013). Mothers' daily person and process praise: Implications for children's theory of intelligence and motivation. *Developmental Psychology, 49*(11), 2040–2046. https://doi.org/10.1037/a0031840

Premier League. 2021. *Premier League players commit to take the knee*. Accessed at www.premierleague.com/news/2204948 on September 27, 2023.

Pressel, D. M. (2003). Nuremberg and Tuskegee: Lessons for contemporary American medicine. *Journal of the National Medical Association, 95*(12), 1216–1225.

Puzio, K., & Colby, G. (2010). *The effects of within class grouping on reading achievement: A meta-analytic synthesis.* Evanston, IL: Society for Research on Educational Effectiveness.

Redfield, D. L., & Rousseau, E. W. (1981). A meta-analysis of experimental research on teacher questioning behavior. *Review of Educational Research, 51*(2), 237–245.

Reeve, J., Nix, G., & Hamm, D. (2003). Testing models of the experience of self-determination in intrinsic motivation and the conundrum of choice. *Journal of Educational Psychology, 95*(2), 375–392.

Rege, M., Hanselman, P., Solli, I. F., Dweck, C. S., Ludvigsen, S., Bettinger, E., et al. (2021). How can we inspire nations of learners? An investigation of growth mindset and challenge-seeking in two countries. *American Psychologist, 76*(5), 755–767.

Risch, N. J. (2002). Searching for genetic determinants in the new millennium. *Nature, 405*(6788), 847–856.

Ritchhart, R. (2023). *Cultures of thinking in action: 10 mindsets to transform our teaching and students' learning.* Hoboken, NJ: Jossey-Bass.

Roediger, H. L., III, Agarwal, P. K., McDaniel, M. A., & McDermott, K. B. (2011). Test-enhanced learning in the classroom: Long-term improvements from quizzing. *Journal of Experimental Psychology: Applied, 17*(4), 382–395.

Rohrer, D., Dedrick, R. F., & Stershic, S. (2015). Interleaved practice improves mathematics learning. *Journal of Educational Psychology, 107*(3), 900–908.

Rohrer, D., & Taylor, K. (2007). The shuffling of mathematics problems improves learning. *Instructional Science, 35*(6), 481–498. https://doi.org/10.1007/s11251-007-9015-8

Rosenshine, B. (2012). Principles of instruction: Research-based principles that all teachers should know. *American Educator, 36*(1), 12–19, 39.

Rothbart, M. K., & Bates, J. E. (2006). In N. Eisenberg (Ed.), *Handbook of child psychology: Social, emotional, and personality development* (Vol. 3, 6th ed., pp. 99–166). Hoboken, NJ: John Wiley & Sons.

Rothstein, D., & Santana, L. (2011). *Make just one change: Teach students to ask their own questions.* Cambridge, MA: Harvard Education Press.

Rowe, M. B. (1986). Wait time: Slowing down may be a way of speeding up! *Journal of Teacher Education, 37*(1), 43–50.

Rubie-Davies, C. M. (2006). Teacher expectations and student self-perceptions: Exploring relationships. *Psychology in the Schools, 43*(5), 537–552. https://doi.org/10.1002/pits.20169

Russell, B. (1985). *On education.* London: Routledge.

Sabarwal, S., Abu-Jawdeh, M., & Kapoor, R. (2022). Teacher beliefs: Why they matter and what they are. *World Bank Research Observer, 37*(1), 73–106.

Samson, G. E., Strykowski, B., Weinstein, T., & Walberg, H. J. (1987). The effects of teacher questioning levels on student achievement: A quantitative synthesis. *Journal of Educational Research, 80*(5), 290–295.

Schimmer, T. (2016). *Grading from the inside out: Bringing accuracy to student assessment through a standards-based mindset.* Bloomington, IN: Solution Tree Press.

Scriven, M. (1967). The methodology of evaluation. In R. W. Tyler, R. M. Gagne, & M. Scriven (Eds.), *Perspectives of curriculum evaluation* (pp. 39–83). Chicago: Rand McNally.

Shea, J. B., & Morgan, R. L. (1979). Contextual interference effects on the acquisition, retention, and transfer of a motor skill. *Journal of Experimental Psychology: Human Learning and Memory, 5*(2), 179–187.

Shernoff, D. J., Csikszentmihalyi, M., Shneider, B., & Shernoff, E. S. (2003). Student engagement in high school classrooms from the perspective of flow theory. *School Psychology Quarterly, 18*(2), 158–176.

Siegler, R. S. (1992). The other Alfred Binet. *Developmental Psychology, 28*(2), 179–190.

Sinek, S. (2009a, September). *How great leaders inspire action* [Video file]. TEDxPuget Sound. Accessed at www.ted.com/talks/simon_sinek_how_great_leaders_inspire_action?language=en on August 28, 2023.

Sinek, S. (2009b). *Start with why: How great leaders inspire everyone to take action.* New York: Portfolio.

Sirotnik, K. A. (1983). What you see is what you get: Consistency, persistency, and mediocrity in classrooms. *Harvard Educational Review, 53*(1), 16–31.

Sisk, V. F., Burgoyne, A. P., Sun, J., Butler, J. L., & Macnamara, B. N. (2018). To what extent and under which circumstances are growth mind-sets important to academic achievement? Two meta-analyses. *Psychological Science, 29*(4), 549–571. https://doi.org/10.1177/0956797617739704

Skinner, B. F. (1948). *Walden Two.* New York: Macmillan.

Smiley, P. A., Buttitta, K. V., Chung, S. Y., Dubon, V. X., & Chang, L. K. (2016). Mediation models of implicit theories and achievement goals predict planning and withdrawal after failure. *Motivation and Emotion, 40*(6), 878–894.

Smith, F., Hardman, F., Wall, K., & Mroz, M. (2004). Interactive whole class teaching in the national literacy and numeracy strategies. *British Educational Research Journal, 30*(3), 395–411.

Snow, C. E. (2014). Input to interaction to instruction: Three key shifts in the history of child language research. *Journal of Child Language, 41*(S1), 117–123. https://doi.org/10.1017/S0305000914000294

Stahl, R. J. (1994). *Using "think-time" and "wait-time" skillfully in the classroom.* (ED370885). ERIC. Accessed at https://files.eric.ed.gov/fulltext/ED370885.pdf on July 27, 2023.

Stanford Center on Poverty and Inequality. (n.d.). *Aristotle quote.* Accessed at https://inequality.stanford.edu/publications/quote/aristotle-0 on August 28, 2023.

Steenbergen-Hu, S., Makel, M. C., & Olszewski-Kubilius, P. (2016). What one hundred years of research says about the effects of ability grouping and acceleration on K–12 students' academic achievement: Findings of two second-order meta-analyses. *Review of Educational Research, 86*(4), 849–899. https://doi.org/10.3102/0034654316675417

Stevens, R. (1912). *The question as a measure of efficiency in instruction: A critical study of classroom practice.* New York: Teachers College, Columbia University.

Stiggins, R. (2005). From formative assessment to assessment for learning: A path to success in standards-based schools. *Phi Delta Kappan, 87*(4), 324–328.

Stipek, D. (2010). *How do teachers' expectations affect student learning.* Washington, D.C. Accessed at www.education.com/reference/article/teachers-expectations-affect-learning on October 1, 2014.

Sullivan, J. [@Webwight]. (2023, April 21). *I used to live in Paris and one of the things I always marveled at was the carving on the Victory of Samothrace. It's amazing to make marble into something that looks like ripples of gauze over a beautiful body* [Post]. X. Accessed at https://twitter.com/Webwight/status/1649337451431837696?s=20 on August 23, 2023.

Sweller, J. (1988). Cognitive load during problem solving: Effects on learning. *Cognitive Science, 12*(2), 257–285.

Sykes, E. D. A., Bell, J. F., & Rodeiro, C. V. (2009). *Birthdate effects: A review of the literature from 1990–on.* Cambridge, England: University of Cambridge Local Examinations Syndicate. Accessed at https://www.cambridgeassessment.org.uk/Images/109784-birthdate-effects-a-review-of-the-literature-from-1990-on.pdf on June 15, 2023.

Tan, X., & Michel, R. (2011). Why do standardized testing programs report scaled scores? *R & D Connections, 16*, 1–6. Accessed at www.ets.org/Media/Research/pdf/RD_Connections16.pdf on September 1, 2023.

Terman, L. M. (1916). The uses of intelligence tests. In L. M. Terman, *The measurement of intelligence* (pp. 3–21). Boston: Houghton Mifflin.

Tienken, C. H., Goldberg, S., & Dirocco, D. (2009). Questioning the questions. *Kappa Delta Pi Record, 46*(1), 39–43.

Tobin, K. (1987). The role of wait time in higher cognitive level learning. *Review of Educational Research, 57*(1), 69–95.

Tolkien, J. R. R. (1954). *The fellowship of the ring.* London: George Allen & Unwin.

Toth, M. D. (2021, March 17). *Why student engagement is important in a post-COVID world—and 5 strategies to improve it* [Blog post]. Accessed at www.learningsciences.com/blog/why-is-student-engagement-important on July 27, 2023.

Trahan, L. H., Stuebing, K. K., Fletcher, J. M., & Hiscock, M. (2014). The Flynn effect: A meta-analysis. *Psychological Bulletin, 140*(5), 1332–1360.

Trautwein, U. (2007). The homework–achievement relation reconsidered: Differentiating homework time, homework frequency, and homework effort. *Learning and Instruction, 17*(3), 372–388.

Tūrangawaewae. (2007). In *Te Ara—the encyclopedia of New Zealand*. Accessed at www.TeAra.govt.nz/en/papatuanuku-the-land/page-5 on September 7, 2023.

Visible Learning Meta[x]. (n.d.). Accessed at www.visiblelearningmetax.com on July 13, 2023.

Vygotsky, L. S. (1962). *Thought and language*. Cambridge, MA: MIT Press.

Vygotsky, L. S. (1978). *Mind in society: The development of higher psychological processes*. Cambridge, MA: Harvard University Press.

Wang, S., Rubie-Davies, C. M., & Meissel, K. (2018). A systematic review of the teacher expectation literature over the past 30 years. *Educational Research and Evaluation*, *24*(3–5), 124–179. https://doi.org/10.1080/13803611.2018.1548798

Wegerif, R. (2013). *Dialogic: Education for the internet age*. London: Routledge.

Wegerif, R. (2015). Toward dialogic literacy education for the internet age. *Literacy Research: Theory, Method, and Practice*, *64*(1), 56–72.

Wegerif, R., Littleton, K., Dawes, L., Mercer, N., & Rowe, D. (2004). Widening access to educational opportunities through teaching children how to reason together. *Westminster Studies in Education*, *27*(2), 143–156.

Wegerif, R., Mercer, N., & Dawes, L. (1999). From social interaction to individual reasoning: An empirical investigation of a possible sociocultural model of cognitive development. *Learning and Instruction*, *9*(6), 493–516.

Wegerif, R., & Scrimshaw, P. (Eds.). (1997). *Computers and talk in the primary classroom*. Philadelphia: Multilingual Matters.

Wells, G. (2000). Dialogic inquiry: Towards a sociocultural practice and theory of education. *Harvard Educational Review*, *70*(2), 228–230.

White, S. H. (2000). Conceptual foundations of IQ testing. *Psychology, Public Policy, and Law*, *6*(1), 33–43. https://doi.org/10.1037/1076-8971.6.1.33

Whyte, L. (2016, February 17). *Active learning: Preparing students for the future* [Blog post]. Accessed at https://blog.cambridgeinternational.org/active-learning-preparing-students-for-the-future on September 1, 2023.

Wiliam, D. (2011). What is assessment for learning? *Studies in Educational Evaluation*, *37*(1), 3–14.

Wiliam, D. (2014). The right questions, the right way. *Educational Leadership*, *71*(6). Accessed at www.ascd.org/el/articles/the-right-questions-the-right-way on August 18, 2023.

Wiliam, D. [@dylanwiliam]. (2017, January 26). *I've come to the conclusion Sweller's Cognitive Load Theory is the single most important thing for teachers to know http://bit.ly/2kouLOq* [Post]. X. Accessed at https://twitter.com/dylanwiliam/status/824682504602943489 on January 26, 2017.

Wiliam, D [@dylanwiliam]. (2020, May 7). *I think we have to distinguish between small, well-established effects (e.g., growth mindset) and those for which there is no reliable evidence (Brain Gym, learning styles)* [Post]. X. Accessed at https://twitter.com/dylanwiliam/status/824682504602943489?s=20 on September 7, 2023.

Williamson, L. & Wright, G. (2023). Andrew Tate charged with rape and human trafficking. Accessed at https://www.bbc.com/news/world-europe-65959097 on December 4, 2023.

Willingham, D. T. (2009). Why don't students like school? Because the mind is not designed for thinking. *American Educator, 33*(1), 4–13. Accessed at www.aft.org/sites/default/files/WILLINGHAM%282%29.pdf on August 18, 2023.

Willingham, D. T. (2021a). Ask the cognitive scientist: Does developing a growth mindset help students learn? *American Educator, Winter 2022–2023*. Accessed at www.aft.org/ae/winter2022-2023/willingham on December 19, 2022.

Willingham, D. T. (2021b). Ask the cognitive scientist: Why do students remember everything that's on television and forget everything I say? *American Educator, Summer 2021*. Accessed at https://www.aft.org/ae/summer2021/Willingham on August 18, 2023.

Willms, J. D. (2003). *Student engagement at school: A sense of belonging and participation—Results from PISA 2000*. Paris: Organisation for Economic Co-operation and Development.

Wilson, R. C., Shenhav, A., Straccia, M., & Cohen, J. D. (2019). The eighty five percent rule for optimal learning. *Nature Communications, 10*(1), 4646.

Winterton, W. A. (1977). The effect of extended wait-time on selected verbal response characteristics on some Pueblo Indian children. *Dissertation Abstracts International Section A: Humanities and Social Sciences, 38*(2-A), 620.

Wolf, M. K., Crosson, A. C., & Resnick, L. B. (2005). Classroom talk for rigorous reading comprehension instruction. *Reading Psychology, 26*(1), 27–53. https://doi.org/10.1080/02702710490897518

Wolfe, S., & Alexander, R. J. (2008). *Argumentation and dialogic teaching: Alternative pedagogies for a changing world*. London: FutureLab.

Wood, D., Bruner, J. S., & Ross, G. (1976). The role of tutoring in problem solving. *Journal of Child Psychology and Psychiatry, 17*(2), 89–100.

Woolley, M. E., Strutchens, M. E., Gilbert, M. C., & Martin, W. G. (2010). Mathematics success of Black middle school students: Direct and indirect effects of teacher expectations and reform practices. *Negro Educational Review, 61*(1–4), 41–59.

Yair, G. (2000). Educational battlefields in America: The tug-of-war over students' engagement with instruction. *Sociology of Education, 73*(4), 247–269.

Yang, Z., & Brindley, S. (2023). Engaging students in dialogic interactions through questioning. *ELT Journal, 77*(2), 217–226.

Yeager, D. S., & Dweck, C. S. (2020). What can be learned from growth mindset controversies? *American Psychologist, 75*(9), 1269–1284.

Yeager, D. S., Hanselman, P., Walton, G. M., Murray, J. S., Crosnoe, R., Muller, C., et al. (2019). A national experiment reveals where a growth mindset improves achievement. *Nature, 573*(7774), 364–369.

Yeager, D. S., Walton, G. M., Brady, S. T., Akcinar, E. N., Paunesku, D., Keane, L., et al. (2016). Teaching a lay theory before college narrows achievement gaps at scale. *Proceedings of the National Academy of Sciences, 113*(24), E3341–E3348.

Youde, J. J. (2019). *A meta-analysis of the effects of reflective self-assessment on academic achievement in primary and secondary populations* [Doctoral dissertation, Seattle Pacific University]. Digital Commons @ SPU. https://digitalcommons.spu.edu/soe_etd/48

Yousafzai, M. (2013, July 12). *16th birthday speech at the United Nations.* Accessed at https://malala.org/newsroom/malala-un-speech on August 28, 2023.

Zepeda, C. D., Martin, R. S., & Butler, A. C. (2020). Motivational strategies to engage learners in desirable difficulties. *Journal of Applied Research in Memory and Cognition, 9*(4), 468–474. https://doi.org/10.1016/j.jarmac.2020.08.007

Zhan, L., Guo, D., Chen, G., & Yang, J. (2018). Effects of repetition learning on associative recognition over time: Role of the hippocampus and prefrontal cortex. *Frontiers in Human Neuroscience, 12*, 277.

Zhang, L. J., Gu, P. Y., & Hu, G. (2008). A cognitive perspective on Singaporean primary school pupils' use of reading strategies in learning to read in English. *British Journal of Educational Psychology, 78*(2), 245–271. https://doi.org/10.1348/000709907X218179

Zimmerman, B. J., Bandura, A., & Martinez-Pons, M. (1992). Self-motivation for academic attainment: The role of self-efficacy beliefs and personal goal setting. *American Educational Research Journal, 29*(3), 663–676.

Index

NUMBERS

80/20 principle
    and challenge, 145–146
    and expectations, 216
    and grouping, 249
    in the Learning Pit, 122
    and setting appropriately challenging goals, 106–108

A

ability and genetics, 220–222
ability grouping, 247, 249, 250. See also grouping
abstract concepts, 126. See also concepts
achievement
    definition of achievers, 218
    relationship between growth mindset and, 236–237
    use of term, 217–218
    wait time and questioning and, 40
advice, feedback's essential qualities, 151–156
agreement and dialogue, 87
Alice's Adventures in Wonderland (Carroll), 130
alternative assessment methods, 150, 190. See also assessments
Angelou, M., 147, 216
Animal Farm (Orwell), 130
annotating books, 243. See also progress
antiracism workshop, 284–286
Aristotle, 83
art
    amplifying progress and, 241–242
    example descriptors for increasing depth of learning, 169
    example success criteria, 173
ASK (attitudes, skills, and knowledge) model
    about, 161–163
    ASK model: attitudes, 163–164
    ASK model: knowledge, 165
    ASK model: skills, 164–165
    example of, 162
    learning intentions and, 179, 203–204
    progress and, 243, 247
assessment for learning, 187–188
assessments. See also tests/testing
    alternative assessment methods, 150, 190
    effect size of, 150
    example progress made between assessments, 224, 225
    example scores achieved by six fictitious students, 223
    peer assessment, 150, 179–185, 193
    self-assessment, 150, 180, 191, 195
at-risk students
    accuracy of effect size and, 8
    expectations and, 216
    growth mindset and, 237, 280, 281
    how-to guides, use of, 274
    reducing cognitive overload, 294
    thinking time/wait time and, 38, 40, 283, 293
    use of term, 271
    worked examples and, 192
attainers, definition of, 218
attainment, use of term, 217–218
attention
    distractions and, 27–28
    engagement and, 22–23
    paying attention to your what, 3–5
    schemas and, 288
authentic questions, 41, 42. See also questioning

B

background music, 10, 13
beating personal bests and amplifying progress, 243. See also progress
beginning, middle, end and amplifying progress, 242. See also progress
beliefs, influence on teaching and learning, 6
Bergmann, J., 273
bias, 8
Binet, A., 228, 230
Binet-Simon test, 227–228, 229
Bjork, E., 44
Bjork, R., 44
Black, P., xi–xii, 194–195
black box, xi–xii, 3, 15, 299–300
Black Lives Matter, 285
Bloom's taxonomy, 35, 36, 161, 176
Boggiano, A., 256

C

Carroll, L., 130
challenge
- about, 91
- being in the habit and, 98
- blueprint for, 91–93
- challenge summary, 145
- desirable difficulties and, 102–106
- expectations and, 100–102
- four pillars of, 96
- giving students control over their learning, 109–113
- goals, setting appropriately challenging, 106–108
- Learning Pit, creating challenge with the, 124–144
- Learning Pit, understanding challenge and the, 113–123
- learning what research says about, 98–99
- making challenge interesting, 111–113
- making challenge more desirable, 95–98
- mindset and, 234–235
- QR codes for, 95
- teach brilliantly top ten: challenge, 145–146
- understanding that without challenge, there is no learning, 93–95
- what gets in the way of, 94–95
- why challenge is important, 93–94

cheating, 80, 207
checks for understanding, 45, 46
choice
- effect size of, 7, 109
- giving students control over their learning, 109–113
- reasons students give for the choices they make, 110
- rewards and, 255–256

chunking, 103
classifying. See strategies to help students sort and classify
classroom discussions, 150, 190. See also dialogue/dialogic teaching; feedback
closed questions, 35. See also questioning
Coe, R., 17
cognitive conflict. See also conflict
- creating through questioning, 131–132
- creating with wobblers, 133–137
- examples of, 130
- features of, 130–131
- Learning Pit and, 129
- types of, 131

cognitive dissonance, 137
cognitive load theory
- about, 287–290
- and cognitive overload, 291–292, 294
- and worked examples, 192

Cohen's d, 15, 281. See also effect size
cold calling, 43
collective efficacy. See also efficacy and expectations; self-efficacy
- about, 266–267
- effect size of, 257
- growth mindset and, 215

comments versus grades, 150, 194–195. See also grades
concepts
- abstract and concrete concepts, 126
- categories of knowledge, 165
- concept lines, 76–77, 140
- concept tables, 78–79
- concept targets, 77–78, 140
- example of concepts for elementary school students, 128
- example of literature and language concepts, 128
- facts or concepts, 127, 129
- in the Learning Pit, 124, 126–129
- and questions to encourage metacognition, 143
- using strategies to help students think about concepts, 76–79

concise writing and cognitive overload, 292
confidence, 39
conflict. See also cognitive conflict
- in the Learning Pit, 124, 129–137
- and questions to encourage metacognition, 143–144

connections. See strategies to help students make connections
consideration/consider
- in the Learning Pit, 124, 142–143
- and questions to encourage metacognition, 144

construction/construct
- construction by being open to other interpretations, 141
- construction by distinguishing differences, 139–140
- construction by refining definitions, 140
- construction by significance, 139
- construction of better answers, 138–139
- eureka experience, 142
- in the Learning Pit, 124, 137–142
- and questions to encourage metacognition, 144
- and way to deal with wrong answers, 137–138

control
- giving students control over their learning, 109–113
- and learning what research says about challenge, 99

cost-benefit analysis, 8

creative thinking, 36
critical thinking, 36, 50, 53, 88, 89
Csikszentmihalyi, M., 108
cumulative talk, 52–53. See also dialogue/dialogic teaching

D

deep learning, 57. See also SOLO Taxonomy (Structure of the Observed Learning Outcome)
deliberate mistakes, 178. See also mistakes and failures
desirable difficulty
    about, 99, 102
    creating desirable difficulties, 102–106
    differences in perceived performance compared to actual performance, 106
    in the Learning Pit, 121
    use of term, 94, 113
detentions, 279
dialogue/dialogic teaching. See also exploratory talk
    about, 6, 49–50
    barriers to dialogue, 50–51
    choosing when and, 6, 56–58
    classroom discussions, 150, 190
    dialogue summary, 88–89
    effect size of, 7, 50
    engagement and, 29, 89, 90
    focusing on the right type of talk, 52–54
    questioning and, 31
    reducing polarization and increasing dialogue, 283–286
    teaching student how to engage in dialogue, 52
diamond ranking, 67, 68. See also ranking
digging for information, 273–274
disadvantaged students, use of term, 271
discipline
    preview detentions, 279
    wait time and questioning and, 39
discovery learning, 138
discussions and dialogue, 52. See also dialogue/dialogic teaching
disputational talk, 20, 52, 53. See also dialogue/dialogic teaching
distractions, 27–29
Dweck, C., 231, 255, 264–265

E

Education Endowment Foundation, 13
Eells, R., 263
effect size
    about, 6–7, 17–18
    checking the reliability of your choices and, 13
    choice and, 7, 109
    collective efficacy and, 257
    dialogue/dialogic teaching and, 7, 50
    expectations and, 99, 100
    feedback and, 7, 149–150. See also specific types of feedback
    glossary of terms, 15–16
    growth mindset and, 12, 235–236
    how effect sizes mislead, 8–9
    jigsaw and, 257
    learning about effect sizes: to use or not to use, 14–15
    preview strategies and, 275
    QR codes for, 9
    understanding why some interventions are more equal than others, 9
    using a benchmark and, 10–13
    why effect sizes are worthwhile, 7–8
efficacy and expectations, 268. See also collective efficacy; self-efficacy
ego depletion, 110
engagement
    about, 19
    attention and, 22–23
    blueprint for, 19–20
    choice and, 109
    definition of, 21
    dialogue, choosing the right time to engage students in, 56–58
    dialogue, using to build engagement, 49–56
    dialogue summary, 88–89
    distractions and, 27–29
    emotions and, 23
    familiarity and, 23–25
    judging engagement, 85–86
    noticing what engagement looks like, 22
    QR codes for, 30
    storytelling and, 25–27
    teach brilliantly top ten: engagement, 89–90
    understanding student engagement, 21–30
    understanding that not all those who wonder are lost, 85–87
    using questioning to boost, 30–49
    using strategies to help students examine opinions, 80–84
    using strategies to help students make connections, 58–66
    using strategies to help students sort and classify, 67–76
    using strategies to help students think about concepts, 76–79
    what's next, 29–30
English learners (ELs), 277, 286–287

equality, definition of, 271
equity
    about, 269
    and cognitive load theory, 287–292
    definition of, 271
    equity, equality, and fairness, 269–271
    equity summary, 292–297
    further strategies to boost equity, 282–287
    and growth mindset for low-socioeconomic-status students, 280–282
    and preview strategies, 272–279
    QR codes for, 272
eugenics, 220, 227, 229
eureka experience/moment, 105, 142
event schemas, 288
examples and success criteria, 178
expectations
    ability and genetics, 220–222
    about, 215
    amplifying progress and, 240–247
    blueprint for, 215–216
    boosting self-efficacy and collective efficacy, 263–267
    continuum of learning and, 222–227
    effect size of, 99, 100
    expectations for all students, 100–102, 216–219
    exploratory talk and, 54–55
    feedback and, 158
    grouping students and, 247–251
    growth mindset and, 230–240
    high expectations versus low expectations, 101
    intelligence testing and, 227–230
    mistakes and failures and, 257–263
    praise and rewards and, 251–256
    student data and a learning continuum and, 226–227
    teach brilliantly top ten: expectations, 267–268
    thinking time, five steps toward improving, 41
    wait time and questioning and, 40
experience and environment
    ability and genetics and, 220–222
    influence of, 267
    mistakes and failures and, 257
exploratory talk. See also dialogue/dialogic teaching
    benefits of, 88–89
    engagement and, 20, 294
    focusing on the right type of talk, 53–54
    group work and, 90
    steps for, 54–56
    use of term, 52
extrinsic rewards, 92. See also rewards
extroverted thinking, 85–86, 89
eye contact, 40–41

F

facts
    categories of knowledge, 165
    facts or concepts, 127, 129
FAIL (first attempt in learning), 262
failure. See mistakes and failures
failure to respond, 39
Fasano, J., 4
feedback. See also Seven Steps to Feedback
    about, 147
    advice and, 151–156
    blueprint for, 147–148
    Education Endowment Foundation on, 13
    effect size of, 7, 149–150
    essential qualities of, 151–165
    examples of, 153, 154, 155, 157
    formative and summative, 186–188
    guiding questions for, 150–151
    learning intentions and success criteria and, 166–179
    learning outcomes and, 158–165
    Learning Pit and, 195–199
    mindset and, 234
    praise and, 252
    QR codes for, 151, 185
    rewards and, 256
    self- and peer feedback, 179–186, 200, 205–206
    self-efficacy and, 266
    statement of purpose, 3
    teach brilliantly top ten: feedback, 213
    types of, 188–195
    use of, 156–158
    using, 145
    what is feedback, 148–149
    why is feedback so complex, 149–150
feedback from students, 149, 191
feedforward, 195
fight-or-flight reactions, 23
films/movies, 223, 274
first attempts, 200, 205, 262
fixed mindset. See also growth mindset; mindsets
    about, 230–231
    comparisons of fixed and growth mindset, 231–233
    example of when growth mindset is poorly implemented, 238
    and failure, 260
    importance of mindset, 233–235
    and maintaining grade levels, 238
    and talents, 239
Fleckenstein, J., 16–17
flexible grouping, 250, 267. See also grouping
flipped learning, 272, 273

flow theory, 108
Flynn, J., 220
formative evaluations and feedback, 150, 185, 186–188, 193. See also assessments

G

generation and testing, 105–106
genetics and abilities, 220–222
geography
    example descriptors for increasing depth of learning, 170
    example success criteria, 173
    self- and peer feedback and, 180–181
glossary of terms, 15–16
goals
    challenge and, 99
    clear goal intentions and effect size of, 150, 192
    in the Learning Pit, 124
    setting appropriately challenging goals, 106–108
    Seven Steps to Feedback and, 200, 201–205
Goldilocks zone, 99, 106, 114, 145, 274, 291
good, the bad, and the ugly for success criteria, 178
grades. See also feedback
    comments versus grades, 150, 194–195
    feedback and, 213
    growth mindset and, 238
    negative responses to, 209
    peer and self-grading, 150, 191
    Seven Steps to Feedback and, 201, 210–213
    teacher feedback and, 208–209
grouping
    ability grouping, 247, 249, 250
    about, 247–249
    criteria for, 250
    effect size of, 248
    exploratory talk and, 90
    flexible grouping, 250, 267
    group work attitudes and skills, 163
    necessity of, 249–251
growth mindset. See also fixed mindset; mindsets
    about, 230–231
    advice and, 152
    comparisons of fixed and, 231–233
    effect size of, 12, 235–236
    example of when growth mindset is poorly implemented, 238
    expectations and, 215
    failure and, 260
    importance of mindset and, 233–235
    is growth mindset worth investing in, 239
    for low-socioeconomic-status students, 280–282, 293
    making growth mindset a reality for your students, 239–240
    mistakes and failures and, 258, 259
    QR codes for, 230
    testing and, 245, 246
    when is mindset most effective, 235–239

H

Harrison, C., 194–195
Hattie, J., 49, 100, 294
higher-order questions, 35, 36–37, 48. See also questioning
higher-order-thinking
    challenge and, 146
    interleaving and, 105
    odd one out and, 60
    questioning and, 35, 36–37, 38, 48
hinge point, 7, 8, 11, 12–13, 16
history
    example descriptors for increasing depth of learning, 170
    example success criteria, 173–174
Hodges, T., 29
homework, 277–278
how-to guides and preview strategies, 274. See also preview strategies
Huelser, B., 257
humility, 131
humor, 131

I

influences, 216
inner circle and outer circle, 87
instruction. See also teaching, adjusting for learning
    preventing cognitive overload and, 292
    using ten principles for effective instruction, 44–46
interleaving, 104–105, 106. See also desirable difficulty
interventions. See also growth mindset
    dialogue/dialogic teaching and, 88
    effect size of, 9, 15, 16, 17
    expectations and, 267
    justifying your choices and, 7, 8
    mindset and, 233
    oral language interventions/oracy, impact of, 50
    understanding why some interventions are more equal than others, 9
    using a benchmark and, 10–11, 12, 13
intrinsic motivation, 29, 109, 111, 256. See also motivation

introduction
  black box, xi–xii
  how this book is organized, xii–xiii
introverted thinking, 85–86, 89
I-R-E pattern/IR-Evaluate approach. See also questioning
  about, 30–31
  effectiveness of, 89
  feedback and, 191
  IR-Explore approach and, 32
  QR codes for, 34
IR-Explore approach. See also questioning
  about, 31–32
  examples for, 33–34
  exploratory talk and, 53
  frequently asked questions for, 32–33
  QR codes for, 34
  three starting points for IR-Exploring questioning, 48–49
is–could be–never would be, 70–73. See also strategies to help students sort and classify

J

jigsaw
  about, 294–295
  effect size of, 257
  as part of your professional learning, 296–297
  using jigsaw in eight easy steps, 295
journals, 243

K

Kawasaki, G., 259
knowledge. See also ASK (attitudes, skills, and knowledge) model
  categories of, 165
  phrases to help design learning intentions, 172
  privileging knowledge, 160
Köller, O., 16–17

L

labeling, 100, 224, 249
learner orientation, 261, 262
learners, definition of, 218
learning. See also teaching, adjusting for learning
  deep learning and surface learning, 57
  discovery learning, 138
  distinction between performance and, 44
  use of term, 217–218
  variations in the conditions of learning and desirable difficulty, 102–103
learning conferences, 243. See also progress
learning intentions. See also feedback; success criteria
  about, 167–169
  connecting and decontextualizing, 202–203
  example descriptors for increasing depth of learning, 169–171
  feedback and, 166–167, 213
  QR codes for, 167
  self- and peer feedback and, 206
  sharing and recording learning intentions, 204
  some final thoughts, 178–179
  summary of learning intention descriptors, 172
  writing learning intentions, 202, 203–204
learning outcomes. See also SOLO Taxonomy (Structure of the Observed Learning Outcome)
  equity and, 270
  feedback and, 158–165
  improvement of application, 160–163
  improvement of learning, 158–160
Learning Pit
  challenge and, 113–123, 146
  choosing when and, 6, 107
  creating challenge with the Learning Pit: a step-by-step guide, 124–144
  English learners and, 287
  eureka experience/moment, 105
  feedback and, 195–199
  foundations of, 115–119
  four stages of, 125
  is–could be–never would be and, 70
  learning is not linear, 114
  Learning Pit social-emotional context words, 127
  Learning Pit, version 1—thought bubbles, 116
  Learning Pit, version 2—progress template for students, 117
  Learning Pit, version 3—detailed descriptions, 118
  Learning Pit, version 4—a bilingual illustration, 119
  original illustration of, 115
  QR codes for, 115, 116, 120
  self-efficacy and, 265–266
  stage 1: concept, 126–129
  stage 2: conflict, 129–137
  stage 3: construct, 137–142
  stage 4: consider, 142–143
  storytelling and, 26–27
  students' introduction to, 120–123
  wrong way and right way to draw a Learning Pit, 120
  zone of proximal development and, 93
learning styles, Education Endowment Foundation on, 13
learning walks, 44, 109, 155, 157, 203

Lee, C., 194–195
line ranking, 67, 68. See also ranking
literacy
    example descriptors for increasing depth of learning, 170
    example success criteria, 174
    self- and peer feedback and, 182–183
long-term memory. See also working memory
    challenge and, 99, 145
    cognitive load theory and, 192, 288, 289, 290, 294
    emotions and, 23
Lord of the Rings, The (Tolkien), 85
lower-order questions, 35, 36, 48. See also questioning
low-socioeconomic status (SES) students
    growth mindset and, 280–282, 293
    reducing cognitive overload, 294
    reducing polarization and increasing dialogue and, 283–286
    thinking time/wait time and, 282
    vocabulary and, 290

M

Makel, M., 248
Mandela, N., 83, 270
mantras, intended purpose of Hattie's hinge point, 12
markup features and amplifying progress, 242. See also progress
Marshall, B., 194–195
marvelous mistakes, 258. See also mistakes and failures
mathematics
    example descriptors for increasing depth of learning, 171
    example success criteria, 174
    self- and peer feedback and, 183–184
meaning, 87
Measurement of Intelligence, The (Terman), 229
memory. See also long-term memory; working memory
    challenge and, 145
    emotions and, 23
    worked examples and, 192
Mercer, N., 53
meta-analysis, glossary of terms, 16
metacognition
    about, 143
    categories of knowledge, 165
    in the Learning Pit, 146
    mistakes and failure and, 257
    peer and self-grading and, 191
    questions to encourage metacognition, 143–144
Metcalfe, J., 257

midway pause and engagement, 86
Mindset (Dweck), 255
mindsets. See also fixed mindset; growth mindset
    importance of, 233–235
    at-risk students and, 216
    when is mindset most effective, 235–239
mini-whiteboards, 43, 44, 45
minority students
    use of term, 271
    wait time and questioning and, 40
mistakes and failures
    dealing with wrong answers, 137–138
    deliberate mistakes, 178
    failure puzzle study, 252–253
    learning from, 257–263, 268
    Learning Pit stage 3 and, 137–138
    mindset and, 235
    QR codes for, 256
    ready-fire-aim, 259–260
    responding to failure, 260–263
    success criteria and, 178
    timing/when and, 5
Möller, O., 16–17
monologic talk, 50, 88. See also dialogue/dialogic teaching
monopolizers, 42
month-of-birth effect, 248
more signal, less noise, 291
motivation. See also intrinsic motivation
    challenge and, 145
    efficacy and, 265
    giving students control over their learning and, 109
    Goldilocks zone and, 114
    praise and rewards and, 251–253
    rewards and, 256
    wait time and questioning and, 39
music
    example descriptors for increasing depth of learning, 171
    example success criteria, 174
    Mozart Effect, 10

N

Newell, A., 143
Nuthall, G., 50

O

odd one out strategy
    about, 60, 62
    construction by distinguishing differences and, 140

examples of categories to use for, 64–65
odd one out examples, 63, 66
odd one out extensions, 66
odd one out options, 62–63
odd one out structure, 63
Show Racism the Red Card, 284–286
Olszewski-Kubilius, P., 248
open questions, 35. See also questioning
opinions
opinion corners, 82–83
opinion lines, 80–82
thinking corners, 83–84
oral language interventions/oracy, impact of, 50
Orwell, G., 130

P

pacing and engagement, 20
participation
exploratory talk and, 88
guidance for, 86–87
rate of questioning and, 37
thinking time/wait time and, 39, 41, 42
pause and reflect time, 87
peer and self-grading, 150, 191
peer assessment, 150, 179–185, 193. See also assessments
peer-to-peer feedback, 180, 186. See also feedback; self- and peer feedback
peer-to-peer talk, 20, 52. See also dialogue/dialogic teaching
performance
differences in perceived performance compared to actual performance, 106
distinction between performance and learning, 44
performance orientation, 261–262
person praise, 252, 254, 266. See also praise
physical education, example descriptors for increasing depth of learning, 171
polarization approach, 284, 293–294
post-tests, 179, 192, 210, 245, 246. See also tests/testing
praise
challenge and, 92, 112
effectiveness of, 267
examples of three types of, 254
feedback and, 156, 189, 195
growth mindset and, 237
guidelines for, 255
knowing how to praise and what to reward, 251–256
self-efficacy and, 266
prejudice and schemas, 288

pretests, 245, 246. See also tests/testing
preview strategies
about, 272–273
effect size of, 275
evidence supporting, 275
five ways to preview, 273–274
homework and, 278
impact of, 292
preview detentions, 279
preview notes, 277–279
why previewing does not spoil the surprise, 275–277
problem solving
exploratory talk and, 89
higher-order questions and, 36
process praise, 252, 254, 266, 267. See also praise
product praise, 252, 254. See also praise
productive failure, 150, 194. See also mistakes and failures
progress
examples of progress, 242–244
examples of Silja's butterfly drawings, 241
expectations and, 267
identification of the type of progress you want, 246–247
improving everyone's learning by amplifying progress, 240–247
tests that show progress, 244–246
provisional language, 87
psychologically privileged, 25
purpose
challenge and, 91–92
engagement and, 19–20
expectations and, 215
feedback and, 147
remembering your why, 2–3
pyramid ranking, 67, 68. See also ranking

Q

QR codes
for challenge, 95
for downloading high-resolution color images for Learning Pit illustrations, 116
for effect size, 9
for engagement, 30
for equity, 272
for exploratory talk, 54
for feedback, 151, 185
for Hattie video regarding dialogue, 49
for introducing the Learning Pit, 115, 120
for IR-Evaluate and IR-Explore, 34
for learning intentions and success criteria, 167
for mistakes, 256

for SOLO Taxonomy (Structure of the Observed Learning Outcome), 167
questioning
    about, 30–31
    asking the right types of questions, 34–38
    authentic questions, 41, 42
    closed questions, 35
    creation of cognitive conflict through, 131–132
    effect size of, 150
    engagement and, 29, 89, 90
    exploring instead of evaluating and, 31–34
    feedback types and effect size of, 191
    feedback's guiding questions, 150–151
    higher-order questions, 35, 36–37, 48
    increasing sample size and, 43–44
    lower-order questions, 35, 36, 48
    open questions, 35
    question stems, 47
    rate of questioning, 37–38
    Socratic questions, 46
    summarizing the questioning process, 47–49
    teaching students how to ask better questions, 46–47
    ten principles for effective instruction, 44–46
    timing and, 38–42
    using questioning to boost engagement, 30–49

R

raised hands, 41, 43–44, 45, 86
ranking, 67–70. See also strategies to help students sort and classify
ready-fire-aim, 178, 259–260
reflection time, 86, 87
reinforcement and cues (feedback), 149, 189. See also feedback
relaxation techniques, 10
repeat-paraphrase-connect, 87
rescue and making challenge interesting, 112–113
revisiting earlier iterations, use of, 242. See also progress
rewards, 92, 255–256
Rowe, M., 38

S

sample size, questioning and increasing, 43–44
Sams, A., 273
scaffolding, 45, 113, 189, 294
schemas, 288–290, 294
science
    example descriptors for increasing depth of learning, 171
    example success criteria, 175

self- and peer feedback. See also feedback
    about, 179–185
    learning intentions and success criteria and, 148, 166
    Seven Steps to Feedback and, 200, 205–206, 211
self-assessment, 150, 180, 191, 195. See also assessments; feedback
self-consciousness, 28. See also engagement
self-determination theory, 109
self-efficacy. See also efficacy and expectations
    boosting self-efficacy and collective efficacy, 263–267
    challenge and, 94, 149
    comparing low and high self-efficacy, 264
    growth mindset and, 215, 234
    how to boost student self-efficacy, 265–266
    impact of, 265
    praise and, 255
    rescuing and, 112
self-schemas, 288
Seven Steps to Feedback. See also feedback
    about, 199–201
    edits and, 200, 206, 209
    first attempts and, 200, 205
    grades and, 201, 210–212
    learning goals and, 108, 200, 201–205
    self- and peer feedback and, 200, 205–206
    teacher feedback and, 200, 206–209
Simon, T., 227
skills
    ASK model: skills, 164–165
    phrases to help design learning intentions, 172
    trying a new skills, 274
Skinner, B., 255–256
small-group discussions, 42. See also dialogue/dialogic teaching
Smiley, P., 233
social schemas, 288
social-emotional learning
    example descriptors for increasing depth of learning, 171
    example success criteria, 175
sociocultural theory, 54
Socratic questions, 46. See also questioning
SOLO Taxonomy (Structure of the Observed Learning Outcome)
    about, 56–58
    example descriptors for increasing depth of learning, 169–171
    example of progress levels matched to the SOLO taxonomy, 159
    and grouping, 250–251
    and improvement of learning outcomes, 158
    and learning goals, 201–202

and learning intentions and success criteria, 168–169, 179
in the Learning Pit, 125
and preview strategies, 276
QR codes for, 167
SOLO taxonomy (abridged), 57
sorting. See strategies to help students sort and classify
spacing effect, 103
speculative thinking, 39
staff-student relationships, 23
stages of the Learning Pit. See also Learning Pit
    stage 1: concept, 126–129
    stage 1: feedback, 195, 197
    stage 2: conflict, 129–137
    stage 2: feedback, 197–198
    stage 3: construct, 137–142
    stage 3: feedback, 198
    stage 4: consider, 142–143
    stage 4: feedback, 198–199
standardized mean differences (SMDs), 281–282
Stanford-Binet intelligence test, 229
Steenbergen-Hu, S., 248
stop and think, 291
storytelling, 25–27
strategies to boost equity. See also equity
    about, 282
    extending thinking time, 282–283
    reducing polarization and increasing dialogue, 283–286
    supporting students who are English learners, 286–287
strategies to help students examine opinions
    about, 80
    opinion corners, 82–83
    opinion lines, 80–82
    thinking corners, 83–84
strategies to help students make connections
    about, 58
    odd one out, 60, 62–63, 66
    what's the difference, 58, 60
strategies to help students sort and classify
    about, 67
    is–could be–never would be, 70–73
    ranking, 67–70
    Venn diagrams, 73–76
strategies to help students think about concepts
    about, 76
    concept lines, 76–77
    concept tables, 78–79
    concept targets, 77–78
student choice. See choice
student data and a learning continuum, 226–227
student engagement. See engagement
students at promise, use of term, 271
student-to-student exchanges, wait time and questioning and, 39
success criteria. See also feedback; learning intentions
    about, 173–175
    choosing success criteria, 204–205
    co-constructing (an understanding of) success criteria, 177–178
    definition of, 167–168
    effect size of, 150
    feedback and, 166–167, 206, 213
    some final thoughts, 178–179
    terms to use when designing success criteria, 176–177
    wide variety of feedback types and effect size of, 190
success of retrieval, 103
summative evaluations and feedback, 185, 186–188
surface learning, 57. See also SOLO Taxonomy (Structure of the Observed Learning Outcome)

T

taking the knee, 285
talents, 223, 235, 239
tasks and procedures (feedback), 149, 189, 190, 213. See also feedback
teach brilliantly top ten for
    challenge, 145–146
    engagement, 89–90
    expectations, 267–268
    feedback, 213
    learning, 17–18
teacher feedback, 200, 206–209. See also feedback
teaching, adjusting for learning
    about, 1–2
    checking the reliability of your choices, 13
    choosing when, 5–6
    glossary of terms, 15–16
    justifying your choices, 6–9
    learning about effect sizes: to use or not to use, 14–15
    next steps, 16–17
    paying attention to your what, 3–5
    remembering your why, 2–3
    teach brilliantly top ten: learning, 17–18
    understanding why some interventions are more equal than others, 9
    using a benchmark, 10–13
teaching staff, definition of, xi
technology (feedback), 149, 190. See also feedback
ten principles for effective instruction, 44–46
Terman, L., 229
tests/testing. See also assessments

desirable difficulty and, 105–106
feedback types and effect size of, 149, 150, 190, 192, 193–194
intelligence testing, 227–230
post-tests, 179, 192, 210, 245, 246
pretests, 245, 246
showing progress, 244–245
tests that show progress, 244–246
thinking corners, 83–84. See also strategies to help students examine opinions
thinking journals, 243. See also progress
thinking rounds, 42
thinking time. See also wait time
extended thinking time, 293
five steps toward improving thinking time, 40–42
guidance for, 86–87
strategies to boost equity, 282–283
use of term, 40
think-pair-share routines, 42
timing. See also feedback; thinking time; wait time
challenge and, 92–93
choosing the right time to engage students in dialogue, 56–58
choosing when, 5–6
engagement and, 20
expectations and, 216
feedback and, 148, 149, 158, 189
reflection time, 86, 87
Seven Steps to Feedback and, 211
Tolkien, J., 85
tourist teaching, 43
tracking/streaming, 248–249
trickery, 131
trust, what gets in the way of challenge, 95
turn and talk, 291. See also dialogue/dialogic teaching

V

Venn diagrams, 73–76, 140. See also strategies to help students sort and classify
Visible Learning, glossary of terms, 16
Visible Learning: The Sequel (Hattie), 100
vision statements, remembering your why and, 3
vulnerable students, use of term, 271

W

WAGOLL (what a good one looks like), 202, 205
wait time. See also thinking time
guidance for, 86–87
impact of increasing, 38–40
increasing, 89
rate of questioning and, 38

summarizing the questioning process, 47, 48
Walden Two (Skinner), 255–256
WALT (we are learning to), 202
Wang, S., 100
what, paying attention to your what, 3–5, 17
what to notice
challenge and, 92
engagement and, 20
expectations and, 216
feedback and, 148
what's the difference, 58–60, 61 140. See also strategies to help students make connections
when challenge is just right, students' abilities improve. See challenge
when expectations are high, everyone prospers. See expectations
when feedback is used brilliantly, it adds significant value. See feedback
when there is equity, there is fairness. See equity
when you adjust your teaching, it transforms students' learning. See teaching, adjusting for learning
when you engage your students, their learning gains purpose. See engagement
why, remembering your why, 2–3, 17
WILF (what I'm looking for), 202
Wiliam, D.
on assessment and engagement, 188
on the black box, xi–xii
on cognitive load theory, 287
on grades, 194–195
on growth mindset, 233
on questions, 34–35
Willingham, D., 23, 25, 138
wobblers, creation of cognitive conflict with wobblers, 133–137
worked examples, 150, 191–192, 292
working memory, 192, 289–290, 291, 294. See also long-term memory
writing
concise writing and cognitive overload, 292
learning intentions and, 202, 203–204
wrong answers and Learning Pit stage 3, 137–138

Y

Yair, G., 293
Yousafzai, M., 83

Z

Zimmermann, F., 16–17
zone of proximal development, 93

Heroes Within
Aaron Hansen
Empower students to break free from attitudes of disengagement, apathy, or passive compliance. Detailing the hero-maker framework, this book speaks directly to overcoming the student motivation challenges teachers face as they work to empower students with purpose, ownership, and self-efficacy to face challenges.
BKF805

30+ Movement Strategies to Boost Cognitive Engagement
Rebecca Stobaugh
Studies show student movement in the classroom is integral to improving cognitive engagement. In this essential instructional guidebook, you'll discover a variety of research-backed strategies for reimaging your teaching to inspire student movement and active learning.
BKG103

Acceleration for All
Sharon V. Kramer and Sarah Schuhl
Overcoming student learning gaps requires a shift in practice from remediation to acceleration. Every student deserves to learn at grade level and beyond. Acceleration for All offers research-informed, ready-to-implement strategies that emphasize core instructional practices to ensure accelerated learning schoolwide.
BKG049

What STEM Can Do for Your Classroom
Jason McKenna
Author and educator Jason McKenna offers examples, tried and tested classroom projects, and collaborative strategies in this innovative resource designed to open up STEM education for K–6 educators in exciting and expansive new ways.
BKG088

Stick the Learning
Eric Saunders
This concise guide bridges brain-based learning theory with everyday instructional practice to maximize teacher effectiveness for visible student achievement. Learn three powerful, doable techniques proven to support long-term retention: spaced repetition, interleaving, and retrieval (SIR).
BKG083

Solution Tree | Press

a division of
Solution Tree

Visit SolutionTree.com or call 800.733.6786 to order.

Tremendous, tremendous, tremendous!

The speaker made me do some very deep internal reflection about the **PLC process** and the personal responsibility I have in making the school improvement process work **for ALL kids.**

—Marc Rodriguez, teacher effectiveness coach, Denver Public Schools, Colorado

PD Services

Our experts draw from decades of research and their own experiences to bring you practical strategies for building and sustaining a high-performing PLC. You can choose from a range of customizable services, from a one-day overview to a multiyear process.

Book your PLC PD today!
888.763.9045

Solution Tree